# THE HIGHEST STATE
# OF CONSCIOUSNESS

*The Right Copy.*

# THE HIGHEST STATE OF CONSCIOUSNESS

## EDITED BY JOHN WHITE

ANCHOR BOOKS

DOUBLEDAY & COMPANY, INC.
GARDEN CITY, NEW YORK
1972

The Anchor Books edition is the first publication of
*The Highest State of Consciousness*

Anchor Books edition: 1972

LIBRARY OF CONGRESS CATALOG CARD NUMBER 70-171340
COPYRIGHT © 1972 BY JOHN WHITE
ALL RIGHTS RESERVED
PRINTED IN THE UNITED STATES OF AMERICA
FIRST EDITION

To A.L.P. and H.C.E.

*Hiara pirlu resh kavawn*
J. R. Salamanca, LILITH

# INTRODUCTION

What is the highest state of consciousness? St. Paul called it the "peace that passeth understanding" and R. M. Bucke named it "cosmic consciousness." In Zen Buddhism, the term for it is *satori* or *kensho,* while in Yoga it is *samadhi* or *moksha,* and in Taoism, "the absolute Tao." Thomas Merton used the phrase "transcendental unconscious" to describe it; Abraham Maslow coined the term "peak experience"; Sufis speak of *fana.* Gurdjieff labeled it "objective consciousness" while the Quakers call it "the Inner Light." Jung referred to individuation, and Buber spoke of the I-Thou relationship. But whatever the name for this old and well-known phenomenon, all are concerned with a state of awareness radically different from our ordinary understanding or normal waking consciousness.

Furthermore, all are agreed in calling it the highest state of consciousness: a self-transforming perception of one's total union with the infinite. It is beyond time and space. It is an experience of the timelessness which is eternity, of unlimited unity with all creation. One's socially conditioned sense of "me" is shattered and swept away by a new definition of the self, the I. In that redefinition of self, I equals all mankind, all life and the universe. The usual ego boundaries break down, and the ego passes beyond the limits of the body. The self becomes integrated with what Emerson called the Oversoul and what Arthur Clarke in *Childhood's End* called the Overmind. Self becomes selfless, ego is seen to be an illusion, and the ego game ends. The *Maitrayana Upanishad* puts it this

Originally published as the lead article in *The Journal for the Study of Consciousness,* Vol. 4, No. 1, January–June 1971. Reprinted by permission.

way: "Having realized his own self as the Self, a man becomes selfless. . . . This is the highest mystery."

## A New Mode of Self-Understanding

This mode of self-understanding may come dramatically, as with St. Paul on the road to Damascus, or it may come with no apparent outward sign of the inner drama. But the resulting experience has been uniform around the world and throughout history. By their own testimony, the "illuminati"— people who have experienced the highest state of consciousness—have felt the deepest sense of peace with others and harmony with the world. They comprehend the universe, as Dante wrote at the end of *The Divine Comedy*, to be moving to the power of Love. They see a cosmic plan, a moral order, to the seeming chaos and accident of intergalactic dust and stellar gas. They see, with Hamlet, "a divinity that shapes our ends." This is the "god" (or Buddha or Tao or Brahma) of countless religions and philosophies. In all cases the self-enveloping awareness that "I" and "the other" are unified, makes new or reborn men. It changes a bleak and hopeless notion of life to one in which everything has a joyful meaning. It changes a gestalt of existential absurdity to a world view of inevitably hopeful exuberance; the subject discovers the fundamental design in what were previously only disconnected, confusing perceptions and experiences.

Just as important as self-testimony have been the observations of others about illuminati. Almost without exception, they have been regarded as saints and visionaries and prophets: Jesus, Buddha, Lao Tse, Jacob Boehme, Ramakrishna, Walt Whitman, Aldous Huxley. Socially revered, they have exhibited exceptional courage, sweetness, compassion, wholeness, and holiness. Even though they have retained the characteristics of men, they have been set apart in a special way and made recognizable by an aura—sometimes literally visible as a glowing light—which affects other men in powerful ways. And they have ceaselessly urged others to prepare themselves through good deeds, study and meditation to receive the highest blessing of life. It is a blessing that cannot be forced or foreseen; it is always a surprise when it happens. Yet they maintain that it should be sought, to use the words of Jesus' commandment, "with all thy heart and with all thy soul and with all thy strength and with all thy mind."

## How to Save the World

It is only through a change of consciousness that the world will be "saved." Everyone must begin with himself. Political action, social work, this *ism*, that *ology*, are all incomplete, futile actions unless accompanied by a new and elevated mode of awareness. The ultimate action, then, is no action at all except to change consciousness. In other words, *the true revolution is revelation.* When that has occurred on a global scale, the old problems and prejudices and inhumanities will vanish, and revolution will become evolution—but not until then.

Where does one begin? The following readings have been chosen from the literature available in English as some of the best descriptions of the highest state of consciousness. But it must be emphasized that they are only guides, not guarantees. Description is not enough. The liberated have continually stressed that words are only *about* truth, not truth itself. Truth cannot be known except through direct experience, through enlightenment. And often language is a barrier to knowing the truth because there is a confusion between beams of non-verbal intuition and that learned arbitrary framework called language. For it is quite clear now that learning to speak a language means learning to think in a language— that is, learning to think in terms of abstract verbal concepts and grammatical categories. Language is symbolic; language-thinking is symbol-thinking. And symbols are always less than the realities for which they stand. As such, language constricts consciousness and places limits on understanding. One must go beyond words and other symbols to a direct, unmediated vision in which perceptions are not filtered through a linguistic screen existing in the mind.

Another aspect of the mystical state is emotion. Francis Younghusband observes in *Modern Mystics* that mystical experience brings "emotionalism to a degree unbelievable by those who have never witnessed it. . . ." But he continues, "There should indeed be no objection to strong emotion in itself. . . . No love of beauty or love of a mother for her child could ever be felt with too deep an intensity. The fact that the mystical state is a highly emotional state must therefore be accepted."

The mystical state, then, is beyond words and is highly emotional. More than that, the unifying principle at work in illumination dissolves the learned semantic categories of "thought" and "feeling" or "reason" and "emotion." In the mystical state, intellect and intuition merge. There is a fusion of insight and instinct which results in a new condition of being. That condition is not the detached, euphoric state commonly referred to as "being high" or "tripping" (although, as some authors report here, psychedelic drugs can give access to truly expanded consciousness, when wisely used). Rather it is holistic; it involves the whole organism. Understanding comes to the one experiencing liberation through the total use of all channels for sensation and perception.

## Difficulties in Altering Consciousness: Culture

Part of the difficulty in altering consciousness, though, resides in those very channels, and the difficulty is both biologically and culturally determined. Those who study perception have learned that our senses are blinded in many ways. They point out that men are generally in a state that I will call "sensory repression." For example, culture can build screens in the mind which usually remain unconscious to a person. Anthropologist Edward T. Hall's investigation of proxemics (*The Hidden Dimension*) shows that different cultures have different sensory worlds. "Selective screening of sensory data," he writes, "admits some things while filtering others, so that experience as it is perceived through one set of culturally patterned sensory screens is quite different from the experience perceived through another." The preface to

Carlos Castaneda's *The Teachings of Don Juan* gives a memorable summary of the matter:

> Anthropology has taught us that the world is differently defined in different places. . . . The very metaphysical presuppositions differ: space does not conform to Euclidean geometry, time does not form a continuous unidirectional flow, causation does not conform to Aristotelian logic, man is not differentiated from non-man or life from death, as in our world. . . . The central importance of entering into worlds other than our own . . . lies in the fact that the experience leads us to understand that our own world is also a cultural construct.

A quest for ultimate knowledge of reality must account for various culturally determined realities.

## Difficulties in Altering Consciousness: Biology

Biology also contributes to our state of sensory repression because sensory processing is the initial stage in determining reality. Consider the fact that vision is more than just an event in which light is passively received by the retina and transmitted to the brain for interpretation. The process of seeing is an active one, in which some signals and perceptions are deliberately blocked or filtered out by the optic nerve and reticular activating system so that others can be attended to by the brain. If a human being were to allow every signal that bombards his senses to rise into consciousness (as seems to be the case when under the influence of LSD and other powerful drugs), he would be unable to focus awareness on the simple tasks for survival. The famous frog's eye experiment performed at MIT by Warren McCullough, *et al.* (available in his *Embodiments of Mind*) showed that a frog's visual attention is caught only by moving objects the size of the average insect, while other visual perceptions are normally repressed. This suggests by extrapolation to *homo sapiens* that nature has constructed us on a basis of sensory repression; it was necessary for evolution.

A biological-cultural process developed our everyday state of consciousness and separated us from animals by giving us a self-concept, by making us aware that we are aware. But by that process we were also separated from that organic unity which animals have with the natural world. Normal self-consciousness (which seems to develop in humans at about the age of two) is both a biological advance and a biological handicap. In terms of development of the race, it was necessary for survival. In terms of development of the individual, it is no longer necessary and now appears, unfortunately, to be the major cause of our rush toward extinction.

## Becoming God-Like

Our normal state of consciousness shuts off awareness of our affinity with creation, our union with the divine. But if we are normally in a state of sensory repression, it is of equal importance in the study of consciousness to note that man's capacity to modify or edit his sensory processes means that he is capable of exaggerating or enhancing them to animal-like sensitivity, as well as inhibiting them. This is what seems to occur in many cases of ecstasy, where the subject becomes hypersensitive to all kinds of stimuli. Ecstasy, *ex stasis*, is the transport out of a biologically and culturally ordered mode of thought and perception. In the mystic mode, man returns to this primal state of affairs. But the return is on a higher level. It is both a circle (revolution) and a linear progression (evolution): an upward spiraling. Man regains his primitive condition, but rather than being unconscious or unaware of it, as animals are, he is superconscious of it. It is paradoxical: *By recovering his animal nature, man becomes God.*

## Enlightenment and the Brain

In terms of the brain, enlightenment seems to involve a repatterning of neural networks. Whereas before there were unconnected or "compartmentalized" areas of the brain's nervous system, in enlightenment there is a breakthrough which results in an integration of the nerve pathways by which we think and feel. Our multiple "brains" become one brain. The neocortex (the "thinking-intellect" part) and the limbic system and thalamus (the "feeling-emotion" part) and the medulla oblongata (the "intuition-unconscious" part) attain a previously non-existent—but always possible—mode of intercellular communication. A threshold is passed—probably explainable in terms of both cellular electrochemical change and growth of new nerve endings. However it is accomplished in neurophysiological terms, though, the result is a new state of consciousness. This, in turn, creates a new mode of perception and feeling which leads to the discovery of non-rational (but not irrational) forms of logic, which are multi-level/integrated/simultaneous, not linear/sequential/either-or.

How can a person attain the highest state of consciousness? There are many doors to the same room. Some have been discovered; others have been developed. Classic trigger-situations have been dance, fasting and diet, self-torture, electric shock, sensory isolation, sensory overload, psychotic episodes, trauma and birth by ordeal, extreme fatigue, sexual relations and simply gazing on natural scenery. The more systematic approaches, often requiring strict adherence and discipline, include prayer, Yoga, Zen, tantra, transcendental meditation, psychedelic drugs, hypnosis and occult methods such as those of Gurdjieff and Madame Blavatsky. Recently, light shows, biofeedback and structural integration ("Rolfing") have also shown potential. An uncompromising introspection—what Gurdjieff called the way of the clever man —has brought some to a state of personal salvation.

But none of these methods is a sure way to attain liberation. Evelyn Underhill, in her monumental *Mysticism*, distinguishes three stages on the way to ecstasy: awakening of the self, purification of the self and illumination of the self. Other terms such as "the meditative stage" and "the purgative stage" may be preferred, but the important point is this: no matter how hard enlightenment is sought, it can never be attained—only discovered. A somewhat discredited and discarded Christian concept applies here: grace.

Here also it is important to assert that enlightenment is *not* hallucination or illusion. Even if it were, experiencing it would be valuable simply in terms of its beneficial effect upon human lives. But, as I will try to show later in this introduction, the highest state of consciousness is far more than pure subjectivity. It is subjective, but in a paradoxical sense: Enlightenment reveals that *what is most deeply personal is also most universal*. In the mystical state, reality and ideality become one.

## Content of Consciousness vs. Consciousness Itself

It may appear that greater attention is given in the following readings to the *content of consciousness* than to the origin or source of consciousness—i.e. *consciousness itself*. Some scientists—Sir Russell Brain, for example—have posited that many things may be learned about consciousness, but consciousness itself cannot be defined on other than a subjective basis or in terms of something less fundamental than consciousness. That is, we may accumulate data on what takes place during consciousness but never on the actual qualities of consciousness itself.

Can consciousness itself be defined? What is the relation between activity of the brain's neural networks and mentation by the mind's cognitive systems? How does electrochemical action become thought and feeling? What are the determinants for each state of human consciousness?

Theories of consciousness are now being developed by scientists and philosophers. Laboratory work in artificial intelligence and in lower animal consciousness may offer exciting discoveries; it may also be a blind alley. For example, Gunther S. Stent, a molecular biologist, states in *The Coming of the Golden Age*: ". . . there now seem to remain only three deep problems yet to be solved: the origin of life, the mechanism of cellular differentiation, and the functional basis of the higher nervous system. . . . I do not [forsee a solution to] the mechanism of consciousness . . . since its epistemological aspects both posit it as *the* central philosophical problem of life and also place it beyond the realm of scientific research." On the other hand, the anthropologist Roger W. Wescott offers the intriguing hypothesis that consciousness is internal bioluminescence, a concept which may prompt investigation of the possibility that enlightenment is a physical and measurable event in the brain. In *The Divine Animal* Wescott proposes that endocranial bioluminescence, "a literal form of light generated in, by, and for the brain," may be the stuff of pure consciousness. ". . . Awareness itself may consist of the internal generation and reception or perceptible radiation—in a word, of light."

## Enlightenment: The Eye Seeing Itself

My own experience leads me to suggest that in the highest state of consciousness, there is no difference between the content of consciousness and consciousness itself. Integration or unity is the principal characteristic of that state, both literally and figuratively. In the highest state, what you are aware of is the vital force, the universal condition which issues forth as intelligent awareness having your own name. It amounts to the eye seeing itself, to thought turning itself inside out and thinking about thinking. Enlightenment is the reflexive act wherein the mind understands itself, including that very experience of understanding. Return to godhead (content of consciousness) is equivalent with awareness of Cosmic Awareness (consciousness itself).

When considered abstractly, consciousness, like light, has both a physical and spiritual aspect. But unification is the concrete reality behind, beneath, above and within it all— subtle but nevertheless real, as recent evidence of plant perception shows. Consciousness as biochemistry may be analyzed in terms of neurons, electrochemical firings across synapses and molecular bundles which permeate membranes. But these too can be analyzed until the atomic level is reached, and then the subatomic level. Where does it end?

Cleve Backster, the rediscoverer of ancient India's knowledge of plant perception, has found that primary perception (the ability of plant and animal cell life to perceive human and animal thoughts and feelings) can be demonstrated with minerals, metals and even triply distilled water. A capacity for perception resides in everything. The whole cosmos is sensitive and (in both meanings) sensible. In the "final" analysis, consciousness can be seen as the interconnectedness of all creation or, more precisely, the fundamental context of that connectedness which makes it possible. Zeno the Greek asked his fellow philosophers, "Why not admit that the world is a living and rational being since it produces animate and rational entities?" A scientific basis for such an observation is given by F. L. Kunz in his essay "On the Symmetry Principle" in the March–April 1966 issue of *Main Currents:*

> Surely consciousness . . . is a localization in a primal field, presumably that one in which all else originates. As we have said, such a proposition can only be justified very slowly. Yet it is already becoming clear that some form of consciousness accompanies all organic life, even the most primitive protoplasmic slime, and there is an accumulating body of evidence which points to its presence below the threshold of life.

From ancient days, Hindu thought declared that the *atman,* man's deepest center, is one with the *Brahman,* the deepest center of creation. Now science confirms it: I am the universe; I am Universal Mind.

## Levels of Existence

This notion may be better understood through the metaphor of levels of existence. Try to conceive creation as having five levels. From bottom to top they are atomic, biological, psychological, social and cosmic. If you search for an answer to that ultimate koan, the question "Who am I?" everything you examine will dissolve into the other categories of this metaphor. Start in the middle. You study psychology and soon the psychological brings you to the social through group psychology. On the social level, group psychology extends into sociology, which in turn leads to a study of religion and philosophy. From there you find yourself concerned with the meaning of existence and the relation of men to the universe. You are now on a study of the cosmic.

Going downward in search of an answer to the question "Who am I?" you soon pass from psychology to a study of biology and chemistry. As you seek to know yourself better you study cellular composition and neural networks and the chemistry of emotion, perception, learning and memory. But in seeking to understand mentality you find that soon you have descended to the atomic level and are considering DNA and double helixes and the transmission of atomic radiation. All of which brings you *down* to the top level! For subatomic physics leads you into the study of matter and anti-matter on a cosmic scale. Cosmology is that branch of metaphysics which treats of the character of the universe as an orderly system. The underlying unity of all things and all knowledge brings you full circle and demonstrates the validity of the ancient occult saying: "As above, so below."

## A New Model of Man

Man appears to be constructed in the manner of Yeats' intersecting gyres or as a miniature model of the doughnut-shaped Van Allen radiation belt surrounding our planet. A local vortex in a sea of energy, man is a visible emblem of the steady-state theory of creation. It is not so much a case of "I think" as "I am being thought" or "I am constantly created." Consciousness as the basis of all bodily activity and mental functioning becomes a sort of internal radiation which is not internal at all, but rather is a focused or concentrated area of external cosmic radiation. The aura of mystics and the stylized halo of saints is then explainable as self-induced electromagnetic energy stepped up and brought into the visible-light area of the spectrum by their "spiritual purity" —that is, by their lack of interfering vibrations from confused thought processes.

From quarks to quasars, from pulse to pulsars—and all because of a question: Who am I? The final analysis turns out to be an original synthesis, and consciousness becomes the interconnectedness of all creation in a great chain of being. Content and process, science and religion converge in the study of self-identity, revealing the true meaning of "psychedelic." *Psyche delos:* mind-manifesting, showing forth the true dimensions of the self-spirit.

Who am I? I am the universe; I am Universal Mind.

# CONTENTS

# Contents

# THE HIGHEST STATE
# OF CONSCIOUSNESS

# ALTERED STATES
# OF CONSCIOUSNESS

## STANLEY KRIPPNER

In general terms, an altered conscious state can be defined as a mental state which can be subjectively recognized by an individual (or by an objective observer of the individual) as representing a *difference* in psychological functioning from that individual's "normal," alert, waking state. Twenty states of consciousness have been tentatively identified (with considerable overlapping) as worthy of further study.[1]

1. *The Dreaming State* can be identified on the electro-encephalograph (EEG) by noting periods of rapid eye movements and the absence of "slow" brain waves. The dreaming state occurs periodically during the night as part of the sleep-dream cycle.

2. *The Sleeping State* can be identified on the EEG by an absence of rapid eye movements and by a gradually emerging

From an unpublished paper entitled "Investigations of 'Extra-sensory' Phenomena in Dreams and Other Altered States of Consciousness." Printed by permission of the author.

[1] Very little experimental work has been done in the area of consciousness—what James referred to as "the stream of thought." It was once thought that the EEG might provide a reliable indicator of states of consciousness, but the wide variety of electrical patterns observed has made the relationship between cortical electrical activity and states of consciousness a very complicated one. Krippner and Meacham, in a 1968 article, suggested that a more fruitful approach for researchers might be the investigation of objects of consciousness, a direct study of the external and internal phenomena which comprise the content of "the stream of thought."

pattern of "slow" brain waves. A person awakened from sleep will usually give a brief verbal report which differs considerably from dream reports; this brief verbal report indicates that mental activity is present during the sleeping state as well as during the dreaming state.

3. *The Hypnagogic State* occurs between wakefulness and sleep at the onset of the sleep-dream cycle. It is often characterized by visual imagery and sometimes includes auditory imagery as well; both types of images differ from mental activity experienced during sleeping and dreaming states.

4. *The Hypnopompic State* occurs between sleep and wakefulness at the end of the sleep-dream cycle. At times it is characterized by visual and/or auditory imagery, differing qualitatively from forms of mental activity which occur during sleeping and dreaming states.

5. *The Hyperalert State* is characterized by prolonged and increased vigilance while one is awake. It can be induced by drugs which stimulate the brain, by activities demanding intense concentration, or by measures necessary for survival during military operations (e.g., crow's nest watch, sentry duty).

6. *The Lethargic State* is characterized by dulled, sluggish mental activity. It can be induced by fatigue, sleep deprivation, malnutrition, dehydration, improper sugar balance, drugs that depress brain activity, or by despondent moods and feelings.

7. *States of Rapture* are characterized by intense feeling and overpowering emotion, subjectively evaluated as pleasurable and positive in nature. These states can be induced by sexual stimulation, frenzied dances (e.g., the "whirling dervishes"), orgiastic rituals (e.g., witchcraft and voodoo), rites of passage (e.g., primitive puberty initiations), religious activities (e.g., conversion, "evangelistic" meetings, "speaking-in-tongues"), and certain drugs.

8. *States of Hysteria* are characterized by intense feeling and overpowering emotion, subjectively evaluated as negative and destructive in nature. These states can be induced by rage, anger, jealousy, panic, fear, terror, horror, fear of being "bewitched" or "possessed," violent mob activity (e.g.,

"lynching parties," "running berserk"), psychoneurotic anxiety, and certain drugs.

9. *States of Fragmentation* are characterized by lack of integration among important segments, aspects, or themes of the total personality. These states parallel conditions referred to as psychosis, severe psychoneurosis, dissociation, "multiple personality," amnesia, and fugue episodes (in which someone forgets his past and begins a new life pattern). These states, which may be either temporary or long lasting, can be induced by certain drugs, physical trauma to the brain, psychological stress, physiological predispositions (which interact with psychological stress in some types of schizophrenia), and experimental manipulation (e.g., sensory deprivation, hypnosis).

10. *Regressive States* are characterized by behavior that is clearly inappropriate in terms of the individual's physiological status and chronological age. These states may be temporary (e.g., a person who has undergone "age regression" as a result of experimental manipulation through hypnosis or drugs) or long lasting (e.g., an individual suffering from various types of senility).

11. *Meditative States* are characterized by minimal mental activity, the lack of visual imagery, and the presence of continuous alpha waves on the EEG. They may be induced by lack of external stimulation, massage, floating in water, or meditative disciplines (e.g., Yoga, Zen).

12. *Trance States* are characterized by the absence of continuous alpha waves on the EEG, hypersuggestibility (but not passivity), alertness, and the concentration of attention on a single stimulus—and feeling "at one" with the stimulus without responding to other stimuli (making possible such phenomena as post-hypnotic suggestions). These states may be induced by the voice of a hypnotist, listening to one's heartbeat, chants, prolonged watching of a revolving object (e.g., drum, metronome, stroboscope), trance-inducing rituals (e.g., mediumistic rites, certain tribal dances), repetitive grilling (e.g., "brainwashing," "getting the third degree") trance-inducing material (a lullaby, certain types of poetry and music, a charismatic speaker), watching a dramatic presentation

and becoming "caught up" in the action, or performing a task which requires attentiveness but which involves little variation in response (e.g., driving a "snowcat" vehicle across the snow for several hours, watching a radar screen, staring at a white line in the middle of a highway while driving).

13. *Reverie* is frequently characterized by rapid eye movements on the EEG but occurs during trance. Typically, the state is experimentally induced by a hypnotist who suggests that the individual will have a dreamlike experience.

14. *The Daydreaming State* is characterized by rapidly occurring thoughts which bear little relation to the external environment. It may occur with the eyes open or closed; when the eyes are closed, visual images may appear and rapid eye movements may occur. Daydreaming may be induced by boredom, social isolation, sensory deprivation, nighttime dream deprivation, psychodynamic needs (e.g., wish fulfillment), or spontaneously occurring periods of reverie and fantasy.

15. *Internal Scanning* is characterized by awareness of bodily feelings in the organs, tissues, muscles, etc. Consciousness is always present but exists on a non-reflective level unless there is a concerted effort on the part of an individual to become aware of these feelings *or* unless the bodily feelings are intensified by pain, hunger, etc.

16. *Stupor* is characterized by a suspended or greatly reduced ability to perceive incoming stimuli. Motor activity may be possible but its efficiency is greatly reduced; language may be used but only in a limited and often non-meaningful way. Stupor may be induced by certain types of psychosis or certain drugs (e.g., opiates, large quantities of alcohol).

17. *Coma* is characterized by an inability to perceive incoming stimuli. There is little motor activity and no use of language. Coma may be induced by illness, toxic agents, epileptic seizures, trauma to the brain, or glandular dysfunction.

18. *Stored Memory* involves past experience which is not immediately available to an individual's reflective awareness. Nevertheless, the memory traces (or "engrams") of past events always exist on some level of the individual's consciousness. They may be recalled by conscious effort, they

may be evoked by electrical or chemical stimulation of the cortex, they may be produced through psychoanalytic free association, or they may emerge spontaneously.

19. *"Expanded" Conscious States* are characterized by a lowered sensory threshold and an abandonment of habitual ways of perceiving the external and/or internal environment. Although these "expanded" states may occur spontaneously or may be induced through hypnosis or sensory bombardment, they are frequently brought about experimentally by the use of psychedelic ("mind-manifesting") drugs and plants. Typically, these states progress along four different levels: sensory, recollective-analytic, symbolic, and integral. At the sensory level, there are subjective reports of alterations in space, time, the body image, and sensory impressions. At the recollective-analytic level, novel ideas and thoughts emerge concerning the individual's psychodynamics or conception of the world and his role in it. At the symbolic level, there is an identification with historical or legendary persons, with evolutionary recapitulation, or with mythical symbols. At the integral level (which relatively few individuals attain), there is a religious and/or mystical experience in which God (or the "Ground of Being") is confronted or in which the individual has the subjective impression of dissolving into the energy field of the universe (e.g., "satori," "samadhi," "oceanic unity," "cosmic consciousness," "peak experience").

20. The twentieth state of consciousness is, of course, the "normal," everyday, waking state, characterized by logic, rationality, cause-and-effect thinking, goal-directedness, and the feeling that one is "in control" of one's mental activity. One engages in "reflective" thinking; in other words, the individual is aware of himself as an experiencing unit. However, there are other states of consciousness which are "nonreflective" (e.g., stupor, coma). These states must also be referred to as conscious states if one agrees with the psychologist Rex Collier, that consciousness is a field of energy processes representing the entire organism.

# THE SEARCH FOR ECSTASY

Wild rites and states of mind verging on madness have played a part in every world religion. In a state of ecstasy, reached by deliberate rituals or long periods of self-denial and contemplation, worshippers experience heightened states of consciousness and unity with their gods. Official leaders of religious movements have often been embarrassed by this tendency among those in their charge. Unable to deny that the founders and saints of most faiths have known ecstasy, they fear the uncontrollable and irresponsible orgies which often accompany ecstatic conditions.

One problem has been that those who have experienced ecstasies always find it hard to describe their experiences. Very often they speak of them as "beyond words," of "unutterable beauty." When they try to describe the indescribable they usually do so in terms of lights and colors and visions. For the religious ecstatics, ecstasy is a union with God, and a sense of wholeness and unity pervades them. Radhakrishnan, a Hindu mystic, described his experiences by saying: "A lightning flash, a sudden flame of incandescence, throws a momentary but eternal gleam on life in time. A strange quietness enters the soul; a great peace invades its being. The vision, the spark, the supreme moment of unification of conscious realization, sets the whole being ablaze with perfect purpose. The supreme awareness, the intimately felt presence, brings with it a rapture beyond joy, a knowledge beyond reason, a sensation more intense than life itself, infinite in peace and harmony."

While throughout history people have experienced ecstatic phenomena unsought, many have deliberately used physical stimulants to trigger off what is essentially a mental experience. Drugs, alcohol, dancing, sexual orgies, sexual abstinence, self-inflicted torture, have all been used for this purpose.

Those who frequently experience ecstatic states often have a history of ill health. Louise Lateau, a Belgian, was a sickly child. At the age of 11 she was severely gored by a bull; at 16 she nursed a dying household in a cholera epidemic and at 17 an attack of angina nearly killed her. A devout Catholic, when she was 18 she felt an urge to suffer the agonies of Christ's crucifixion. On 15 April 1868 she had a vision of the Christ Child and went into an ecstasy. The following month she experienced bleeding from her side and feet—she had become a stigmatic, someone who repeats in their own body the wounds of Christ. The wounds recurred regularly for the next seven years.

St. Catherine of Siena (1347–80), who had "thousands of ecstasies," some of them lasting three days, was always in poor health; Dostoevsky (1821–81), the Russian novelist, was an epileptic and experienced ecstasies preceding his seizures.

In their mystical literature the Persian Sufis continually employ the metaphor of "madness" to describe their ecstasies. They recognize that while ecstatic experience may lead to integration of the personality, it may equally result in a complete breakdown of all accepted values, in total indifference to good and evil, in madness and schizophrenia.

Death may be sometimes preceded by ecstatic experiences. Illusions of levitation (spontaneous rising into the air) may occur, often in elaborate form, some people believing that they are being carried to heaven by angels. It is common for ecstatics to feel that by this experience they have been purified and purged of all their sins.

Undoubtedly, some of Man's earliest religious experiences, particularly fertility rites and dances, led to ecstatic experiences among some members of the tribe or community. The majority would be excited by the dance and rhythms, but the priests or priestesses of such rites might react to the power engendered by falling into trances during which they experienced ecstatic visions.

In Ancient Greece ecstatic experiences were frequently linked with prophetic utterances. The Greeks respected ecstatics, and the great popularity of the Delphic oracle was based on a supposed ability of its priestesses to foretell the future. There were also many groups of ecstatics who danced in honor of the gods. Dionysus, the god of the cultivated vine, was worshipped by dancers who sought divine inspiration in their dancing. Fantastic, orgiastic performances were held in the spring, at the coming of the grape harvest, and in the autumn. The participants, especially the girls, worked themselves into frenzies, often aided by chewing ivy leaves. They would tear animals apart and devour the flesh raw. Even human victims were sometimes destroyed. The Greeks accepted such rites—without them, they feared, the vines would be barren.

In Greek legend Orpheus was the chief representative of the art of song and playing on the lyre. He was supposed to be a minor god, although some believe that he was a real person, a religious reformer from Crete who introduced the doctrine of *ecstasis* without intoxication among the Thracians and who was slain by participants in one frenzied ritual.

Ecstasies and visions were well known to Romans. The Roman author, Juvenal (A.D. 60–140), in his satires, gave an account of the crazed priests of the Syrian rites who slashed and mutilated themselves in orgiastic frenzies. Many Romans experienced the surge of power which comes from ecstatic experiences and felt themselves inspired by the angels. Some practiced perversions so that they would turn in disgust from the natural world; others practiced extreme asceticism . . . to give themselves the power needed for their mystical experiences.

One great Roman ecstatic was Simon Magus, who disputed with St. Paul. He claimed to have the power of levitation—an art known well to religious mystics who, on the whole, have found it rather embarrassing.

Following the entry into the promised land of Canaan the Jews produced a long line of prophets, who were ecstatic seers, seized upon by forces which they did not understand and by which they were forced to prophesy. Generally speaking, the Jews favored ascetical practices—principally fasting and sexual abstinence—to bring about an ecstatic union with the great unknown.

However, ritual flogging was also used by some Jewish sects to obtain ecstatic experiences and was one of the great ceremonies of the Day of Pardon. Voluntary flogging, as a form of exalted or ecstatic devotion occurs in almost all religions. Egyptians beat themselves during the annual festivals in honor of their god Isis; in Sparta children were flogged before the altar of Artemis Orthia until the blood flowed. At Alea in the Peloponnese, women were flogged in the temple of Dionysus, and at the Roman festival of Lupercalia women were flogged at a purificatory ceremony.

Flagellation was taken up enthusiastically by the early Christian Churches—as a penance, but also as a means of achieving ecstatic union with God. The custom of collective flagellation was introduced into monastic houses, after which some of the flagellants fell into trances and claimed they saw the Beatific Vision.

In Italy in the thirteenth century, flagellant fraternities became common and long processions of people, headed by priests carrying crosses and banners, walked the streets in double file reciting prayers and drawing the blood from their bodies with leather thongs.

In Medieval times mass ecstasy was a well-known phenomenon. It was often a mental release of energy in the great festivals of Martinmas in November, Lammas on 2 February, May Day and Lady Day (1 August). While the ordinary villagers would celebrate with gay parties, drinking, dancing and sexual by-play, those who belonged to witches' covens would slip away for their own ceremonies. They sought out the powers of nature in an ecstatic dance with much leaping and screaming, spinning in an anti-clockwise direction (widdershins). They tried to reach ecstasy in the dance so they could tune in to the spirit world about them, and to achieve this power by a sense of sexual strain induced by the naked dancers, by unfulfilled sexual contacts, and sometimes by drugs such as hellebore or vervain. Witches, frequently supposed to be evil in intent, were often simply nature worshippers seeking power.

European witchcraft is not dissimilar from the Haitian cult of Vodun or Voodoo. Here worship lays special emphasis on the Earth Mother. Dances in her honor are rhythmic and accompanied by drums. They produce ecstatic states in which the devotees are quite unaware of the outside world and suffer the torments of spirit possession with convulsions and frothing at the mouth.

A curious form of medieval ecstasy was tarantism—believed to be due to the bite of the tarantula spider. According to traditional accounts, the first symptom was a state of depression curable only by music, which excited an overpowering desire to dance. Tarantism frequently induced mass hysteria and whole villages were affected by the "dancing ecstasy"—though no one had necessarily been bitten.

The dervish fraternities of Islam were particularly strong during the fifteenth, sixteenth and seventeenth centuries. They resembled Christian monastic orders in form, with a "rule" and a set ritual. This ritual always emphasized the emotional aspect of the Moslem religion, and the well-known "dancing dervishes" in ecstasy cut themselves with knives, ate live coals and glass, handled red-hot spears and devoured serpents.

Ranters, and Quakers in the early days of the movement, were two seventeenth-century English sects in revolt from the Established Church, and insisted on an inward spiritual experience which was manifested in the actions of their bodies. Ranters spoke "in tongues" and threw themselves about when they were "possessed of the holy spirit." They were widely punished for their "blasphemous and immoral views." Many of them were absorbed into the Quakers, who were given their name because they trembled and shook at the intensity of their religious experiences.

In the nineteenth century, many of the ecstatic manifestations known so well to Europe were repeated in America, where Negroes understood the rhythmic dancing and trance ecstasies as no white man ever could. In the history of ecstatic phenomena it would seem that ecstatic experiences stem from a conflict or strain. This conflict may be of the mind or induced by some other cause. Such conditions existed on a racial scale where colored populations lived under the strain of existence in the white man's society, and gave rise to mass religious convulsions such as those experienced by the Holy Rollers.

Meanwhile in Europe, while a few poets and artists such as Charles Baudelaire (1821–67), Théophile Gautier (1811–72) and Eugène Delacroix (1798–1863) experimented with hashish to achieve a "sense of detachment from oneself, of loss of all impulse towards action, and of widespread indifference to other persons as to all worldly ties," in the nineteenth century the major expression of ecstatic experiences came from mediums who sought a trance-like state and were "possessed" by the spirits of the dead.

The orthodox religious mystic tends to differentiate between "sacred" and "profane" ecstasy—the latter being frequently noted for its extreme physical manifestations—but admits the validity of mystical and ecstatic experience.

The Hindu, for example, believes that he does not attain union with his God, Brahman, by means of any achievements of his natural powers, but only by quitting the world of the senses in a state of ecstasy and thus learning the reality of pure being.

Ecstasy figures large in the history of the Christian Church, although it is generally realized that ecstasy is not the only way to spiritual life and that while all experience of God when it becomes intense is ecstatic, ecstatic emotion is not necessarily an experience of God.

St. Paul's conversion was founded on a vision when he traveled from Jerusalem to Damascus, saw a blinding light and heard Jesus Christ speak to him. According to the Acts he often saw visions and heard voices during the course of his missionary wanderings, and in the second Epistle to the Corinthians he records the ecstatic vision in which he was "caught up into the third heaven" and saw things ineffable.

St. Bernard of Clairvaux, Lady Julian of Norwich, St. Teresa of Avila, St. John of the Cross—these are just four great names in the history of the Church whose souls were nourished by direct contact with God.

Sometimes ecstatic manifestations got out of hand; then they were held to be from the devil. The seventeenth-century nuns of Loudun created a first-class scandal by their behavior. A contemporary writer said:

"The nuns struck their chests and backs with their hands, as if they had their necks broken, and with inconceivable rapidity. Their tongues issued suddenly from their mouths, horrible swollen, black, hard and covered with pimples and yet while in this state they spoke distinctly."

The search for ecstasy is by no means dead and often very old forms of it reappear in the twentieth century. There are, for example, witches' covens in Britain today.

Until very recently an old African method of achieving ecstasy—snake handling—was practiced in the southern states of America. As recently as 1956 an eyewitness wrote:

"Several people were fondling rattlesnakes and copperheads with apparent confidence. One deacon of the church twisted a snake round his head and arm and held the snake's head close to or just brushing his mouth. About twenty or thirty people were shaking violently. Many were dancing around, either alone or with others. Some were sobbing, shouting and singing."

Modern snake-handlers say that the snake is supposed to represent the devil and the faith of the faithful protects them from harm. Snake cults have been known for centuries in Africa, and in any group ritual of such psychological intensity one must surely expect to find both inner meanings and the emotional communication of these meanings. There is much discernible phallic symbolism in the snake-handling cult, although in the twentieth century it is unconscious, or at least pre-conscious.

In this century there have been two exceptionally vocal protagonists of the ecstatic experience: D. H. Lawrence (1885–1930) and Aldous Huxley (1894–1963). The former used sexual experience as the trigger for ecstasy and returned to the old, primitive gods of earth and sky and water. Aldous Huxley sought his experiences in mescaline and claimed that under its influence he attained a vision of ultimate reality.

The search for ecstasy, the need for something above normal everyday experience, seems rooted in man. "Civilization" has not killed the primitive need—it continues today in the use of LSD and other drugs, in the revolt of the "flower people" away from accepted social standards and their search for a new outlet and a new vision. Perhaps they do not have the vitality, the burning power of their forefathers who danced in covens and practiced their nature rites, but their purpose is the same. And even if penance, mysticism and ecstasy are a little out of fashion in the Christian Church today, the traditions are alive and strong in the East.

# THE SUPRA-CONSCIOUS STATE

## KENNETH WALKER

"The greatest happiness of the thinking man is to have fathomed those things which are fathomable and to reserve those things that are not fathomable for reverence in quietude."

To that great poet and thinker, Goethe, religious beliefs were essential to the well-being of humanity. They necessitated a man's emergence from the narrow, restricted thoughts of everyday life, and his entry into a more spacious world. But in order to reach this ampler world a man had to escape first from the egocentric thinking of his personality and then to establish contact with a larger and more conscious "Self" than his usual "self."

Religion is one of the several methods by which an individual may establish contact with a higher level of consciousness. But before this is discussed something must first be said on the subject of "consciousness," for even the meaning of that word is often misunderstood in the West. *Consciousness* has often been equated with "thought" in Western writings, but consciousness is no more thought than it is emotion, sensation or movement. It is none of our functions but is an awareness of our various activities at the moment at which they are occurring in us. A little self-observation will be sufficient to prove to us that we usually think, feel, move and respond to the stimulations acting on us, without our being aware of what is happening within us. In other words, we react entirely automatically to the various stimulations which provoke our reactions. Often we are not even aware of these reactions.

From *Image*, Vol. 10, 1964. Reprinted by permission of *Image* Roche Medical Photo Reports, Hoffman-LaRoche Limited.

There are several different ways of classifying degrees or levels of awareness. Gurdjieff describes five different levels of consciousness, namely (1) the level of deep sleep devoid of all dreams; (2) lighter sleep troubled by dreams; (3) the ordinary level of consciousness, a state of waking sleep, maintained during the day; (4) the state of true Self-awareness which we may seldom attain even momentarily; (5) the highest level of Cosmic or Universal Consciousness, that is to say, a state of Supra-consciousness. The fourth and fifth states of consciousness do not occur automatically and they are comparatively rare experiences. Some readers may deny that Self-awareness is an unusual state of consciousness. They will declare that they are often self-aware, in the real sense of that term. Now, it is quite true that occasionally we are less caught up in what we are doing and become aware of our existence in the "here" and the "now." But it is a fleeting experience, for life soon swallows us again and we slip back into unawareness of our own existence.

What is a state of Supra-consciousness? Some psychologists deny the existence of higher states of consciousness, and dismiss them as "dream-states," regarding the experiences of the mystics as entirely illusory. It is strange that Freud, who discovered so much about subconscious states, should not have postulated the existence of levels of consciousness *above* as well as *below* the level on which we usually live. But Jung, Freud's gifted disciple, recognized the importance of mystical phenomena. In his opinion the great majority of his middle-aged patients were suffering because they had lost their earlier religious beliefs.

In order to reach the more silent areas of consciousness we have to get beyond the noisy regions of our minds in which we spend so much of our time. This necessitates a control over our thoughts. We may then be able to reach that silent area which is the dwelling place of the Spirit, for I know of no better definition of the word Spirit than that it is pure Consciousness devoid of all thought and words. The attainment of higher levels of consciousness is closely related to certain religious practices and more particularly to the practices of meditation and contemplation. These are the first steps to the disciplining of the mind, which in course of time may lead to an acquirement of higher levels of consciousness. Meditation is also the gateway to a new and a much more *direct* way of knowing, a way in which the "known" and the "thing known" become one and the same thing. It is a difficult path to tread because our attention is repeatedly being caught again by the ceaseless chattering taking place in our heads. But eventually we may, for a short time, succeed in reaching a state of pure consciousness without thought, a state in which truth is revealed to us *directly* and without the use of words.

In those moments we *see* rather than *think*, and it is only afterwards that we start to fumble for words in which we try to express what was revealed to us. There is nothing "personal" or even *individual* in the direct knowledge which comes to us in a Supra-conscious state. Our individual consciousness merged with a much wider consciousness, which we felt to be Universal. So also were we aware of the presence within us of something much higher than ourselves, of something which, for lack of any other name, we were forced to call God.

Supra-conscious states may, or may not, come, as a reward for the self-disciplining of meditation. Although they never last for very long, during them we seem to be dwelling in an "eternal now." But soon the intensity of our new sense of "being" weakens, the level of our consciousness drops, our personalities reassert themselves, and we are back again in the world of time and of inner chatterings. All that remains of what has been is a sense of gratitude for what has happened. Then life swallows us again and we disappear. But we are unlikely ever to forget what has happened to us. Our experience of the Supra-conscious state remains for us the most important psychic event in our lives.

# STATES OF CONSCIOUSNESS

## ROGER W. WESCOTT

If . . . we divide the individual mind into three functional layers, these will be—reading . . . from the outside in—the "nice," the "nasty," and the "natural," respectively.

While the equivalence is far from complete, this nice-nasty-natural triad inevitably reminds us of three other tripartitions of the mind advanced by psychoanalysis. The first of these is the early Freudian distinction between the *conscious,* the *preconscious,* and the *unconscious* minds, the first of which is characterized by full awareness, the second by fluctuating awareness, and the third by unawareness. The second such tripartition is the Jungian distinction between *imago, persona,* and *shadow,* of which the first is one's ideal of the opposite sex, the second the social role one habitually plays, and the third is one's potential for demonic behavior. The third tripartition is the late Freudian distinction between *superego, ego,* and *id,* of which the first is conscience, the second is self-awareness, and the third is instinct.

When we combine these four trifurcations, what we arrive at are the following synthesized strata:

1. On the surface, a polite, decent, and well-adjusted subpersonality, of which the individual is half aware (but not fully aware, because he is unable to observe his own external behavior with the clarity, objectivity, and completeness possible to other observers)
2. Below the surface, a lonely, selfish, and suspicious subpersonality, of which the individual is keenly aware (but

which he tends grossly to misperceive in the image of the external subpersonality, partly out of wishfulness and partly out of an honest inability to see his inner image in perspective, in the absence of psychic distance between himself and that image)

3. In the depths, a spontaneous, childlike, and sensual subpersonality, of which the individual is rarely aware (partly because of its remoteness and partly because of its unacceptability to the other subpersonalities)

. . . The third of these—the shadowy, unconscious, and natural id—seems, predictably enough, to be the oldest. Zoologically, this is hardly surprising, since there is no evidence of anything resembling an ego or superego among any animals except mammals. And ontogenetic analogy supports this assumption, since those few psychoanalysts who have given any sort of developmental consideration to the id have attributed to it a birthless, deathless, and seemingly changeless character verbally reminiscent of Hindu descriptions of Brahman, the "world soul."

The next to appear was probably the first of the above mental entities—the imaginal, half-conscious, and "nice" superego. Students of animal psychology, such as Kortlandt and Etkin, maintain that man is not the only mammal with a conscience. Domestic dogs and free-living wolves also exhibit it—the wolves, surprisingly enough, more strongly than the dogs. (From what is known about the domesticability of the coyote and the jackal, I would guess that they too are "conscientious." This certainly seems true of the coyote, which can even be employed as a sheep dog.) Since the earliest remains of the genus *Canis,* to which they belong, come from the Upper Pliocene Epoch of about 5 million years ago, it seems reasonable to grant at least this antiquity to conscience itself. . . .

## Ego and Anxiety

The last member of man's inner spiritual trinity to make its appearance was almost certainly the ego, or conscious individual self. The ego differs from the unconscious id in its keen, almost painful, awareness of social reality and from the group-oriented superego in its isolative, often antagonistic, relation toward other psychic entities—toward the superego and the id attached to itself no less than toward the egos of other individuals.

Dating the genesis of the ego is a hazardous undertaking, but I am inclined to correlate its development with the appearance of language, religion, and kinship systems. This would mean that the earliest hominid species to possess an ego was the Neanderthal; the earliest culture to embody it, the Mousterian; and the earliest era to behold it, the Middle Paleolithic. Chronometrically, it would mean that the ego is about 100,000 years old—antique in comparison with civilization but newborn in comparison with conscience. (The probability that ego followed conscience in hominian phylogeny is increased by the fact that it seems to do so in the psychic ontogeny of the child.)

As the specific and characteristic emotion of the conscience is guilt, so the specific and characteristic emotion of the ego is *anxiety*. Most students of personality distinguish anxiety from fear in terms of the palpability of its object, defining fear as an animal's realistic apprehension of a concrete threat to its welfare and anxiety as its vague apprehension of an abstract threat to something connected with, but not actually constituting, itself. In those terms, then, the discipline termed ego psychology by Anna Freud and her coworkers becomes, not just tangentially but characteristically and primarily, the study of anxiety.

The "unreal" threat of which the ego is most apprehensive is, of course, death, or the cessation of its being. Although all higher animals fear and avoid injury, man appears to be the only animal who fears death even when it is unaccompanied by injury. And the earliest expression of man's anxiety over nonexistence is the Mousterian funerary cult of Neanderthal Man, with its evident attempt to arrest and ritually reverse the processes of devitalization and decay.

While pre-Neanderthalian men must have undergone conflict between superego and id, there is no evidence that they were aware of it. Neanderthal Man, however, seems to have been conscious of the clash between self and other. It looks as though he strove manfully (how else?) to resolve this conflict by building propitiatory shrines of the skulls of the animals he killed—by treating with gentle reverence what he had previously handled with rapacious disregard.

Neanderthalian panic in the uncanny face of death is but one facet of a more generalized malaise that Austrian psychoanalyst Otto Rank called "separation anxiety." This anxiety, which he attributed to the traumatic experience of birth (for every infant, he maintained, an "Expulsion from the Garden"), he saw reactivated in every life crisis from weaning through marriage to retirement from active social involvement.

If, however, ego evolved when and as we earlier described it as having done, then anxiety is not a product of birth (for the infant is as egoless as he is speechless) but a condition of egohood. To be egoed, as to be sexed, means being set off in opposition to others. In the case of sex, this opposition is, exclusively at first and primarily at all times, anatomical in nature. But, in the case of ego, the opposition has no perceptive organic basis beyond the physical discontinuity between individuals. It not only involves but essentially consists of a sense of antithesis between self and unself, of contrast between identity and otherness.

From this it follows that both alienation and altruism (each of which, significantly, comes from the Latin root al-, meaning "other") are inseparable from ego, rather than being, as is generally assumed, an overdevelopment of egotism in the first case and an antidote to egotism in the second. For the egoless, altruism is as impossible as alienation, since each requires an awareness of the distinction between "I" and "not-I." The she-bear defending her cubs is not altruistic—nor could she be, unless she first felt and then somehow bridged an emotional chasm between herself and them. And there is no evidence or even likelihood that she does either.

Once the habit of thinking in terms of mutually exclusive alternatives is well established, it then tends to pervade culture. The hominine polarity of ego versus non-ego ramifies to

produce—or at least to reinforce—such comparable polarities
as that between the sacred and the profane, the proximate
and the obviate, or the consanguine and the affinal. That is,
the distinction between "mine" and "thine" came to be paralleled by such distinctions as those between "mind" and "body,"
"this" and "that," and "sister" and "wife." To be sure, such
dichotomies as these were doubtless built on the natural model
of such readily observable dichotomies as those between male
and female, adult and child, or living and lifeless. But the
habit of thinking in antitheses—of bifurcating the world of
experience—is, as French ethnologist Claude Lévi-Strauss
points out, a cultivated one. Only a creature already committed to the intricate system of implicit contrasts (such as
those of frontal versus dorsal or vocalic versus consonantal)
which constitute a phonemic system, would be likely to create
an explicit system of collective oppositions between kin groups
known as "totemism" (which symbolizes the distinction between clans by calling one, for example, by the name of an
animal and another by the name of a plant).

Ego, of course, is not an all-or-none phenomenon. On the
individual level, at least, there are marked variations in the
degree of ego awareness exhibited by different hominian
groups. The most conspicuous connection between self-
awareness and social conditions is the generally positive cor-
relation between egocentricity and the progress of economic
technology. On the whole, hunters and gatherers show minimal development of individual self-interest and self-consciousness. The Arunta of Australia, as described by French sociologist Emile Durkheim, are representative of this minimal
level of economic development, in which the kin group rather
than the individual is the primary focus—quite certainly of
behavior and apparently also of consciousness.

When the herding or tilling stage is reached, and food is
produced rather than merely extracted, an economic surplus
accumulates. This surplus becomes property—a term which,
in Classical Latin, meant (among other things) "selfhood."
It also, of course, meant "ownership"; but even this rendering brings us back to the ego, since ownership in turn means
"possessing something as one's *own*." In most parts of the

world, it is true, farmland is owned not by individuals but by kin groups (ranging in size from families to tribes). Since, however, food production leads to an increase in political authority as well as in economic welfare, group property tends to be administered by powerful individuals who treat both it and their dependent kinsmen as extensions of their own personalities.

The noun "property" itself, like the adjective "proprietary" and the verb "expropriate," comes from Latin *proprius*, "exclusive," from which we also derive the term "proper" with its many and varied usages. Latin *proprius* apparently comes from the phrase *pro privo*, "on one's own behalf." *Privus* by itself meant "special" or "not public." From it come English "privy," "private," and "privacy." The Latin verb corresponding to *privus* was *privare*, "to segregate," from which we derive the words "privation" and "deprive." The interesting realization that arises from this etymological excursus is that the concept of property has been a primarily negative one as far back as we can trace it, laying far more emphasis on exclusion from possession than on enjoyment of possession. (By contrast, the Chinese *Tao Teh Ching*, which is perhaps the earliest book known that advocates a deliberate reversal of the ego trend, never employs a proper name—that is, a name belonging to one individual but not to another. By implication, then, it is a book by Man for all men, rather than a book by Lao-tse for pure-bred Chinese, for celebrated rulers, or for orthodox Taoists.)

When the next stage of economic development is reached, agriculture is supervised and coordinated from literate urban centers of metallurgical industry. At this point, ego awareness grows still keener. Rulers can call still more subjects and property their "own" and can now project their egos in both space and time by means of edicts and monuments. Yet, paradoxically perhaps, their subjects also become more self-conscious, chiefly because the conditions of urban life weaken kinship ties and leave individuals feeling isolated. This very aloneness, in turn, forces urbanites to compensate for their isolation by thinking more about themselves, relying more on themselves, and striving more effectively to advance their own interests.

In one respect—that of ego consciousness—the outlooks of the three economic levels just outlined correspond rather well to those of the three globally sequential culture types posited by sociologist Pitirim Sorokin—the "Ideational," the "Idealistic," and the "Sensate." Ideational cultures, according to Sorokin, are characterized by selfless altruism and sensate cultures by selfish materialism, with idealistic cultures striking a balance between the two. Ideational creations and inventions are usually anonymous offerings to God or Society, while sensate accomplishments are essentially demonstrations of the prowess of this or that individual ego.

Predictably enough, however, there is considerable variation in ego intensity from one culture to another, even on the same economic level. Since the time of Pericles, European urbanites, for example, seem to have been more self-affirmative and their civilization as a whole less anonymous than in comparable urban centers on other continents. (Yet, even in this case, it could be argued that Europeans are more egocentric because they are more urban—that is, more literate, more inventive, and hence more aware—than the indigenes of other continents.)

## Collective Ego

Nonetheless, since ego is not an intrinsically individual phenomenon but may function on a collective level, we ought not to regard it as a foregone conclusion that the civilized West is the most ego-oriented culture that has ever existed. Indeed, there is considerable evidence that familial consciousness, or "kin-group ego," is weaker among urbanites generally than among preliterates anywhere, for most of whom some extension of the family is not merely larger and more persistent but also in a profound sense "realer" than the individual himself. Among the majority of hunting or gardening peoples—which means most of the nonwhites of Africa, Australia, and Latin America—the question is not one of whether the kin group is more focal than the individual but only of which particular kin level is the focus of maximal collective awareness and collective identification. Moving from the narrowest to the broadest such groups, the consanguine and/or affinal bodies of preurban society are:

1. the nuclear family (typically, a man, his wife, and their children)
2. the extended family (typically, an older man, controlling a number of married women, who may be either his wives or those of his sons)
3. the lineage (a group of extended families whose common ancestor is personally remembered by the lineage elders)
4. the clan (a group of lineages whose common ancestor, though not many decades dead, is not personally remembered by its living members)
5. the phratry (a group of clans whose common ancestor may be mythical yet who treat one another as relatives)
6. the moiety (a group of phratries composing half a tribe)
7. the tribe (a group of phratries or a pair of moieties whose members are expected to treat one another as at least fictive relatives)

Of these seven, the two that are most likely to be foci of ego identification for members of industrialized societies are those at the peripheries—namely the first (usually referred to simply as "*the* family") and the last (in its urbanized form, that of the nation-state). For preliterates, the reverse is true: it is the intermediate kin groups that are the foci of identification. It is they that give the preliterate individual wholeness —they without whom he is not a person at all but only a peripheral primate.

## Ideology as Ego Extension

On the other hand, though he lacks the kin-group egotism of the primitive, civilized man readily develops an ego identification of a type apparently unknown to the preliterate world—namely, ideological commitment. Instead of being a

Child of the Lineage, he becomes a Servant of the Cause. Psychologically, such immersion in a larger selfhood shows a functional unity, whether the cause be religious, political, or philosophical in nature. Commitment to causes functions as ego affirmation whether it is labeled "Christian selflessness," "scientific objectivity," or (more revealingly, in the words of Benito Mussolini) "sacred egoism." In each case, the human mind is literally as well as figuratively enthralled to what social psychologist Erving Goffman calls "the sacred self."

All things considered, then, it does seem that literate, urban Western man exhibits a more highly developed ego overall than does ancient, primitive, or non-Western man. For, above and beyond his uniquely egocentric individualism (itself an ideology at least since Renaissance times), Western man also shows as much ego involvement in such supra-familial movements as Lutheranism, Freudianism, or Marxism (all significantly named after persistently ego-assertive individuals) as does non-Western man in his extended kin groups.

So extensive, indeed, is the development of the Western ego that one may well ask if it has not undergone hypertrophy, to the point of constituting a dangerous tumor on the modern mind. If so, it may be that some degree of "ego resorption" may prove necessary if humanity is to survive the stimulating but disrupting experience of Westernization without suffering self-incineration. . . .

It does seem that the progressive expansion of ego that has apparently characterized our species since at least the inception of the Neolithic Era is now reaching an impasse: unleashed collective egoism, whether racial, national, or credal in nature, can only result in unleashed collective aggression on a scale that the species is progressively less able to sustain. Ethnocentrism in every form is egotism, just as surely as is the competitive individualism of the most highly industrialized capitalist nations.

Yet how can the threat of the ballooning ego be contained? Not by "self-abnegation," for this in effect means punishing the ego—a procedure which may be expected to be about as effective as punishing a brain tumor. Nor by self-subordination, for immersing the individual ego in the larger ego of family, tribe, or ideological communion does not eliminate ego but only transfers it to a higher and, if anything, more dangerous level. Even submission to the will of God, as practiced (or, at any rate, pursued) by monastics and mendicants of many faiths, can hardly produce a state of overall ego transcendence, since God (at least as understood by the adherents of the three great Hebraic religions) is himself an ego. Indeed, God is the Ego of egos: untrammeled by id, unsupervised by any higher will, and unlimited in knowledge, power, and longevity.

But if the Lord himself cannot save us from ego, who or what can? The question is a legitimate one that deserves a careful answer. Our answer, however, depends on a more extensive analysis of the stratification of the mind than we have as yet undertaken. For the moment, suffice it to observe that, in many respects, ego—like war and like civilization (with both of which it may be more than accidentally associated)—seems to be an institution. And, if it is such, we can hardly expect that it will succumb to de-institutionalization overnight.

## Unself and Unperson

Impersonality . . . is of several quite different kinds. The most widespread of these, obviously, is the impersonality of nonhominian animals and of hominian infants. This we might call *prepersonality*. The kind most familiar in the contemporary industrial world is that in which personality has been eroded or destroyed by excessive regimentation. This we might call *depersonality*.

The third type of impersonality is the type most rarely observed, most incompletely experienced, and therefore most difficult to understand in our modern life. It has been sporadically reported by artists, mystics, and philosophers since the first millennium B.C. and frequently credited as the source of their inspiration. More precisely, they have described it as a relatively sudden and transitory experience of spiritual growth, too dramatic in nature to be called "learning" in any ordinary sense, although it has much in common with intellectual insight. Many have employed such images as the removal of a blindfold or the disintegration of prison walls to express their sensation on these occasions. And nearly all have commented on the extraordinary difference between the self that underwent these illuminations and the ordinary self that each of them normally was. The illuminated self always seemed larger, more cosmic, and less personal than the common self. And, most striking, despite the brevity of these experiences (some of which, in stopwatch terms, lasted no longer than does a lightning flash), nearly all of them have reported a feeling of certainty that the illuminated self was eternal—or, at the least, that it constituted a part of something far more durable than any separate ego or any individual body. This aspect of mind we shall call *transpersonality*.

The three forms of impersonality—the prepersonal, the depersonal, and the transpersonal—are, though easily confused, fundamentally different, both in genesis and in significance. In functional terms, prepersonality and transpersonality seem to resemble each other far more than either resembles depersonality. For both the prepersonal and the transpersonal states are apparently free of anxiety, while the depersonal state is typified by a complex of wholly negative emotions, ranging from resignation through apathy, depression, and intimidation to impotently rebellious rage. In emotional tone, depersonality resembles personality more than it resembles either of the other two forms of impersonality. For, although personality is affectively more variable than depersonality, exhibiting considerable, if sporadic exuberance, its most persistent mood is one of apprehension. And this, after all, is only what might be expected in view of the fact that personality, being both transitory and self-conscious, inevitably anticipates and fears its own dissolution.

What makes depersonalization painful, of course, is the element of more or less overt coercion involved in it. The depersonalized employee, recruit, or prisoner is forced by irresistible institutional pressure to divest himself of most of the symbols and artifacts of his distinctive personality. The fact that personality itself is characterized by predominantly negative affect, even in the absence of blatant institutional manipulation, suggests that the process of personalization is probably carried on under conditions of more or less covert coercion and that men (which is to say, children) everywhere have to be personalized somewhat against their wills.

However, just as it would be a mistake to equate personality and depersonality, despite their shared disadvantages, so also it would be erroneous to identify prepersonality with transpersonality, despite their common freedom from these disadvantages. For prepersonality is, almost by definition, less conscious than personality, while transpersonality is, by all accounts, more conscious (being, subjectively at least, "cosmic" in scope).

My own guess—and, at present, one can do no more than guess—is that, psychically, transpersonality is "the wave of the future." The evidence for this is not so much an increase in general transpersonal experience (which, outside the confines of the recently developed LSD cult, is scarcely observable) as an obvious and increasing sense of personal malaise among the most highly educated and economically secure members of the industrialized societies. As ever larger numbers of intellectual leaders and cultural innovators resort with ever-increasing frequency to psychotherapists, in order to rid their personalities of neuroses, searching and disturbing questions inevitably arise. One answer which can hardly help but suggest itself is that personalities are not being "repaired" to a degree commensurate with the time, effort, and money being expended on their repair. Most psychiatry is palliative rather than curative in its effect. This consideration may in turn lead to the suspicion that *it is not the distortions of personality but personality itself that produces the intense and persistent emotional conflict with which human culture generally and modern culture particularly is cursed*. Rephrasing this insight in psychoanalytic terms, we might say that all neurosis is character neurosis, or alternatively, that character (here termed personality) *is* neurosis.

Once personality ceases to be regarded as man's most prized possession and begins to be perceived as a burden, transpersonal inclinations—already experienced but still generally resisted—may be expected to make themselves felt with steadily growing force. . . .

## The Waking, Sleeping, Dreaming, Entranced, and Released States

Whatever the ultimate substance of consciousness may prove to be, however, we shall here treat the various states of consciousness in the order of their relative familiarity in our own culture, which is as follows:

1. waking
2. sleeping
3. dreaming
4. entranced
5. released

. . . The last and least familiar state of consciousness in modern Western society is what I have chosen to call the released state. Precisely because it is least familiar, it is also least easy to describe. In terms of subjective intensity, the released state is most like the waking state. In fact, that religious leader whose Illumination Experience is often taken as the paradigm of the released state—Gautama Siddharta, founder of Buddhism—is most commonly known by the honorific title of Buddha, "the Awakened One." What this elliptical sobriquet meant, of course, was not merely that Gautama was an exponent of the waking state, since this could have been said of any alert and thoughtful person. It meant rather that the Buddha's consciousness exceeded that of the ordinary man to the same degree that the waking state exceeds the dreaming state in clarity and completeness.

In objective behavioral terms, however, the released state seems rather to resemble the sleeping state, in that release from the psychic restrictions of the normal waking state is usually achieved when the body is in a state of rest. But, since awareness remains keen in the released state and often involves feelings of bliss as intensely positive as nightmare feelings are negative, it might be fairer to compare released consciousness to dreaming consciousness. For in both the individual, while deeply perceptive, is relatively passive toward his surroundings. Yet (to bring our discussion full circle) the released state resembles the waking state in this, that just as an individual when awake tends to regard his dreams—no matter how intense—as fragmentary and distorted, so that same individual when released tends to regard his unreleased waking consciousness as an equally fragmentary and distorted version of the larger reality that he now apprehends.

The only way in which the released state seems to resemble the entranced state is in their common impersonality. Dreams are generally more personal than is the released state, in that more dream elements are referable, even in the Freudian schema, to the ego and superego than to the id and superid. Of the two impersonal entities—id and superid—there is little doubt, if one may judge by autobiographical descriptions, that it is the superid that contributes more to the released state.

The content of the released state is difficult to describe. Even those mystics who claim to have experienced it rarely claim to have attained this state solely by their own deliberate volition or effort. About the only aspect of released consciousness concerning which nearly all reports agree is its ineffability—the impossibility of translating it into words. Most other descriptions are similarly negative: the released state has no temporal or spatial dimensions; it lacks the separations and divisions of waking life; it cannot be formulated without being distorted. It is the Great Emptiness, the Divine Nothing, Unconditioned Being. Novelist Aldous Huxley called it Mind-at-Large, that in which all particular minds are contained and their contradictions resolved. Lao-tse called it Tao (*"The Way"*—that is, the route which is its own destination rather than a means to some other destination).

The Sanskrit word for this state of consciousness is *moksha*, "release," and the individual who has achieved it is *mukta*, "released." The Proto-Aryan root of these words is *meu-*, "to liquify," from which we get, through Anglo-Saxon, English *mud*, through Latin, English *mucus*, and through Greek, English *myriad*. The common semantic element in all these terms seems to be the idea of "flow." In the released state, the waking intellect no longer attempts to stay the cosmic process by chopping it into segments or rigidifying it into an entity. Instead it flows—and glows—like the world movement of which it is a part.

The notion of fluidity suggests still another image in terms of which the released state has been described. In his discussion of "the Nirvana-Principle" (which, however, he considered a manifestation of the death instinct), Freud referred repeatedly to the "oceanic feeling" experienced and frequently reported by psychotics, sometimes by religious worshipers, and occasionally even by skeptical scientific investigators. The common element in all these reports was a sensation of pleasurable engulfment in a mysterious mindlike something without the spatio-temporal limitations of ordinary individual consciousness. In Europe, as in most of the modern world, such an experience was, at the very least, exotic. In India, however, it had been commonplace for centuries to describe self-realization in terms not of differentiation but of merger. Atman, the individual soul, was pictured as being released from the unending cycle of futile rebirths by reabsorption into Brahman, the world spirit, "like a rain drop into the sea." After considerable soul searching of his own, however, Freud finally concluded that "the ocean of spirituality" was at best an illusion and at worst symptomatic of a schizoid trend in the emotions or an epileptoid tendency in the brain. . . .

The notoriety of the drug cult . . . inevitably raises the question of the extent to which any or all of the states of consciousness we have been discussing can be biochemically induced. The answer is that all of them have been so induced—the waking state by amphetamines, the sleeping state by barbiturates, the dreaming state by opiates, the entranced state by sodium pentathol, and the released state by indoles ranging from mescaline to lysergic acid diethylamide. Yet none of these states occur solely as the result of ingestion or injection of such psychopharmaceuticals; and the evidence is that, for most peoples at most periods, all five types of consciousness have usually been attained druglessly, as a result of either environmental or internal stimuli.

The order in which we have thus far presented and discussed states of consciousness is, of course, an arbitrary one, reflecting only the habits and prejudices of our own contemporary Western culture. From an evolutionary standpoint, a far more logical sequence is one which begins with minimal consciousness (that of the sleeping state) and ends with maximal consciousness (that of the released state).

The intermediate stages of the sequence, however, differ according to whether the development traced is phylogenetic (that of man's ancestry since the Pre-Cambrian Era) or ontogenetic (that of the individual human being from conception on). On the former scale, the order of states of consciousness is probably this:

1. sleeping
2. entranced
3. waking
4. dreaming
5. released

The reason for the preceding arrangement is that, after the minimal awareness which we must ascribe to plants and protozoans, the most probable state of such rudimentary metazoans as worms and coelenterates is one of rigidly stereotyped activity—of a kind which, among men, is observed only in somnambulism and kindred conditions. With cephalopods and vertebrates, however, we encounter an alertness and an adaptability which exceed the capacities of a sleepwalker (although, of course, many such animals can and do regress to such a cataleptic state when immobilized and stroked for a period of time). Dreaming, as we have seen, is confined to warm-blooded animals and persists over long stretches of sleeping time only in mammals. The released state, finally, seems to be unique to man; at any rate, there is as yet no evidence for its occurrence in other species.

While it might at first seem that the ontogeny of consciousness would be far easier to trace than its phylogeny—since ontogeny is contemporary, whereas phylogeny is prehistoric—in actuality the reverse is probably true. For extinct ancestors of ours like the dryopithecines or the crossopterygians have living equivalents in the pongids and the coelacanths, but the hominian embryo had equivalents only among the embryos of other mammals which are almost equally difficult to subject to intrauterine observation. And there is little doubt that some levels of hominian consciousness develop before birth. On this assumption, we may rearrange the evolutionary sequence of states of consciousness in the individual as follows:

1. sleeping
2. dreaming
3. entranced
4. waking
5. released

Our assumption that the dreaming state is the first one attained by the unborn infant after the sleeping state seems justified by two facts. First, the proportion of sleep time taken up by dreaming declines steadily throughout postnatal life, from a maximum of 50 percent just after birth to a minimum of 10 percent or less in the elderly; from which it may be inferred (with some probability, though hardly with certainty) that, in the last few months before its birth, the hominian infant dreams more than half the time. And second, although limb movement also begins before birth, it is intrinsically unlikely that, in our species, prenatal limb exercise would begin as early as prenatal brain exercise. For the tasks that man's brain must perform, even in infancy, far exceed those required of the limbs. It seems plausible, however, that entranced consciousness preceded waking consciousness in all of us, on the grounds that one's sense organs must be fully operative if one is to exhibit the alertness associated with the waking state; whereas an entranced subject can engage in coordinated motor activity even when his sensitivity to sensory stimuli is very slight. We awake, then, only when we are born. And I would further assert, aprioristically, that one must have known the waking state before he can attain the released state, since *striving for release can occur only in one who has achieved awareness of confinement.*

# VISIONARY EXPERIENCE

## ALDOUS HUXLEY

Mr. Chairman, ladies and gentlemen, I feel a little dubious about being here in a group of distinguished scientists. However, I console myself by the thought that the people in my profession have been occupied with the problems of psychology for three or four thousand years before your profession was invented. You have, of course, systematized what people in the literary field have seen in a rather vague and intuitive and spasmodic way, and of course we in our turn can learn a great deal from you.

My excuse for being here, really, can be summed up in the phrase of Alexander Pope that "fools rush in where angels fear to tread." Amid so many academic angels who are of course completely inhibited by their surroundings, by their intellectual vested interests, by their Ph.D.'s, it is very important, I think, that there should break in, every now and then, a literary fool who is not inhibited in any of these ways and who does start ranging about over this immense field and is not afraid of making a fool of himself, or of getting into some kind of academic trouble. I think that in spite of the fact that the literary man cannot contribute anything of solid scientific interest, he may nevertheless be of some value inasmuch as he does explore areas of this fantastic universe of the human mind, which the more cautious academic psychologist is rather nervous of getting into. And with this brief introduc-

From a speech delivered at the XIV International Congress of Applied Psychology, Copenhagen, Denmark, 1961. Copyright © 1972 by Laura Huxley and printed by her permission.

tion let me get on to this fascinating subject of Visionary Experience.

## Why Are Precious Stones Precious?

I shall begin by asking one of those questions which children ask of their parents and which leaves them completely stumped—a question like Why is grass green? This question is: Why are precious stones precious? It is very peculiar, when you think of the subject: Why should human beings have spent an immense amount of time, energy and money in collecting colored pebbles? There is no conceivable economic value in this and they are rather pretty in their way, but it seems very strange that this enormous amount of energy should have been put forth on the collection of precious stones, and also that such an immense mythology and folklore as has arisen and has been crystallized around precious stones, should have ever come into existence.

Why should precious stones have always been regarded as extremely precious? This question was asked some fifty years ago by the distinguished American philosopher, George Santayana, and he came up with this answer. He said . . . that they are precious because, of all objects in this world of transience, this world of perpetual perishing, they seem to be the nearest to absolute permanence; they give us, so to say, a kind of visible image of eternity or unchangeableness. I think there is something in this answer, but I don't think it is by any means the whole answer to our problem. It is important because it seems to go back to some deep psychological factor in the mind, but I don't think it goes back far enough; I don't think it goes to the most important psychological factor, which determines the preciousness of precious stones. And here I shall quote from another philosopher of antiquity, Plotinus, the great neoplatonic philosopher, who in a very interesting and profoundly significant passage says, "In the intelligible world, which is the world of platonic ideas, everything shines; consequently, the most beautiful thing in our world is fire."

This remark is significant in several ways. First of all, it interests me profoundly as showing that a great metaphysical structure, the platonic and neoplatonic structure, was essentially built up on a quasi-sensory experience. The world of Ideas shines, it is a world which can be seen; and this curious fact that the ideal world can actually be seen, can be discovered also in Plato himself. In the *Phaedo,* Socrates speaks about the posthumous world to which good men go after they are dead, and it is rather difficult from the dialogue itself to make out whether this is simply a paradise world, or whether it is also in a sense the world of Ideas. But anyhow, what Socrates says about this world—which he calls the other earth— is again that in this other earth everything shines, that the very stones of the road and on the mountains have the quality of precious stones; and he ends up by saying that the precious stones of our earth, our highly valued emeralds, rubies, and so on, are but infinitesimal fragments of the stones which are to be seen in this other earth; and this other earth, where everything is brighter and clearer and more real than in our world, is, he says, a vision of blessed beholders. Here again is another indication that a great metaphysical idea, the platonic Idea, the platonic system of an ideal world, is also based upon a world of vision. It is a vision of blessed beholders, and I think we now begin to see why precious stones are precious: they are precious because in some way they remind us of something which is already there in our minds. They remind us of this paradisal, more-than-real world which sometimes is glimpsed consciously by some people and which I think most people have had slight glimpses of, and which we are all, in some obscure way, aware of on an unconscious level. And as Plotinus says, it is because of the existence of this other world, this luminous other world, that the most beautiful thing on earth is fire.

Now it is an interesting fact that we still speak about diamonds having fire, that the most precious, most valuable diamonds are those with the greatest amount of fire, and the whole art of cutting diamonds is of course the art of making them as brilliant as possible and making them show off the greatest amount of fire within. And indeed it can be said that all precious stones are in a sense crystallized fire. It is very significant in this context that we find that in the *Book of Ezekiel*, when he is describing the Garden of Eden, he says it is full of stones of fire—which are simply precious stones—so that we see, I think quite definitely, that the reason why precious stones are precious is precisely this, that they remind us of this strange other world at the back of our heads to which some people can obtain access, and to which some people are given access spontaneously.

## Access to the Visionary World

### *Spontaneous Access*

Before I go on to talk about the actual nature of this internal visionary world, let me say a little about the means of access to that world. Some people spontaneously go there; they seem to be able to move back and forth without any difficulty between the visionary world and the workaday, biologically useful world of our ordinary experience. You get people, for example, like William Blake, who is constantly moving back and forth between the two worlds. Blake had a period in middle life when he was unable to visit the visionary world. For about twenty years he didn't see it. He used to see it in his youth, and then again in his old age he was able to go into it quite freely. And we have, I think, plenty of cases of poets and artists who have gone back and forth from one world to another. There are very beautiful and very detailed descriptions of the visionary world given to the Irish poet, George Russell—who wrote under the name of A. E.—where he describes his own experiences of going back and forth into this luminous world within the mind.

There are these spontaneous cases where a privileged few are able to visit the other world and come back again safe and sound. Then I think we can also say that, in a very large number of children—I don't know what the proportion is; I don't think it has ever been systematically investigated—but in a good number of children, there is this capacity to live in a kind of visionary world. They see both within and without this transfigured luminous world. It is of course the world described by Wordsworth in his famous *Ode on the Intimations of Immortality from Recollections of Early Childhood*. I think a great many children have exactly the kind of intimations of immortality which Wordsworth described. Then in due course, as they are subjected to our system of analytical and conceptual education, they lose the capacity of seeing this other world which gradually, in Wordsworth's words, "fades into the light of common day." From having lived in a world which had "the glory and the freshness of a dream," they return to this rather boring, rather drab world in which most of us pass our lives. I would say, in passing, that one of the major problems of education is: How do we help children to make the best of both worlds? How do we help them to make the best of the world of primary experience (and of this extension of primary experience: visionary experience) and at the same time help them to make the best of the world of language and the best of the world of concepts and general ideas? At present our system of education seems almost a guarantee that while we teach them how to use words and concepts, we wipe out this other world of beauty and higher reality which so many children live in.

These are two cases of spontaneous awareness of the other world, of the visionary world. Another class of people who have this awareness spontaneously is the class of the dying. Readers of Tolstoi will remember in that extraordinary story *The Death of Ivan Ilyitch*, that at the end of his unutterable sufferings and miseries, this wretched man feels that he is being pushed into a black sack, deeper and deeper, and suddenly, within a few hours before he dies, he perceives that the bottom of the sack is open and at the end of it is a light.

This is not merely a literary invention. In recent months Dr. Karlis Osis,[1] of the Parapsychology Foundation of New

[1] Karlis Osis, *Deathbed Observations by Physicians and Nurses*. "Parapsychological Monographs," No. 3. N.Y.: Parapsychology Foundation, Inc. (29 West 57th St.), 1961. Pp. 113. (Condensed in *International Journal of Parapsychology* (N.Y.), Vol. 4, No. 2, Spring, 1962, pp. 27–56. See also Duncan Blewett, "Psychedelic Drugs in Parapsychological Research," *ibid.*, Vol. 5, No. 1, Winter, 1963, pp. 43–74.)

York, has been sending out questionnaires to a large number of doctors and nurses getting them to give reports of the state of mind of patients on their deathbed. The interesting thing is that he has . . . about 800 answers from doctors and nurses who report that, spontaneously, patients on the verge of death did have these tremendous visionary experiences of light, of luminous figures. It is a most interesting fact to find that this phenomenon, which has been reported of course in literature in the past, is now statistically confirmed. This is one of the most fascinating things that professional psychologists are doing now. They are confirming, by questionnaires and in the laboratory, all kinds of things which were intuitively known, and known by observation, and recorded in a casual way by literary men and philosophers in the past.

This represents a third class of spontaneous cases. Now we have to go on to the induced cases.

## Induced Access

The fact that visionary experience has always, at all times and everywhere been very highly valued, means that at all times and in all cultures systematic efforts have been made to induce this experience.

The experience can be induced in a variety of ways. . . . One method is hypnosis. Under deep hypnosis a certain number of people (not very many, but I have seen a few) do evidently enter this world and report very strange and interesting happenings: they see figures, they see luminous landscapes, and so on. These are not very common phenomena, but it is interesting to know that there are a certain number of people who can be transported into this other world by hypnosis.

There are other psychological methods for getting into the other world, and one of the best known in the Orient of course is the method of one-pointed concentration, the traditional Yoga method of excluding everything except one particular point on which the attention is concentrated. This in many cases does seem to result in breaking through the barrier surrounding our ordinary, day-to-day, biologically utilitarian world of consciousness, and breaking through into another mode of consciousness, the visionary mode. There is yet another method which has been practiced of course within all the great religious traditions, the method of what is now called sensory deprivation, or the limited environment. Here again it is most interesting to find professional psychologists repeating, in the laboratory, work which was done for metaphysical and religious reasons by hermits and saints living in caves in the mountains or in the desert. It is a very extraordinary fact that when we do limit the number of external stimuli or cut them out altogether, as can be done with some difficulty, then in a relatively short time the mind starts producing tremendous visionary experiences. Historically we see such figures as St. Anthony and the monks of the Thebaid in the fourth century in the Egyptian desert, and we see again the hermits of the Himalayas, the Tibetan and the Hindu hermits who lived in complete isolation in the caves. For example, if you read the life of Milarepa, the great Tibetan hermit, or if you read the lives of St. Anthony and St. Paul, the hermit in the Christian tradition, you will see that this isolation did in fact produce visionary experiences. And it is interesting, as I say, to see these facts confirmed by such contemporary workers as D. O. Hebb at McGill in Canada, [and] Dr. John Lilly . . . Lilly has probably gone further than anyone else in creating a limited environment. He immerses himself in a bath at the temperature of 96, has himself fastened into a harness so that he can hardly move, breathes only through a snorkel so that even his face is covered with water and there is no differentiation of sensation on any part of his body, and within three or four hours he is having tremendous visionary experiences. Now the interesting thing is that like St. Anthony's, most of these visionary experiences are extraordinarily unpleasant. I have asked Dr. Lilly to describe these experiences, but he would never tell me exactly what they were, except that they were very, very unpleasant indeed. St. Anthony, as anybody who has ever visited any picture gallery knows, was also subjected to extremely unpleasant experiences, but he occasionally evidently had genuine mystical and divine experiences. It is interesting too that, in all the religious traditions, deserts and places where there is a minimum of sensory stimulation have always been regarded in an ambivalent way, first of all as the places where God is nearest and secondly as the places where devils abound. We find in the New Testament, for example, that the devils who are cast out by Jesus go into the desert because this is the natural place, the habitat, of devils. But again, hermits who lived in the deserts in the fourth century say they went there because this is the place where one can get nearer to God than anywhere else. As I say, it is extremely interesting to find that these ancient religious practices can be and have been confirmed in the laboratory by modern psychological workers.

Another method of getting into the other world is the method of systematic breathing. Breathing exercises were of course developed most systematically in India, and we find traces of them in the Western tradition, particularly in the Greek Orthodox Church tradition where people did evidently employ some breathing methods, and even in individual Western mystics. I am thinking of Father Surin, the French seventeenth-century Jesuit, who speaks about the different modes of breathing, though he doesn't exactly describe what they were. The significant fact about breathing is that I think one can say that all these elaborate breathing exercises tend to end up in prolonged suspensions of breath. A prolonged suspension of breath necessarily means a growing concentration of carbon dioxide in the blood. Again, it is well known that high concentrations of carbon dioxide do produce very remarkable and startling visionary experiences in the mind, so that we see here, in an empirical way, that people in all the religious traditions of the past made use of methods for changing the body chemistry, in such a way that visionary experiences would become facilitated. This again is the physiological reason, not the metaphysical or the ethical reason, for such practices as fasting.

Fasting has been employed in virtually all the cultural traditions, among other things for the purpose of inducing visions. For example, in a primitive Indian society in America this was a regular part of the initiation of the adolescent young men. They went out into the forest or into the prairie and fasted until they got a vision of the god they were looking for, and in due course they always did get a vision. The methods of fasting of course have been used in every religious tradition. These psychological effects of fasting have been confirmed in the large study by Keys called *The Biology of Human Starvation*.[2] There is a most elaborate description of what happens after a long period of abstention from food, and among the things that happen are these visionary experiences. We know too that the inadequate amounts of vitamins as well as merely inadequate amounts of calories also produce profound psychological changes. There are profound psychological changes in pellagra, for example, and in beriberi. Here again it is interesting, with the knowledge that we now have, to look back over history and to see why a period like the Middle Ages was probably far more fruitful in vision than a period of the present time. The reason very simply is that we are simply stuffed with vitamins and they were not. After all, every winter in the Middle Ages there was a period of extreme vitamin deficiency: pellagra and the other deficiency diseases were very common. On top of a long period of involuntary fasting came the forty days of Lent where voluntary fasting was imposed upon involuntary fasting, so that by the time Easter came around, the mind was completely ready for any kind of vision. I think there is no doubt at all that this is one of the reasons why spontaneous visionary experiences are a good deal less common now than they were; it is simply a dietary factor. In the past, in earlier civilizations, a rather deficient diet tended to make certain types of visionary experiences possible, whereas now our very full diet tends to block them off.

Among other methods of transporting the mind to the other world was the deprivation of sleep. You find this in all the religious traditions: the sleep is reduced and the mind is made open and ripe for visionary experience. Here again it is interesting to see the professional psychologist confirming the find-

[2] Ancel Keys, *et al.*, *The Biology of Human Starvation*. Minneapolis: Univ. of Minnesota Press, 1950.

ings of the past. . . . Dr. J. West a year or two ago had the occasion to supervise the sleeplessness period of a man who was a disc jockey on an American radio station. For a bet he had resolved to go without sleep for . . . ten or twelve days. Dr. West supervised this and he told me that . . . after about seven or eight days . . . this man was living in a completely visionary world with breakings in of every kind of strange visions, some horrible and some rather beautiful. So here again we see an interesting confirmation of old empirical findings, in the modern laboratory.

Even the medieval habit of austerities of self-imposed punishment was probably also extremely conducive to visions. Self-flagellation, for example: if you analyze what the effects of this sort of proceeding were, it is quite clear that they all made for visionary experiences. They first of all released a great deal of adrenalin, a great deal of histamine, both of which have very strange effects on the mind, and then in the Middle Ages, when neither soaps nor antiseptics existed, any wound which could fester, did fester, and the breakdown products of protein got into the bloodstream. We also know that these things do have very strange and interesting psychological effects. In confirmation of this it is very curious to read of the remark by the great French nineteenth-century Curé d'Ars (and now canonized as St. Jean Vianney) who was forbidden by his bishop to indulge in the extremely severe austerities, the self-beatings which he had practiced as a young man, and he said nostalgically, "When I was allowed to do what I liked with my body, God would refuse me nothing." This is a very interesting psychological statement, that evidently there are psychological reactions on the biochemical level which, connected with this kind of self-torture, do tend towards the production of visions.

## Chemical Access

Let us now pass to a final class of vision-inducing procedures; these have to do with the ingestion of various chemicals. As the French anthropologist Philippe de Félice showed some twenty years ago in his book *Poisons Sacrés, Ivresses*

*Divines*,[3] virtually in every religious tradition, both civilized and primitive, use has been made of mind-changing drugs used for the purposes of inducing visionary experiences. Every kind of chemical substance has been used for this purpose. The most anciently recorded, I suppose, is the *soma* of the Indians. Nobody knows, I think, what the plant soma was. It has been identified as the asclepias or milkweed, but the descriptions in the sacred text don't seem to fit in with the milkweed identification. From the ancient text it seems that this was a creeping plant which the Aryan invaders of India in 1000 B.C. brought down with them from Central Asia, and it became more and more difficult to get hold of the plant as they penetrated further and further into India. Philippe de Félice has a very interesting hypothesis that the development of Yoga (which evidently took place probably about this time, although it may have started earlier with the pre-Aryan people in India), the taking over of Yoga by the Aryan invaders may have been forced upon them by the fact that it was impossible for them to obtain supplies of soma so that, as they couldn't induce visions by biochemical means, they were forced to resort to purely psychological and breathing exercises to get to the same place. It is an interesting hypothesis which may perhaps be true . . . Then among the other drugs, which of course have been used in the past, are such extremely dangerous mind-changing drugs as opium and as coca, from which cocaine is derived, and such relatively dangerous drugs as hashish—and alcohol, which was used by the Greeks, later by the Persians, and used by the Celts in Europe as a mind-changing drug and worshipped as a god. This is the interesting thing: the substance which produces the change of mind is regarded as divine and is then hypostatized as a person projected into the external universe as a divine person. We get the same phenomenon in Central America where recently the archaeologists have dug up in the highlands of Guatamala a large number of small stone figures which represent mushrooms out of whose stem emerges the head of a

[3] Philippe de Félice, *Poisons Sacrés, Ivresses Divines.* Essai sur quelques formes inférieures de la mystique. Paris: A. Michel, 1936. P. 395.

god. It is a very significant fact that this mind-changing mushroom which . . . has now entered European life, was actually hypostatized as a deity.

## The Mushroom Access

Among the more harmless mind-changing drugs used by people in their religious rites in the past are peyote, the Mexican cactus, which is used in the southwestern states of America and over large parts of Mexico, then the banisteria of South America, and now of course the Mexican mushroom.

In modern times pharmacology has produced, partly by more refined methods of extraction and partly by methods of synthesis, a number of mind-changing drugs of extraordinary power, but remarkable for the fact that they have very little harmful effect upon the body. Peyote, among the natural drugs, has almost no harmful effect upon the body; it is not addictive, and Indians 80 years old take no more of the drug than they did when they were young, nor do they feel any desire to take it more frequently than once every month or six weeks when the religious rites take place. The extract from peyote which is now the active principle, which is now synthesized mescaline, has the same qualities. Among the more recent additions to the armamentarium of the pharmacologists, the psychopharmacologists, are LSD-25 (lysergic acid diethylamide) which was synthesized by Dr. Albert Hofmann of Basel in 1938, and more recently psilocybin . . . which was synthesized I think not more than 2 or 3 years ago, also by Dr. Hofmann, who began by extracting the active principles of the Mexican mushroom which had been brought back by Professor Heim from his expedition to Mexico with Mr. Gordon Wasson.[4] I recently had the interesting experi-

[4] Roger Heim and R. Gordon Wasson, *Les Champignons Hallucinogènes du Mexique:* Etudes Ethnologiques, Taxinomiques, Biologiques, Physiologiques et Chimiques. With the collaboration of Albert Hofmann, Roger Cailleux, A. Cerletti, Arthur Brack, Hans Kobel, Jean Delay, Pierre Pichot, Th. Lemperière, and J. Nicolas-Charles. (*Archives du Muséum National d'Histoire Naturelle,* 1958. Series 7, Vol. VI.) Paris: Muséum National d'Histoire Naturelle, 1959. P. 322.

ence of reading a letter which Professor Heim had written to my brother and said, "I have just come back from Mexico and as a great triumph I took with me a number of Hofmann's capsules of psilocybin and I gave a dose to the old lady—the curandera, the medicine woman—with whom we had originally done our experiments with the mushrooms—and she was quite delighted because the effects were exactly the same as the mushrooms and she said, 'Now I can do my magic all the year round, I don't have to wait for the mushroom season!'" So this perhaps is one of the great triumphs of modern science, that one of these days perhaps Professor Hofmann at Basel will receive a telegram saying, "Please airmail one hundred capsules to southern Mexico, have very important magic to perform next week"—and the capsules will go and the magic will be performed.

These biochemical methods are, I suppose, the most powerful and the most foolproof, so to say, of all the methods for transporting us to this other world that at present exist. I think . . . that there is here a very large field for systematic experimentation by psychologists, because it is now possible to explore areas of the mind at a minimum expense to the body, areas which were almost impossible to get at before, except either by the use of extremely dangerous drugs or else by looking around for the rather rare people who spontaneously can go into this world. (Of course it is very difficult for them to go in on demand, "the Spirit bloweth where it listeth," we can never be sure that the people with the spontaneous gift of visionary experience will have it on demand.) With such drugs as psilocybin it is possible for the majority of people to go into this other world with very little trouble and with almost no harm to themselves.

## The Nature of Visionary Experience

Having discussed the means of access to this world of visionary experience, let me begin to talk about the nature of the world. What is the nature of visionary experience?

## Light

The highest common factor, I think, in all these experiences is the factor of light. There can be both negative, bad light, and good light. In *Paradise Lost,* Milton talks about the illumination of hell which he says is darkness visible. This I think is probably a very good psychological description of the kind of sinister light which sometimes visionaries do see, and it is a light which I think many schizophrenics see. In Dr. Séchehaye's volume *Journal d'une Schizophrène,*[5] her patient describes precisely this appalling light which she lives in: it is a kind of hellish light, it is a light like the glare inside a factory, the hideous glare of modern electric lighting gleaming upon machines. But on the other hand, those who go into a positive experience say this light is of incredible beauty and significance.

The light experience on the positive side may be divided, I think, into two main types. There is the experience of what may be called undifferentiated light, an experience just of light, of everything being flooded with light. And there is the experience of differentiated light, that is to say of objects, of people, of landscapes which seem to be impregnated and shining with their own light.

In general I think it is possible to say that the experience of undifferentiated light tends to be the experience associated with the fullblown mystical experience. The mystical experience, I think, may be defined in a rather simple way as the experience in which the subject-object relationship is transcended, in which there is a sense of complete solidarity of the subject with other human beings and with the universe in general. There is also a sense of what may be called the ultimate allrightness of the universe, the fact that in spite of pain,

[5] Marguerite A. Séchehaye, *Journal d'une Schizophrène.* Autoobservation d'une schizophrène pendant le traitement psychothérapique. Paris: Presses Universitaires de Frances, 1950. Pp. 138. (Transl. by G. Rubin-Rabson: *Reality Lost and Regained.* Autobiography of a Schizophrenic Girl, with Analytic Interpretation. N.Y.: Grune & Stratton, 1951. P. 161.)

in spite of death, in spite of all the horrors which go on all around us, this universe somehow is all right, and there is a direct understanding of such phrases as we find, for example, in the *Book of Job,* phrases which in our ordinary state we certainly cannot understand. I mean when Job says, "Yea, though he slay me, yet will I trust in Him," this is incomprehensible on our ordinary biological level, and yet it becomes perfectly comprehensible on the mystical level, even on the level of induced mysticism.

Then there is another very characteristic psychological feature in the mystical experience: the sense of an intense gratitude, an intense gratitude for the privilege of being alive in a universe as extraordinary as this, as altogether wonderful. Here again one finds phrases in the mystical literature which are completely incomprehensible on the ordinary, everyday, biological level but which become completely comprehensible on the visionary and mystical level. For example, there is a phrase of William Blake's where he says "Gratitude is Heaven itself." What does this mean? It is very difficult to imagine in our ordinary state of mind, but it becomes perfectly clear in the induced or spontaneous mystical condition: gratitude *is* Heaven itself, gratitude is intense, and the actual experience of gratitude has an uplifting and joyous quality which is beyond all words.

The light experience is of course described again and again in the religious literature. After all, the most celebrated cases, (the light experience by St. Paul on the road to Damascus; a tremendous explosion of light which woke Mohammed out of sleep and which made him faint from its intensity; the experience of tremendous light which Plotinus described as having three or four times in his life)—you will find this again and again in literature. And don't imagine that these experiences of light are confined only to remarkable and outstanding men and women; they are not. A great many quite ordinary people have had them, and this is one of the great merits of the most recent book of Professor Raynor C. Johnson, the book called *Watcher on the Hills,*[6] where he brings

[6] Raynor C. Johnson, *Watcher on the Hills.* A Study of Some Mystical Experiences of Ordinary People. London: Hodder & Stoughton, 1959. P. 188. (N.Y.: Harper, 1960.)

together a great many case histories of perfectly ordinary people who had this tremendous experience of undifferentiated light. If I may quote from a letter I received recently from an unknown correspondent—this is a woman in her sixties who wrote to me saying that she had had an experience as a school girl which had affected her throughout her life—she said, "I was a girl of 15 or 16, I was in the kitchen toasting bread for tea and suddenly on a dark November afternoon the whole place was flooded with light, and for a minute by clock time I was immersed in this, and I had a sense that in some unutterable way the universe was all right. This has affected me for the rest of my life, I have lost all fear of death, I have a passion for light, but I am in no way afraid of death, because this light experience has been a kind of conviction to me that everything *is* all right in some way."

These experiences are relatively common; many more people have them than at present let on; I mean we live now in a period when people don't like to talk about these experiences. If you have these experiences, you keep your mouth shut for fear of being told to go to a psychoanalyst. In the past, when visions were regarded as creditable, people talked about them. They did run, of course, a considerable risk because most visions in the past were regarded as being inspired by the devil, but if you had the luck to convince your fellows that your visions were divine, then you achieved a great deal of credit. But now . . . the case has altered and people don't like talking about these things. This is the value, I think, of Professor Maslow's recent work on what he calls peak experiences.[7] He is collecting a very large number of cases of this kind of experience, and he reassures his students that he is not going to regard them as crazy if they tell him about these things, and he says it is surprising what a number of them do come out with fact that they have had these kinds of experiences.

So much for the undifferentiated light, and here let me point out an interesting fact. I think one can say that in all the religions, both primitive and developed, light is the sort of

[7] Abraham H. Maslow, *Toward a Psychology of Being.* Princeton, N.J.: Van Nostrand, 1962. P. 214. ("Insight Books," No. 5—paperback.)

predominant divine symbol, but the interesting fact is that this symbol is based upon a psychological fact, that the light of the world, the inner light, enlightenment, the clear light of the void in the Buddhist literature, all these are symbols. But they are also psychological facts. Just as the great metaphysical systems—so it seems to me—take their origin in many cases from psychological experiences, so again do we see these great primary symbols of religious life also take their origin from psychological experiences. This quasi-sensory experience of light is something which has run through many, I think one can say all, religions and has become . . . the primary symbol.

From undifferentiated light we pass to differentiated light, that is to say, light contained in objects, shining out of things and people. On its simplest level this is a kind of luminous living geometry. There is something rather interesting here. I think here again we can say that certain symbols are based on psychological facts. For example the Mandalas of India, about which the late Dr. Jung was so keen—these too are based, I think, on psychological facts. In what may be called the early stages of the visionary experience, people do see with the closed eyes things which are exactly like Mandalas. These great symbolic constructs are again based upon immediate psychological experiences.

Beyond these, of course, there are all kinds of more realistic, naturalistic visionary experiences—experiences of architectures, of landscapes, of figures. It is interesting to find that again and again in the accounts given by people of visionary experiences, we find the same elements described; for example, in Heinrich Klüver's book on peyotl where he sums up most of the material which had been published up to the time that he wrote it.[8] We find again and again this description of luminous landscapes and architectures encrusted with gems. The doors and windows are surrounded by gems, the whole world of landscape is filled with what Ezekiel calls the stones

---

[8] Heinrich Klüver, *Mescal*. The 'Divine' Plant and Its Psychological Effects. London: Kegan Paul, Trench, Trubner & Co., 1928. P. 111. (Soon to be republished by the University of Chicago Press.)

of fire. These descriptions of course very closely parallel all the accounts of paradises, posthumous worlds and fairylands which are found in all the traditions of the world. . . . I think it is important to point out that here again there is a psychological basis to a great deal of material which is to be found in the traditional literature of religion and folklore.

## Visionary Figures

We come now to the visionary figures. These also occur—and here again there is a very curious and interesting fact which has been recorded again and again in the literature both of spontaneous experiences and induced experiences—that when a figure is seen, it virtually never has a face which we recognize. Our fathers and mothers and wives and children do not appear. What we see is a complete stranger.

Here again I think this fact accounts for some interesting theological speculations. For example, angels are not, as now theoretically supposed, the departed spirits of the dead; they belong to another species altogether. This exactly confirms what the psychologists have found in relation to induced or spontaneous experiences; these are always figures of strangers.

When one starts to think about the neurology and the psychology of this state of affairs, it is most extraordinary that there is something in our brain/mind, some part of our brain/mind, which uses the memories of visual experiences and recombines them in such a way as to present to the consciousness something absolutely novel, which has nothing to do with our private life and very little to do, as far as one can see, with the life of humanity in general. Personally I find it extremely comforting to think that I have somewhere at the back of my skull something which is absolutely indifferent to me and even absolutely indifferent to the human race. I think this is something very satisfying, that there is an area of the mind which doesn't care about what I am doing, but which is concerned with something quite, quite different. And why this should be and what the neurological basis is, I cannot imagine, but this is something which I think requires investigation.

## Transfigurations

Now we come to another aspect of differentiated light which may be described as the spilling out from the interior world into the external world. There is a kind of visionary experience which people have with the eyes open and which consists in a transfiguration of the external world so that it seems overwhelmingly beautiful and alive and shining. This of course is what Wordsworth described so beautifully and so accurately in his great *Ode on the Intimations of Immortality,* and similar experiences can be found in the works of the mystics, in the work of the Anglican mystic, Traherne, who gives an incredibly beautiful description of the kind of transfigured world in which he lived in childhood. This description ends up with the most beautiful passage where he describes this wonderful world, and he says, "And so with much ado I was taught the dirty devices of the world which now I unlearn and become as a little child again so that I now enter once more the Kingdom of God."

And here . . . is surely one of the great challenges to modern education: How do we keep alive this world of immense value which people have had during childhood and which certain privileged people retain throughout their lives? How do we keep this alive and at the same time impart a sufficient amount of conceptual education to make them efficient citizens and scientists? This I don't know, but I am absolutely certain that *this* is one of the important challenges confronting modern education.

This transfigured external vision is very important in relation to art. By no means is all art visionary art; there is wonderful art which is essentially not visionary art. But there is also wonderful art which is essentially visionary art, which is the product either of the artist's vision, so to say, with the eyes closed, of what is happening inside his head, this extraordinary other world; or else a vision of the external world transfigured either for the good or for the evil. In the works of van Gogh, for example, one can find extraordinary examples of both negative and of positive transfiguration. One can see in the same exhibition two pictures, one of which quite clearly is the most blissful picture of the most blissful experience of a positively transfigured world, and next to it will be a picture which is absolutely terrifying in its sinisterness, where he has perceived the world as indeed transfigured, but transfigured in a purely diabolic way. One can understand the sufferings of this unfortunate man who could be precipitated out of a real paradise into something absolutely infernal, and it is not surprising that he ended up as a suicide. When one sees a large collection of his pictures it is quite easy to trace the ups and downs of his extraordinary experience, both of positive and of negative transfiguration.

## Visionary Experience, Religion and Folklore

Now very briefly let us touch on some of the significances of visionary experience for religion and folklore. One finds, in all the traditions, descriptions of paradise, of the golden age, of the future life, which one places side by side with the descriptions of visionary experience, either spontaneous or induced, and sees that they are exactly the same; that the world described in popular religion, these other worlds, are simply descriptions of visionary experiences that men have projected from the inside into the universe. In all the traditions we find the same confusion of gems, and where gems are not used we find glass which, of course, was regarded as a very precious and strange material in the past. We find this in the *Book of Revelation*, a sea of glass in the New Jerusalem, the walls of which were gold and yet transparent, a kind of gold and transparent glass, and we find the same emphasis on glass as a marvelous magical material in the Northern traditions. We find it in the Celtic tradition, in the Welsh tradition; for example the home of the dead is called Ynisvitrin, the Isle of Glass, and in the Teutonic tradition the dead live in a place called Glasberg, the mountain of glass. And it is most curious to find, from Japan to Western Europe, these same images coming through again and again, showing how universal and how uniform this kind of visionary experience has been and how it has constantly been regarded as of immense importance and has been projected out into the cosmos in the various religious traditions.

## Visionary Arts

Let me talk very briefly about some of the arts which are visionary in nature. Needless to say, one of the most extraordinary which reached its pitch of excellence in the twelfth and thirteenth centuries is the art of stained glass. Anybody who has been inside Chartres Cathedral or inside the Sainte-Chapelle in Paris will realize how extraordinary this art could be, that inside the Sainte-Chapelle, for example, one is inside an immense gem, a most elaborate kind of jeweled vision which one is at the heart of. It is a very interesting historical fact that in the twelfth century the famous Abbot of St. Denis, Suger, says that in his time, in all the churches, there were two collecting boxes, one for the poor, and one for making stained-glass windows, and whereas the collecting box for the poor was generally empty, the collecting box for stained-glass windows was always full, showing that people did immensely value this kind of visionary experience.

Another interesting fact is that visionary art is very often popular art, and many popular arts are very often visionary arts, for example the art of pageantry and processions of dressing up. All Kings and Popes and every member of the aristocracy, of the religious hierarchies of the past, have always understood perfectly well the enormous power of this kind of visionary display on human beings. These pageants, the entry of Kings into cities, the coronation of Popes, have always been immensely popular and have been, I think, among the most powerful instruments for persuading people that *de facto* authority was also *de jure, de jure divino* authority. And it is by creating a kind of visionary surrounding, visionary environment to the symbol of naked authority, that naked authority comes to be accepted as legitimate.

Another kind of popular art which is visionary is, of course, the art of fireworks. Fireworks had an enormous development even in the Roman empire, and after the invention of gunpowder they went much further than they could ever go in the past. But these have always been enormously popular forms of art and are essentially visionary arts.

Similarly the art of spectacle in the theater: the great Elizabethan and Jacobean masques of the sixteenth and seventeenth centuries on which fantastic sums were spent. There is the record of one masque put on by the lawyers of the Inns of Court in London which cost twenty thousand pounds in money at that period, which is an absolutely gigantic sum now, probably at least a quarter of a million pounds for one night's entertainment. I am showing the enormous interest and excitement which this kind of display evoked. Needless to say, this kind of popular art, depending upon luminous display, is largely contingent upon the current development of technology. In the past, I am sure, with candles, extremely poor illumination was possible, and it is interesting to note that since the invention of the parabolic mirror at the end of the eighteenth century, then the invention of gas, then limelight, then electricity, it has become possible to produce visionary effects in the world of the theater which were quite out of the question in the past.

Here again popular etymology is very interesting. It is interesting, for example, to find that Athanasius Kircher's invention in the seventeenth century was immediately called Lanterna Magica; his projection of a luminous image in a dark room on a white screen was immediately felt to be in some way magical. The word "magic lantern" was felt to be completely appropriate to this kind of visionary experience.

I find it very touching to think that one can trace a complete spectrum of visionary experience from fireworks through the magic lantern, through the modern review or colored movie, colored spectacle, right up through the visions of the Saints and finally the undifferentiated light of the mystics. This whole thing follows a continuous curve, and throughout there has been this immediate sense on the part of almost everyone concerned that there was something intrinsically valuable and important in this kind of experience.

And this leads me to my conclusion—what is the value of visionary experience?

## The Value of Visionary Experience

I suppose in a certain sense one can say the value is absolute. In a sense one can say that visionary experience is . . . a manifestation simultaneously of the beautiful and the true, of intense beauty and intense reality, and as such it doesn't have to be justified in any other way. After all, the Good, the True and the Beautiful are absolute values, and in a certain sense one can say that visionary experience has always been regarded as an absolute value, that it has been always felt to be intrinsically of immense significance and importance and worth having at a very great price.

But it is also important to point out that, although they are in some sense intrinsically valuable and in some sense absolutely valuable, yet I think we can speak about visionary experiences in terms of their value within the frame of reference of goodness and spirituality. In this context I think it is very important to think of the theological definition of such experiences. The theological definition of a vision or even of a spontaneous mystical experience is "a gratuitous grace." These things are graces. They are given to us; we don't work for them. They come to us and they are gratuitous, which means to say that they are neither necessary nor sufficient for salvation or for enlightenment, whatever you like to call it. But if they are properly used, if they are co-operated with, if the memory of them is felt to be important and people work along the lines laid down during the vision, then they can be of immense value to us and of great importance in changing our lives. This idea of the gratuitous grace which takes on importance if we co-operate with it, is very significant in all the range of visionary experience, both spontaneous and induced.

We shall hear [much] about the induction of such experiences by such substances as psilocybin, and I would certainly say that this kind of induced experience may be of no value at all, it may be just like going to the movies and seeing an interesting film. Or on the contrary, if it is co-operated with, if we perceive this has some sort of deep significance and we do something about it, then it may be very, very important in changing our lives, changing our mode of consciousness, perceiving that there are other ways of looking at the world than the ordinary utilitarian manner, and it may also result in significant changes of behavior.

We now come to the philosophical problem: What is the metaphysical status of visions, what is the ontological status? . . . For the time being we can say, I think, that the value, apart from their intrinsic value, so to say the ethical, sociological and spiritual value of the visionary experience, is that, if it is well used, it can result in a significant and important change in the mode of consciousness and perhaps also in a change in behavior for the good.

# THE PERENNIAL PHILOSOPHY

## ALDOUS HUXLEY

*Philosophia perennis*—the phrase was coined by Leibniz; but the thing—the metaphysic that recognizes a divine Reality substantial to the world of things and lives and minds; the psychology that finds in the soul something similar to, or even identical with, divine Reality; the ethic that places man's final end in the knowledge of the immanent and transcendent Ground of all being—the thing is immemorial and universal. Rudiments of the Perennial Philosophy may be found among the traditional lore of primitive peoples in every region of the world, and in its fully developed forms it has a place in every one of the higher religions. A version of this Highest Common Factor in all preceding and subsequent theologies was first committed to writing more than twenty-five centuries ago, and since that time the inexhaustible theme has been treated again and again, from the standpoint of every religious tradition and in all the principal languages of Asia and Europe. . . .

Knowledge is a function of being. When there is a change in the being of the knower, there is a corresponding change in the nature and amount of knowing. For example, the being of a child is transformed by growth and education into that of a man; among the results of this transformation is a revolutionary change in the way of knowing and the amount

From pp. vii–xi ("Introduction") and pp. 1–21 ("That Art Thou," Chapter 1) in *The Perennial Philosophy*, by Aldous Huxley. Copyright 1944, 1945 by Aldous Huxley. Reprinted by permission of Harper & Row, Publishers, Inc. and Chatto and Windus Ltd.

and character of the things known. As the individual grows up, his knowledge becomes more conceptual and systematic in form, and its factual, utilitarian content is enormously increased. But these gains are offset by a certain deterioration in the quality of immediate apprehension, a blunting and a loss of intuitive power. Or consider the change in his being which the scientist is able to induce mechanically by means of his instruments. Equipped with a spectroscope and a sixty-inch reflector an astronomer becomes, so far as eyesight is concerned, a superhuman creature; and, as we should naturally expect, the knowledge possessed by this superhuman creature is very different, both in quantity and quality, from that which can be acquired by a star-gazer with unmodified, merely human eyes.

Nor are changes in the knower's physiological or intellectual being the only ones to affect his knowledge. What we know depends also on what, as moral beings, we choose to make ourselves. "Practice," in the words of William James, "may change our theoretical horizon, and this in a twofold way: it may lead into new worlds and secure new powers. Knowledge we could never attain, remaining what we are, may be attainable in consequences of higher powers and a higher life, which we may morally achieve." To put the matter more succinctly, "Blessed are the pure in heart, for they shall see God." And the same idea has been expressed by the Sufi poet, Jalal-uddin Rumi, in terms of a scientific metaphor: "The astrolabe of the mysteries of God is love."

. . . The Perennial Philosophy is primarily concerned with the one, divine Reality substantial to the manifold world of things and lives and minds. But the nature of this one Reality is such that it cannot be directly and immediately apprehended except by those who have chosen to fulfill certain conditions, making themselves loving, pure in heart, and poor in spirit. Why should this be so? We do not know. It is just one of those facts which we have to accept, whether we like them or not and however implausible and unlikely they may seem. Nothing in our everyday experience gives us any reason for supposing that water is made up of hydrogen and oxygen; and yet when we subject water to certain rather drastic treatments, the nature of its constituent elements becomes manifest. Similarly, nothing in our everyday experience gives us much reason for supposing that the mind of the average sensual man has, as one of its constituents, something resembling, or identical with, the Reality substantial to the manifold world; and yet, when that mind is subjected to certain rather drastic treatments, the divine element, of which it is in part at least composed, becomes manifest, not only to the mind itself, but also, by its reflection in external behaviour, to other minds. It is only by making physical experiments that we can discover the intimate nature of matter and its potentialities. And it is only by making psychological and moral experiments that we can discover the intimate nature of mind and its potentialities. In the ordinary circumstances of average sensual life these potentialities of the mind remain latent and unmanifested. If we would realize them, we must fulfill certain conditions and obey certain rules, which experience has shown empirically to be valid.

In regard to few professional philosophers and men of letters is there any evidence that they did very much in the way of fulfilling the necessary conditions of direct spiritual knowledge. When poets or metaphysicians talk about the subject matter of the Perennial Philosophy, it is generally at second hand. But in every age there have been some men and women who chose to fulfil the conditions upon which alone, as a matter of brute empirical fact, such immediate knowledge can be had; and of these a few have left accounts of the Reality they were thus enabled to apprehend and have tried to relate, in one comprehensive system of thought, the given facts of this experience with the given facts of their other experiences. To such first-hand exponents of the Perennial Philosophy those who knew them have generally given the name of "saint" or "prophet," "sage" or "enlightened one." . . .

[We] shall here confine our attention to but a single feature of this traditional psychology—the most important, the most emphatically insisted upon by all exponents of the Perennial Philosophy and, we may add, the least psychological. For the doctrine that is to be illustrated in this section belongs to autology rather than psychology—to the science, not of the personal ego, but of that eternal Self in the depth of particular, individualized selves, and identical with, or at least akin to, the divine Ground. Based upon the direct experience of those who have fulfilled the necessary conditions of such knowledge, this teaching is expressed most succinctly in the Sanskrit formula, *tat tvam asi* ("That art thou"); the Atman, or immanent eternal Self, is one with Brahman, the Absolute Principle of all existence; and the last end of every human being is to discover the fact for himself, to find out Who he really is.

> The more God is in all things, the more He is outside them. The more He is within, the more without.
>
> ECKHART

Only the transcendent, the completely other, can be immanent without being modified by the becoming of that in which it dwells. The Perennial Philosophy teaches that it is desirable and indeed necessary to know the spiritual Ground of things, not only within the soul, but also outside in the world and, beyond world and soul, in its transcendent otherness—"in heaven."

> Though GOD is everywhere present, yet He is only present to thee in the deepest and most central part of thy soul. The natural senses cannot possess God or unite thee to Him; nay, thy inward faculties of understanding, will and memory can only reach after God, but cannot be the place of his habitation in thee. But there is a root or depth of thee from whence all these faculties come forth, as lines from a centre, or as branches from the body of the tree. This depth is called the centre, the fund or bottom of the soul. This depth is the unity, the eternity—I had almost said the infinity—of thy soul; for it is so infinite that nothing can satisfy it or give it rest but the infinity of God.
>
> WILLIAM LAW

This extract seems to contradict what was said above; but the contradiction is not a real one. God within and God without —these are two abstract notions, which can be entertained by the understanding and expressed in words. But the facts to which these notions refer cannot be realized and experienced except in "the deepest and most central part of the soul." And this is true no less of God without than of God within. But though the two abstract notions have to be realized (to use a spatial metaphor) in the same place, the intrinsic nature of the realization of God within is qualitatively different from that of the realization of God without, and each in turn is different from that of the realization of the Ground as simultaneously within and without—as the Self of the perceiver and at the same time (in the words of the Bhagavad-Gita) as "That by which all this world is pervaded." . . .

The man who wishes to know the "That" which is "thou" may set to work in any one of three ways. He may begin by looking inwards into his own particular *thou* and, by a process of "dying to self"—self in reasoning, self in willing, self in feeling—come at last to a knowledge of the Self, the Kingdom of God that is within. Or else he may begin with the *thous* existing outside himself, and may try to realize their essential unity with God and, through God, with one another and with his own being. Or, finally (and this is doubtless the best way), he may seek to approach the ultimate That both from within and from without, so that he comes to realize God experimentally as at once the principle of his own *thou* and of all other *thous*, animate and inanimate. The completely illuminated human being knows, with Law, that God "is present in the deepest and most central part of his own soul"; but he is also and at the same time one of those who, in the words of Plotinus,

> see all things, not in process of becoming, but in Being, and see themselves in the other. Each being contains in itself the whole intelligible world. Therefore All is everywhere. Each is there All, and All is each. Man as he now is has ceased to be the All. But when he ceases to be an individual, he raises himself again and penetrates the whole world.

It is from the more or less obscure intuition of the oneness that is the ground and principle of all multiplicity that philosophy takes its source. And not alone philosophy, but natural science as well. All science, in Meyerson's phrase, is the reduction of multiplicities to identities. Divining the One within and beyond the many, we find an intrinsic plausibility in any explanation of the diverse in terms of a single principle.

The philosophy of the Upanishads reappears, developed and enriched, in the Bhagavad-Gita and was finally systematized, in the ninth century of our era, by Shankara. Shankara's teaching (simultaneously theoretical and practical, as is that of all true exponents of the Perennial Philosophy) is summarized in his versified treaties, *Viveka-Chudamani* ("The Crest-Jewel of Wisdom"). All the following passages are taken from this conveniently brief and untechnical work.

The Atman is that by which the universe is pervaded, but which nothing pervades; which causes all things to shine, but which all things cannot make to shine. . . .

The nature of the one Reality must be known by one's own clear spiritual perception; it cannot be known through a pandit (learned man). Similarly the form of the moon can only be known through one's own eyes. How can it be known through others? . . .

Liberation cannot be achieved except by the perception of the identity of the individual spirit with the universal Spirit. It can be achieved neither by Yoga (physical training), nor by Sankhya (speculative philosophy), nor by the practice of religious ceremonies, nor by mere learning. . . .

Disease is not cured by pronouncing the name of medicine, but by taking medicine. Deliverance is not achieved by repeating the word "Brahman," but by directly experiencing Brahman. . . .

The wise man is one who understands that the essence of Brahman and of Atman is Pure Consciousness, and who realizes their absolute identity. The identity of Brahman and Atman is affirmed in hundreds of sacred texts. . . .

Caste, creed, family and lineage do not exist in Brahman. Brahman has neither name nor form, transcends merit and demerit, is beyond time, space and the objects of sense-experience. Such is Brahman, and "thou art That." Meditate upon this truth within your consciousness.

Supreme, beyond the power of speech to express, Brahman may yet be apprehended by the eye of pure illumination. Pure, absolute and eternal Reality—such is Brahman, and "thou art That." Meditate upon this truth within your consciousness. . . .

Though One, Brahman is the cause of the many. There is no other cause. And yet Brahman is independent of the law of causation. Such is Brahman, and "thou art That." Meditate upon this truth within your consciousness. . . .

It is ignorance that causes us to identify ourselves with the body, the ego, the senses, or anything that is not the Atman. He is a wise man who overcomes this ignorance by devotion to the Atman. . . .

SHANKARA

In the Taoist formulations of the Perennial Philosophy there is an insistence, no less forcible than in the Upanishads, the Gita and the writings of Shankara, upon the universal immanence of the transcendent spiritual Ground of all existence. What follows is an extract from one of the great classics of Taoist literature, the Book of Chuang Tzu, most of which seems to have been written around the turn of the fourth and third centuries B.C.

Do not ask whether the Principle is in this or in that; it is in all beings. It is on this account that we apply to it the epithets of supreme, universal, total. . . . It has ordained that all things should be limited, but is Itself unlimited, infinite. As to what pertains to manifestation, the Principle causes the succession of its phases, but is not this succession. It is the author of causes and effects, but is not the causes and effects. It is the author of condensations and dissipations (birth and death, changes of state), but is not itself condensations and dissipations. All proceeds from It and is under its influence. It is in all things, but is not identical with beings, for it is neither differentiated nor limited.

CHUANG TZU

From Taoism we pass to that Mahayana Buddhism which, in the Far East, came to be so closely associated with Taoism, borrowing and bestowing until the two came at last to be fused in what is known as Zen. The Lankavatara Sutra, from which the following extract is taken, was the scripture which the founder of Zen Buddhism expressly recommended to his first disciples.

> Those who vainly reason without understanding the truth are lost in the jungle of the Vijnanas (the various forms of relative knowledge), running about here and there and trying to justify their view of ego-substance.
>
> The self realized in your inmost consciousness appears in its purity; this is the Tathagata-garbha (literally, Buddha-womb), which is not the realm of those given over to mere reasoning. . . .
>
> Pure in its own nature and free from the category of finite and infinite, Universal Mind is the undefiled Buddha-womb, which is wrongly apprehended by sentient beings.
>
> LANKAVATARA SUTRA

> One Nature, perfect and pervading, circulates in all natures,
> One Reality, all-comprehensive, contains within itself all realities.
> The one Moon reflects itself wherever there is a sheet of water,
> And all the moons in the waters are embraced within the one Moon.
> The Dharma-body (the Absolute) of all the Buddhas enters into my own being.
> And my own being is found in union with theirs. . . .
> The Inner Light is beyond praise and blame;
> Like space it knows no boundaries,
> Yet it is even here, within us, ever retaining its serenity and fullness.
> It is only when you hunt for it that you lose it;
> You cannot take hold of it, but equally you cannot get rid of it,
> And while you can do neither, it goes on its own way.
> You remain silent and it speaks; you speak, and it is dumb;
> The great gate of charity is wide open, with no obstacles before it.
>
> YUNG-CHIA TA-SHIH

I am not competent . . . to discuss the doctrinal differences between Buddhism and Hinduism. Let it suffice to point out that, when he insisted that human beings are by nature "non-Atman," the Buddha was evidently speaking about the personal self and not the universal Self. The Brahman controversialists, who appear in certain of the Pali scriptures, never so much as mention the Vedanta doctrine of the identity of Atman and Godhead and the non-identity of ego and Atman. What they maintain and Gautama denies is the substantial nature and eternal persistence of the individual psyche. "As an unintelligent man seeks for the abode of music in the body of the lute, so does he look for a soul within the *skandhas* (the material and psychic aggregates, of which the individual mind-body is composed)." About the existence of the Atman that is Brahman, as about most other metaphysical matters, the Buddha declines to speak, on the ground that such discussions do not tend to edification or spiritual progress among the members of a monastic order, such as he had founded. But though it has its dangers, though it may become the most absorbing, because the most serious and noblest, of distractions, metaphysical thinking is unavoidable and finally necessary. Even the Hinayanists found this, and the later Mahayanists were to develop, in connection with the practice of their religion, a splendid and imposing system of cosmological, ethical and psychological thought. This system was based upon the postulates of a strict idealism and professed to dispense with the idea of God. But moral and spiritual experience was too strong for philosophical theory, and under the inspiration of direct experience, the writers of the Mahayana sutras found themselves using all their ingenuity to explain why the Tathagata and the Bodhisattvas display an infinite charity towards beings that do not really exist. At the same time they stretched the framework of subjective idealism so as to make room for Universal Mind; qualified the idea of soullessness with the doctrine that, if purified, the individual mind can identify itself with the Universal Mind or Buddha-womb; and, while maintaining godlessness, asserted that this realizable Universal Mind is the inner consciousness of the eternal Buddha and that the Buddha-mind is associated with "a great compassionate heart" which desires the liberation of every sentient being and bestows divine grace on all who make a serious effort to achieve man's final end. In a word, despite their inauspicious vocabulary, the best of the Mahayana sutras contain an authentic formulation of the Perennial Philosophy—a formulation which in some respects (as we shall see when we come to the section, "God in the World") is more complete than any other.

In India, as in Persia, Mohammedan thought came to be enriched by the doctrine that God is immanent as well as transcendent, while to Mohammedan practice were added the moral disciplines and "spiritual exercises," by means of which the soul is prepared for contemplation or the unitive knowledge of the Godhead. It is a significant historical fact that the poet-saint Kabir is claimed as a co-religionist both by Moslems and Hindus. The politics of those whose goal is beyond time are always pacific; it is the idolaters of past and future, of reactionary memory and Utopian dream, who do the persecuting and make the wars.

> Behold but One in all things; it is the second that leads you astray.
>
> KABIR

That this insight into the nature of things and the origin of good and evil is not confined exclusively to the saint, but is recognized obscurely by every human being, is proved by the very structure of our language. For language, as Richard Trench pointed out long ago, is often "wiser, not merely than the vulgar, but even than the wisest of those who speak it. Sometimes it locks up truths which were once well known, but have been forgotten. In other cases it holds the germs of truths which, though they were never plainly discerned, the genius of its framers caught a glimpse of in a happy moment of divination." For example, how significant it is that in the Indo-European languages, as Darmsteter has pointed out, the root meaning "two" should connote badness. The Greek prefix dys- (as in dyspepsia) and the Latin dis- (as in dishonorable) are both derived from "duo." The cognate bis- gives a pejorative sense to such modern French words as *bévue* ("blunder," literally "two-sight"). Traces of that "second which leads you astray" can be found in "dubious," "doubt" and *Zweifel*—for to doubt is to be double-minded. Bunyan has his Mr. Facing-both-ways, and modern American slang its "two-timers." Obscurely and unconsciously wise, our language confirms the findings of the mystics and proclaims the essential badness of division—a word, incidentally, in which our old enemy "two" makes another decisive appearance.

Here it may be remarked that the cult of unity on the political level is only an idolatrous *ersatz* for the genuine religion of unity on the personal and spiritual levels. Totalitarian regimes justify their existence by means of a philosophy of political monism, according to which the state is God on earth, unification under the heel of the divine state is salvation, and all means to such unification, however intrinsically wicked, are right and may be used without scruple. This political monism leads in practice to excessive privilege and power for the few and oppression for the many, to discontent at home and war abroad. But excessive privilege and power are standing temptations to pride, greed, vanity and cruelty; oppression results in fear and envy; war breeds hatred, misery and despair. All such negative emotions are fatal to the spiritual life. Only the pure in heart and poor in spirit can come to the unitive knowledge of God. Hence, the attempt to impose more unity upon societies than their individual members are ready for makes it psychologically almost impossible for those individuals to realize their unity with the divine Ground and with one another.

Among the Christians and the Sufis, to whose writings we now return, the concern is primarily with the human mind and its divine essence.

> My Me is God, nor do I recognize any other Me except my God Himself.
>
> ST. CATHERINE OF GENOA

> In those respects in which the soul is unlike God, it is also unlike itself.
>
> ST. BERNARD

> I went from God to God, until they cried from me in me, "O thou I!"
>
> BAYAZID OF BISTUN

Two of the recorded anecdotes about this Sufi saint deserve to be quoted here. "When Bayazid was asked how old he was, he replied, 'Four years.' They said, 'How can that be?' He answered, 'I have been veiled from God by the world for seventy years, but I have seen Him during the last four years. The period during which one is veiled does not belong to one's life.'" On another occasion someone knocked at the saint's door and cried, "Is Bayazid here?" Bayazid answered, "Is anybody here except God?"

> To gauge the soul we must gauge it with God, for the Ground of God and the Ground of the Soul are one and the same.
>
> ECKHART

> The spirit possesses God essentially in naked nature, and God the spirit.
>
> RUYSBROECK

> The knower and the known are one. Simple people imagine that they should see God, as if He stood there and they here. This is not so. God and I, we are one in knowledge.
>
> ECKHART

"I live, yet not I, but Christ in me." Or perhaps it might be more accurate to use the verb transitively and say, "I live, yet not I; for it is the Logos who *lives me*"—lives me as an actor lives his part. In such a case, of course, the actor is always infinitely superior to the role. Where real life is concerned, there are no Shakespearean characters, there are only Addisonian Catos or, more often, grotesque Monsieur Perrichons and Charlie's Aunts mistaking themselves for Julius Caesar or the Prince of Denmark. But by a merciful dispensation it is always in the power of every *dramatis persona* to get his low, stupid lines pronounced and supernaturally transfigured by the divine equivalent of a Garrick.

> O my God, how does it happen in this poor old world that Thou art so great and yet nobody finds Thee, that Thou callest so loudly and nobody hears Thee, that Thou art so near and nobody feels Thee, that Thou givest Thyself to everybody and nobody knows Thy name? Men flee from Thee and say they cannot find Thee; they turn their backs and say they cannot see Thee; they stop their ears and say they cannot hear Thee.
>
> HANS DENK

Between the Catholic mystics of the fourteenth and fifteenth centuries and the Quakers of the seventeenth there yawns a wide gap of time made hideous, so far as religion is concerned, with interdenominational wars and persecutions. But the gulf was bridged by a succession of men, whom Rufus Jones, in the only accessible English work devoted to their lives and teachings, has called the "Spiritual Reformers." Denk, Franck, Castellio, Weigel, Everard, the Cambridge Platonists—in spite of the murdering and the madness, the apostolic succession remains unbroken. The truths that had been spoken in the *Theologia Germanica*—that book which Luther professed to love so much and from which, if we may judge from his career, he learned so singularly little—were being uttered once again by Englishmen during the Civil War and under the Cromwellian dictatorship. The mystical tradition, perpetuated by the Protestant Spiritual Reformers, had become diffused, as it were, in the religious atmosphere of the time when George Fox had his first great "opening" and knew by direct experience

> that Every Man was enlightened by the Divine Light of Christ, and I saw it shine through all; And that they that believed in it came out of Condemnation and came to the Light of Life, and became the Children of it; And that they that hated it and did not believe in it, were condemned by it, though they made a profession of Christ. This I saw in the pure Openings of Light, without the help of any Man, neither did I then know where to find it in the Scriptures, though afterwards, searching the Scriptures, I found it.
>
> From Fox's JOURNAL

The doctrine of the Inner Light achieved a clearer formulation in the writings of the second generation of Quakers. "There is," wrote William Penn, "something nearer to us than Scriptures, to wit, the Word in the heart from which all Scriptures come." And a little later Robert Barclay sought to explain the direct experience of *tat tvam asi* in terms of an Augustinian theology that had, of course, to be considerably stretched and trimmed before it could fit the facts. Man, he declared in his famous theses, is a fallen being, incapable of good, unless united to the Divine Light. This Divine Light is

Christ within the human soul, and is as universal as the seed of sin. All men, heathen as well as Christian, are endowed with the Inward Light, even though they may know nothing of the outward history of Christ's life. Justification is for those who do not resist the Inner Light and so permit of a new birth of holiness within them.

> Goodness needeth not to enter into the soul, for it is there already, only it is unperceived.
>
> THEOLOGIA GERMANICA

> When the Ten Thousand things are viewed in their oneness, we return to the Origin and remain where we have always been.
>
> SEN T'SEN

It is because we don't know Who we are, because we are unaware that the Kingdom of Heaven is within us, that we behave in the generally silly, the often insane, the sometimes criminal ways that are so characteristically human. We are saved, we are liberated and enlightened, by perceiving the hitherto unperceived good that is already within us, by returning to our eternal Ground and remaining where, without knowing it, we have always been. Plato speaks in the same sense when he says, in the *Republic,* that "the virtue of wisdom more than anything else contains a divine element which always remains." And in the *Theaetetus* he makes the point, so frequently insisted upon by those who have practiced spiritual religion, that it is only by becoming Godlike that we can know God—and to become Godlike is to identify ourselves with the divine element which in fact constitutes our essential nature, but of which, in our mainly voluntary ignorance, we choose to remain unaware.

> They are on the way to truth who apprehend God by means of the divine, Light by the light.
>
> PHILO

Philo was the exponent of the Hellenistic Mystery Religion which grew up, as Professor Goodenough has shown, among the Jews of the Dispersion, between about 200 B.C. and A.D. 100. Reinterpreting the Pentateuch in terms of a metaphysical system derived from Platonism, Neo-Pythagoreanism and

Stoicism, Philo transformed the wholly transcendental and almost anthropomorphically personal God of the Old Testament into the immanent-transcendent Absolute Mind of the Perennial Philosophy. But even from the orthodox scribes and Pharisees of that momentous century which witnessed, along with the dissemination of Philo's doctrines, the first beginnings of Christianity and the destruction of the Temple at Jerusalem, even from the guardians of the Law we hear significantly mystical utterances. Hillel, the great rabbi whose teachings on humility and the love of God and man read like an earlier, cruder version of some of the Gospel sermons, is reported to have spoken these words to an assemblage in the courts of the Temple. "If I am here," (it is Jehovah who is speaking through the mouth of his prophet) "everyone is here. If I am not here, no one is here."

> The Beloved is all in all; the lover merely veils Him;
> The Beloved is all that lives, the lover a dead thing.
>
> JALAL-UDDIN RUMI

> There is a spirit in the soul, untouched by time and flesh, flowing from the Spirit, remaining in the Spirit, itself wholly spiritual. In this principle is God, ever verdant, ever flowering in all the joy and glory of His actual Self. Sometimes I have called this principle the Tabernacle of the soul, sometimes a spiritual Light, anon I say it is a Spark. But now I say that it is more exalted over this and that than the heavens are exalted above the earth. So now I name it in a nobler fashion. . . . It is free of all names and void of all forms. It is one and simple, as God is one and simple, and no man can in any wise behold it.
>
> ECKHART

Crude formulations of some of the doctrines of the Perennial Philosophy are to be found in the thought-systems of the uncivilized and so-called primitive peoples of the world. Among the Maoris, for example, every human being is regarded as a compound of four elements—a divine eternal principle, known as the *toiora;* an ego, which disappears at death; a ghost-shadow, or psyche, which survives death; and finally a body. Among the Oglala Indians the divine element is called the *sican,* and this is regarded as identical with the *ton,* or divine essence of the world. Other elements of the self are the *nagi,* or personality, and *niya,* or vital soul. After death the *sican* is reunited with the divine Ground of all things, the *nagi* survives in the ghost world of psychic phenomena and the *niya* disappears into the material universe.

In regard to no twentieth-century "primitive" society can we rule out the possibility of influence by, or borrowing from, some higher culture. Consequently, we have no right to argue from the present to the past. Because many contemporary savages have an esoteric philosophy that is monotheistic with a monotheism that is sometimes of the "That art thou" variety, we are not entitled to infer offhand that neolithic or palaeolithic men held similar views.

More legitimate and more intrinsically plausible are the inferences that may be drawn from what we know about our own physiology and psychology. We know that human minds have proved themselves capable of everything from imbecility to Quantum Theory, from *Mein Kampf* and sadism to the sanctity of Philip Neri, from metaphysics to crossword puzzles, power politics and the *Missa Solemnis.* We also know that human minds are in some way associated with human brains, and we have fairly good reasons for supposing that there have been no considerable changes in the size and conformation of human brains for a good many thousands of years. Consequently it seems justifiable to infer that human minds in the remote past were capable of as many and as various kinds and degrees of activity as are minds at the present time.

It is, however, certain that many activities undertaken by some minds at the present time were not, in the remote past, undertaken by any minds at all. For this there are several obvious reasons. Certain thoughts are practically unthinkable except in terms of an appropriate language and within the framework of an appropriate system of classification. Where these necessary instruments do not exist, the thoughts in question are not expressed and not even conceived. Nor is this all: the incentive to develop the instruments of certain kinds of thinking is not always present. For long periods of history and prehistory it would seem that men and women, though perfectly capable of doing so, did not wish to pay attention to problems, which their descendants found absorbingly interesting. For example, there is no reason to suppose that, between the thirteenth century and the twentieth, the human mind underwent any kind of evolutionary change, comparable to the change, let us say, in the physical structure of the horse's foot during an incomparably longer span of geological time. What happened was that men turned their attention from certain aspects of reality to certain other aspects. The result, among other things, was the development of the natural sciences. Our perceptions and our understanding are directed, in large measure, by our will. We are aware of, and we think about, the things which, for one reason or another, we want to see and understand. Where there's a will there is always an intellectual way. The capacities of the human mind are almost indefinitely great. Whatever we will to do, whether it be to come to the unitive knowledge of the Godhead, or to manufacture self-propelled flame-throwers—that we are able to do, provided always that the willing be sufficiently intense and sustained. It is clear that many of the things to which modern men have chosen to pay attention were ignored by their predecessors. Consequently the very means for thinking clearly and fruitfully about those things remained uninvented, not merely during prehistoric times, but even to the opening of the modern era.

The lack of a suitable vocabulary and an adequate frame of reference, and the absence of any strong and sustained desire to invent these necessary instruments of thought—here are two sufficient reasons why so many of the almost endless potentialities of the human mind remained for so long unactualized. Another and, on its own level, equally cogent reason is this: much of the world's most original and fruitful thinking is done by people of poor physique and of a thoroughly unpractical turn of mind. Because this is so, and because the value of pure thought, whether analytical or integral, has everywhere been more or less clearly recognized, provision was and still is made by every civilized society for giving thinkers a measure of protection from the ordinary strains and stresses of social life. The hermitage, the monastery, the

college, the academy and the research laboratory; the begging
bowl, the endowment, patronage and the grant of taxpayers'
money—such are the principal devices that have been used by
actives to conserve that rare bird, the religious, philosophical, artistic or scientific contemplative. In many primitive societies conditions are hard and there is no surplus wealth.
The born contemplative has to face the struggle for existence
and social predominance without protection. The result, in
most cases, is that he either dies young or is too desperately
busy merely keeping alive to be able to devote his attention
to anything else. When this happens the prevailing philosophy
will be that of the hardy, extraverted man of action.

All this sheds some light—dim, it is true, and merely infer-
ential—on the problem of the perennialness of the Perennial
Philosophy. In India the scriptures were regarded, not as revelations made at some given moment of history, but as eternal gospels, existent from everlasting to everlasting, inasmuch
as coeval with man, or for that matter with any other kind of
corporeal or incorporeal being possessed of reason. A similar
point of view is expressed by Aristotle, who regards the fundamental truths of religion as everlasting and indestructible.
There have been ascents and falls, periods (literally "roads
around" or cycles) of progress and regress; but the great
fact of God as the First Mover of a universe which partakes
of His divinity has always been recognized. In the light of
what we know about prehistoric man (and what we know
amounts to nothing more than a few chipped stones, some
paintings, drawings and sculptures) and of what we may legitimately infer from other, better documented fields of
knowledge, what are we to think of these traditional doctrines? My own view is that they may be true. We know that
born contemplatives in the realm both of analytic and of integral thought have turned up in fair numbers and at frequent
intervals during recorded history. There is therefore every
reason to suppose that they turned up before history was recorded. That many of these people died young or were unable
to exercise their talents is certain. But a few of them must
have survived. In this context it is highly significant that,
among many contemporary primitives, two thought patterns

are found—an exoteric pattern for the unphilosophic many and an esoteric pattern (often monotheistic, with a belief in a God not merely of power, but of goodness and wisdom) for the initiated few. There is no reason to suppose that circumstances were any harder for prehistoric men than they are for many contemporary savages. But if an esoteric monotheism of the kind that seems to come natural to the born thinker is possible in modern savage societies, the majority of whose members accept the sort of polytheistic philosophy that seems to come natural to men of action, a similar esoteric doctrine might have been current in prehistoric societies. True, the modern esoteric doctrines may have been derived from higher cultures. But the significant fact remains that, if so derived, they yet had a meaning for certain members of the primitive society and were considered valuable enough to be carefully preserved. We have seen that many thoughts are unthinkable apart from an appropriate vocabulary and frame of reference. But the fundamental ideas of the Perennial Philosophy can be formulated in a very simple vocabulary, and the experiences to which the ideas refer can and indeed must be had immediately and apart from any vocabulary whatsoever. Strange openings and theophanies are granted to quite small children, who are often profoundly and permanently affected by these experiences. We have no reason to suppose that what happens now to persons with small vocabularies did not happen in remote antiquity. In the modern world (as Vaughan and Traherne and Wordsworth, among others, have told us) the child tends to grow out of his direct awareness of the one Ground of things; for the habit of analytical thought is fatal to the intuitions of integral thinking, whether on the "psychic" or the spiritual level. Psychic preoccupations may be and often are a major obstacle in the way of genuine spirituality. In primitive societies now (and, presumably, in the remote past) there is much preoccupation with, and a widespread talent for, psychic thinking. But a few people may have worked their way through psychic into genuinely spiritual experience—just as, even in modern industrialized societies, a few people work their way out of the prevailing preoccupation with matter and through the prevailing habits of analytical thought into the direct experience of the spiritual Ground of things.

Such, then, very briefly are the reasons for supposing that the historical traditions of oriental and our own classical antiquity may be true. It is interesting to find that at least one distinguished contemporary ethnologist is in agreement with Aristotle and the Vedantists. "Orthodox ethnology," writes Dr. Paul Radin in his *Primitive Man as Philosopher,* "has been nothing but an enthusiastic and quite uncritical attempt to apply the Darwinian theory of evolution to the facts of social experience." And he adds that "no progress in ethnology will be achieved until scholars rid themselves once and for all of the curious notion that everything possesses a history; until they realize that certain ideas and certain concepts are as ultimate for man, as a social being, as specific physiological reactions are ultimate for him, as a biological being." Among these ultimate concepts, in Dr. Radin's view, is that of monotheism. Such monotheism is often no more than the recognition of a single dark and numinous Power ruling the world. But it may sometimes be genuinely ethical and spiritual.

The nineteenth century's mania for history and prophetic Utopianism tended to blind the eyes of even its acutest thinkers to the timeless facts of eternity. Thus we find T. H. Green writing of mystical union as though it were an evolutionary process and not, as all the evidence seems to show, a state which man, as man, has always had it in his power to realize. "An animal organism, which has its history in time, gradually becomes the vehicle of an eternally complete consciousness, which in itself can have no history, but a history of the process by which the animal organism becomes its vehicle." But in actual fact it is only in regard to peripheral knowledge that there has been a genuine historical development. Without much lapse of time and much accumulation of skills and information, there can be but an imperfect knowledge of the material world. But direct awareness of the "eternally complete consciousness," which is the ground of the material world, is a possibility occasionally actualized by some human beings at almost any stage of their own personal development, from childhood to old age, and at any period of the race's history.

# FROM SELF TO COSMIC
# CONSCIOUSNESS

### RICHARD M. BUCKE

## I

. . . If we are right in [the] assumption [that human evolution has not ceased] new faculties will from time to time
arise in the mind as, in the past, new faculties have arisen.
This being granted, let us assume that what in this book is
called Cosmic Consciousness is such a nascent . . . faculty.
And now let us see what we know about this new sense, state,
faculty, or whatever it may be called. And, first, it may be
noted that the new sense does not appear by chance in this
man or that. It is necessary for its appearance that an exalted
human personality should exist and supply the pre-conditions
for its birth. In the great cases especially is there an exceptional development of some or all of the ordinary human
faculties. Note particularly, since that case is unmistakably
known to us, the singular perfection of the intellectual and
moral faculties and of the special senses in Walt Whitman.
It is probable that an approximation to this evolutionary excellence is necessary in all cases. Then certainly in some,
probably in all, cases the person has an exceptional physique
—exceptional beauty of build and carriage, exceptionally
handsome features, exceptional health, exceptional sweetness
of temper, exceptional magnetism.

From the book *Cosmic Consciousness* by Richard Maurice
Bucke. Copyright 1901, 1923 by E. P. Dutton & Co., Inc., and reprinted with their permission.

## II

The faculty itself has many names, but they have not been understood or recognized. It will be well to give some of them here. They will be better understood as we advance. Either Gautama himself, or some one of his early disciples, called it "Nirvâna" because of the "extinction" of certain lower mental faculties (such as the sense of sin, fear of death, desire of wealth, etc., etc.) which is directly incident upon its birth. This subjugation of the old personality along with the birth of the new is, in fact, almost equivalent to the annihilation of the old and the creation of a new self. The word Nirvâna is defined as "the state to which the Buddhist saint is to aspire as the highest aim and highest good." Jesus called the new condition "the Kingdom of God" or the "Kingdom of Heaven," because of the peace and happiness which belong to it and which are perhaps its most characteristic features. Paul called it "Christ." He speaks of himself as "a man in Christ," of "them that are in Christ." He also calls it "the Spirit" and "the Spirit of God." After Paul had entered Cosmic Consciousness he knew that Jesus had possessed the Cosmic Sense and that he was living (as it were) the life of Jesus —that another individuality, another self, lived in him. This second self he called Christ (the divinely sent deliverer), identifying it not so much with the man Jesus, as with the deliverer which was to be sent and which had been sent in his person, who was both Jesus (the ordinary Self Conscious man) and Messiah (the herald and exemplar of the new, higher race). The duplex personality of men having Cosmic Consciousness will appear many times as we proceed and will be seen to be a constant and prominent phenomenon. Mohammed called the Cosmic Sense "Gabriel," and seems to have looked upon it as a distinctly separate person who lived in him and spoke to him. Dante called it "Beatrice" ("Making Happy"), a name almost or quite equivalent to "Kingdom of Heaven." Balzac called the new man a "specialist" and the new condition "Specialism." Whitman called Cosmic Consciousness "My Soul," but spoke of it as if it were another person; for instance:

> *O soul repressless, I with thee and thou with me.* . . . .
> *We too take ship O soul.* . . . .
> *With laugh and many a kiss* . . .
> *O soul thou pleasest me, I thee.*

Bacon (in the Sonnets) has treated the cosmic sense so emphatically as a distinct person that the world for three hundred years has taken him at his word and has agreed that the "person" in question (whatever his name may have been) was a young friend of the poet's! . . .

## III

It has already been incidentally mentioned that a race entering upon the possession of a new faculty, especially if this be in the line of the direct ascent of the race, as is certainly the case with Cosmic Consciousness, the new faculty will necessarily be acquired at first not only by the best specimens of the race but also when these are at their best—that is, at full maturity and before the decline incident to age has set in. What, now, are the facts in this regard as to the coming of the Cosmic Sense?

They may be summarized in a few words as follows: Of thirty-four cases, in which illumination was instantaneous and the period at which it occurred was with some degree of certainty known, the age at which the person passed into Cosmic Consciousness was in one instance twenty-four years; in three, thirty years; in two, thirty-one years; in two, thirty-one and a half years; in three, thirty-two years; in one, thirty-three years; in two, thirty-four years; in eight, thirty-five years; in two, thirty-six years; in two, thirty-seven years; in two, thirty-eight years; in three, thirty-nine years; in one, forty years; in one, forty-nine years, and, in one, fifty-four years. . . .

## IV

Cosmic Consciousness, then, appears in individuals mostly of the male sex, who are otherwise highly developed—men of good intellect, of high moral qualities, of superior physique. It appears at about that time of life when the organism is at its high-water mark of efficiency, at the age of thirty to forty years. It must have been that the immediate precursor of Cosmic Consciousness—Self Consciousness—also appeared at first in mid-life, here and there, in isolated cases, in the most advanced specimens of the race, becoming more and more nearly universal (as the race grew up to it), manifesting itself at an earlier and earlier age, until (as we see) it declares itself now in every fairly constituted individual, at about the age of three years.

Analogy, then, would lead us to believe that the step in promotion . . . also awaits the whole race—that a time will come when to be without the faculty in question will be a mark of inferiority parallel to the absence at present of the moral nature. The presumption seems to be that the new sense will become more and more common and show itself earlier in life, until after many generations it will appear in each normal individual at the age of puberty or even earlier; then go on becoming still more universal, and appearing at a still earlier age, until, after many thousands of generations, it shows itself immediately after infancy in nearly every member of the race.

## V

It must be clearly understood that all cases of Cosmic Consciousness are not on the same plane. Or, if we speak of Simple Consciousness, Self Consciousness and Cosmic Consciousness as each occupying a plane, then, as the range of Self Consciousness on *its plane* (where one man may be an Aristotle, a Cæsar, a Newton, or a Comte, while his neighbor on the next street may be intellectually and morally, to all appearance, little if at all above the animal in his stable) is far greater than the range of Simple Consciousness *in any given species* on its plane, so we must suppose that the range of Cosmic Consciousness (given millions of cases, as on the other planes) is greater than that of Self Consciousness, and it probably is in fact very much greater both in kind and degree: that is to say, given a world peopled with men having Cosmic Consciousness, they would vary both in the way of greater and less intellectual ability, and greater and less moral and spiritual elevation, and also in the way of variety of character, more than would the inhabitants of a planet on the plane of Self Consciousness. Within the plane of Cosmic Consciousness one man shall be a god while another shall not be, to casual observation, lifted so very much above ordinary humanity, however much his inward life may be exalted, strengthened and purified by the new sense. But, as the Self Conscious man (however degraded) is in fact almost infinitely above the animal with merely Simple Consciousness, so any man permanently endowed with the Cosmic Sense would be almost infinitely higher and nobler than any man who is Self Conscious merely. And not only so, but the man who has had the Cosmic Sense for even a few moments only will probably never again descend to the spiritual level of the merely Self Conscious man, but twenty, thirty or forty years afterwards he will still feel within him the purifying, strengthening and exalting effect of that divine illumination, and many of those about him will recognize that his spiritual stature is above that of the average man.

## VI

The hypothesis adopted by the present writer requires that cases of Cosmic Consciousness should become more numerous from age to age, and not only so but that they should become more perfect, more pronounced. What are the facts? Putting aside minor cases, such as must have appeared and been forgotten by hundreds in the last few millenniums, of those given above at least thirteen are so great that they can never fade from human memory—namely: Gautama, Jesus, Paul, Plotinus, Mohammed, Dante, Las Casas, John Yepes, Francis Bacon, Jacob Behmen, William Blake, Balzac, Walt Whitman.

From Gautama to Dante we count eighteen hundred years, within which period we have five cases. Again from Dante to the present day we count six hundred years, in which we have eight cases. That is to say, while in the earlier period there was one case to every three hundred and sixty years, in the later there was a case to each seventy-five years. In other words, Cosmic Consciousness has been 4.8 times more frequent during the latter period than it was during the former. And before the time of Gautama? There were probably no, or few and imperfectly developed, cases.

We know that at present there are many of what may be called lesser cases, but the number of these cannot be compared with the number of similar cases in the past, for the reason that the latter are lost. It must also be remembered that the thirteen "great cases" given above are only perhaps a small fraction of cases just as great which have occurred since the time of Gautama, for probably only a small proportion of the "great cases" undertake and carry through work which ensures them remembrance. How easily might the memory even of Jesus have been obliterated from the minds of his contemporaries and followers almost before it was born. Many today think that, all else granted, if he had not been immediately followed by Paul, his work and name would have expired together almost with the generation that heard him speak. . . .

## VII

It seems that in every, or nearly every, man who enters into Cosmic Consciousness apprehension is at first more or less excited, the person doubting whether the new sense may not be a symptom or form of insanity. Mohammed was greatly alarmed. I think it is clear that Paul was, and others to be mentioned further on were similarly affected.

The first thing each person asks himself upon experiencing the new sense is: Does what I see and feel represent reality or am I suffering from a delusion? The fact that the new experience seems even more real than the old teachings of simple and Self Consciousness does not at first fully reassure him, because he probably knows that delusions, when present, possess the mind just as firmly as do actual facts.

True or not true, each person who has the experience in question eventually, perforce, believes in its teachings, accepting them as absolutely as any other teachings whatsoever. This, however, would not prove them true, since the same might be said of the delusions of the insane.

How, then, shall we know that this is a new sense, revealing fact, and not a form of insanity, plunging its subject into delusion? In the first place, the tendencies of the condition in question are entirely unlike, even opposite to, those of mental alienation, these last being distinctly amoral or even immoral, while the former are moral in a very high degree. In the second place, while in all forms of insanity self-restraint —inhibition—is greatly reduced, sometimes even abolished, in Cosmic Consciousness it is enormously increased. The absolute proof of this last statement can be found in the lives of the men here cited as examples. In the third place (whatever the scoffers of religion may say) it is certain that modern civilization (speaking broadly) rests (as already said) very largely on the teachings of the new sense. The *masters* are taught by it and the rest of the world by them through their books, followers and disciples, so that if what is here called Cosmic Consciousness is a form of insanity, we are confronted by the terrible fact (were it not an absurdity) that our civilization, including all our highest religions, rests on delusion. But (in the fourth place), far from granting, or for a moment entertaining, such an awful alternative, it can be maintained that we have the same evidence of the objective reality which corresponds to this faculty that we have of the reality which tallies any other sense or faculty whatever. Sight, for instance: You know that the tree standing there, across the field, half a mile away, is real and not an hallucination, because all other persons having the sense of sight to whom you have spoken about it also see it, while if it were an hallucination it would be visible to no one but yourself. By the same method of reasoning do we establish the reality of the objective universe tallying Cosmic Consciousness. Each

person who has the faculty is made aware by it of essentially
the same fact or facts. If three men looked at the tree and
were asked half an hour afterwards to draw or describe it
the three drafts or descriptions would not tally in detail, but
in general outline would correspond. Just in the same way
do the reports of those who have had Cosmic Consciousness
correspond in all essentials, though in detail they doubtless
more or less diverge (but these divergences are fully as much
in our misunderstanding of the reports as in the reports themselves). So there is no instance of a person who has been
illumined denying or disputing the teaching of another who
has passed through the same experience. . . .

## VIII

As has been either said or implied already, in order that a
man may enter into Cosmic Consciousness he must belong
(so to speak) to the top layer of the world of Self Consciousness. Not that he need have an extraordinary intellect (this
faculty is rated, usually far above its real value and does not
seem nearly so important, from this point of view, as do some
others) though he must not be deficient in this respect, either.
He must have a good physique, good health, but above all
he must have an exalted moral nature, strong sympathies, a
warm heart, courage, strong and earnest religious feeling.
All these being granted, and the man having reached the age
necessary to bring him to the top of the Self Conscious mental
stratum, some day he enters Cosmic Consciousness. What is
his experience? Details must be given with diffidence, as
they are only known to the writer in a few cases, and doubtless
the phenomena are varied and diverse. What is said here,
however, may be depended on as far as it goes. It is true of
certain cases, and certainly touches upon the full truth in
certain other cases, so that it may be looked upon as being
provisionally correct.

*a.* The person, suddenly, without warning, has a sense of
being immersed in a flame, or rose-colored cloud, or perhaps
rather a sense that the mind is itself filled with such a cloud of
haze.

*b.* At the same instant he is, as it were, bathed in an emotion of joy, assurance, triumph, "salvation." The last word is not strictly correct if taken in its ordinary sense, for the feeling, when fully developed, is not that a particular act of salvation is effected, but that no special "salvation" is needed, the scheme upon which the world is built being itself sufficient. It is this ecstasy, far beyond any that belongs to the merely Self Conscious life, with which the *poets,* as such, especially occupy themselves: As Gautama, in his discourses, preserved in the "Suttas"; Jesus in the "Parables"; Paul in the "Epistles"; Dante at the end of the "Purgatorio" and beginning of "Paradiso"; "Shakespeare" in the "Sonnets"; Balzac in "Seraphita"; Whitman in the "Leaves"; Edward Carpenter in "Towards Democracy"; leaving to the *singers* the pleasures and pains, loves and hates, joys and sorrows, peace and war, life and death, of Self Conscious man; though the *poets* may treat of these, too, but from the new point of view, as expressed in the "Leaves": "I will never again mention love or death inside a house"—that is, from the old point of view, with the old connotations.

*c.* Simultaneously or instantly following the above sense and emotional experiences there comes to the person an intellectual illumination quite impossible to describe. Like a flash there is presented to his consciousness a clear conception (a vision) in outline of the meaning and drift of the universe. He does not come to believe merely; but he sees and knows that the cosmos, which to the Self Conscious mind seems made up of dead matter, is in fact far otherwise—is in very truth a living presence. He sees that instead of men being, as it were, patches of life scattered through an infinite sea of non-living substance, they are in reality specks of relative death in an infinite ocean of life. He sees that the life which is in man is eternal, as all life is eternal; that the soul of man is as immortal as God is; that the universe is so built and ordered that without any peradventure all things work together for the good of each and all; that the foundation principle of the world is what we call love, and that the happiness of every individual is in the long run absolutely certain. The person who passes through this experience will learn in the few minutes, or even moments, of its continuance more than in months or years of study, and he will learn much that no study ever taught or can teach. Especially does he obtain such a conception of *the whole,* or at least of an immense *whole,* as dwarfs all conception, imagination or speculation, springing from and belonging to ordinary Self Consciousness, such a conception as makes the old attempts to mentally grasp the universe and its meaning petty and even ridiculous.

This awakening of the intellect has been well described by a writer upon Jacob Behmen in these words: "The mysteries of which he discoursed were not reported to him, he *beheld* them. He saw the root of all mysteries, the *Ungrund* or *Urgrund,* whence issue all contrasts and discordant principles, hardness and softness, severity and mildness, sweet and bitter, love and sorrow, heaven and hell. These he *saw* in their origin; these he attempted to describe in their issue and to reconcile in their eternal results. He saw into the being of God; whence the birth or going forth of the divine manifestation. Nature lay unveiled to him—he was at home in the heart of things. His own book, which he himself was (so Whitman: 'This is no book; who touches this touches a man') the microcosm of man, with his three-fold life, was patent to his vision."

*d.* Along with moral elevation and intellectual illumination comes what must be called, for want of a better term, a sense of immortality. This is not an intellectual conviction, such as comes with the solution of a problem, nor is it an experience such as learning something unknown before. It is far more simple and elementary, and could better be compared to that certainty of distinct individuality, possessed by each one, which comes with and belongs to Self Consciousness.

*e.* With illumination the fear of death which haunts so many men and women at times all their lives falls off like an old cloak—not, however, as a result of reasoning—it simply vanishes.

*f.* The same may be said of the sense of sin. It is not that the person escapes from sin; but he no longer sees that there is any sin in the world from which to escape.

*g.* The instantaneousness of the illumination is one of its most striking features. It can be compared with nothing so well as with a dazzling flash of lightning in a dark night, bringing the landscape which had been hidden into clear view.

*h.* The previous character of the man who enters the new life is an important element in the case.

*i.* So is the age at which illumination occurs. Should we hear of a case of Cosmic Consciousness occurring at twenty, for instance, we should at first doubt the truth of the account, and if forced to believe it we should expect the man (if he lived) to prove himself, in some way, a veritable spiritual giant.

*j.* The added charm to the personality of the person who attains to Cosmic Consciousness is always, it is believed, a feature in the case.

*k.* There seems to the writer to be sufficient evidence that, with Cosmic Consciousness, while it is actually present, and lasting (gradually passing away) a short time thereafter, a change takes place in the appearance of the subject of illumination. This change is similar to that caused in a person's appearance by great joy, but at times (that is, in pronounced cases) it seems to be much more marked than that. In these great cases in which illumination is intense the change in question is also intense and may amount to a veritable "transfiguration." Dante says that he was "transhumanized into a God." There seems to be a strong probability that could he have been seen at that moment he would have exhibited what could only have been called "transfiguration." . . .

## IX

The passage from Self to Cosmic Consciousness, considered from the point of view of the intellect, seems to be a phenomenon strictly parallel to the passage from Simple to Self Consciousness.

As in the latter, so in the former, there are two chief elements:

    *a.* Added consciousness;
    *b.* Added faculty.

*a.* When an organism which possesses Simple Consciousness only, attains to Self Consciousness, it becomes aware for the first time that it is a separate creature, or *self* existing in a world which is apart from it. That is, the oncoming of the new faculty instructs it without any new experience or process of learning.

*b.* It, at the same time, acquires enormously increased powers of accumulating knowledge and of initiating action.

So when a person who was Self Conscious only, enters into Cosmic Consciousness—

*a.* He knows without learning (from the mere fact of illumination) certain things, as, for instance: (1) that the universe is not a dead machine but a living presence; (2) that in its essence and tendency it is infinitely good; (3) that individual existence is continuous beyond what is called death. At the same time:

*b.* He takes on enormously greater capacity both for learning and initiating.

# X

The parallel holds also from the point of view of the moral nature. For the animal that has Simple Consciousness merely cannot possibly know anything of the pure delight in simply living that is possessed (at least part of the time) by every healthy, well-constituted young or middle-aged man or woman. "Cannot possibly," for this feeling depends on Self Consciousness and without that can have no existence. The horse or dog enjoys life while experiencing an agreeable sensation or when stimulated by an agreeable activity (really the same thing), but cannot realize that everyday calm in the enjoyment of life, independent of the senses, and of outward things, which belongs to the moral nature (the basic fact, indeed, of the *positive* side of this), starting, as may be truly said, from the central well-spring of the life of the organism (the sense of *bien-être*—"well-being") that belongs to man as man and is in truth one of his most valued heritages. This constitutes a plain or plateau, in the region of the moral nature, upon which the sentient creature steps when passing, or as it passes, from Simple to Self Consciousness.

Corresponding with this moral ascent and with those steps, above noted, taken by the intellect from Simple to Self, and from Self to Cosmic Consciousness, is the moral ascent that belongs to the passage from Self to Cosmic Consciousness. This can only be realized, therefore only described, by those who have passed through the experience. What do they say about it? Well, read what Gautama and the illuminati of the Buddhists tell us of Nirvâna; namely, that it is the "highest happiness." Says the unknown, but unquestionably illumined writer, in the Mahabbharata: "The devotee, whose happiness is within himself, and whose light [of knowledge] also is within himself, becoming one with the Brahman, obtains the Brahmic bliss." Note the dicta of Jesus on the value of the "Kingdom of Heaven," to purchase which a man sells all that he has; remember the worth that Paul ascribes to "Christ," and how he was caught up into the third heaven; reflect on Dante's "transhumanization" from a man "into a God," and on the name he gives the cosmic sense: Beatrice —"Making Happy." Here, too, is his distinct statement of the joy that belongs to it: "That which I was seeing seemed to me a smile of the universe, for my inebriation was entering through the hearing and through the sight. O joy! O ineffable gladness! O life entire of love and of peace! O riches secure without longing!" See what Behmen says on the same subject: "Earthly language is entirely insufficient to describe what there is of joy, happiness, and loveliness contained in the inner wonders of God. Even if the eternal Virgin pictures them to our minds, man's constitution is too cold and dark to be able to express even a spark of it in his language." Observe Elukhanam's oft-repeated exclamation: "Sandosiam, Sandosiam Eppotham"—"Joy, always joy." And again Edward Carpenter's "All sorrow finished," "The deep, deep ocean of joy within," "Being filled with joy," "singing joy unending." Above all, bear in mind the testimony of Walt Whitman—testimony unvarying, though given in ever varying language, and upon almost every page of the "Leaves," covering forty years of life: "I am satisfied—I see, dance, laugh, sing." "Wandering, amazed at my own lightness and glee." "O the joy of my spirit—it is uncaged—it darts like lightning." "I float this carol with joy, with joy to thee, O death." And that forecast of the future taken from his own heart—that future "when through these states walk a hundred millions of superb persons"—that is, persons possessed of the Cosmic Sense. And finally: "The ocean filled with joy—the atmosphere all joy! Joy, joy, in freedom, worship, love! Joy in the ecstasy of life: Enough to merely be! Enough to breathe! Joy, Joy! All over joy!"

## XI

"Well," some one will say, "if these people see and know and feel so much, why don't they come out with it in plain language and give the world the benefit of it?" This is what "speech" said to Whitman: "Walt, you contain enough, why don't you let it out, then?" But he tells us:

> *"When I undertake to tell the best I find I cannot,*
> *My tongue is ineffectual on its pivots,*
> *My breath will not be obedient to its organs,*
> *I become a dumb man."*

So Paul, when he was "caught up into paradise," heard "unspeakable words." And Dante was not able to recount the things he saw in heaven. "My vision," he says, "was greater than *our speech,* which yields to such a sight." And so of the rest. The fact of the matter is not difficult to understand; it is that speech (as fully explained above) is the tally of the Self Conscious intellect, can express that and nothing but that, does not tally and cannot express the Cosmic Sense—or, if at all, only in so far as this may be translated into terms of the Self Conscious intellect.

## XII

It will be well to state here (partly in recapitulation) for the benefit of the reader . . . briefly and explicitly, the marks of the Cosmic Sense. They are:

*a.* The subjective light.

*b.* The moral elevation.

*c.* The intellectual illumination.

*d.* The sense of immortality.

*e.* The loss of the fear of death.

*f.* The loss of the sense of sin.

*g.* The suddenness, instantaneousness, of the awakening.

*h.* The previous character of the man—intellectual, moral and physical.

*i.* The age of illumination.

*j.* The added charm to the personality so that men and women are always (?) strongly attracted to the person.

*k.* The transfiguration of the subject of the change as seen by others when the Cosmic Sense is actually present.

# SELF-TRANSCENDENCE
# AND BEYOND

## ROBERT S. DE ROPP

. . . Man's ordinary state of consciousness is not the highest level of consciousness of which he is capable. In fact, it is so defective that the condition has been defined as little better than somnambulism. Man does not really know what he is doing or where he is going. He lives in dreams. He inhabits a world of delusions and, because of these delusions, makes dangers for himself and others. If this is accepted, then we ask the next questions: What can be done about it? Can man really awaken? What other states of consciousness are possible for him and what must he do to attain these states?

Let us repeat an oft-quoted passage from *The Varieties of Religious Experience:*

> One conclusion was forced upon my mind at that time, and my impression of its truth has ever since remained unshaken. It is that our normal waking consciousness, rational consciousness as we call it, is but one special type of consciousness, whilst all about it, parted from it by the filmiest of screens, there lie potential forms of consciousness entirely different. We may go through life without suspecting their existence, but apply the requisite stimulus, and at a touch they are there in all their completeness. . . . No account of the universe in its totality can be final which leaves these other forms of consciousness quite disregarded.

William James was actually describing effects he obtained while experimenting with nitrous oxide. The statement, however, need not be limited to drug-induced states of altered awareness. One can, in fact, be far more specific than was James in the above passage. One can affirm, on the basis of considerable evidence, that roughly five levels of consciousness are possible for man:

| | |
|---|---|
| 1) Deep sleep without dreams. | The First Level |
| 2) Sleep with dreams. | The Second Level |
| 3) Waking sleep (identification). | The Third Level |
| 4) Self-transcendence (self-remembering). | The Fourth Level |
| 5) Objective Consciousness (cosmic consciousness). | The Fifth Level |

Nature guarantees that man shall experience the first, second and third levels of consciousness. These are necessary for life, for the maintenance of the physical body and for the perpetuation of the species. She does not guarantee that he shall experience the fourth and fifth states. In fact, it appears, owing to an error in the pattern of man's evolution, that mechanisms have developed in him which make it difficult for him to attain the two higher states of consciousness. . . .

## Waking Sleep

The third state of consciousness is experienced when man awakens from physical sleep and plunges at once into the condition called "identification." Identification is the essence of the third state of consciousness. In this state, man has no separate awareness. He is lost in whatever he happens to be doing, feeling, thinking. Because he is lost, immersed, not present in himself, this condition, the third state of consciousness, is referred to in the Gurdjieffian system as the state of "waking sleep." Man in this state is described not as the real man but as a machine, without inner unity, real will or permanent I, acted upon and manipulated by external forces as a puppet is activated by the puppeteer.

For many people, this concept of waking sleep makes no sense at all. They firmly maintain that, once they "wake up," they are responsible beings, masters of themselves, fully conscious, and that anyone who tells them that they are not is a fool or a liar. It is almost impossible to convince such people that they are deceiving themselves because, when a man is told that he is not really conscious, a mechanism is activated within him which awakens him for a moment. He replies, indignantly, "But I *am* fully conscious," and because of this "trick of Nature" as Ouspensky used to call it, he does become conscious for a moment. He moves from the third room to the threshold of the fourth room, answers the challenge, and at once goes to sleep again, firmly convinced that he is a fully awakened being. . . .

It was exactly this reaction that Plato described in his account of the prisoners in the cave . . . Suppose, says Plato in his *Republic* (Loeb edition), that one of the prisoners in the cave, whose only impression of reality is derived from watching shadows on the walls, escapes into the world outside. Suppose he is of an altruistic disposition and returns to tell the other prisoners of the bright and varied world that lies beyond their prison. Suppose he announces that all things they have ever seen are merely shadows. Will they welcome that message? Not likely!

> There will certainly be laughter at his expense and it will be said that the only result of his escapade up there is that he has come back with his eyesight ruined. Moral: it's a fool's game even to make the attempt to go up aloft; and as for the busybody who goes in for all the liberating and translating to higher spheres, if ever we have a chance to catch and kill him we will certainly take it.

The fact is that man in the third state of consciousness is in a situation from which it is hard to escape. He does not recognize the state as waking sleep, does not understand the meaning of identification. If anyone tells him that he is not fully conscious, he replies that he *is* conscious and, by the "trick of Nature," becomes conscious for a moment. He is like a man surrounded by distorting mirrors which offer him an image of himself that in no way corresponds to reality. If he is fat, they tell him he is slender. If he is old, they tell him he is young. He is very happy to believe the mirrors for they save him from that hardest of all tasks, the struggle to know himself as he really is.

Furthermore, this sleeping man is surrounded by other sleeping people and the whole culture in which he lives serves to perpetuate that state of sleep. Its ethics, morality, value systems are all based on the idea that it is lawful and desirable for man to spend his life in the third room rather than in a struggle to enter the fourth. Teachings that exhort men to awaken, to adopt a system of values based on *levels of being* rather than material possessions are distrusted. *Theoretically,* in the United States at least, what are loosely called "spiritual values" are accepted as valid, but practically they do not carry much weight.

## Self-transcendence

A man's chance of attaining the fourth state of consciousness depends on whether or not he has experienced this state. If he does not even know it exists, he will not long for it any more than a bird born and raised in captivity can know what freedom is like or long for freedom. Man can, and from time to time does, experience the fourth state as a result of some religious emotion, under the influence of a work of art, in the rapture of sexual love or in situations of great danger and difficulty. In these circumstances it is said that he "remembers himself." This term is not entirely descriptive of the fourth state but it is the best available. Self-remembering is a certain separation of awareness from whatever a man happens to be doing, thinking, feeling. It is symbolized by a two-headed arrow suggesting double awareness. There is actor and observer, there is an objective awareness of self. There is a feeling of being outside of, separated from, the confines of the physical body; there is a sense of detachment, a state of nonidentification. For identification and self-remembering can no more exist together than a room can simultaneously be illuminated and dark. One excludes the other.

Several characteristics of the fourth state of consciousness have been described by A. Maslow in a chapter [of *Toward a Psychology of Being*] entitled "Peak Experiences as Acute Identity Experiences." He emphasizes the paradoxical quality of this state: "The greatest attainment of identity, autonomy or selfhood is itself simultaneously a transcending of itself, a going beyond and above selfhood. The person can then become relatively egoless."

One statement in this chapter by Maslow calls for some elaboration: "Peaks are not planned or brought about by design; they happen." This may be perfectly true, but does not have to be. The whole practice of Creative Psychology is based on the hypothesis that man *can* change his level of being through intentional effort properly guided and persistently exerted. As a result of this effort, he will attain the fourth state of consciousness (roughly corresponding to Maslow's peak experience)[1] with increasing frequency. He will also get glimpses of the fifth state of consciousness. The difference between experiencing these states by accident and inducing them deliberately is like that between finding money in the street and earning it by the sweat of one's brow. One may find money now and then, but it is not an event to be relied upon. In the same way, some drug experiences may produce a state akin to self-remembering and generate what Baudelaire called "The Taste of the Infinite." There are several ways of getting glimpses of the interior of the fourth room or even the fifth which a person may stumble upon more or less accidentally. This is not at all the same thing as finding the key and unlocking these chambers. For this, both effort and knowledge are required.

Once a man knows that the fourth room exists, he reaches a parting of ways so far as his life is concerned. He can either try to forget all about the fourth room, behave as if it does not exist, lapse again into the state of total identification, or he can decide to play the Master Game and set about looking for someone to teach him the technique. Two factors will in-

[1] Maslow actually has two senses for this term, and it is in the sense of a low-order ecstasy (relative)—not cosmic consciousness (absolute)—that it is used here. [J.W.]

fluence his decision: the intensity of his dislike of sleep and the intensity of his longing for real awakening. These are the stick and the carrot which between them get the donkey moving. The struggle to unlock and enter the fourth room and, having entered it, to remain there, is a task so difficult under the conditions of modern life that few undertake it and even fewer succeed. It may well be that even the appetite for this adventure is gradually disappearing from the psyche of man. In this respect, the words of Nietzsche in *Thus Spake Zarathustra* may be relevant:

> Alas! there comes the time when man will no longer launch the arrow of his longing beyond man. . . .
> Lo! I show you the last man.
> The earth has become small and on it hops the last man who makes everything small. His species is ineradicable like the ground flea; the last man lives longest.

It may be asked at this point why should one make great efforts to enter the fourth room when things have been made so easy and pleasant in the third room. For there is no doubt about it; we of the so-called advanced nations live, on the whole, like kings. Better than kings. Not all the wealth of Croesus could have brought him even so commonplace an experience as a flight through the air, nor did all the riches of Egypt suffice to give Cleopatra freedom from the pangs of childbirth. The great ones of antiquity were as prone to pestilence as the meanest of their slaves. Even for the rich, life was dangerous and uncomfortable. For the poor, it was one long struggle to keep body and soul together.

Things are very different now. Watched over from cradle to grave by a paternalistic government, protected from overwork by unions, from hunger by the bounty of a scientific agriculture, from pestilence by an art of medicine so advanced that all the great plagues of antiquity have been conquered, soothed by tranquilizers or stimulated by antidepressants, perpetually hypnotized by the unending circuses offered by television, radio, the movies, why should we ask for more? When the third room is comfortable, safe and full of delights, why should we strive to ascend to the fourth? What does it have to offer that the third room does not?

The answer, of course, is freedom. Only when he enters the fourth room does a man become free. Only in the fourth state of consciousness is he liberated from the tyranny of the personal ego and all the fears and miseries that this entity generates. Once he has attained the fourth room and learned to live in it, a man becomes fearless. The words "I" and "mine" have ceased to be meaningful. He does not identify the self with the physical body or attach much importance to the possessions of that body. He feeds it, dresses it, cares for it and regulates its behavior. In due course he leaves it. One of the powers conferred by entry into the fourth room is the capacity to die at will.

Man in the third room may think he is his own master but actually has no control over his actions. He cannot so much as walk down a street without losing his attention in every stray impression that "takes his fancy." Man in the fourth room really is his own master. He knows where he is going, what he is doing, why he is doing it. His secret is that he remains unattached to the results of his activity, measures his success and failure not in terms of outward achievement, but in terms of inner awareness. He is able, as a result of his knowledge of forces at work about him, to know what is possible and what is impossible, what can be achieved and what cannot be achieved.

This may sound like a small accomplishment but it is actually a very large one. Dabblers in various forms of occultism and theosophy, dilettantes who play with what they imagine to be yoga, show a pathetic naïveté when it comes to evaluating what can and what cannot be obtained by these means. All sorts of miraculous achievements are accepted as possible, for man in the third state of consciousness tends to love miracles and to believe all sorts of nonsense that could not possibly happen. In the fourth state of consciousness such naïveté disappears. A man knows what combination of forces can produce what sort of result. He knows that everything happens in accordance with certain laws governing the relations of matter and energy. He knows that there is no miracle and anything that appears to be a miracle is merely a manifestation of some rare combination of forces, like the rare combination of skill and knowledge that enabled the master magician, Houdini, to extricate himself from every form of restraint that was ever applied to him.

## Cosmic Consciousness

In addition to the fourth room, there is said by some commentators on this subject to exist a fifth room, corresponding to the fifth level of consciousness. It is related to that condition which R. M. Bucke described in *Cosmic Consciousness,* the "prime characteristic of which" was "a consciousness of the cosmos, that is, of the life and order of the universe." Flashes of this state of consciousness may be experienced by certain people for no apparent reason. They may also be induced by psychedelics. Much of the material described by Alan Watts in *The Joyous Cosmology* could have been obtained as a result of his having entered the fifth room. The cosmic vision offered to Arjuna by Krishna and described in the eleventh chapter of the *Bhagavad Gita* is another example of the working of the fifth state of consciousness.

It must be understood, however, that this state, cosmic consciousness, is impossible for man to sustain without long and special training. The normal course of development demands that man must learn to enter and live in the fourth room before he can safely ascend to the fifth. If he enters the fifth room unlawfully, either by the use of drugs or any other means, he may suffer permanent damage as a result of the force of the impressions poured into his unprepared awareness. His situation is akin to that of an electrical machine suddenly subjected to a current much more powerful than that for which it was designed. The result at best is a blown fuse, at worst a burned out machine. Fortunately the physiological equivalent of a fuse does exist in man. Its operation results in the loss of consciousness when a man accidentally enters the fifth room. He is simply overwhelmed by the terrific rush of awareness and "blacks out," retaining afterwards scarcely a memory of that extraordinary moment.

This concept of the five rooms, or five levels of consciousness, is the theoretical basis of the whole teaching of Creative

Psychology. We say "theoretical" because, unless a man has experienced the five states, they must remain for him theoretical possibilities only. No one, no matter how great his skill, can communicate to another the feeling of a different level of consciousness. Man in the fourth room cannot communicate his condition to man in the third room, nor can man in the third room communicate with man in the second.

## Samadhi and Satori

Those familiar with the terminology of Zen Buddhism and yoga may ask what relationship the states called *satori* and *samadhi* have to the fourth and fifth states of consciousness. The answer is that neither *satori* nor *samadhi* represents one condition. They may range all the way from a brief experience of the fourth state to a profound experience of the fifth. *Satori* is the psychological result of the practice of *zazen* or "wall gazing," which, combined as it is in most Zen monasteries with strenuous physical work and certain types of physical exercises, induces the "objective awareness of the self" characteristic of the fourth state of consciousness. *Satori* is not a trancelike condition but *a new mode of awareness*. It does not, in the early stages at least, occur all the time but only in flashes, induced perhaps by a struggle with some *koan* or by some shock or stimulus supplied by the Zen Master.

*Samadhi* is a state of consciousness beyond name and form and, for this reason, cannot be described in words. "As salt being dissolved in water becomes one with it, so when *atma* and mind become one, it is called *samadhi*."[2] It is further stated, in this same text:

> The whole of this world and all the schemes of the mind are but the creations of thought. Discarding these thoughts and taking leave of all conjectures, obtain peace. As camphor disappears in fire, and rock salt in water, so the mind united with the *atma* loses its identity. All that appears is the knowable, the mind is called

[2] Sinh, Pancham, translator, *Hatha Yoga Pradipika* (Allahabad: The Panini Office, 1932).

knowledge. When the knowable and the knowledge are both destroyed equally, then duality is destroyed.[3]

Commenting on these passages, Theos Bernard wrote:

> *Samadhi* cannot be experienced until a condition of mindlessness has been created. All modifications of the thinking principle must cease; all thought forms must be removed, yet some form of awareness must remain. Without yoga experience it is difficult to imagine what is meant; that is why teachers do not even try to explain.[4]

*Samadhi,* as generally described, involves a trancelike state, in which awareness of the body and its surroundings is lost. Is this an essential accompaniment of the state? Is it possible to "enter *samadhi*" and still maintain some sort of external activity? Is *samadhi* the fifth state of consciousness, the ultimate level above which no man can ascend and still remain linked to the physical body? All these questions can be answered only by experiment and observation. Words, definitions, commentaries merely serve to confuse the issue. If one wants to find out what lies beyond the frontier, the only way to do so is to go beyond it and see. On this journey one will do well to obtain both a map and a guide but he will have to travel every step by his own efforts.

[3] *Ibid.*
[4] Bernard, Theos, *Hatha Yoga* (London: Rider and Co., 1950).

# TRANSCENDENTAL EXPERIENCE

### R. D. LAING

We are living in an age in which the ground is shifting and the foundations are shaking. I cannot answer for other times and places. Perhaps it has always been so. We know it is true today.

In these circumstances, we have every reason to be insecure. When the ultimate basis of our world is in question, we run to different holes in the ground, we scurry into roles, statuses, identities, interpersonal relations. We attempt to live in castles that can only be in the air because there is no firm ground in the social cosmos on which to build. We are all witnesses to this state of affairs. Each sometimes sees the same fragment of the whole situation differently; often our concern is with different presentations of the original catastrophe.

In this chapter I wish to relate the transcendental experiences that *sometimes* break through in psychosis, to those experiences of the divine that are the living fount of all religion.

. . . If we can begin to understand sanity and madness in existential social terms, we shall be more able to see clearly the extent to which we all confront common problems and share common dilemmas.

Experience may be judged as invalidly mad or as validly mystical. The distinction is not easy. In either case, from a social point of view, such judgments characterize different forms of behavior, regarded in our society as deviant. People

From *The Politics of Experience*, Chapter 6, by R. D. Laing. Reprinted by permission of Penguin Books Ltd.

behave in such ways because their experience of themselves is different. It is on the existential meaning of such unusual experience that I wish to focus.

Psychotic experience goes beyond the horizons of our common, that is, our communal, sense.

What regions of experience does this lead to? It entails a loss of the usual foundations of the "sense" of the world that we share with one another. Old purposes no longer seem viable; old meanings are senseless; the distinctions between imagination, dream, external perceptions often seem no longer to apply in the old way. External events may seem magically conjured up. Dreams may seem to be direct communications from others; imagination may seem to be objective reality.

But most radical of all, the very ontological foundations are shaken. The being of phenomena shifts and the phenomenon of being may no longer present itself to us as before. There are no supports, nothing to cling to, except perhaps some fragments from the wreck, a few memories, names, sounds, one or two objects, that retain a link with a world long lost. This void may not be empty. It may be peopled by visions and voices, ghosts, strange shapes and apparitions. No one who has not experienced how insubstantial the pageant of external reality can be, how it may fade, can fully realize the sublime and grotesque presences that can replace it, or that can exist alongside it.

When a person goes mad, a profound transposition of his place in relation to all domains of being occurs. His center of experience moves from ego to self. Mundane time becomes merely anecdotal, only the eternal matters. The madman is, however, confused. He muddles ego with self, inner with outer, natural and supernatural. Nevertheless, he can often be to us, even through his profound wretchedness and disintegration, the heirophant of the sacred. An exile from the scene of being as we know it, he is an alien, a stranger signaling to us from the void in which he is foundering, a void which may be peopled by presences that we do not even dream of. They used to be called demons and spirits, and they used to be known and named. He has lost his sense of self, his feelings, his place in the world as we know it. He tells us he is dead. But we are distracted from our cozy security by this mad ghost who haunts us with his visions and voices which seem so senseless and of which we feel impelled to rid him, cleanse him, cure him.

Madness need not be all breakdown. It may also be breakthrough. It is potentially liberation and renewal as well as enslavement and existential death.

There are now a growing number of accounts by people who have been through the experience of madness.[1]

The following is part of one of the earlier contemporary accounts, as recorded by Karl Jaspers in his *General Psychopathology*.[2]

> I believe I caused the illness myself. In my attempt to penetrate the other world I met its natural guardians, the embodiment of my own weaknesses and faults. I first thought these demons were lowly inhabitants of the other world who could play me like a ball because I went into these regions unprepared and lost my way. Later I thought they were split-off parts of my own mind (passions) which existed near me in free space and thrived on my feelings. I believed everyone else had these too but did not perceive them, thanks to the protective successful deceit of the feeling of personal existence. I thought the latter was an artifact of memory, thought-complexes, etc., a doll that was nice enough to look at from outside but nothing real inside it.
>
> In my case the personal self had grown porous because of my dimmed consciousness. Through it I wanted to bring myself closer to the higher sources of life. I should have prepared myself for this over a long period by invoking in me a higher, impersonal self, since "nectar" is not for mortal lips. It acted destructively on the animal-human self, split it up into its parts. These gradually disintegrated, the doll was really broken and the body damaged. I had forced untimely access to the "source of life," the curse of the "gods" descended on me. I recognized too late that murky elements had taken

[1] See, for example, the anthology *The Inner World of Mental Illness,* edited by Bert Kaplan (New York and London: Harper and Row, 1964), and *Beyond All Reason,* by Morag Coate (London: Constable and Co., 1964; Philadelphia: Lippincott, 1965).

[2] Manchester: Manchester University Press, 1962, pages 417–18.

a hand. I got to know them after they had already too much power. There was no way back. I now had the world of spirits I had wanted to see. The demons came up from the abyss, as guardian Cerberi, denying admission to the unauthorized. I decided to take up the life-and-death struggle. This meant for me in the end a decision to die, since I had to put aside everything that maintained the enemy, but this was also everything that maintained life. I wanted to enter death without going mad and stood before the Sphinx: either thou into the abyss or I!

Then came illumination. I fasted and so penetrated into the true nature of my seducers. They were pimps and deceivers of my dear personal self which seemed as much a thing of naught as they. A larger and more comprehensive self emerged and I could abandon the previous personality with its entire entourage. I saw this earlier personality could never enter transcendental realms. I felt as a result a terrible pain, like an annihilating blow, but I was rescued, the demons shriveled, vanished and perished. A new life began for me and from now on I felt different from other people. A self that consisted of conventional lies, shams, self-deceptions, memory images, a self just like that of other people, grew in me again but behind and above it stood a greater and more comprehensive self which impressed me with something of what is eternal, unchanging, immortal and inviolable and which ever since that time has been my protector and refuge. I believe it would be good for many if they were acquainted with such a higher self and that there are people who have attained this goal in fact by kinder means.

Jaspers comments:

Such self-interpretations are obviously made under the influence of delusion-like tendencies and deep psychic forces. They originate from profound experiences and the wealth of such schizophrenic experience calls on the observer as well as on the reflective patient not to take all this merely as a chaotic jumble of contents. Mind and spirit are present in the morbid psychic life as well as in the healthy. But interpretations of this sort must be divested of any casual importance. All they can do is to throw light on content and bring it into some sort of context.

This patient has described, with a lucidity I could not improve upon, a very ancient quest, with its pitfalls and dangers. Jaspers still speaks of this experience as morbid and tends to discount the patient's own construction. Yet both the experience and the construction may be valid in their own terms.

Certain *transcendental experiences* seem to me to be the original wellspring of all religions. Some psychotic people have transcendental experiences. Often (to the best of their recollection), they have never had such experiences before, and frequently they will never have them again. I am not saying, however, that psychotic experience necessarily contains this element more manifestly than sane experience.

We experience in different modes. We perceive external realities, we dream, imagine, have semiconscious reveries. Some people have visions, hallucinations, experience faces transfigured, see auras and so on. Most people most of the time experience themselves and others in one or another way that I shall call *egoic*. That is, centrally or peripherally, they experience the world and themselves in terms of a consistent identity, a me-here over against a you-there, within a framework of certain ground structures of space and time shared with other members of their society.

This identity-anchored, space-and-time-bound experience has been studied philosophically by Kant, and later by the phenomenologists, e.g. Husserl, Merleau-Ponty. Its historical and ontological relativity should be fully realized by any contemporary student of the human scene. Its cultural, socioeconomic relativity has become a commonplace among anthropologists and a platitude to the Marxists and neo-Marxists. And yet, with the consensual and interpersonal confirmation it offers, it gives us a sense of ontological security, whose validity we *experience* as self-validating, although metaphysically-historically-ontologically-socioeconomically-culturally we know its apparent absolute validity as an illusion.

In fact, all religious and all existential philosophies have agreed that such *egoic experience* is a preliminary illusion, a veil, a film of *maya*—a dream to Heraclitus, and to Lao-Tzu, the fundamental illusion of all Buddhism, a state of sleep, of death, of socially accepted madness, a womb state to which one has to die, from which one has to be born.

The person going through ego-loss or transcendental experiences may or may not become in different ways confused. Then he might legitimately be regarded as mad. But to be mad is not necessarily to be ill, notwithstanding that in our culture the two categories have become confused. It is assumed that if a person is mad (whatever that means) then *ipso facto* he is ill (whatever that means). The experience that a person may be absorbed in, while to others he appears simply ill-mad, may be for him veritable manna from heaven. The person's whole life may be changed, but it is difficult not to doubt the validity of such vision. Also, not everyone comes back to us again.

Are these experiences simply the effulgence of a pathological process or of a particular alienation? I do not think they are.

In certain cases, a man blind from birth may have an operation performed which gives him his sight. The result—frequently misery, confusion, disorientation. The light that illumines the madman is an unearthly light. It is not always a distorted refraction of his mundane life situation. He may be irradiated by light from other worlds. It may burn him out.

This "other" world is not essentially a battlefield wherein psychological forces, derived or diverted, displaced or sublimated from their original object-cathexes, are engaged in an illusionary fight—although such forces may obscure these realities, just as they may obscure so-called external realities. When Ivan in *The Brothers Karamazov* says, "If God does not exist, everything is permissible," he is *not* saying, "If my super-ego, in projected form, can be abolished, I can do anything with a good conscience." He *is* saying, "If there is *only* my conscience, then there is no ultimate validity for my will."

Among physicians and priests there should be some who are guides, who can educt the person from this world and induct him to the other. To guide him in it and to lead him back again.

One enters the other world by breaking a shell: or through

a door: through a partition: the curtains part or rise: a veil is lifted. Seven veils: seven seals, seven heavens.

The "ego" is the instrument for living in *this* world. If the "ego" is broken up or destroyed (by the insurmountable contradictions of certain life situations, by toxins, chemical changes, etc.), then the person may be exposed to other worlds, "real" in different ways from the more familiar territory of dreams, imagination, perception or fantasy.

The world that one enters, one's capacity to experience it, seem to be partly conditional on the state of one's "ego."

Our time has been distinguished, more than by anything else, by a drive to control the external world, and by an almost total forgetfulness of the internal world. If one estimates human evolution from the point of view of knowledge of the external world, then we are in many respects progressing.

If our estimate is from the point of view of the internal world and of oneness of internal and external, then the judgment must be very different.

Phenomenologically the terms "internal" and "external" have little validity. But in this whole realm one is reduced to mere verbal expedients—words are simply the finger pointing at the moon. One of the difficulties of talking in the present day of these matters is that the very existence of inner realities is now called in question.

By "inner" I mean our way of seeing the external world and all those realities that have no "external," "objective" presence—imagination, dreams, fantasies, trances, the realities of contemplative and meditative states, realities of which modern man, for the most part, has not the slightest direct awareness.

For example, nowhere in the Bible is there any argument about the *existence* of gods, demons, angels. People did not first "believe in" God: they experienced His presence, as was true of other spiritual agencies. The question was not whether God existed, but whether this particular God was the greatest god of all, or the only God; and what was the relation of the various spiritual agencies to each other. Today, there is a public debate, not as to the trustworthiness of God, the particular place in the spiritual hierarchy of different spirits, etc., but whether God or such spirits *even exist* or ever have existed.

Sanity today appears to rest very largely on a capacity to adapt to the external world—the interpersonal world, and the realm of human collectivities.

As this external human world is almost completely and totally estranged from the inner, any personal direct awareness of the inner world already has grave risks.

But since society, without knowing it, is *starving* for the inner, the demands on people to evoke its presence in a "safe" way, in a way that need not be taken seriously, etc., is tremendous—while the ambivalence is equally intense. Small wonder that the list of artists, in say the last 150 years, who have become shipwrecked on these reefs is so long—Hölderlin, John Clare, Rimbaud, Van Gogh, Nietzsche, Antonin Artaud. . . .

Those who survived have had exceptional qualities—a capacity for secrecy, slyness, cunning—a thoroughly realistic appraisal of the risks they run, not only from the spiritual realms they frequent, but from the hatred of their fellows for anyone engaged in this pursuit.

Let us *cure* them. The poet who mistakes a real woman for his Muse and acts accordingly. . . . The young man who sets off in a yacht in search of God. . . .

The outer divorced from any illumination from the inner is in a state of darkness. We are in an age of darkness. The state of outer darkness is a state of sin—i.e., alienation or estrangement from the *inner light*.[3] Certain actions lead to greater estrangement; certain others help one not to be so far removed. The former used to be called sinful.

The ways of losing one's way are legion. Madness is certainly not the least unambiguous. The countermadness of Kraepelinian psychiatry is the exact counterpart of "official" psychosis. Literally, and absolutely seriously, it is as *mad,* if by madness we mean any radical estrangement from the totality of what is the case. Remember Kierkegaard's objective madness.

[3] M. Eliade, *The Two and the One* (London: Harvill Press, 1965), especially Chapter I.

As we experience the world, so we act. We conduct ourselves in the light of our view of what is the case and what is not the case. That is, each person is a more or less naïve ontologist. Each person has views of what is and what is not.

There is no doubt, it seems to me, that there have been profound changes in the experience of man in the last thousand years. In some ways this is more evident than changes in the patterns of his behavior. There is everything to suggest that man experienced God. Faith was never a matter of believing. He existed, but of trusting, in the presence that was experienced and known to exist as a self-validating datum. It seems likely that far more people in our time experience neither the presence of God, nor the presence of his absence, but the absence of his presence.

We require a history of phenomena, not simply more phenomena of history.

As it is, the secular psychotherapist is often in the role of the blind leading the half-blind.

The fountain has not played itself out, the frame still shines, the river still flows, the spring still bubbles forth, the light has not faded. But between *us* and It, there is a veil which is more like fifty feet of solid concrete. *Deus absconditus.* Or we have absconded.

Already everything in our time is directed to categorizing and segregating this reality from objective facts. This is precisely the concrete wall. Intellectually, emotionally, interpersonally, organizationally, intuitively, theoretically, we have to blast our way through the solid wall, even if at the risk of chaos, madness and death. For from *this* side of the wall, this is the risk. There are no assurances, no guarantees.

Many people are prepared to have faith in the sense of scientifically indefensible belief in an untested hypothesis. Few have trust enough to test it. Many people make-believe what they experience. Few are made to believe by their experience. Paul of Tarsus was picked up by the scruff of the neck, thrown to the ground and blinded for three days. This direct experience was self-validating.

We live in a secular world. To adapt to this world the child abdicates its ecstasy. (*"L'enfant abdique son extase"*: Malarmé.) Having lost our experience of the spirit, we are expected to have faith. But this faith comes to be a belief in a reality which is not evident. There is a prophecy in Amos that a time will come when there will be a famine in the land, "not a famine for bread, nor a thirst for water, but of *hearing* the words of the Lord." That time has now come to pass. It is the present age.

From the alienated starting point of our pseudosanity, everything is equivocal. Our sanity is not "true" sanity. Their madness is not "true" madness. The madness of our patients is an artifact of the destruction wreaked on them by us and by them on themselves. Let no one suppose that we meet "true" madness any more than that we are truly sane. The madness that we encounter in "patients" is a gross travesty, a mockery, a grotesque caricature of what the natural healing of that estranged integration we call sanity might be. True sanity entails in one way or another the dissolution of the normal ego, that false self competently adjusted to our alienated social reality; the emergence of the "inner" archetypal mediators of divine power, and through this death a rebirth, and the eventual re-establishment of a new kind of ego-functioning, the ego now being the servant of the divine, no longer its betrayer.

# MYSTICAL STATES AND
# THE CONCEPT OF REGRESSION

## RAYMOND PRINCE and CHARLES SAVAGE

Many authorities on mysticism consider the mystical state to be a transitory elevation to a higher type of consciousness. Bucke (1) considered this "higher level" to be a final step in man's evolutionary development. First, there is simple consciousness as in animals and young children; next emerges self-consciousness as it exists in human adults; finally, there is the stage called "cosmic consciousness" reached by but a few men in the mystical state. Bucke predicted that increasing numbers would attain the state of cosmic consciousness. This point of view is difficult to reconcile with the observation that mystical states have much in common with certain psychotic states. For example, many psychotics describe states of ecstasy, of positive knowledge and of union with the "world soul" that are highly reminiscent of the subjective experiences of mystics. One patient (2) wrote concerning the early stages of psychosis:

> I was suddenly confronted by an overwhelming conviction that I had discovered the secrets of the universe, which were rapidly made plain with incredible lucidity. The truths discovered seemed to be known immediately and directly with absolute certainty.

Similarly, the group of psychedelic drugs is alleged by some to produce model psychoses, but, by others, to produce mys-

From *Psychedelic Review*, No. 8, 1966. Reprinted by permission of *Psychedelic Review* and the authors.

tical states. This puzzling situation is somewhat akin to that relating genius and mental illness.

It is an alternative hypothesis about the nature of the mystical experience that we wish to present. It is based upon a psychoanalytic model. The hypothesis is that mystical states represent regressions in the service of the ego. In presenting this hypothesis we will touch briefly upon the four following areas: (1) the concept of regression, emphasizing its function in health; (2) neurophysiological data relevant to regression; (3) the subjective experience of early infancy; and (4) several characteristic features of the mystical state in the light of the present hypothesis.

## The Concept of Regression

In the simplest terms, regression means a return to an earlier level of functioning. Let us give some examples:

This first instance (3) describes the behavior of a two-year-old boy when he was taken to a hospital. He was a well-developed child with a good relation to his mother. For the first week the mother visited him daily; the second week she visited only twice and then did not return:

> He became listless, often sat in a corner sucking and dreaming, at other times he was very aggressive. He almost completely stopped talking. He was dirty and wet continually. He sat in front of his plate eating very little, without pleasure, and started smearing his food over the table.

Comment is hardly necessary. We have a stress—abandonment in hospital—and a child of normal two-year development returns to behavior characteristic of a much younger child: (1) he stops talking, (2) eating habits deteriorate, (3) he sucks a good deal, and (4) there is a loss of bladder and bowel control. The picture is a familiar one to anyone with a family, observed to a lesser degree in the youngest child when a new baby enters the family circle. The next example is the account of an LSD experience (the result of a dose of 100 gamma given to a normal subject) recorded two days afterwards:

> About one and a half hours after ingestion, the psychosis seemed to be at its height, and there was a great struggle to cling to reality. I had a coin and a pin in my wallet that had been given to me as good luck charms. I took these out and looked at them and they seemed to have a protective function as amulets. I seemed to be struggling against complete annihilation and nothingness.
>
> During this period words seem to have lost their meaning. I asked constantly if there was such a thing as "a chair," or as "truth" or "craziness." I seemed to be crossing the river Styx on words . . . At one point in the depth of the psychosis, I can't remember just when, I half-purposefully conjured up a visual image of a woman I had recently seen in a photography exhibition. She was a very motherly woman suckling a child at her ample breast . . . I replaced the woman in the picture with my own mother . . . her large nose, her fatness, and particularly the odor of her perspiration. I hallucinated her nipple in my mouth. This again was a protection against annihilation and a comfort. By about four hours following ingestion, I was beginning to recover. I felt completely exhausted physically and emotionally and felt as though I had been swimming through uncharted seas; I flung myself exhausted on the bank. I was Lazarus back from the dead; I was a prisoner consigned to death and given a reprieve. A whole new crop of words had sprouted and I had a strong sense of having a new personality—tender, defenseless—just pulling myself out of the primeval slime and sunning myself on the bank.

In this example we have an anxiety-laden regression to the preverbal level. Other regressive features are (1) a return to magical modes of thinking, the use of the pin and the coin as protective amulets, (2) a return to hallucinatory thinking. Unlike the child in the first example, this regression is largely subjective and of short duration. He does not, for example, lose bowel or bladder control, nor does he suck at his fingers or engage in other childlike behavior. Of particular interest here is the symbolism of death and rebirth. He speaks of crossing the river Styx, and when the effects are wearing off, he feels like Lazarus back from the dead, a whole new crop of words has sprung up and he has a strong sense of having a new personality—tender, defenseless, "just pulling myself out of the primeval slime and sunning myself on the bank." Here, then, is a withdrawal and a return, a regression of at least some part of the self back to the age of one or two years, then the regression is terminated and there is a feeling of rebirth and a successful return to adulthood.

Our final example is a regression of a different type, or at least a regression that serves a different function. It is not escape from a painful reality with an undesirable outcome, nor is it drug-induced. Rather it is an example of regression in the service of the ego—a technique employed by the ego in problem solving. We quote from Henri Poincare's (4) description of his discovery of certain mathematical equations:

> For fifteen days I strove to prove that there could not be any functions like those I have since called Fuchsian functions. I was then very ignorant, every day I seated myself at the work table, stayed an hour or two, tried a great number of combinations and reached no results. One evening, contrary to my custom, I drank black coffee and could not sleep. Ideas rose in crowds; I felt them collide until pairs interlocked, so to speak, making a stable combination. By the next morning I had established the existence of a class of Fuchsian functions . . . I had only to write out the results, which took but a few hours.

and further:

> . . . when, above, I made certain personal observations, I spoke of a night of excitement, when I worked in spite of myself. Such cases are frequent, and it is not necessary that the abnormal cerebral activity be caused by physical excitement as in that I mentioned. It seemed that, in such cases, that one is present at his own unconscious work, made partially perceptible to the overexcited consciousness, yet without having changed its nature. Then we vaguely comprehend what distinguishes the two mechanisms or, if you wish, the working methods of the two egos.

In this example the higher conscious logical modes of thinking are given up and a more random trial-and-error kind of dream thinking takes over.

These examples by no means exhaust the range of phenomena designated regressive. Many hypnotists claim that genuine age regressions can be produced by hypnosis. Some of regression is present in all psychiatric disorder. Schizophrenia provides perhaps the best example of the deepest regression over the most prolonged period. To mention one example, Arieti (5) has described a group of chronic schizophrenics in mental hospitals whose behavior is highly reminiscent of six-months to two-year-old children:

> . . . They manifest the habit of grabbing every small object and putting it into the mouth, pay no attention at all to the edible or non-edible nature of it. If they are not restrained, these patients pick up crumbs, cockroaches, stones, rags, paper, wood, coal, pencils and leaves from the floor and put them in the mouth. Generally they eat these things; occasionally they swallow them with great risk.

These patients were also severely regressed in other ways: if they spoke at all their words were unintelligible; there was loss of bowel and bladder control and complete absence of social graces.

These pathological types of regression are probably too well known to require further description. Regression in the service of the ego, on the other hand, is perhaps less familiar and is indeed more relevant to our present subject. One of the commonest instances of regression in the service of the ego is sleep. Freud described how, before sleep, we strip off all the bric-a-brac of civilization: our false teeth, wigs, spectacles and clothes—and return to our primal state of nudity. We return to our prenatal condition of unconsciousness. Even more to the point are the regressive phenomena that we experience along the borderlines of sleep, the hypnagogic imagery, the loosening of thought processes, the preverbal hallucinatory phenomena of dreams with their archaic logic. And each morning we experience a rejuvenation and rebirth. Kris has discussed the regressive nature of humor and of many types of games and play. (6) Psychoanalysis makes extensive use of regression; over the months of treatment the patient during his hour-long sessions makes a fluctuating regression into his past. He re-experiences situations within his family and projects his reactivated feelings upon his analyst. The responses of his analyst are different from those of his pathological family figures and he is able to correct his feelings and move on to other situations, stripping each one of its painful affects. He comes to terms with the specters from his past.

Let us now fill out and broaden our definition of regression. Regression is a return to an earlier level of functioning—it may involve only part of the self (as with the regressive modes of thought of Poincare) or it may be more complete, as in the severely regressed schizophrenics described by Arieti. The regression may be of a few minutes' duration or may be permanent; it may be in response to stress—a retreat from painful reality—or it may be more or less consciously undertaken as a means of recreation, or as a step in the creative process, or as a form of treatment for psychoneuroses.

## Neurophysiology and Regression

There are many neurophysiological experiments with animals, and some with humans, which shed light on the nature of regression in physiological terms. We would like to touch briefly on four types of study:

The concept of regression suggests that the human brain contains complete records of at least some of the past experiences of the individual. We do not here mean simply memory. We mean that the entire experience, including the way the individual reacted to it, the experience and the matrix in which it is embedded, have been recorded—like a video tape with sound track, olfactory, pain and temperature track as well as affect track.

Wilder Penfield's (7) work with cortical stimulation provides evidence that this is so. The cortex of an epileptic patient was exposed; the patient remained conscious. Various cortical areas were stimulated to seek that area which would produce the aura that heralded the patient's seizure. During these explorations, Penfield was surprised to find that his patient would relive with hallucinatory vividness, long forgotten experiences:

> These hallucinations are made up of elements from the individual's past experience. They may seem to him so

strange that he calls them dreams but when they can be carefully analyzed it is evident that the hallucination is a shorter or longer sequence of past experience. The subject relives a period of the past, although he is still aware of the present. Movement goes forward again as it did in that interval of time that has now been by chance, revived, and all of the elements of his previous consciousness seem to be there—sight, sound, interpretations, emotions. The hallucinations include those things that were within the focus of attention. The things he ignored then are missing now.

Penfield does not mention the reactivation of experience from early preverbal periods. Perhaps the upper surfaces of the cortex do not store these very early experiences. There is evidence, as we shall see presently, that early experiences may be related to phylogenetically older brain areas.

Let us now turn to cognitive functions—the area of perception, and concept and symbol formation. As Piaget and others have demonstrated, the child develops the symbolic function by gradually differentiating the signifier from the thing signified; the word from the object. There is first the hallucinatory image of the chair, then the word "chair" attached to a specific chair, and finally the general category of chair—the platonic idea of a chair; the child gradually transforms a signal into a symbol. All this takes place in the first three years of life. In regressive phenomena we find the reverse process; conceptual abilities disappear first and subsequently there is a re-emergence of hallucinatory phenomena. We have already seen in the LSD-induced regression how the subject reported that words had lost their meaning and later that hallucinatory phenomena appeared. A similar sequence has been demonstrated in animals by several workers. Bridger (8) dealt with the effects of mescaline on conditioned responses of dogs. Normally, the dogs would lift a paw at the onset of a conditioned stimulus (buzzer) that had previously been paired with the unconditioned stimulus (shock). They would howl and bark when they received the shock. Under the effects of mescaline, the specific motor act of lifting the paw was inhibited. However, they howled and barked to the conditioned stimulus, even though no shock was applied. It appeared that the buzzer produced the hallucination of the shock. In a similar study in rats, Courvoisier (9) reported a "veritable hallucinatory crisis." Under mescaline, in response to each presentation of the conditioned stimulus (bell), the rats squealed and jumped up and down "as if they were being shocked," an event that never appeared in the "unmescalinized state."

How do the hallucinogens act to produce this regressed state? There is growing evidence that both LSD and mescaline dampen the activity of the most highly evolved areas of the brain and activate the more archaic areas. A description of the experimental evidence for these statements is not sufficiently relevant to this paper to warrant presentation, but the interested reader is referred to the writings of Gastaut (10), Rowland (11), Killam (12) and the summary by Bridger (8).

As a final piece of experimental evidence we would like to mention the findings of Lustman. (13) He and his associates studied 46 newborn infants under 8 days old during circumstances regarded to be the extremes of pleasure and pain, i.e., during active suckling and during colic. They observed that during these experiences the infants were completely unresponsive to auditory, tactile and electrical stimulation. They developed the hypothesis that the newborn ego has at its disposal a very limited amount of "psychic energy" which is completely absorbed in the pleasant or unpleasant experience. No energy remains for other sensory avenues. "This lack of available energy forms an inborn primary defense mechanism which is called the defense of imperceptivity." We mention these observations because of their possible connection to the well-known states of imperceptivity associated with yoga and other mystical states. St. Teresa (14) writes, for example:

> While seeking God in this way, the soul is conscious that it is fainting almost completely away in a kind of swoon. It can hardly stir its hands without great effort, the eyes close involuntarily; if they remain open, they scarcely see anything. If a person reads, he can scarcely make out a single letter; it is as much as he can do even to recognize one. He sees that there are letters, but as the understanding does not help, he cannot read them if he

wanted to. He hears but he doesn't understand what he hears.

Recently, electroencephalographic studies of yoga practitioners during "samadhi" have been carried out. In idle waking consciousness, cortical electrodes demonstrate what is known as alpha rhythm (8 to 12 cycles per second) and when an individual concentrates, this alpha rhythm is blocked. It returns with the return to the idle state. Anand *et al.* (15) took EEG tracings of 4 yoga practitioners in "samadhi." Their rhythms were of the normal alpha type except that there was some increased amplitude modulation. However, the alpha activity could not be blocked by sensory stimulation; for example, the alpha rhythm was unaffected when the subject's hands were placed in ice water for three-quarters of an hour. The yogi seemed to have effectively cut himself off from the external world, a fact of which he himself was aware and which could also be demonstrated objectively in this way.

Of possible relevance here are some further observations of Arieti (16) on his group of regressed schizophrenics. They seemed almost insensitive to pain.

> They appear analgesic not only to pinprick but to much more painful stimuli. When they are in need of surgical intervention and require sutures in such sensitive regions as the lips, face, skull, or hands, they act as though they cannot feel anything, even in the absence of any anesthetic procedure . . . The same anesthesia is noted for temperature. The patient may hold a piece of ice in his hands without showing any reaction. Pieces of ice may be placed over the breast, abdomen or other sensitive regions without eliciting any reaction or defensive movement . . . They may sit near the radiator and if they are not moved they may continue to stay there even when, as a result of close contact, they are burned.

We do not know, of course, whether these phenomena, which are somewhat similar on the surface, really have any neurophysiologic resemblance. It would be interesting to repeat Anand's electroencephalographic studies on Arieti's schizophrenics. The hypothesis we put forward is that the defensive imperceptivity to be observed in the newborn returns in the schizophrenics as a result of a deep regression. The yogi has in some way gained conscious control of this archaic physiological process during a temporary regression in the service of the ego.

## The Phenomenology of the Infantile State

What does it feel like to be a newborn child? Of course we can never know, any more than we can ever know what the subjective life of a caterpillar or a dog is like—or, for that matter, that of even those people closest to us. As far as the subjective life is concerned, each is an island unto himself.

This very fundamental difficulty has not prevented speculation or, should we say, assertions about the phenomenology of the infant, particularly by members of the analytic school. (17) Such descriptions are not entirely imaginary, but are pieced together from observations on young children, the recollections of adults, and abnormal states of patients.

> It would appear that the earliest mode of relationship between the infant and the outer world of things is by participation—or perhaps it would be more correct to say, in this early stage, the self and the world have not yet been separated from one another. In the newborn's relationship with the thing, he is that thing; he doesn't see and feel the breast: he doesn't hear the sound of the train whistle, he is the sound of the train whistle . . . We can perhaps think of the infant's stream of consciousness at this time as being a succession of concrete things—hunger, pain, breast, mother odor, side bar of crib, etc. At this stage there would be no separation between I and it—all would be one. Subsequently, when the infant's ego has attained some degree of autonomy, the stream of consciousness becomes one of perception, and hallucinations of perception. At first we may think of the hallucinatory experience as being indistinguishable from genuine perception. One may consider the sleeping child; physiological conditions of hunger occur and the child rises to the more superficial levels of sleep, then the hallucination of the breast emerges and the child may be observed to make sucking motions with his mouth and then sink back into the deeper levels of sleep. At this level, the image of the breast is equal to the real breast. (18)

We have already drawn attention to the interesting regressive phenomena that occur at the fringes of sleep. They may take the form of curious body image distortions—one's mouth seems huge and swollen or one's hands or buttocks are very large and heavy. There may be visual hallucinations, or there may be humming sounds or the babbling of indistinguishable voices. There may be pages of print which one strains to read. They seem to have meaning at the time, but upon emerging to a higher level of consciousness the words seem to have been mere nonsense. These phenomena, of course, merge with dream experiences of one kind or another. We do not know how widely these phenomena are distributed in the population but it is probable that there are at least some of the readers of this paper who have experienced them. They are unstable; one has but to move a limb and they collapse.

In 1938 Isakower (19) described that particular cluster of such hypnogogic experience which now bears his name—the Isakower phenomenon. The experience occurs just as the patient is falling asleep or, rarely, just as he is waking up. A large, round, dark mass seems to approach the beginning sleeper, or it may be like a gray cloud, it envelops him, at the same time producing a rough, doughy, corrugated feeling in the mouth and in the skin, so that he loses his sense of the self-boundary and cannot say where the division is between his own body and the mass. At times there is a feeling of giddiness, as though the sleeper were on a rotating disc. There is something large in the mouth, a lump that cannot be swallowed. There may be a heaviness lying on top of him, and perhaps a humming, babbling or murmuring of unintelligible speech. This phenomenon has since been widely commented upon by others. Isakower believed it to be a hallucinatory revival of the nursing experience. It is a state of regression and reactivation of the time when self and breast were indistinguishable. In 1946 Bertram Lewin (20) described his concept of the dream screen:

> The baby, after nursing, falls into a presumably dream-less sleep. Theoretically it may be more correct to speak of the babies having a "blank dream," a vision of uni-

form blankness which is a persistent after-image of the breast. Later in life this blank picture of the flattened breast, preserved in dreams as a sort of backdrop or projective screen, like its analogue in the cinema, comes to have projected upon it the picture that we call the visual manifest content of the dream. The fulfillment of the wish to sleep produces only sound sleep and the dream screen. So far as falling asleep reproduces the infant's first sleep after nursing, it reproduces the fusion of the ego and the breast. The primitive sleeping ego is id, except for the dream screen, the erstwhile breast sole and first representative of the environment.

We have here then in the works of Isakower and Lewin the concept that each night the individual regresses to the primary nursing experience. One of the reasons we introduced Lewin's concept of the dream screen was to suggest that the dream screen might be related to the mandala. Jung (21) has made us very conscious of the mandala. The word is Sanskrit for magic circle. It is generally a circular symbol with a figure, frequently female—the *anima mundi*—at the center. One of our patients produced in dreams such a mandala. The female figure in the center was clothed in white and she carried in one hand a torch and in the other a dove; around her waist was a serpent swallowing its own tail; at the periphery were panels showing the sun, moon, stars, fields, etc. The patient felt that the female figure was a source of great power and that all the meaning in the world had its source in her. Mandala symbolism is, of course, extremely diverse, and of very widespread distribution in the religions of the world. It is frequently used as a focus for contemplation by mystics.

We know of only one instance of the dream screen or the mandala in literature. It is in those gold mines of psychopathology, the short stories of Edgar Allan Poe. *The Narrative of A. Gordon Pym* concerns a series of harrowing adventures at sea. The story is full of oral imagery and pathology—starvation, cannibalism, sleep disturbances, etc. At the end of the story the protagonist is adrift in a canoe in some exotic and unexplored part of the globe. The sea water is of a milky hue and in his canoe he approaches a strange white curtain.

I can liken it to nothing but a limitless cataract, rolling silently into the sea from some immense and far-distant ramparts in the heavens. The gigantic curtain ranged along the whole extent of the southern horizon. It emitted no sound . . . at intervals there were visible in it yawning, momentary rents, and from out these rents, within which was a chaos of flitting and indistinct images, there came rushing and mighty, but soundless winds, tearing up the enkindled ocean in their course . . . and now we rushed into the embraces of the cataract, where a chasm threw itself open to receive us. But there arose in our pathway a shrouded human figure, very far larger in its proportions than any dweller among men. And the hue of the skin of the figure was of the perfect whiteness of snow.

## Mystical States as Regressions in the Service of the Ego

We have now dwelt sufficiently on the concept of regression and the variety of its manifestations. Let us now turn to a description of the mystical state. Mystical states of altered consciousness are of relatively short duration—a few minutes to a few hours, exceptionally to a few days. They may occur spontaneously or may be actively sought by the subject using a variety of techniques, including prayer, contemplation, fasting, and various bodily activities or postures. Not all are successful; even with considerable effort some individuals are not to attain the mystical state. There is no doubt a variety of such states with a wide range of phenomenology. Zaehner (22) describes the following three types: (1) the state of feeling at one with nature; (2) the feeling of fusion of the self with Deity but with the maintenance of the self-feeling; (3) a loss of self-feeling—the fusion of the self with the other so that there is only the one all-pervading element. Unlike the states of possession that occur in primitive groups, most of these states seem to occur in a more or less clear consciousness so that the experience can be recalled after the return to ordinary consciousness. In many instances a definite change in personality or attitude results. Such changes are by no means automatic, however, and seem to depend a good deal upon the setting in which the state occurs and the attitudes of the subject. Changes may be along the line of a reduction in self-concern, an increased placidity, a loss of interest in material possessions, an increase of passivity in the face of adversity, etc. The nature of these changes, their extent and stability have not been adequately studied, at least in the Western world.

In spite of the diversity of these states, a number of common features has been described. These include, (1) renunciation of worldly attachments as a prelude, (2) the ineffability of the experience itself, (3) the noetic quality, (4) the ecstatic feeling, and (5) the experience of fusion.

As we have already said, the hypothesis we are proposing is that mystical states are examples of regressions in the service of the ego. They are, therefore, to be considered in the same class as certain creative experiences and certain types of psychotherapy; they are also close kin to the psychoses. More specifically, we propose that mystical states represent regressions to very early periods of infancy. The basic characteristic—that of ecstatic union—suggests a regression to early nursing experience. Possibly the variation in phenomenology represents variations in depth of the regression to earlier or later types of nursing experience. It is possible too that the outcome of the experience—either the successful return to the real world or the entry into psychoses—depends in part whether these early feeding experiences were pleasurable or frightening. The exploration of this line of thought is, however, beyond the scope of the present paper. Now we would like to examine the above-listed characteristics in the light of this hypothesis.

## *(1) The Renunciation of Worldly Interests*

When mystical states are aspired to, the first stage is the stripping of the self of all material encumbrances; there is renunciation and detachment.

This renunciation seems a common prelude to regressive experiences in general. The preparation for sleep involves the putting aside of all the trappings of adult life, as we have shown: the room is darkened and we must disengage ourselves from the concerns of the day; it is a well-known feature of the beginning stages of schizophrenia that the patient gradually loses interest in his friends, his work, and the external world in general; regressive experiences produced by sensory deprivation could also be mentioned. (23)

## (2) Ineffability

Upon return, mystics commonly have difficulty in clothing their experiences in words. When they do refer to the content, they feel that the words they are using do not really express the nature of their experience. In the light of our hypothesis, the difficulty could be explained by the fact that the experience recaptured is a preverbal one. Words are linked with states of consciousness typical of two years of age and older. When they are pressed into service to describe earlier modes of experience they seem to fall short. Jacob Boehme, (24) the great 16th century Christian mystic wrote:

> . . . Who can express it?
> Or why and what do I write, whose tongue does but stammer like a child which is learning to speak? With what shall I compare it? Or to what shall I liken it? Shall I compare it with the love of this world? No, that is but a mere dark valley to it.
> O immense Greatness! I cannot compare it with any thing, but only with resurrection from the dead; there will the Love-Fire rise up again in us, and rekindle again our astringent, bitter, and cold, dark and dead powers, and embrace us most courteously and friendly.

## (3) The Noetic Quality

Mystics believe they have grasped profound truths during their experiences. They have drunk deeply at the fountain of meaning. As Happold (25) says:

> (Mystical experiences) result in insight into depths of truth unplumbed by the discursive intellect, insights which carry with them a tremendous sense of authority. Things take on a new pattern, and a new, often unsuspected, significance.

How are we to explain this noetic quality? It is a common psychological principle that first experiences are the most significant in any series. Clearly, one of the first conscious experiences is that of feeding at the breast. Lewin (26) writes:

> A similar element in many ecstasies is the allegation of direct inspiration, pure and immediate perception of inexpressible truth . . . this certainty reflects the realness of the breast experience. This experience is what one knows because it is primal, immediate, and unquestioned experience. It was not learned by seeing or hearsay, but represents the primitive narcissistic trust in sensory experience.

It will be recalled that our patient commented that the female center in her mandala was the source of all the meaning in the world. Plotinus (27) wrote:

> Things there flow in a way from a single source, not like one particular breath or warmth, but as if there were a single quality containing in itself and preserving all qualities, sweet taste and smell and the quality of wine with all other flavors, visions of colors and all that touch perceives, all, too, that hearing hears, all tunes and every rhythm.

It is as though all the realities of the world are dim reflections of that primal Reality.

## (4) Ecstasy

A feeling of preternatural joyfulness seems to be a characteristic of many mystical states—particularly those of the type called nature mysticism and deistic mysticism. There are two ways of looking at the ecstasy of these states: (a) we could regard them as a pure regression and re-experience of the bliss of nursing; (b) we could regard them as similar to the elation associated with certain psychotic states, notably mania.

The psychopathology of mania requires clarification. We have chosen an episode from the novel *Frankenstein* by way of illustration. Frankenstein has succeeded in constructing a monster from human body parts garnered from a graveyard.

Moreover, he succeeds in bringing his monster to life. It is appalling to look upon, Frankenstein is horrified and he rushes from the laboratory. Some days later he returns and is immeasurably relieved to find the monster gone. He has a brief manic attack:

> It was not joy only that possessed me; I felt my flesh tingle with excess of sensitiveness, and my pulse beat rapidly. I was unable to remain for a single instant in the same place; I jumped over chairs, clapped my hands and laughed aloud. Clerval at first attributed my unusual spirits to joy on his arrival; but when he observed me more attentively, he saw a wildness in my eyes for which he could not account; and my loud, unrestrained, heartless laughter frightened and astonished him.

This is a good description of the uneasy elation of mania. Of course the monster had not really gone; he returned to haunt Frankenstein for the balance of the novel. This passage also illustrates the defense mechanism of denial which is so commonly associated with mania. It is a kind of defense of imperceptivity raised to a psychological level. It is at best an unstable elation—a kind of ostrich technique. Mania as a psychiatric disorder is often associated with periods of depression. The mania may then be regarded as associated with the denial of the horror of the depressed state.

If we are to seriously consider the possibility that mystical ecstasies may be of the manic type, we must look for possible painful elements in the nursing situation. We do not have far to seek. It is clear that the state of rage and fear of a child kept waiting to be fed would be such a painful circumstance; the anxiety or irritation of a harassed mother communicated to the tender ego of the newborn would be a second example.

We must now return to our original question. Which type of bliss are we dealing with in mystical experiences—(1) the simple elation of nursing, (2) the elation associated with denial, a manic elation? Let us examine some descriptions of mystical states to see which type seems the best fit.

Certainly, in many descriptions by Christian mystics, the simple elation of fulfillment seems most appropriate. I choose a few at random. Jacob Boehme (28) writes:

> O gracious amiable Blessedness and great Love, how sweet art thou! . . . How pleasant and lovely is the relish and taste! . . . How ravishing sweetly dost thou smell!

Richard St. Victor wrote:

> In this state the Lord often visits the hungry and thirsty soul, often He fills her with inward delight and makes her drink with the sweetness of His spirit.

And now a passage from St. Francis de Sales, (29) in which he describes the "orison of quietude":

> In this state the soul is like a little child still at the breast whose mother, to caress him while he is still in her arms, makes her milk distill into his mouth without even moving his lips. So it is here . . . our Lord desires that our world should be satisfied with sucking the milk which His Majesty pours into our mouth, and that we should relish the sweetness without even knowing that it cometh from the Lord.

From these examples we can see that at least in some instances the mystical ecstasy seems closest to the simple regression to nursing. This is not, we think, the whole story. There is the depressive condition known to mystics as the dark night of the soul and there are periods of temptation. The question of the nature of mystical elation must be left in abeyance at this time.

## (5) *The Fusion Experience*

The experience of fusion is, as we have seen, typical of all kinds of mystical experience. It is a feeling that one's individuality, one's self-boundaries have disappeared—the self and nature are interfused. One's being is fused with a greater being of some type, sometimes to the extent that there are no longer two things but only one all-pervading thing.

We have already dealt at some length with the phenomenology of the infantile state and the gradual emergence of the self as distinct from the rest of the world. The feeling of loss of boundaries, then, can be regarded simply as a regression to this earlier state.

## Conclusion

In an article entitled "The Supra-Conscious State," Kenneth Walker, (30) the well-known British surgeon and student of mysticism, recently expressed a commonly held belief about the psychiatric view of mystical states:

> Some psychologists deny the existence of higher states of consciousness, and dismiss them as "dream states," regarding the experiences of the mystics as entirely illusory. It is strange that Freud, who discovered so much about subconscious states, should not have postulated the existence of levels of consciousness *above* as well as *below* the level on which we usually live.

We hope in this paper that we have at least convinced the reader that the psychoanalyst does have something significant to say about the mystical state, and that it is not simply dismissed as illusion or "dream state." Indeed, we doubt that other hypotheses explain the observed facts nearly as satisfactorily. The concept of regression is particularly helpful in providing a plausible link between psychoses and mystical states. A psychosis is a pressured withdrawal with—in many cases—an incomplete return. A mystical state is a controlled withdrawal and return; a death and rebirth, often a rebirth into a world with a radical shift in its iconography—a death and transfiguration.

REFERENCES

1. BUCKE, R. M. *Cosmic Consciousness* (New York: Dutton Co., 1951).
2. ANONYMOUS, "Case Report: An Autobiography of a Schizophrenic Experience," *Journal of Abnormal Social Psychology,* 51:677–689, 1956.
3. BURLINGHAM, D. et al., "Monthly Report of Hampstead Nurseries for May 1944." Quoted in Bowlby, J., *Child Care and the Growth of Love* (Pelican, 1954), p. 27.
4. POINCARE, H., "Mathematical Creation," in Brewster Ghiselin (ed.), *The Creative Process* (New York: Mentor Books, 1955), p. 36–42.
5. ARIETI, S., *Interpretation of Schizophrenia* (New York: Brunner, 1955), p. 363.

6. KRIS, E., *Psychoanalytic Explorations in Art*, Part 3 (New York: International Universities Press, 1952).

7. PENFIELD, W., *The Excitable Cortex in Conscious Man* (Liverpool: Liverpool University Press, 1958), p. 23.

8. BRIDGER, W. H., "Contributions of Conditioning Principles to Psychiatry," in *Symposium No. 9. Group for the Advancement of Psychiatry*, 1964, pp. 181–98.

9. COURVOISIER, S., "Pharmacodynamic Basis for the Use of Chlorpromazine in Psychiatry," *Journal of Clinical Experimental Psychopathology, 17:25*, 1956.

10. GASTAUT, H., "Some Aspects of the Neurophysiological Basis of Conditioned Reflexes and Behavior," in G. E. W. Wolstenholme and C. M. O'Connor (eds.), *Neurological Basis of Behavior* (London: Ciba Foundation, 1958).

11. ROWLAND, V., "Differential Electroencephalographic Response to Conditioned Auditory Stimuli in Arousal from Sleep," *EEG Clinical Neurophysiology, 9:585–94*, 1957.

12. KILLAM, L. R. & E. K., "The Action of Lysergic Acid Diethylamide on the Central Afferent System in the Cat," *Journal of Pharmacology and Experimental Therapeutics, 116:35–42*, 1956.

13. LUSTMAN, S. L., "Psychic Energy and Mechanisms of Defense," *Psychoanalytic Study of the Child, 12:151–65*, 1957.

14. ST. TERESA, *The Life of Saint Teresa of Avila*, translated by J. M. Cohen (Penguin, 1957), p. 125.

15. ANAND, B. K. et al., "Some Aspects of Electroencephalographic Studies of Yogis," *EEG Clinical Neurophysiology, 13:452*, 1961.

16. ARIETI, S., *op. cit.*, p. 373.

17. FREUD, S., *Civilization and Its Discontents*, Standard Edition, Vol. XXI (London: Hogarth Press), pp. 64–73.

18. BURROW, T., *Preconscious Foundations of Human Experience* (New York: Basic Books), 1964.

19. ISAKOWER, O., "A Contribution to the Psychopathology of Phenomena Associated with Falling Asleep," *International Journal of Psychoanalysis, 19:331–45*, 1938.

20. LEWIN, B. D., "Sleep, Mouth, and Dream Screen," *Psychoanalytical Quarterly, 15:419–43*, 1946; "Reconsiderations of the Dream Screen," *Psychoanalytical Quarterly, 22:174–99*; quotation from *The Psychoanalysis of Elation* (New York: Norton, 1950), p. 89.

21. JUNG, C. G., "Concerning Mandala Symbolism," *Collected Works*, Bollingen Series XX, Vol. 9, Part 1, pp. 355–84, 1959.

22. ZAEHNER, R. C., *Mysticism, Sacred and Profane* (New York: Oxford University Press, 1961).

23. BEXTON, W. H., HERON, W. & SCOTT, T. H., "Effects of Decreased Variation in the Sensory Environment," *Canadian Journal of Psychology, 8:70–76*, 1954; for review see following reference.

THORPE, J. G., "Sensory Deprivation," *Journal of Mental Science,* 107:1047–59, 1961.

24. BOEHME, J., in W. Scott Palmer (ed.), *The Confessions of Jacob Boehme,* New York: Harper, 1954, pp. 43–44.

25. HAPPOLD, F. C., *Mysticism: A Study and an Anthology* (Penguin 1963), p. 45.

26. LEWIN, B. D., *The Psychoanalysis of Elation, op. cit.,* p. 149.

27. HAPPOLD, F. C., *op. cit.,* p. 187, quotation.

28. BOEHME, J., *op. cit.,* p. 43.

29. JAMES, W., *The Varieties of Religious Experience* (New York: Modern Library, 1902), p. 12, quotation.

30. WALKER, K., "The Supra-Conscious State," *Image* (*Hoffman LaRoche*) 10:11–14, 1964; also in this volume.

# THE MYSTICAL EXPERIENCE: FACTS AND VALUES

## CLAIRE MYERS OWENS

Today the mystic state is considered by many Third Force psychologists to be part of the whole process of self-realization. It is often a vital step in the actualization of man's potentialities—a matter of ultimate concern to every thoughtful person. The value of mystical experience to the individual and to society can be more clearly discerned when viewed in this broader frame of reference.

Most Freudian psychologists, on the other hand, dismiss the mystic state as an illusion. Dr. R. H. Prince of McGill University's Department of Psychiatry, however, proposes that it is regression in service of the ego, but lays particular emphasis on the hypothesis that it represents regression to the state of early infancy or is often akin to the psychotic state (1). Here we should like to raise the question whether evidence supports these hypotheses. Are not Prince's conclusions based on superficial resemblances, leaving untouched the *values* of the experience?

Prince, who is a doctor of medicine, had the collaboration of Charles Savage, M. D., an analyst, in the preparation of the paper which he read before a conference held by the R. M. Bucke Memorial Society, under the general subject of "Personality Change and Religious Experience." In the subsequent discussion, Dr. Walter H. Clark, who has elsewhere (2) written about the central importance of mystical experience

Reprinted by permission from *Main Currents in Modern Thought*, Vol. 23, No. 4, March–April 1967.

to religion, expressed gratitude for the serious attention given this neglected subject. He remarked, however, that when the Freudians point out a few similarities between mysticism and early infancy they believe they have said enough to damn this most intense of all human experiences (3).

It is true that Prince's paper is persuasive, well-documented, and couched in scientific terms. For these reasons it might be devastating to anyone who is on the verge of accepting the validity of mystical experience, and therefore a detailed consideration of his arguments seems warranted.

Even a quick reading of Prince's paper reveals his bias, for the similarities of the mystic state to the infantile or psychotic state are carefully presented, while the differences are scarcely mentioned. For example, several cases of pathological regression are cited and documented in detail. Then, as examples of regression in service of the ego, are listed sleep, the creative process, the state occurring in psychoanalysis, and the mystical state. Prince questions whether regression occurs in the cortex, or in the archaic area of the brain, and recalls Wilder Penfield's experiments in stimulating the cortex of an epileptic patient, thus inducing him to re-experience long-forgotten incidents. Further, he suggests that the so-called mystical experience induced by ingestion of LSD offers evidence that the psychedelic chemicals suppress the activity of the cortex, the most highly evolved part of the brain, and activate the more archaic area, leaving the impression that it is obviously retrograde.

As characteristics of the mystical experience, Prince lists a feeling of oneness with nature or Deity, decrease in self-concern and interest in material things, increase in placidity and passivity in adversity. Others which he enumerates in detail, i.e., imperceptivity, participation, renunciation of the world, ineffability, noetic quality, ecstasy and fusion, he regards as regression to an infantile or pathological state. His implication seems to be that the activities of the older brain are ipso facto infantile or psychotic.

These examples may reveal analogous behavior between some cases of infantile regression and pathological states, and some cases of mystical experience. Against these observations, however, it seems only fair to place in evidence innumerable cases wherein the mystical experience has led to permanent transformation of the psyche in the direction of wholeness, health and self-actualization.

It is here that the question of *value* must be taken into consideration—a question which Prince has largely ignored. It has been shown even in the physical sciences, however, that complete objectivity is unattainable. And in the study of subjective states the problem of value is intrinsic—as indeed it is in everything which touches man closely. One of the greatest scientists, Einstein, reminded us that the scientific method teaches us facts but that the ultimate goal of life and the longing to reach it must come from another source. Our existence acquires meaning only by setting up such a goal with appropriate values (4). Mankind rises or falls according to its value system, as is evidenced by today's destruction of values and evident increase in mental illness, fear, crime and devastating war. To the humanist, value derives from man's intrinsic nature; to the religionist, value derives from the eternal ground of being. Both definitions are embraced by mysticism, wherein values are no longer abstractions, but living experience.

Years ago, Bertrand Russell wrote that the person who has had mystical experience is above logic. He has been there; he knows. While it is true that such experience carries its own affirmation, the mystic feels himself intensely one with humanity, and therefore he seeks continuously for ways to communicate to others the realities he has found. He keeps on trying to describe in rational terms what may be beyond reason to comprehend. In the context of our scientific age, therefore, the mystic welcomes the help that science can give to furnish a natural (not a supernatural nor a psychotic) explanation for his intuitive insights. Fortunately, not all scientists regard mystical experience as merely aberrant; some believe it may disclose phases of man's knowing process.

For is the only valid knowledge scientific or rational? Northrop has indicated that there are two kinds of knowledge: theoretic, which is scientifically verifiable, and aesthetic, which is immediately apprehensible. Complete knowledge requires a synthesis of the two (5).

Thus, to understand mysticism properly, we should have scientific observation and facts, and experiential knowledge, which delivers values. In such an enquiry into subjective states, the personal experience of the mystic—the testimony of a life—should be admissible as valid evidence.

## The Unconscious Source

Confusion seems to arise because the contents of the unconscious have not been sufficiently differentiated. The Freudians usually concern themselves with the personal unconscious only, that is, with the upper layer where personal neurosis may occur. As Jung has pointed out, however, there is a deeper level which he called the collective unconscious. Here is the source of the highest good, of mystical and religious experience; here lie the springs of creativity. Here too is the dark seat of psychosis. And it may be said that at birth the infant is immersed in this collective unconscious (6, 7). It is obvious from these statements that the unconscious is the rich and fertile source of many different elements in man's conscious life; it is also apparent that there are no water-tight compartments in this hidden area. All the more reason why great care should be taken to distinguish and evaluate the divergent contents of the unconscious. Yet the psychoanalytic psychologist is inclined to lump all these manifestations together.

My intention here is to show that despite some superficial similarities between the mystical state and the infant or psychotic state, their dissimilarities in cause, consequence and content, and therefore in *value*, put the transcendent experience in an entirely different category. I hope to prove that the mystic state derives from the deeper levels of the unconscious, and that in the balanced and mature individual it is healthy and deeply beneficial.

Prince lists several characteristics of the mystic state which he considers to be closely akin to that of the infant or psychotic. I shall attempt to differentiate these, to demonstrate that fragments of the human psyche, as presented by the good doctor, do not represent its totality, and to show that the conclusions he draws from a few selected details presented out of context are inadequate to explain the whole range of the experience. My argument is that in the mystic experience the center of gravity is transferred from the ego, which is the center of consciousness, to the self, which is the center of the whole psyche, and therefore of the person.

The value of the mystical condition, however, cannot be presented properly except in relation to the larger problems of man and society. One present danger we face is the dichotomy that afflicts man, that is, the dissociation between the conscious and the unconscious which causes so many people to suffer from the meaninglessness of life. Jung believed that this dissociation causes a general cultural sickness that manifests itself among men otherwise normal, leading to a breakdown of society. The question is how to transform man into the harmonious whole which nature intended him to be, and thus give meaning and purpose to his life. I hold that the mystical state, which can be instrumental in the release of unconscious energy and potential, offers a clue to meaning, wholeness and individual self-realization.

The tragic events and cultural dislocation that darken the world today are all man-made. It is becoming apparent that governmental or intergovernmental actions are insufficient to halt the current march toward violence and destruction. Improvements in man's physical environment do not necessarily change and improve his behavior. As Jung pointed out, society cannot be regenerated unless man is regenerated. It is becoming painfully obvious that it is man himself who must be changed. This change is not easily effected by laws, by punishment, by exhortations, or even by education in the ordinary sense of that word. Then how? Man's hidden potential, his "undiscovered self," must be discovered *by him*. He will then understand for himself that the good of society is his own good. I believe that the psychological state called mystical can illuminate this inner self which, when fully realized and released, can lead to regeneration, and reveal man's latent capacities to create a peaceful and just world.

Therefore I am grateful to Dr. Prince, even while I disagree with his findings, for his working hypotheses concerning the mystic state can serve as a welcome stimulus to this whole discussion, and a challenge to the data offered by others.

## Other Testimony

Maslow, the humanistic psychologist, prefers to speak of "peak-experience" rather than mystical experience, but both the psychological process and the results he describes are similar. It is the interpretations after the event that vary. Maslow has discovered that the peak-experience brings the individual fusion of facts and values, resolution of conflicts, loss of anxiety, discovery of the real self, a sense of unity, detachment, selflessness, happiness, and love (8). In another survey of contemporary subjects, he found that during the peak-experience the subject perceives intrinsic values of being, such as wholeness, simplicity, honesty, goodness, effortlessness, playfulness, justice and self-sufficiency (9).

Bucke, whose *Cosmic Consciousness* is a classic in the field, maintains that mystical awareness is a new, third form of consciousness which may constitute the next evolutionary step, and that all men may eventually be endowed with it (10).

Teilhard de Chardin foresees a conjunction of reason and mysticism, for science and religion will inevitably converge as they draw nearer to the whole. As I understand it, Teilhard's science, philosophy and religion all contribute to his statement that biological evolution has attained its ceiling in man, and to his prediction that the man of tomorrow must aid in his own mental and spiritual evolution into a New Being (11).

Carl Jung has made one of the most extensive scientific investigations of the mystical experience. His life-long study of the unconscious in hundreds of subjects—normal, neurotic, psychotic—proved to him that mysticism is the natural tendency of the deeper unconscious. He believed that if modern man regards the mystical state as pathological, this is only because of a lack of understanding. Jung himself wrote of the mystical experience as a discovery of buried treasures in the collective unconscious, entailing union with the impersonal source of life, both attained through regression (12).

Jung's concept of regression is clarified by Freida Fordham (13). Psychic energy or the libido flows between two opposite poles. Human life operates on the principle of *enantiodromia,* the law of the reconciliation of opposites. All life is rhythmic, swinging between sleep and waking, rest and activity, dark and light; so also has psychic energy its natural rhythmic movement forward to the conscious mind and backward into the unconscious. It resembles the ebb and flow of the ocean tides. Seen in this light, regression is part of life's rhythmic movement between the pairs of opposites. The forward, outgoing movement, or progression, Jung found, satisfies the needs of the conscious mind, whereas the backward, inturning movement, or regression, satisfies the demands of the unconscious. The former aids man in adapting to his external environment, the latter in adapting to his inner needs.

In these terms, regression is as normal a counterpart to progression as sleep is to waking. It may sometimes be a reversion to an earlier stage of man's development, but when it occurs in the healthy individual it is a restorative measure. Jung maintained that only when there is repression of the libido may the flow of psychic energy back into the unconscious emerge as a neurotic symptom, infantile behavior, or psychosis. This then constitutes pathological regression, quite different from the normal regression which is a necessity for mental health.

Furthermore, Jung discovered that psychic energy regresses not only back into childhood, that is, to the preverbal level, but inasmuch as the personal stratum terminates at the earliest memories of infancy, regression continues on back into the deeper collective unconscious—into the pre-infantile period which contains residues of man's ancestral life. When psychic energy regresses beyond infancy, a whole new inner spiritual world—whose existence the individual may not even have suspected—opens up.

It may be said, in view of the above testimony, that if regression is the appropriate term to use in describing mystical experience, it is that kind of regression which offers the same refreshment to man as does sleep after wakefulness, quiet after noise, solitude after being in the company of others, and deep reflection after mental activity.

The hypothesis which I should like to put forward is that the mystical state can be described as regression to the earlier pre-infantile level of the collective unconscious which is the matrix of man, wherein lie the seeds of his creativity, his sense of being, his source of integrity and inner harmony, his identity with mankind, and his profound inner union with the integrating principle of the universe. The value of contact with this resource, however achieved, is obviously in an entirely different category from that of the infant state.

## Characteristics of the Mystical State

At this point we might look at the characteristics which Prince offers in support of his contention that the mystical state is similar to the infant or psychotic. These, as previously mentioned, are imperceptivity, participation, renunciation, ineffability, noesis, ecstasy, and fusion. They are worth considering in detail.

### Imperceptivity

In discussing what he calls "defense imperceptivity," Prince cites S. L. Lustman's experiments with forty-six infants under eight days old during extremes of pleasure and pain; in these states the infants were unresponsive to auditory, tactile or even electrical stimulation. Arieti's similar experiments with a group of schizophrenics have led Prince to suggest that some schizophrenics in a condition of imperceptivity return to the infantile state in deep regression. In making his comparison with imperceptivity in mystics, Prince uses the words of the mystics themselves as evidence against them. Thus, St. Theresa wrote that at the time of ecstasy the mystic is insensible to external distractions. Scientific studies of yogis in samadhi show them to be oblivious to noise or to being touched or even to pain.

Prince's implication seems to be that anyone who is imperceptive to sensory stimuli has regressed to the infant state. But such imperceptivity also results from deep abstraction or concentration upon intellectual problems, when the individual is often undistracted by noise or environmental disturbances. To offer an illustration, Socrates was in a state of imperceptivity when Aristodemus observed him standing motionless in a neighbor's porch when he was supposed to be on his way to a banquet at Agathon's house. On emerging from this trance, Socrates' brilliant dialectic during the world's most famous symposium suggests that while in his state of imperceptivity he was able to touch the springs of his inmost life and thought. For it was then that he developed his dialogue concerning the five rungs of the ladder leading toward that perfection achieved through man's love of beauty which may finally lift him to love of "absolute beauty, separate, simple and everlasting." It should seem obvious, therefore, that imperceptivity is not only the result of extreme sensory excitation; it can result from the purposive withdrawal of awareness, its disengagement with sense perception.

## Renunciation

Another characteristic which Prince regards as common to the schizophrenic and the mystic is the renunciation of worldly attachments. However, the schizophrenic abandons his work and his family not through choice but because he is too ill to accept responsibility or to cope with life. The mystic, on the other hand, voluntarily and in full awareness gives up the pleasures and rewards of mundane life in search of what is for him a greater good. So the Buddha renounced his kingly heritage in order to find the causes of human suffering and the ways to alleviate it.

A modern example of worldly renunciation may be found in the life of Albert Schweitzer, who gave up an established career in Europe to establish a hospital in the depths of the African jungle. He has testified that the keystone of his philosophy, "reverence for life," presented itself to him in a mystical flash of insight. A similar act of voluntary renunciation was Thoreau's decision to abandon the opportunity of acquiring wealth from his discovery of a new method of making graphite, in order to seek self-understanding in the Walden woods.

The list of those who have consciously rejected material values and comforts to pursue an ideal is not limited to those religiously oriented. The transcendent moment which transforms attitudes and life habits knows no boundaries of place or time; it can touch the man who is active in the world as well as the philosopher. History has preserved for us the names of countless persons who have given up personal security, love and wealth in order to devote themselves to the service of others, which brings nothing but its own reward.

The life of a mentally ill person, immersed for years in a catatonic stupor, out of reach of all human contact, is a tragic waste. How is it possible to compare such withdrawal from the world with the full and rewarding lives that have resulted from conscious renunciation of personal satisfactions—lives that often have enormously benefitted mankind?

## Ineffability

Mystics have always proclaimed that their experience is indescribable. Prince suggests that this is due to the fact that the experience is preverbal. (Others have held it to be *non-*verbal.) It may be admitted that the older unconscious is not designed by nature to express itself in the conscious verbalization of the newer cortex. Man's unconscious mind conveys its meanings chiefly through symbols and images, dreams and archetypes, visions, intuitions and insights which may later be conceptualized.

As proof of his contention, Prince offers a quotation from Jacob Boehme, in which this famous mystic exclaims that he cannot describe the mystical experience in words, but can only "stammer like a child." He says further that it is "so immense a greatness" it is like the "resurrection from the dead." To Prince, of course, anything which is not verbal is infantile. But this point of view is being seriously challenged by many investigators today, as for example in Michael Polanyi's book,

*The Tacit Dimension,* whose thesis is that we "know more than we can say." His and other studies of intuition and imagination in creative endeavor reveal the major role of these two modes of knowing.

It is true that mystical experience is ineffable, beyond the reaches of discursive thought—but it is non-rational, not irrational. It appears able to open the mind to new insights, new meaning, and new understanding. Despite its ineffability, mystical or direct religious experience has produced the world's greatest religious literature: the Upanishads, the Tao Te Ching, the teachings of the Compassionate Buddha, the Kabala, the Koran, the books of the Bible, and, on a lesser scale, the mystical poems of the Sufis and the writings of St. Theresa, Meister Eckhart, Ruysbroeck, and many others. What is more, flashes of creative insight have produced works of genius in the fields of art, music and science; they have resulted in some of the marvelous discoveries of deductive science as well as those of "intuitive" mathematics. Such men as Bohr, Heisenberg, Poincaré and de Broglie, to name only a few, have acknowledged that their theories stemmed from an original intuitive perception. Faraday's discoveries in the field of electromagnetism resulted from a vision; Kepler perceived the "harmony of the universe."

Nor are such moments restricted to saints and genuises. As Maslow has discovered, many an obscure person has had a peak moment which transformed his life. If a personal note may be introduced, I myself have experienced such a moment, which spontaneously awakened dormant qualities whose existence I never suspected. Life undoubtedly prepares us for such moments, but they may come at the most unexpected times and places. As Arthur Koestler has related out of his experience of imprisonment in Spain as a Communist, a wave of "wordless essence . . . a fragrance of eternity" can wash over a personality, leaving it newborn (14).

## Noesis

Both the infant and the mystic apprehend self-evident truth directly and immediately; Prince seems to believe that this equates the noetic quality in them. He states, for example, that it is a common psychological principle that first experience is the most impressive, and a child's first experience is feeding at the breast. On the other hand, he quotes the statement by F. C. Happold that the transcendent experiences of mystics produce insights into truths unplumbed by the discursive intellect. And in referring to Plotinus, he remarks (as if himself half-persuaded) that to the mystic all the appearances of the world are "but dim reflections of a primal Reality."

The kind of reality apprehended by an infant may certainly be this "primal Reality." Prince, however, does not make quite clear what kind of reality the infant does experience, except for a "narcissistic trust" which results from an erotic feeling aroused by his own body, immersion in concern for himself. In contrast, the mystic's encounter with ultimate reality renders him oblivious of the body and its sensual responses, and results in a purification of narcissistic tendencies and indeed an impersonalization of the personal in all its aspects. It seems fantastic to equate the noetic quality in the infant with the unitive knowledge of universals exemplified in the philosophy of Patanjali, Shankara, Socrates and Pascal, and in the knowledge of the laws of nature revealed to great scientists intuitively.

The dictionary definition of mysticism is that it is the obtaining "of direct knowledge of reality . . . differing from ordinary sense perception or the use of logical reasoning." Thus, even if infants achieve noesis, the significance of their knowledge is lost in the amorphous content of their psyches, unavailable to consciousness. Perhaps the infant's noetic experience may be the "clouds of glory" of which Wordsworth spoke, but alas, it vanishes in the wake of later experience. Not so the mystic's, the effects of whose vision endures throughout life.

## Ecstasy

A universally attested result of mystical experience is ecstasy, bliss or joy. In Prince's view, this is merely regression to the blissful re-experience of nursing, or a condition similar to the false elation of psychotic states. Here again his limited understanding is communicated to his readers through a misleading quotation from Francis de Sales, taken out of context: "In this state [the orison of quietude] the soul is like a little child still at the breast of the mother."

Prince's oversimplification is the result of contemporary reliance upon Freudian techniques, wherein symbolic configurations lose some of their meaning. Familiarity with the literature of mysticism, on the other hand, reveals the degree to which those who have experienced the state of expanded consciousness are forced to rely upon symbol, parable, image and analogy in their efforts to communicate in formal language the essential quality of a formless reality.

The child motif is one such attempt to put the nature of mystical experience in terms which can be understood by the majority of men; it has been so employed for centuries. It is an archetype; it is numinous; it possesses a redemptive effect. The image of innocence and purity, uncontaminated by worldly or selfish interest, meeting reality with fresh, spontaneous and untroubled vision, has been evoked again and again to convey the state of mind and heart required of the aspirant for spiritual knowledge. So Jesus said, "Unless you become as a little child you cannot enter the kingdom of heaven."

Judging from this background, de Sales might have meant that the mystic, like the suckling child, feels he is returning to his source—cosmic, not maternal; that he too is surrendering safely to a power infinitely stronger than himself—a power universal rather than personal; that he is participating in a primary, elemental nourishment natural to man and superior to all others—sustenance for the mind and spirit, rather than the body; and that his ecstasy purifies him so that he feels himself once again as fresh and innocent as a babe.

The ecstasy of the mystic has been a source of redemptive power, purging him of self-doubt and vacillation. Moses' experience of the burning bush lent him strength and courage to lead the Israelites out of bondage. Pascal's vision of a great fire and a flaming cross altered his philosophy and his life. Even though we recognize that these symbolic visions are psychological projections, we cannot dismiss the historical testimony of their transforming power.

The psychotic may have momentary feelings of ecstasy or excitation and believe that he has discovered the secrets of the universe, but his fantasies may generate no new grasp on truth or reality. The schizophrenic may reveal distortions and exaggerations of the underlying patterns of the collective unconscious which he shares with all men; but these distortions alone do not determine the essential character of the unconscious.

Of more interest is Prince's contention that not only the elation but also the depressive condition which the mystic calls the "dark night of the soul" are common to both the mystic and the manic states. It is true that many mystics have testified to this condition of spiritual sterility. It seems to me, following Prince's comparison, that the psychotic loses touch with the so-called reality (actuality is perhaps a better term) of the world. The mystic, however, in his "dark night" loses touch with the ultimate reality he has known. All that remains to him in this period of dryness is the phenomenal world, which by contrast is dull, limited, and without savor. The door to his deeper unconscious, that communicates with the universal integrating principle, has been closed to him; he feels shut out, and the result can be deep depression. Mystics are human beings, after all, with human weaknesses. After a spontaneous awakening of some duration there may come a natural period of reaction, the result of the little-understood ebb and flow of psychic life. It is interesting to note that those who have written with passionate sorrow of their "dark night" are generally those who have had sudden and spontaneous experiences for which they were unprepared. References to this condition in the literature of Hinduism and Buddhism occur in a context so systematized, by reason of their methods of preparation for self-discovery, that they are accepted as part of the process of growth.

## Fusion

The last feature which Prince cites as being common to the mystic and the infant state is fusion. In this state, he maintains, the subject loses all awareness of his individuality, of his body and his surroundings; he feels a complete dissolution of boundaries. Prince believes that this participation is regression to the infantile state, since the infant relates to the world by participation: he *is* his mother's breast; he *is* the sound of the train whistle.

Ironically enough it may be a fact that the fusion experienced by infant and mystic is more alike than Prince indicates. He bases the infant's unity on the physical, omitting possible fusion with the *pre*-infantile level and the value of merging with his cosmic source. Even so, the infant's fusion does not lead to better overt behavior. And his personal identity asserts itself at the age of two, according to Gesell (15). In contrast, the kind of fusion which represents the higher knowledge described in eastern literature is epitomized in the sentence: "The knower and the known are one." The subject-object relationship, with its fundamental dichotomy, dissolves in this unitive knowledge, which neglects no facet of the whole and appreciates qualitative as well as quantitative elements in all things—their aesthetic as well as their theoretic character, their *is-ness,* as well as their relationship to everything else in the universe.

The universality which the mystic experiences may temporarily result in a loss of personal identity; afterward, there is a deepening of the perception of self in the knowledge that all selves are one. Thoreau, for example, lived alone in the woods for two years, losing himself in participation in something much larger than his own personality. The result was an intensely personal yet universal statement, *Walden,* which has been a source of strength to readers because it rings so true, without a false note. He who can truly participate in nature, or fuse with the universality of life, touches a source of serenity, order, beauty and harmony which breathes through all his days. The lives of Lao-Tzu, Socrates, Ramakrishna bear witness.

## Conclusions

The study of the unconscious nature of man has scarcely begun, and while we have incomplete knowledge we must expect misjudgments about what we do know. Prince's thesis that the mystical state is similar to that of the infant is but one example of such confusion, which results, I believe, from a misapprehension of the nature of the unconscious. Further study is obviously needed. The mystical, psychotic and infant states will continue to be confused until we are willing to accept the fact that the contents of the unconscious are multiplex, and that oversimplifications made for the purpose of easy categorization are premature.

The infant may be said to be born immersed in the collective unconscious. But how does individual conscious man, in his unique self-development, relate to this source? How are we to resolve, in rational terms, the old paradox of individuality and oneness? Further investigation may show that the mystic is probing an area of his nature which is common to all men—a chronologically earlier, pre-infantile, deep unconscious level of being, the matrix of his own identity as well as the source of his humanity.

Prince expresses the desire of the Bucke Society to communicate across the boundaries of two disciplines, psychoanalysis and religion. This is an admirable goal. The issue, however, is greater. The fate of modern man may ultimately depend upon a synthesis of science with religion and philosophy. Religious concepts cannot be valid today unless they correspond with knowledge of natural law. The new science does not support pluralism. What it does support, however, is a much larger view than the merely factual or data-ridden.

Obviously, if man is to achieve inner peace and world peace he must do so according to his own nature; he must become what he already is, potentially. The inner process of self-realization frees in him the unifying energy needed for harmonious relationships with all things and all people. Fortunately, there is today discernible, beneath all our violence and sensationalism, a quiet wave of the future: a momentum is being generated in the direction of integration—personal, social, educational. Should we not be encouraged that the integrative education movement proposes to teach children that they are part of the universal continuum which Einstein found to be a reality? This is a truth all mystics have known.

The mystic state, whether spontaneous or induced through meditation and other practices, produces a release of energy from the unconscious which permits the actualization of man's highest potentialities. Therefore, it seems proper that the mystic state be studied by science without prejudice, in an effort to discover whether it may indeed offer clues to the good life, for the individual and for society.

REFERENCES

1. PRINCE, R. H., "Mystical States and the Concept of Regression," *Proceedings* of the R. M. Bucke Memorial Society, McGill Univ. Medical School, Montreal, 1965, pp. 36–55.

2. CLARK, W. H. *Psychology of Religion* (New York: Macmillan, 1965), pp. 261–90.

3. CLARK, W. H. *Proceedings* of the R. M. Bucke Memorial Society, p. 56.

4. EINSTEIN, ALBERT, *Out of My Later Years* (New York: Philos. Library, 1950), pp. 21, 22.

5. NORTHROP, F. S. C., *The Meeting of East and West* (New York: Macmillan, 1950), pp. 163, 446.

6. JUNG, CARL G., *Practice of Psychotherapy* (New York: Bollingen, 1958), p. 490.

7. JUNG, C. G. *Two Essays on Analytical Psychology* (New York: Bollingen, 1953), p. 167.

8. MASLOW, ABRAHAM, *Religion, Values and Peak-Experiences* (Ohio State Univ. Press, 1964), pp. 65–67.

9. MASLOW, A., *Toward a Psychology of Being* (Princeton, D. Van Nostrand, 1962), p. 78.

10. BUCKE, R. M., *Cosmic Consciousness* (New York: Dutton, 1901), pp. 1, 61–82.

11. TEILHARD DE CHARDIN, PIERRE, *Phenomenon of Man* (New York: Harper & Row, 1963), pp. 30, 304.

12. JUNG, C. G., *Psychology and Religion* (New York: Bollingen), p. 184.

13. FORDHAM, FREIDA, *Introduction to Jung's Psychology* (London: Penguin, 1953), pp. 18, 19.

14. KOESTLER, ARTHUR, *The Invisible Writing* (New York: Macmillan, 1954), pp. 350–54.

15. GESELL, ARNOLD, *Infant and Child in the Culture of Today* (New York: Harper & Row, 1943), p. 337.

# MYSTICISM AND SCHIZOPHRENIA[1]

## KENNETH WAPNICK

## Introduction

Mysticism and schizophrenia have often been linked in psychiatric literature. Some writers have suggested that mystics demonstrate a special form of schizophrenia or other psychopathology. (See, for example, Alexander, 1931; Freud, 1961; and Menninger, 1938.) Others write of schizophrenia in highly metaphorical, quasi-mystical language focusing on the experience of psychosis, which leads many to conclude that they are proselytizing for schizophrenia as a valuable and even desirable experience (Bateson, 1961; Laing, 1965, 1967). In a more objective tone, William James noted the similarity between the mystic and schizophrenic experience as far back as 1902. He distinguished between two kinds of mysticism; a higher and a lower. The former included the classic mystical experiences, while the latter James identified with insanity, which he termed a "diabolical mysticism." James (1958) concluded that in both forms is found,

> The same sense of ineffable importance in the smallest events, the same texts and words coming with new meanings, the same voices and visions and leadings and missions, the same controlling by extraneous powers. . . . It is evident that from the point of view of their psychological mechanism, the classic mysticism and these lower

[1] I am grateful to Drs. Gordon F. Derner, Kenneth A. Fisher, and Joel Rudley for their comments on an earlier version of the manuscript. The paper in its present form benefited greatly from the suggestions of Dr. Paul Z. Frisch.

mysticisms spring from the same mental level, from that great subliminal or transmarginal region of which science is beginning to admit the existence, but of which so little is really known. That region contains every kind of matter: "seraph and snake" abide there side by side [p. 326].

In a 1965 paper delivered before the R. M. Bucke Memorial Society, Prince and Savage discussed the mystical experience in terms of Kris' concept of regression in the service of the ego (Prince & Savage, 1965). Almost parenthetically, the authors noted a "plausible link" between psychosis and mysticism, and suggested that psychosis was a "pressured withdrawal" with an incomplete return, while the mystic's withdrawal was more controlled and his return more complete.

Though the similarity of many aspects of these two experiences is striking, it should not obscure the significant differences between them. It is the purpose of the present paper to clarify these similarities and differences so as to more fully understand the nature of these two processes. The nature of mysticism will be presented through an outline of the "typical" mystical experience and the mystical life of St. Teresa of Avila, a 16th-century Spanish Catholic. The schizophrenic experience will be illustrated by excerpts from a first-person account of a schizophrenic episode.

Due to the nature of the experiences to be described below, it will be necessary to use the original metaphoric language of the reported experiences. These words and terms, though personal and experiential, are nonetheless more expressive of the particular experiences than precise, objective language that inevitably transforms the experience.

However, it must be remembered that words like "inner," "outer," "death and rebirth of self," "God," etc. are metaphors that attempt to express the experience in words, but are not to be taken literally as the experience itself. Indeed, the very struggle of John Perceval during his psychosis was to realize that the voices he heard were metaphorical, not literal. As he wrote:

The spirit speaks poetically, but the man understands it literally. Thus, you will hear one lunatic declare that he is made of iron, and that nothing can break him; another, that he is a china vessel, and that he runs in danger of being destroyed every minute. The meaning of the spirit is that this man is strong as iron, the other frail as an earthen vessel; but the lunatic takes the literal sense [Bateson, 1961, p. 271].

## Mysticism

Mysticism is usually characterized as the experience of Unity, or what Stace (1960) has called, "the apprehension of *an ultimate nonsensuous unity in all things,* a oneness or a One to which neither the sense nor the reason can penetrate [pp. 14–15]." Equally characteristic, however, is the orderly quality of the mystic's development. In a classic statement, Underhill (1961) described mysticism as:

the name of that organic process which . . . is the art of [man's] establishing his conscious relation with the Absolute. The movement of the mystic consciousness towards this consummation, is not merely the sudden admission to an overwhelming vision of Truth: though such dazzling glimpses may from time to time be vouchsafed to the soul. It is rather an *ordered movement* towards ever higher levels of reality, ever closer identification with the Infinite [author's emphasis; pp. 81–82].

Every mystic appears to undergo the same basic "ordered movement," and it is this commonality that binds the Christian mystic to the Hindu, the atheist to the Sufi. For purposes of discussion, commentators have found it convenient to delineate the successive stages of this movement. These stages, which as described in the literature vary in number from three to eight, are not to be taken literally, nor as descriptive of the experience of any one mystic; rather, they are intended to be diagrammatic of the "typical" mystical experience. The five stages described by Underhill (1961) provide a framework that lends itself to a workable outline of the mystic's experience and is used as the basis for the present discussion. A sixth stage seems necessary to describe the process completely and is added to Underhill's five stages.

1. As experienced and reported by the mystics, this is the sudden conversion that follows a long period of great unrest and disquiet. Known as "The Awakening of the Self," it is the sudden realization of a strikingly new and different emotional experience that seems to exist beyond sensation, and that carries with it the awareness of a "higher," more desirable level of experience. James referred to this conversion as the break-through of the transmarginal consciousness, the sudden "possession of an active subliminal self."

2. After the mystic experiences this deeper level of consciousness, he finds that his former patterns of living are no longer satisfying. He feels that they must be purged or mortified, what Underhill refers to as "The Purification of the Self." In the language of James' dichotomy of levels of consciousness, the new subliminal consciousness with which the person has just come into contact is markedly different from the everyday consciousness of his ordinary experience. Thus, the behaviors that involved his everyday functioning in the social world are not applicable to this more personal experience and so must be discarded.

The extreme ascetic practices of many mystics that occur during this stage are designed to purge the individual of his need for his old connections to the social reality. Once this is accomplished, the process of purgation or mortification ceases. As Underhill points out, despite its etymology, the goal of mortification for the mystic is life, but this life can only come through the "death" of the "old self."

3. After the person has purged himself of his former interest and involvement with the social world, he enters the third stage or what Underhill terms "The Illumination of the Self." Here, he experiences more fully what lays beyond the boundaries of his immediate senses. The main reported characteristic of this stage is the joyous apprehension of what the mystic experiences to be the Absolute, including effulgent outpourings of ecstasy and rapture in which the individual glories in his relationship to the Absolute. What distinguishes this stage from later stages, however, is that the person still experiences himself as a separate entity, not yet unified with

what he considers to be the Ultimate. There is yet a sense of I-hood, of ego, of self.

4. This is perhaps the most striking stage of the mystical process. Although it may be found in all mystic experiences, its emotional expression appears only in the Western tradition, where it has taken its name from the evocative phrase of St. John of the Cross: "The Dark Night of the Soul." Here, there is the total negation and rejection of the joy of the preceding stage. The person feels totally removed and alienated from his previous experiences and feels very much alone and depressed. It is as if he were thrown into the middle of a vast wasteland or desert, with no hope of survival. During the first purgative period, the individual had to purge himself of his former attachments to the social world. Now, he must purge himself of his experience of self. His very will must become totally submerged to the unknown "force" he experiences to be within. As long as he asserts his own will or individuality, he is maintaining distance or separateness from what he feels to be the Ultimate.

5. Though not the final stage, this is the culmination of the mystic's quest: the complete and total absorption in the asocial, personal world, what has been called "The Unitive Life." It consists of the obliteration of the senses, and even the sense of self, resulting in the experience of unity with the universe. This state has been described as a state of pure consciousness, in which the individual experiences nothing—no thing. The individual has seemingly made contact with the deepest regions of his consciousness and experiences the process as having been completed. Emotionally, the person feels totally tranquil and at peace.

6. *Though not mentioned as an independent stage by commentators, the return of the mystic from the experience of oneness with the universe to the requirements of social living constitutes the most important part of his path. In most mystics, it may be observed that they renew their practical involvement in social situations with a new vitality and strength. As St. Teresa* (St. Teresa, 1961) *observed: "Mar-*

*tha and Mary must work together when they offer the Lord lodging," implying that material and spiritual involvement are equally important* (St. Teresa p. 231). *The lives of Sts. Teresa, Francis and Ignatius, to name just three, bear testimony to the important practical role the mystics have played in the world. In the classical Eastern tradition, the same emphasis on returning to the world is found. The prime example is the Buddha, who returned from his ecstasy underneath the Bo tree to the social world from which he had "fled"* (*Campbell, 1956*).

*The mystic now no longer finds his involvement with the world to be abhorrent, but, in fact, seems to welcome the opportunity to move in the social world he had abandoned. This seeming paradox becomes understandable when one considers that it was not the world that the mystic was renouncing, but merely his attachments and needs relating to it, which precluded the development of his personal, asocial experience. Once he was able to abandon these dependent, social needs, and felt freed of the pull of the social world, he experienced the freedom to live within society in conjunction with his inner strivings, rather than experiencing society's customs and institutions as obstacles to his self-fulfillment.*

The following review of St. Teresa's mystical experiences is largely based upon her *Interior Castle,* one of the most widely known mystical treatises, written in 1577 (St. Teresa, 1961). Using the metaphor of a castle and writing in the third person, Teresa systematically described her own mystical development.

As Teresa experienced it, inside of herself was a soul that she represented as a castle in which there were many rooms or mansions, at the innermost of which was God. The castle was constructed like a palmito—a Spanish shrub consisting of several thick layers of leaves enclosing a succulent kernel at its center, and whose layers had to be removed before the kernel could be eaten. In like manner, the room where God dwelt was surrounded by many mansions, and to reach the center, Teresa had first to travel through the surrounding rooms. Teresa believed that despite the great beauty of these rooms most people chose not to enter the castle, which Teresa equated with being interested and involved in the social world. The path outlined by Teresa corresponds in general to the one outlined above. To avoid confusion, however, Teresa's stages will be referred to by her descriptive names, rather than by number.

Teresa's early mansions correspond roughly to the period of disquiet that precedes the conversion labeled above as the first stage. As Teresa experienced the conversion, the feeling seemed to radiate from deep within her, from a source beyond her awareness and control. This source Teresa called God.

Teresa's preparation for her further experiences was called the Prayer of Recollection. For her it consisted of abandoning her involvement with the social world as a source of pleasure and gratification and concentrating (recollecting) her faculties and attention inward to this inner source.

> [The person] involuntarily closes his eyes and desires solitude; and, without the display of any human skill there seems gradually to be built for him a temple in which he can make the prayer already described; the senses and all external things seem gradually to lose their hold on him, while the soul, on the other hand, regains its lost control [p. 85].[2]

Through the Prayer of Recollection, Teresa prepared herself for movement into the next mansion, what she referred to as the Prayer of Quiet, comparable to the "Illumination" described above. She likened the indescribable feelings of great joy that resulted from her withdrawal of concern in matters external to her to the water in an overflowing basin:

> . . . as this heavenly water begins to flow from this source of which I am speaking—that is, from our very depths—it proceeds to spread within us, and cause an interior dilation and produce ineffable blessings, so that the soul itself cannot understand all that it receives there. The fragrance it experiences, we might say, is as if in those interior depths there were a brazier on which were

[2] Unless otherwise noted, all quotes from this section are from St. Teresa (St. Teresa, 1961).

> cast sweet perfumes; the light cannot be seen, nor the place where it dwells, but the fragrant smoke and the heat penetrates the entire soul, and very often, as I have said, the effects extend even to the body [p. 82].

Teresa cautioned others to be wary of the good feeling of this mansion because they might believe that the Ultimate had been achieved and leave the castle without progressing further.

> For as yet the soul is not even weaned but is like a child beginning to suck the breast. If it be taken from its mother, what can it be expected to do but die? That, I am very much afraid, will be the lot of anyone to whom God has granted this favour if he gives up prayer. . . . [p. 91].

As the delights of this period increased, Teresa moved into the next mansion, the Prayer of Union. Here, she completely gave up all investments in the social world, and totally surrendered herself to what she experienced as God. It was as if she were asleep to everything external to her, and even to herself. She was without consciousness and had seemingly "completely died to the world so that . . . [she] may live more fully in God [p. 98]."

Because of her great difficulty in verbalizing her experiences during this period and those to follow, Teresa employed the metaphor of the Spiritual Marriage to aid her in communicating. The marriage is between herself and God, and was a "union of love with love." During the Prayer of Union, the two met for the first time, became acquainted, and drew up the marriage contract: a Spiritual Betrothal. After those brief "encounters," Teresa experienced a hunger and yearning for the experience of God.

> . . . the soul has been wounded with love for the Spouse and seeks more opportunity of being alone, trying, so far as is possible to one in its state, to renounce everything which can disturb it in this its solitude [p. 126].

However, in the words of the metaphor, God was still withholding the consummation of the Betrothal and, instead, inflicted great pain and trials on Teresa, [disregarding her] yearnings for the conclusion of the Betrothal, desiring that they should become still deeper and that this greatest of all blessings should be won by the soul at some cost to itself [p. 126].

These trials—the most difficult and painful that Teresa had yet to experience ("The Dark Night of the Soul")—included the following: people accusing her of being deceitful or collaborating with the devil; rejection by her friends; tremendous bodily pains; and feelings of great loneliness, when she felt herself apart, not only from others, but from herself. During the latter times, she would be unable to pray, nor to experience God inside of her.

Some of her most excruciating physical pains came during these moments known as "Raptures," when Teresa would experience a "meeting with God." At those moments, she would feel physically freed of her body. This experience brought with it a strange kind of detachment, more than what Teresa experienced during earlier periods. It produced a profound loneliness as she had severed all attachments to the social world, but was still, in the metaphor of the Marriage, not united with God:

no comfort comes to it [Teresa] from Heaven, and it is not in Heaven, and when it desires no earthly comfort, and is not on earth either, but is, as it were, crucified between Heaven and earth; and it suffers greatly, for no help comes to it either from the one hand or from the other [St. Teresa, 1957, p. 123].

Teresa experienced this period as the most difficult for her because it required that she completely relinquish control over herself and be able to withstand the complete independence from the social world.

For, happen what may, we must risk everything, and resign ourselves into the hands of God and go willingly wherever we are carried away [St. Teresa, 1957, p. 120].

Once Teresa was able to do this, she experienced the final union, the consummation of the Spiritual Marriage, the state of "pure spirituality." This experience of union was markedly different from that of the earlier "betrothal." There, although there was an experience of union, there was still separation between herself and the innermost source. Not so, however, in the final stage:

> . . . it is like rain falling from the heavens into a river or a spring; there is nothing but water there and it is impossible to divide or separate the water belonging to the river from that which fell from the heavens. Or it is as if a tiny streamlet enters the sea, from which it will find no way of separating itself, or as if in a room there were two large windows through which the light streamed in: it enters in different places but it all becomes one.

Teresa found herself in an almost perpetual state of tranquillity, even when performing social functions. She now no longer felt overwhelmed by what she previously experienced as the evil in the world. Contrary to what had existed to date, Teresa fervently desired to live in the world and spread the word of God. The remainder of her life was spent in active participation in the Reform of the Spanish Carmelites, which included the founding of 18 convents. Throughout, Teresa's inner experiences continued and she would frequently feel herself to be at one with God.

Summarizing the crucial aspects of Teresa's experience, it is found that as she was able to abandon her dependent involvements with the social world, she had more lasting contact with the asocial, personal experience of herself that she called God. The process was lifelong, entailed tremendous pain, both physical and mental, and culminated in the complete cessation of external involvement and the experience of "Union with God." The most painful stage of the process occurred immediately before the experience of Union. At this time Teresa had severed her ties with the social world, but had yet to experience the Unity with God. She felt tremendous panic and fear of being completely alone, but this feeling was soon replaced by the experience of Union and feelings of the highest peace and joy. Teresa was then able to renew her activity in the social world, deriving greater satisfaction and fulfillment in these activities than before.

## Schizophrenia

Schizophrenia is a condition wherein the individual experiences himself and the world about him in a manner distinctly different from that of most members of society. The schizophrenic's conception of time, space, and the relationship between social situations and inner feelings are often not those shared by the social world. His behavior, accordingly, is often socially inappropriate and strange and incomprehensible to others. The intensely personal, asocial quality of this experience has made schizophrenia most resistant to consensus concerning its etiology and treatment. Indeed, there are almost as many theories and therapeutic approaches as there are theorists and therapists.

Recently in psychology a new direction in the understanding and treatment of schizophrenia has developed. A primary tenet of this position is that the psychosis is part of an ongoing, constructive process, wherein the individual attempts to correct the inadequacy of his functioning. This position has been summarized by Kaplan (1964), who writes that the

> so-called "symptoms," rather than being ego-alien manifestations of a disease process that has somehow gotten a grip on the person, are instead purposeful acts of the individual, which have intentionality and are motivated. The "illness" is something the individual "wills" to happen (p. x).

Similarly, Bateson (1961), in his introduction to John Perceval's autobiographical account of his psychosis, writes of the *process* of schizophrenia and its purposeful quality: ". . . the mind contains, in some form, such wisdom that it can create that *attack* upon itself that will lead to a later resolution of the pathology [p. xii]."

Perhaps the most prominent spokesman of this position is Laing. In his 1966 lectures before the William Alanson White Institute, Laing proposed a new name for schizophrenia: "metanoia," which translated literally from the Greek means "beyond the mind." (In the King James version of the New Testament, "metanoia" is translated as "redemption." See Lara Jefferson's account of her psychosis in the following discussion.) Schizophrenia, thus redefined, denotes a process or experience of the individual that moves beyond the mind or what we conceptualize as the ego, "beyond the horizons of our communal sense [Laing, 1967, p. 92]." The behavioral accompaniments to this movement according to Laing are neither unintelligible nor bizarre, but are rather expressive of the unusual experiences the individual is undergoing; moreover, Laing (1967) states, these experiences sometimes "appear to be part of a potentially orderly, natural sequence of experiences . . . the behavioral expressions of an experiential drama [p. 85]."

One of the principal contributions of this movement has been to focus attention on the experiences of the schizophrenic as being expressive of the individual's personal, asocial, "otherworldly" experiences, rather than merely the manifestations of a deranged mind. As Haley (1959) demonstrated, when the behavior and communications can be understood in the context of the individual's own personal logic and situation, as opposed to that of social convention, they become meaningful and comprehensible. Publications containing firsthand accounts of psychotic episodes and phenomenological analyses of these experiences have advanced the understanding of this condition, as well as having fostered its identification with mystical experiences that are also movements "beyond the horizons of our communal sense." (See, for example, Bateson, 1961; Coate, 1964; Kaplan, 1964; and Laing, 1965, 1967.) The following excerpt from a firstperson account of a schizophrenic episode will demonstrate the phenomenological similarity between aspects of the schizophrenic and mystic experiences, as well as illustrate the differences between them in terms of the meaning each experience has within the context of the individual's life.

Lara Jefferson was a psychiatric patient in a mid-western state hospital during the 1940's. During her psychosis, she wrote of her experiences. These were subsequently found and published as *These Are My Sisters*. Substantial excerpts from this book are contained in Kaplan's anthology (1964), from which this digest is taken.

Lara's experience of her psychosis was that "something has broken loose within"; and what differentiated her from most other psychotics was that she was aware of this process taking place.

> Something has happened to me—I do not know what. All that was my former self has crumbled and fallen together and a creature has emerged of whom I know nothing. She is a stranger to me . . . My whole former life has fallen away . . . All I could do was to feel—startlingly—nakedly—starkly—things no words can describe [pp. 6–8].

This former self was as:

> a pitiful creature who could not cope with life as she found it—nor could she escape it—nor adjust herself to it. So she became mad, and died in anguish—of frustration and raving [p. 9].

Thus, madness became the agent of the "death" of her "former self." With this "death,"

> There is nothing solid to stand on—nothing beneath me but a vast treacherous quagmire of despondency—followed by periods of exultation and ecstasy; and neither condition has any foundation in logic . . . Reason has slipped—altogether . . . [p. 9].

Through her madness, Lara understood that the reason her former self had to be abandoned was because it was ignorant of the true meaning of living:

> . . . I have concerned myself with externals only, and have missed all the meanings of the great inner significance . . . I became mad—not because of some inner deformity—but because of too close supervision and trying—Trying to force the thing I was into an unnatural mold [p. 11].

The "second self" that had been created in the madness now suggested to Lara that:

> the best weapon with which to fight fire—is fire. And suggests fighting madness with madness. Perhaps she is not so insane as I think—perhaps she is saner than I was before she came to me. She presents her idea with so much logic she makes me think that instead of losing reason

in madness—and finding insanity on the other side—that,
in reality, I will lose insanity in madness—and find a
sound mind on the other side [p. 10].

The consequences of this decision were that:

I cannot escape from the Madness by the door I came
in, that is certain . . . I cannot go back—I shall have to
go onwards—even though the path leads to "Three Building"—where the hopeless incurables walk and wail and
wait for the death of their bodies. I cannot escape it—I
cannot face it—how can I endure it [p. 7].

Having "decided" to pursue this course, despite its "intoler-
able horror," Lara experienced a 5-day period of "total madness." It began with the feeling that something was about to
erupt inside of her.

So the monster was out and the ghost of some old
beserker ancestor rose up within me and suggested that
I could do something about it, and the fierce hatred exalted that it had possessed itself of a massive and powerful body. And the thing that was in me was not I at all
—but another—and I knew that no power on earth but a
strait-jacket could hold her [p. 33].

Lara requested a jacket, and it was granted to her. Now
protected against herself and secure in the feeling that she
could not harm or destroy others, Lara could release the
bonds that were holding her back.

And once the great Madness in me found a voice, there
was no stopping it. It rolled out in such a tumult I was
amazed at it myself; wondered where it all came from.
It seemed obscene and terrible that I should answer in
adult language, things said to me in my childhood.
Things I had forgotten, until they again began to pour
about me in a flood of bitter memories. Even incidents
I remembered clearly came back so warped and twisted
they seemed like evil changelings . . .
I felt so much better that I had at last found the courage to look and see things as they were (not camouflag-
ing them in the rosy light of a meaning they did not
have) that I wanted to shout and sing.
That voice was reason making a last desperate stand—
but it was just a shadow and had no power to check the
things I was feeling. Still it held me silent for a few short

minutes and forced me to consider the thing I knew was happening to me . . .

But not for long:

> All my human fear of pain and death and loss of reason was drowned in wild exultation . . . So the last connected and coherent thing in my thinking gave way—and the Madness filling me rejoiced. Because at last there was nothing to stay it, it shouted and exulted with a noise that tore my throat out, charging through me till it nearly dragged the life out of me. Part of my mind stood there and took in the whole situation, yet could know nothing about it. The thing that was raging did not seem wrong to me then—but the rightest thing in the world— a magnificent accomplishment [pp. 36–37].

Lara hardly slept through the night, despite two shots of morphine. But after finally falling asleep near morning she was awakened by a patient screaming about wanting to be on a lake. And then suddenly Lara felt herself alongside a lake:

> It was not imagination—but something stronger. Mere imagination, however vivid, cannot transport a person tied down hand and foot in an insane asylum to set them free in some far place. I found I was standing somewhere on a pebbly beach at dawn . . . I had never seen a dawn so lovely. For I had never been on a lake before which did not exist—nor had I ever experienced a dawn that had not reached me through my dull sense organs —and this was something different—so poignant and perfect it was an ecstasy . . .
> There was such rest and freedom in floating in the current of my thoughts without the struggle of forcing my thinking to continue in the channels I had been taught were right! So I let them run wild and free . . .
> As singing is the natural, spontaneous expression of freedom, I felt an urge to sing—for I was free. And I did sing—song after song. Nothing mattered [pp. 37–39].

The nurses came in at this point, transferred Lara to solitary confinement, and placed her into a new strait jacket, extrastrong, and strapped her to the bedrail. However, the flow continued unabated. Lara began to hallucinate and this continued for at least a day. Then, despite the tight binding of the jacket, she felt a sense of liberation and experienced her arms as free. By the morning of the third day, Lara "was far away in the real heights of ecstasy" and she began to emerge from the Madness.

> By the morning of the fourth day I had settled down into something of the person I still am to this day . . .
>
> The fifth morning they took me out of the jacket. I had been wringing wet with perspiration most of the time during those five days and nights and the odor . . . which assailed me when that jacket was loosened, was asphyxiating. Truly, something had died, and was de-composing! There was a timbre to the odor of that per-spiration which was totally unfamiliar. Even the sweat glands had become a voice in that conflict. My hands were filled with a heavy glutinous substance. Every nerve and fibre in my whole body registered the effect of what I had been through. My whole chemistry was changed. Truly I was a different person [p. 41].

Reflecting back on her experience, Lara offered the fol-lowing advice to those who one day may undergo a similar experience:

> I who stand on the other side of this phenomenon called Madness, would like to stretch a hand across to those who may some day, go through it . . .
>
> To those I would speak and say; (because I know, I have been there) "Remember, when a soul sails out on that unmarked sea called Madness they have gained release . . . Though the need which brought it cannot well be known by those who have not felt it. For what the sane call 'ruin'—because they do not know—those who have experienced what I am speaking of, know the wild hysteria of Madness means salvation. Release. Es-cape. Salvation from a much greater pain than the stark pain of Madness. Escape—from that which could not be endured. And that is why the Madness came. Deliver-ance; pure, simple, deliverance . . . Nothing in this world can stay it when it has claimed its own . . . I have felt it sweep me and take me—where—I do not know, (all the way through Hell, and far, on the other side; and give me keener sense of feeling than the dull edge of reason has)"—still, I have no way of telling about the things experienced on that weird journey [pp. 31–32].

In summary, Lara reported a dichotomy between two lev-els of experience; one was identified with the pre-psychotic self—concerned with reason and "externals only"—while the other was the intense emotions Lara had never expressed. Her psychosis consisted of the breakdown of her control, which enabled these feelings to emerge. These impulses erupted with an explosive power that terrified her; at the same time their liberation filled her with exultation. This loss of control marked the complete withdrawal of her involvement with the social world. Lara expressed this shift in attitude toward her relationship to society as the death of her former self. With the end of the 5-day "total madness," Lara felt an inner peace, which she described as the emergence of a new self. She was now able to "return" to the social world, and was subsequently released from the hospital.

## Discussion

Though coming from vastly different cultures and separated in time by almost four centuries, the experiences of St. Teresa and Lara Jefferson appear to have much in common. These include: their experience of a dichotomy between two levels of experience—the outer or social, as opposed to the inner or personal; the breakdown of their attachments to the social world; their experience of pain and terror as they "entered the inner world"; their feeling of peace following the end of the terror; and their "return" to the social world, deriving more satisfaction in their social functioning than before their experiences.

However, there were important differences as well: the mystical process of St. Teresa was lifelong, whereas Lara Jefferson's experience of the "inner world" was compressed into a much shorter period of time. Teresa's mystic life culminated in the experience of Unity, while Lara had no such experience.[3] Throughout the process, Teresa was able to maintain some degree of social contact, though living in a cloister. Moreover, her decisions to isolate herself were

---

[3] At least one self-report of a schizophrenic episode included an awareness of a greater experience—perhaps the experience of Unity —which the person did not allow to occur (Laing, 1967, pp. 108–12).

within her conscious control. Lara, on the other hand, experienced a loss of conscious control and breakdown in her social functioning, necessitating her hospitalization.

Though Lara Jefferson is an example of a schizophrenic who "came back" to the social world from the terrors of the personal world, her experience of the overwhelming power of its fantasies and images totally incapacitated her from functioning socially during the psychosis. The schizophrenic's inability to manage this inner experience and his break with social reality strikingly contrasts with the mystic's tolerance for the inner experience. This becomes understandable in light of the differing preparations for the experience.

The entire mystic path may be understood to be a strengthening process whereby the mystic gradually develops the "muscles" to withstand the experiences of this "inner world." It is this strengthening that is responsible for the long periods of suffering and fallowness that are often the mystic's fate, as well as the mystic's faith in the positive outcome of his experience. Al Ghazzali, 11th-century Persian mystic, writes of his seclusion and purgation:

> I went to Syria, where I remained more than two years;
> without any other object than that of living in seclusion
> and solitude, conquering my desires, struggling with my
> passions, striving to purify my soul, to perfect my character, and to prepare my heart to meditate upon God
> [Underhill, 1961, p. 226].

Underhill, employing the metaphor of the child, describes the strengthening process thus:

> . . . the Divine Child which was, in the hour of the mystic conversion, born in the spark of the soul, must learn like other children to walk. Though it is true that the spiritual self must never lose its sense of utter dependence on the Invisible; yet within that supporting atmosphere, and fed by its gifts, it must "find its feet." Each effort to stand brings first a glorious sense of growth, and then a fall: each fall means another struggle to obtain the difficult balance which comes when infancy is past. There are many eager trials, many hopes, many disappointments. At last, as it seems suddenly, the moment comes: tottering is over, the muscles have learnt their

lesson, they adjust themselves automatically, and the new self suddenly finds itself—it knows not how—standing upright and secure.

The schizophrenic undergoes no such training or strengthening. His "muscles" are undeveloped and when "thrown" into this "inner world" he is overwhelmed, with no means of dealing with his experience and no conviction that he will survive it.

Writing of the mystic's renunciation of his societal attachments that insulate him from the experience of God, Underhill (1961) uses the image of the mollusk with its hard shell, thereby illustrating the nature of the person's "shell of attachments [pp. 98–99]." Likewise, Schachtel (1959) employs Hebb's image of a cocoon to describe the world of embeddedness that seals off the person's capacity for growth. *Borrowing this imagery, it can be seen that the schizophrenic is one whose protective shell has been suddenly and prematurely broken.* (The etiology of this break will not be discussed in the present paper.) Because of this, he is totally unable to deal with the sudden onrush of the asocial, personal feelings he experiences and his social functioning breaks down. The mystic, on the other hand, through his long training process, is able to slough the shell off gradually. As he increases his tolerance for those new feelings, he is able to incorporate them into his social living. As the mystic becomes strengthened, he becomes ready for the next step and removes another part of his shell.

In writing of his own experiences of the terror of his "confrontation with the unconscious," Jung (1961) stressed the importance of his external life in protecting him from the too-sudden exposure to the inner world of the unconscious.

> Particularly at this time, when I was working on the fantasies, I needed a point of support in "this world," and I may say that my family and my professional work were that to me. It was most essential for me to have a normal life in the real world as a counterpoise to that strange inner world. My family and my profession remained the base to which I could always return, assuring me that I was an actually existing, ordinary person. The unconscious contents could have driven me out of my wits . . .

[as they did Nietzsche] who was a blank page whirling about in the winds of the spirit . . . [who] had lost the ground under his feet because he possessed nothing more than the inner world of his thoughts—which incidentally possessed him more than he it. He was uprooted and hovered above the earth, and therefore he succumbed to exaggeration and irreality. For me, such irreality was the quintessence of horror, for I aimed, after all, at *this* world and *this* life. No matter how deeply absorbed or how blown about I was, I always knew that everything I was experiencing was ultimately directed at this real life of mine [p. 189].

These differences in the preparation reflect the essential difference between the mystic and the schizophrenic. The mystic's goal, as manifested in his lifelong dedication to the Absolute, is to gradually expand his consciousness by moving more deeply into the "inner world" of his personal feelings, until its innermost depth is reached, what he usually refers to as the Self or God, wherein he feels at one with the universe. Though the mystic and schizophrenic ostensibly share the same flight from the social world, the mystic's abandonment is merely of his own dependent attachments to it. Thus, the mystic's life is in essence a process of freeing himself from those habits and customs that had been adopted as security measures to protect against the anxiety that inevitably accompanies any growth or movement toward independence.[4] Once the state of total freedom has been achieved, the mystic is able to once again involve himself in social activities. (To a certain degree, such participation is always necessary. A life lived totally in the "inner world," with no contact with the "outer world," would inevitably lead to physical death, as there could be no search for protection against overexposure nor acquisition of food or drink.)

The schizophrenic, on the other hand, has as the "purpose" of his psychosis the escape from the social world within which he is totally unable to function. The "inner world" be-

[4] For an excellent discussion of how these habits prevent one's development, see Schachtel, 1959. A more extensive discussion of the mystic process from this and other points of view may be found in Wapnick, 1968.

comes his refuge from the impossibility of existing in the "outer world." Unlike the mystic, whose inner experiences are consciously chosen over a period of time and developed within the cultural context, the schizophrenic's experience of his deepest feelings is sudden and occurs in the denial of his social functioning. The flight into psychosis, if successful, restores his capacity to function as a productive member of society, but it does not necessarily prepare him for the life-long process of movement between inner experience and social functioning, nor for the elimination of those learned habits that preclude the development of his inner potential. There is nothing in the reports of recovered schizophrenics to suggest that once having freed themselves from the pathological patterns of their pre-morbid living they continue to explore those inner experiences that had previously overwhelmed them.

In summary, the mystic's life may be seen as a recognition of the existence of the inner, personal experience, which though independent of, and even antagonistic to, the social reality, cannot be fully developed unless the individual also affirms his role in society. Beautiful and powerful feelings are not sufficient to improve one's functioning in the social world. What is needed is the integration of these inner experiences with the various social roles one adopts. The mystic provides the example of the method whereby the inner and outer may be joined; the schizophrenic, the tragic result when they are separated.

#### REFERENCES

ALEXANDER, F. "Buddhistic Training as an Artificial Catatonia," *Psychoanalytical Review*, 1931, *18*, 129–45.

BATESON, G. (ed.) *Perceval's Narrative: A Patient's Account of His Psychosis* (Stanford: Stanford University Press, 1961).

CAMPBELL, J. *The Hero With a Thousand Faces* (New York: Meridian Books, 1956).

COATE, M. *Beyond All Reason* (London: Constable & Co., 1964).

FREUD, S. *Civilization and Its Discontents* (New York: Norton, 1961).

HALEY, J. "An Interactional Description of Schizophrenia," *Psychiatry*, 1959, *22*, 321–32.

174    THE HIGHEST STATE OF CONSCIOUSNESS

JAMES, W. *The Varieties of Religious Experience* (New York: New American Library, 1958).

JUNG, C. G. *Memories, Dreams, Reflections* (New York: Pantheon, 1961).

KAPLAN, B. (ed.) *The Inner World of Mental Illness* (New York: Harper, 1964).

LAING, R. D. *The Divided Self* (Baltimore: Penguin, 1965).

——, *The Politics of Experience* (New York: Pantheon, 1967).

MENNINGER, K. *Man Against Himself* (New York: Harcourt, Brace & World, 1938).

PRINCE, R. & SAVAGE, C. "Mystical States and the Concept of Regression," Paper delivered at the First Annual Meeting, R. M. Bucke Soc., Montreal, Jan. 1965. Also in this volume.

SCHACHTEL, E. G. *Metamorphosis* (New York: Basic Books, 1959).

STACE, W. *The Teachings of the Mystics* (New York: New American Library, 1960).

ST. TERESA, *The Complete Works of St. Teresa,* Vol. 1 (New York: Sheed and Ward, 1957).

——, *Interior Castle* (New York: Image Books, 1961).

UNDERHILL, E. *Mysticism* (New York: E. P. Dutton & Co., 1961).

WAPNICK, K. "The Psychology of the Mystical Experience," Unpublished doctoral dissertation, Adelphi University, 1968.

# ON CREATIVE, PSYCHOTIC AND ECSTATIC STATES

## ROLAND FISCHER

### Biological Models of Creativity

It is the contention of this chapter that "normality," "creativity," and "schizophrenia" represent states of increasing arousal and, therefore, can be conceived as lying on a continuum. Creativity is an excited-exalted state of arousal with a characteristic increase in both *data content* and *rate of data processing*. The acute schizophrenic state is marked by an even higher level of arousal, but the increase in data content is not matched by a corresponding increase in the rate of data processing. The creative state is conducive to the evolution of novel relations and new meaning, whereas the schizophrenic, "jammed computer" state itself interferes—through "protective inhibition" and a narrowing of the field of attention—with the individual's symbolic interpretation of his own central nervous system activity.

## *The Model*

But what are the data which are the content of consciousness, or *con-scientia*? What is permanence within change? Or, in the words of Plato: "What is that which always is and has no becoming, and what is that which is always becoming and never is?"

From *Art Interpretation and Art Therapy*, ed. I. Jakab, *Psychiatry and Art*, Vol. 2, Vth Int. Coll. Psychopathology of Expression, Los Angeles, Calif., 1968 (New York: Karger, Basel, 1969).

These questions shall be answered by the introduction and exposition of a steady-state model which depicts *geometrico modo* "what there is." The model consists of an equilateral triangle with its base standing for *invariant stimulus configurations* (or objects), its left side for *information* (or percept), and the right side for organismic *matching response*. The base of the triangle extends between the two foci of an ellipse, while the vertex of the triangle is lying on the ellipse (fig. 1 a). One can visualize exponentially *increasing states* of *arousal* by shifting the vertex to the left (fig. 1 b) which results in *decreased information* and an *increased matching response*, i.e., an intensification of meaning and total response manifested as a high sensory to motor ratio. The amplification of sensing, knowing and attending by the organism is an experience of increased meaning or, in Gelpke's words, "a torrential flood of inner sensation."

High sensory to motor ratio, that is the predominance of the sensory here over the motor component, is characteristic of daydreaming, the REM stage of sleep, hallucinations, the psychodysleptic (psychotomimetic) drug produced sleepless dream state and other phenomena of motor deprivation which customary language inaccurately terms sensory deprivation. The relations obtained under *increasing tranquilization* are illustrated by the transformations of the triangle toward the right side in fig. 1 b; they display a need for more information and a substantial *decrease* in the *matching response* or meaning. Such a state is exemplified by the patient who was frightened by his image of the devil; after tranquilization, he could still see the devil but was no longer frightened.

Matching response within the model, thus, assumes a *dual* character: on the one hand it stands for the experience of *meaning;* on the other it denotes a specific *sensory to motor ratio*. A particular sensory to motor ratio is the reflection of the subjective and objective facets of our nature. With eyes closed we can experience the universe inside ourselves in sensation, that is, subjectively, whereas with eyes open we can change "what there is" outside ourselves through voluntary motor performance, that is, objectively. These experiential and experimental facets are implicit in the nature of self-

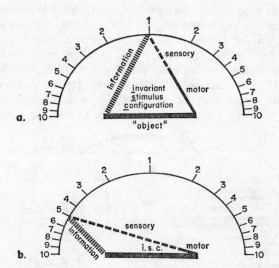

FIG. 1 A and B. Geometrico modo *representation of steady-state between 1. invariant stimulus configuration—commonly called the "object" in physical space-time—; 2. information in sensory space-time, i.e., the irreflexive imprinting of structure on structure and the ability to discriminate a just noticeable sensory difference, and 3. matching response, the latter designating meaning in cerebral space-time as well as a specific sensory to motor ratio. Fig. 1 a represents a subject's state of equanimity, whereas fig. 1 b depicts the model of a control system with non-linear transfer functions during a state of increasing excitation-exaltation along the left logarithmic scale of the ellipse. Departure from the state of equanimity (see equilateral triangle in part a) to the left (part b) marks not only increasing levels of arousal but also the gradual withdrawal from physical space-time to a combined sensory and cerebral space-time and finally at scale 10 to cerebral space-time only.*

referential, self-organizing systems. Self-reference implies that the universe exists subjectively, that is, in reference to the self, whereas self-organization, or goal seeking, refers to the ability to rearrange the outside-universe.

The ratio of the experiential or sensory to the experimental or motor component within the large matching response of a high level of arousal, expresses the type of experience an individual has. High or low sensory to motor ratios within a sensorimotor performance—behavioral state—can be illustrated by the extreme examples of either the catatonic hallucinatory state with its extremely high sensory involvement and no motor performance, as opposed to the sprinter's per-

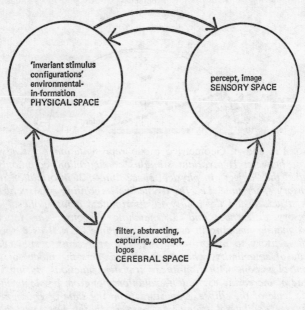

FIG. 2. *The three space-times within the circuitry scheme of a healthy self-organizing, self-reflecting system. Invariant stimulus configurations from* physical *space arrive as information in* sensory *space and finally proceed to* cerebral *space as imageless meaning-schemata for waking and dreaming reference. As a result of the self-reflecting process, information and meaning are externalized as objects in Euclidean physical space, a survival or engineering space of decision-making and action with the externalized objects defined as stimuli arriving in the speech dominant hemisphere.*

formance during a running race with his very high motor to sensory ratio. There is, of course, an infinite variety of behavioral states between these two extremes.

The steady-state system model (fig. 1) can be made even more useful by rebuilding it into the context of three space-times, and by postulating that the fabric of experience is synchronized in *cerebral, sensory,* and *physical* (survival) space-times (fig. 2).

The *cerebral space* of thought, dreaming and hallucination stores memories of imageless schemata for waking and dreaming reference with feedback to sensory space. Meaning, as perceived-created by self-referential systems, is most likely multivalued in its logical form, and, being without dimension, has no geometry.

Immediate—raw—and uninterpreted, i.e., a-logical, sensations are the content of experience in non-Euclidean, hyperbolic *sensory space-time,* whereas *survival space-time* is the realm of active waking experience, a modified sensory space constructed by and reflecting life experience. Euclidean geometry, two-valued language, and logic are operative here, and decision-making with regard to survival is the dominant activity.[1]

---

[1] A flower, for example, within this context is the "invariant stimulus configuration," in physical space-time, filtered through cerebral—conceptual—space-time and visualized as the image of the flower in sensory space-time. In Aristotelian, two-valued, conventional language there is no such tripartition but only a dichotomy between perceiving subject and perceived object, the flower. Evidently, such a dichotomy does not provide for a differentiation between an "invariant stimulus configuration" and its replicated image. In Aristotelian ontology, after having created-replicated the flower, we exclaim: "The flower is!" In cybernetic ontology, we know that the "is" in the previous exclamation mainly designates the self-referential system, i.e., the flower-replicator.

The concept is not new: in the Middle Ages paintings and sculptures were not thought of in relation to a natural object which they sought to imitate but rather in relation to the formative process by which they came into being, namely, the projection of an "idea" existing in—though by no means "created" by—the artist's mind into a visible and tangible substance. Master Ekkehard's painter painted a rose, as Dante drew the figure of an angel, not "from life" but from the "image of his soul."

In this broadened version of the new model comprised of the equilateral triangle model (fig. 1 a and b) and the three space-times circuitry (fig. 2), objects, information, and matching response also stand for physical, sensory, and cerebral space-times respectively.

This enlarged model is well suited for illustrating increasing levels of arousal on a continuum. Starting from the healthy, normal state of equanimity (Scale 1 of fig. 1 a)—characterized by an average amount of data content and an average rate of data processing—a point of creativity is reached (arbitrarily set between divisions 2 and 3 on the left logarithmic scale of fig. 1 b), a point at which an increase in data content is matched by a corresponding increase in the rate of data processing. Further arousal, however, results in a state of schizophrenic hyperarousal or exaltation (set at division 5 on the left scale of fig. 1 b), a state which can be defined as a subject's experience of an increased data content unaccompanied by an increase in the rate of data processing. This situation can also be defined as time contraction or *chronosystole* since more data can be experienced within a chronological time unit by the self-referential system.

Such is the case during psychodysleptic drug-produced, schizophrenic states in which perceptual acuity is increased: for instance, one needs less sensory, specifically chemical, gustatory information to perceive a just noticeable difference, or "jnd," in taste. These findings also agree with the observation of an increase in neural firing in sensory pathways independent of sensed inputs during the psilocybin or LSD-produced hyperarousal. The shortening of the information side of the triangle illustrates not only this facet but also the subject's gradual withdrawal from physical space-time—the space-time of decision making—to an existence in sensory and cerebral space-time only (fig. 3). States of still higher arousal are depicted by the left logarithmic scale of the ellipse; thus, the state of being and experiencing solely in cerebral space-time is illustrated by the coalescence of the three sides of the triangle into one horizontal line, indicating that the highest attainable arousal has been reached.

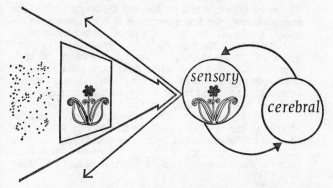

FIG. 3. *The limitation—or withdrawal—to* sensory *and* cerebral *space-times only, i.e., the split from physical space-time, of a self-reflecting system during a schizophrenic reaction and the psychodysleptic, as well as the religious and creative experiences.*

What I propose is that normality, creativity, schizophrenia, and mystical states, though seemingly disparate, actually lie on a continuum. Furthermore, they represent increasing levels of arousal and a gradual withdrawal from the synchronized physical-sensory-cerebral space-times of the normal state. Specifically, there is retreat first to a sensory-cerebral space-time and, ultimately, to cerebral space-time only. The gradual withdrawal from physical space-time is an expression of the dissolution of ego boundaries, that is, the fusion of objects and subject, and it implies that an existence solely in cerebral space-time is an oceanic experience, the most intense mirroring of the ego in his own meaning.

Since cerebral space-time is the most time-like and the least space-like dimension, it is understandable that genuine mystical experiences have been described as being timeless, lasting for only moments, or of infinite duration. The widely varying estimates of time, I propose, arise from the impossibility of referring to spatial change while existing in the most time-like dimension.

The more intensely and profoundly the contact with God is experienced, the less susceptible it is of objective definition, for by its very nature it transcends the categories of subject and object which [in Aristotelian logic] every definition presupposes. . . . At the beginning of their path, mystics tend to describe their experience in forms drawn from the world of perception. At later stages, corresponding to different levels of consciousness, the world of nature recedes, and these "natural" forms are gradually replaced by specifically mystical structures. Nearly all the mystics known to us describe such structures as configurations of lights and sounds. At still later stages, as the mystic's experience progresses toward the ultimate formlessness, these structures dissolve in their turn.[2]

That existence in cerebral space-time—"cet espace sans es-pace"—can be shielded against stimulation from sensory and physical space-times has been demonstrated by both Zen and Yoga practitioners. Habituation to auditory stimulation does not occur at the peak of meditation in Zen experts as measured by the EEG, whereas non-meditating control subjects show marked habituation of alpha blocking to repetitive stimulation. The effect of a distracting stimulus, as measured by the disappearance of alpha rhythm, is most prominent in the novices, less prominent in those of intermediate training, and almost absent in the master. Moreover, electroencephalographic studies have shown that during deep meditation attained through the constant practice of various postures (Asana), breathing exercises (Pranayama), and meditation (Dharana and Dhyana) within the traditional Indian framework, the alpha rhythm is not altered by opening the eyes or by a painful stimulus.

Such evidence is well in line with the self observations of Saint Teresa of Ávila in 1565:

. . . when the rapture is at its height; and by "its height" I mean those times when the faculties are lost, because closely united with God. Then, in my opinion, [the soul] neither sees nor hears nor feels. But as I said in describing the previous prayer of union. . . . While it lasts,

---

[2] G. G. Scholem, *On the Kabbalah and its Symbolism,* tr. R. Manheim (London: Routledge and Kegan Paul, 1965).

however, none of the senses perceives or knows what is taking place. . . . The eyes are generally closed, although we may not wish to close them, and if occasionally they remain open, the soul, as I have just said, does not perceive anything or pay attention to what it sees.[3]

The vivid sensory phenomena which accompany acute psychodysleptic drug-produced excitatory states should not be compared to that even higher aroused (hyperaroused) state marked by complete withdrawal of the mystic to his cerebral space, since the latter phase is the most intense state of hyperarousal, the last step on the continuum. In this most time-like and least space-like dimension, cerebral space-time, the ego is without boundaries and mirrors itself in the most intense experience of its own meaning; *"se ipsum per se ipsum videt"* —the soul sees itself through itself—(St. Augustine). Or in biocybernetic terminology, there is no data content from without, and therefore, no rate of data processing; the only content of the ecstatic experience of the mystic at the height of his rapture is a reflecting of himself in his own "program."

Since intense meaning is devoid of specificity, one of the few means of communicating its intensity is through the use of the metaphor; only metaphorically can the artist give us a glimpse of the intensity of gnostic experience. Marcel Proust, in the chapter "Cambray" in *Swann's Way*, rendered the evanescent impressions of the sensory life into a flowing consciousness of the hawthorn blossoms, using all the splendors of language. As the hawthorn hedge heaps flower upon flower, so Proust adds metaphor to metaphor in a profusion of radiant images—of flamboyant churches, of music, of altars adorned, of the sea, of cups of pink marble, of confections, of masterpieces of painting—that express the Bergsonian intuition of duration in terms of unfolding realization in time of beauty itself.

Regardless of whether these states of arousal are drug-produced or natural, they potentiate only those faculties already present in an individual. Baudelaire, the poet, correctly observed that drugs can add nothing new to a man but can

[3] Saint Teresa, *The Life of Saint Teresa by Herself*, tr. J. M. Cohen (Edinburgh: Clark, 1957).

only raise to a higher power what is already within him, and Hess, the scientist, could only reaffirm about a century later that psychodysleptic drugs "only provoke symptoms which are already potentially present within the cerebral organization." Evidently, colorful people when hyperaroused will radiate in colorful splendor, whereas bores will be more borish. These relationships also hold true for the naturally talented mystic: a Saint Francis of Assisi or a Saint Teresa of Ávila will be able to fill his exalted experience in cerebral space with the meaningful artistic data of a genius—whereas the maximum a Teresa of Konnersreut, a simple peasant girl, can offer is ephemeral stigmata. For the profane, non-creative, but sensitive hyperaroused subject who has the talent to dissolve gradually his ego boundaries at will, the culmination of the experience equivalent to the mystical rapture or the physical stigmata could be the orgasm.

From these examples, it is apparent that two distinct factors are essential. The first is a necessary but not sufficient hereditary "cause" which facilitates hyperarousal and is most likely polygenic in nature, being closely related or possibly identical with that implicated in schizophrenia. The other factor is an endowment or capacity to make the hyperaroused state meaningful, that is, the talent to interpret symbolically one's own central nervous system activity.

## Information and Meaning

The basic difficulty of communicating meaning is that meaning is a function of the level of arousal at which it is experienced. More specifically, the symbolic interpretation of one's own central nervous system activity, that is, the integration of information to systemic meaning depends on the level of arousal. Higher levels of arousal, and thus more complete withdrawal from physical space-time into cerebral space-time, narrow the field of attention and deepen the experience of meaning. This is paralleled by a decrease in relevance of the Aristotelian binary logic and language, a language otherwise so eminently suited for survival purposes in physical space-time.

Let us analyze at this point what could be called the complementarity of information and meaning on different levels of organization—in physical space-time—bearing in mind that meaning results from *integration* of information within the systemic context of a self-referential, self-organizing system.

The fusion of two stereoscopic pictures into one spatialized image is such an integration—or in Polanyi's terms: the fusion of clues to the image—and whether illusory or not, it is the outcome of a "tacit inference," i.e., a systemic, organismic matching response.

Information and meaning appear to form a dualism within an endless series of integrated pairs of levels whereby on each consecutive level the principles governing the lower level are controlled by the higher level. Since the principles structuring the units of a lower level are non-linear, knowledge of them is irrelevant for the prediction of the structuring on the next higher level. Determinism and chance then underlie each other in a series of integrative levels, each containing both the principles which operate from below and lead to an arbitrariness of freedom above. Consequently the operations of a higher level cannot be accounted for by the laws governing the organization of the units forming the next lower level. Each pair of levels presents its own dualism and complementarity, such as the Democritean primary and secondary qualities, or mind and body in the macro-physical realm—while position and velocity, or time and energy, are examples of micro-physical dualisms. These dualisms prevail between every pair of successive ontological levels because our systemic integration to meaning on one level follows rules of composition which exclude simultaneous integration on another level. The limiting factor seems to be "an uncertainty principle" *in vivo* inherent in the spatio-temporal constraint of our biological organization (structure). Equipped with rules of composition—which reflect our own self-referential organization—we interpret information and project meaning onto a particular ontological level for the few milliseconds during which a particular set of our nervous network fires *"now,"* excluding the interpretation and experience of everything else.

Although the future course of operations on a higher level

cannot be predicted from the "non-linear, superadditive" rule of composition prevailing on the level below, we always try to explain the higher plane based on behavior of the parts of the plane below.[4] "Such is the kind of universe that we have inherited from the Copernican Revolution. In it no essentially higher things exist, nor can intangible things be real. To understand the world then consists in representing throughout all that is of greater significance in terms of less meaningful elements." And we do this at average low levels of arousal in the so-called normal state while classifying the world into objects and subjects! It is easy to see then that at higher levels of arousal and hyperarousal, that is, during withdrawal from physical space-time, such representation completely lacks relevance and meaning. For instance I have repeatedly been told by volunteer subjects participating in psychodysleptic drug experimentation that questions which otherwise appear relevant in physical space-time and can easily be answered true or false are often "ridiculous, childish, or simply inapplicable." One of the volunteers quite concisely remarked that

[4] The relationship between information and meaning can also be conceptualized within the intent for self-preservation by an organism. Organisms or systems are both objective or goal-seeking and subjective, or self-referential, i.e., feedback systems with first order purposes related to immediate satisfaction, second order purposes related to self-preservation, third order purposes related to preservation of the group or species, and fourth order purposes related to the preservation of a process of purpose seeking beyond the preservation of any particular group or species of nets.

By disregarding the hierarchy implied in Deutsch's model, we can conceptualize on each of these ordered levels of purpose a transformation of input by output so as to render an initially independent variable partially dependent in accordance with some rule of convergence whose amplitude oscillates within fixed bounds about a certain standard or limit. We may now add meta-levels and the foregoing process may be rendered more complex through another but inverse transformation that can change the standard itself. I would submit that the function of these inverse transformations is the *transformation of information to meaning*. Purposes then are to be regarded as ordered levels with the information of a lower level being always transformed to the meaning of the next higher level; that meaning again represents the information with respect to the meaning of the next higher level, and so forth.

at the peak of the drug experience many items of the Minnesota Multiphasic Personality Inventory (MMPI) appear as "redundant, offensive and ambiguous baby-talk." In all fairness to the MMPI, it should be added that *after* the drug experience, however, the volunteer disagrees with his own critical comments made while under the influence of the drug.

These observations are not new. According to William James:

> Nitrous oxide and ether, especially nitrous oxide, when sufficiently diluted with air, stimulate the mystical consciousness in an extraordinary degree. Depth beyond depth of truth seems revealed to the inhaler. This truth fades out, however, or escapes, at the moment of coming to; and if any words remain over in which it seemed to clothe itself, they prove to be the veriest nonsense. Nevertheless, the sense of a profound meaning having been there persists; and I know more than one person who is persuaded that in the nitrous oxide trance we have a genuine metaphysical revelation.
>
> Some years ago I myself made some observations on this aspect of nitrous oxide intoxication, and reported them in print. One conclusion was forced upon my mind at that time, and my impression of its truth has ever since remained unshaken. It is that our normal waking consciousness, rational consciousness as we call it, is but one special type of consciousness, whilst all about it, parted from it by the filmiest of screens, there lie potential forms of consciousness entirely different. We may go through life without suspecting their existence; but apply the requisite stimulus, and at a touch they are there in all their completeness, definite types of mentality which probably somewhere have their field of application and adaptation.[5]

James's report is all the more interesting since the experiential effects of nitrous oxide resemble those seen with a variety of psychotomimetic drugs. It appears that meaning on a particular level of arousal is meaningless on another level, and that each level of arousal and hyperarousal has its own space-time coordinates, information-content, meaning, and logic, all of

[5] William James, *The Varieties of Religious Experience* (New York: Random House Modern Library, 1902).

which is relevant to that level. Due to this hierarchical stratification, inter- or intra-personal communication is restricted to a particular level of arousal. Meaningful communication flows easily between volunteer subjects of similar background and personality at the peak of a psilocybin or LSD experience as it does in dreams: not much of anything needs to be said since everything is intuitively understood.

Assuming that communication could occur at different levels of arousal, the linkage could be effected by the Jacob's ladder of a meta language. Without some such interpreter, metaphor remains the only vehicle of meaning. A suggestion of such a meta language is in the following note composed after a psilocybin experience by one of my talented, sensitive volunteer subjects in which she refers to a few moments during the waning of the drug experience:

> Just briefly I wanted
>     to touch the pool of light in your hair
>     that had melted in the sun and threatened
>     to spill over and run down your cheek.
> But I wasn't sure you'd understand
>     that it was just a gesture, not a commitment,
>     and I didn't want to burden the others in the room with
> it.
> So instead I poured myself another cup of coffee
>     and sat down cross-legged on the tile floor
>     and returned my attention to the questions
>     the others were asking. . . .

## Creative Arousal and Schizophrenic Hyperarousal

Creativity is an aroused state of lesser intensity than the schizophrenic state (see fig. 4). However, that these two states are proximate implies that schizophrenia may lead to a creative manner of symbolically interpreting the individual's own central nervous system activity, when—in my terminology —the schizophrenic "jammed computer" state subsides, giving way to increased data content and concomitant increase in rate of data processing. Of course, one can also reach the creatively aroused state from the opposite direction, that is, from the normal level (see fig. 4). Since both the creative and the schizophrenic states are "diagnosed" mainly from the vantage point of the "average" normal level, they are always subject to reformulation by the *Zeitgeist,* as well as by individuals. The theory of the "divine madness" of poets—first mentioned in Plato's *Phaidros*—must have had its origin in the difficulty of making a clear-cut "diagnosis." Curtius traces the history of the idea of "divine madness" into the Middle Ages when the poetic *uavía* found expression also on the popular level; to make poetry was to be mad, with a *cervello bizzarro,* as Manzoni puts it. Wilhelm Lange-Eichbaum in a unique book, *Genius, Madness and Fame,* enlarged by W. Kurth in the fifth edition, conceives the most complete bibliography of the creative genius evaluating 3,500 references and compiling the pathographies of an inordinate number of creative individuals from Aristotle to the present day. It is, of course, impossible to find a normal creative individual in this lexicon of madness and creativity, again reinforcing my contention that a clear-cut "diagnosis" of either stage is difficult or even impossible.

Regardless of the difficulty in "diagnosis," a higher state of arousal *is* a necessary prerequisite for creative activity. This should be documented if only by two examples of outstanding men, Henri Poincaré, the mathematician, and Max Ernst, the artist. Poincaré, once when unable to sleep after drinking coffee, became a spectator of some ordinarily hidden aspects of his own spontaneous creative activity: "Ideas rose in crowds; I felt them collide until pairs interlocked, so to speak, making a stable combination." A similar incident is recounted by Ernst:

> It all started on August 10, 1925, by my recalling an incident of my childhood when the sight of an imitation mahogany panel opposite my bed had induced one of those dreams between sleeping and waking. And happening to be at a seaside inn in wet weather I was struck by the way the floor, its grain accentuated by many scrubbings, obsessed my nervously excited gaze. So I decided to explore the symbolism of the obsession, and to encourage my powers of meditation and hallucination I took a series of drawings from the floorboards by dropping pieces of paper on them at random and then

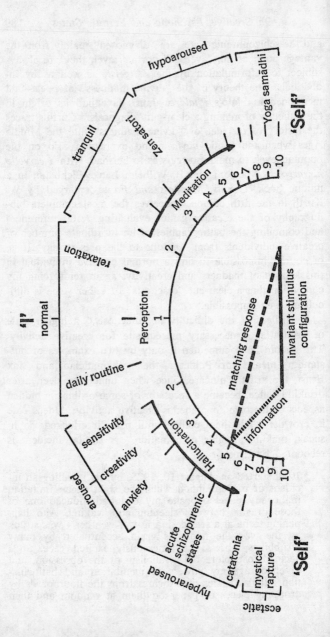

'I'

normal

daily routine

hypoaroused

tranquil

relaxation

Zen satori

Meditation

1  2  3  4  5  6  7  8  9  10

Yoga samādhi

'Self'

Perception

matching response

invariant stimulus configuration

information

1  2  3  4  5  6  7  8  9  10

Hallucination

sensitivity

creativity

anxiety

aroused

acute schizophrenic states

catatonia

hyperaroused

mystical rapture

ecstatic

'Self'

rubbing the paper with blacklead. As I looked carefully at the drawings that I got in this way—some dark, others smudgily dim—I was surprised by the sudden heighten-

---

FIG. 4. *Model of the continuous but opposing states of excitation and tranquilization depicted as a control system with non-linear transfer functions. Invariant stimulus configuration, i.e., the "object" in physical space-time, is represented here by the base of an equilateral triangle which connects the foci of an ellipse. The left and right legs of the triangle stand for input, or sensory information, and output, or matching response, respectively. The latter expresses an increasing sensory-to-motor ratio (indicating a more hallucinatory experience) with movement of the triangle's vertex along the ellipse to the left, i.e., during increasing states of excitation, and also expresses the increased meaningfulness of such experience.*

*Normal, creative, schizophrenic and ecstatic states, are conceived as symbolic interpretations (i.e., perception-behavior) on the perception-hallucination continuum (left half) of increasingly higher states of arousal. These states are experienced in terms of increasing data content and increasing rate of data processing, and may result in a creative (artistic or religious) state. Eventually, however, the rate of processing cannot keep step with the ever-increasing data content—"the torrential flood of inner sensation"—and results in the schizophrenic "jammed computer" state. At the peak of ecstatic states, interpretive activity ceases or, in biocybernetic terminology, there is no data content from without, and, therefore, no rate of data processing from within, the only content of the experience at the height of rapture being the reflection of the mystic in his own "program."*

*The right half of the model depicts decreasing levels of arousal on the perception-meditation continuum with the meditative states of satori and samadhi representing peak experiences. Samadhi, at the extreme right, can be conceptualized as an experience of pure self-reference without a program.*

*The "Self," the knower and image-maker most fully aware of itself during samadhi and ecstasy, projects the "I," a representation or model of known images and events "out there": the world of the normal state. This individual Self-awareness in the world is the basis of our con-scientia, or consensual validation of experience (consciousness).*

ing of my visionary powers, and by the dreamlike succession of contradictory images that came one on top of another with the persistence and rapidity peculiar to memories of love.

Now my curiosity was aroused and excited, and I began an impartial exploration. . . .

I stress the fact that, through a series of suggestions and transmutations arrived at spontaneously like hypnotic visions, drawings obtained in this way lose more and more of the character of the material being explored. . . . They begin to appear as the kind of unexpectedly clear images most likely to throw light on the first cause of the obsession, or at least to provide a substitute for it.

And so the *frottage* process simply depends on intensifying the mind's capacity for nervous excitement, using the appropriate technical means, excluding all conscious directing of the mind. . . . The author is present as a spectator, indifferent or impassioned, at the birth of his own work, and observes the phases of his own development.[6]

A few comments [about] the levels of arousal during Stage 4 as well as REM sleep. Let it be recalled that the latter is an organismic condition comparable in intensity and variability of internal events only to the most aroused wakefulness. Neuronal discharge during sleep may, at times, even reach convulsive intensity and, as is well known, convulsivelike phenomena can occur in PT neurons[7] during REM sleep. According to Evarts the segmented motor level is "uncoupled" from the cortical level during sleep. However, when sleep is considered from Hebb's point of view that it is a reorganization rather than an absence of neuronal activity, it would follow that sleep is a protective mechanism against stress produced by fatigue, for the neurons which become less active with sleep are those which are most active during waking. The REM stage specifically can be characterized by an almost complete tonic inhibition of the somatic musculature and many other features related to increased levels of arousal in

[6] B. Ghiselin, ed., *The Creative Process,* Mentor, 1955.

[7] Those motor cortex neurons which have axons passing through the medullary pyramid and respond antidromically to the medullary stimulus can be identified as PT neurons.

the experimental as well as the experiential dimensions. These features are also shared by the psychodysleptic experience, which is a sleepless dream state with all the manifestations of the "excitation syndrome." It is no wonder then that daily we experience during the transition stages from waking to sleeping, and vice versa, a complete range of psychopathology —the features common to all psychoses. The range of phenomena experienced during these transition stages are the source of nightmares, myths and fairy tales, that is, prophetic, poetic, and religious symbolism. The high level of arousal of Stage 1, REM sleep, fits well the low levels of EEG variability data of Goldstein, data which are again similar to those obtained under hallucinations (either in patients or in volunteers under the influence of psychodysleptic drugs) in anxiety states and during creative activity.

It should be remembered that with drowsiness as a starting point a vertical movement in either direction, i.e., toward Stage 1, REM sleep, on the one hand, or toward catatonia, on the other, there is an increase in the tonic inhibition of the somatic musculature or, in other words, an *increase* in the *sensory to motor ratio*, a prerequisite for hallucinatory and dreamy experiences. By going one step further, and by discarding the Cartesian dualism—the terminology of which defines hallucinations as "perceptions without an object"—it is postulated that sensations, eidetic imagery and entoptic phenomena in dreams and hallucinations are the result of inhibition of the motor component within the steady state of sensori-motor performance. Therefore, hallucinations[8] are redefined as intensely active sensations with blocked peripheral motor manifestations.[9]

It is apparent from the model that schizophrenic reactions need not necessarily be regarded as pathological just as the drug-produced experience in volunteers can take form as a model of a psychosis, a mystical experience, a "kick," an intensification of the religious, a therapeutic, self-enlightening experience, or a panic-ridden "trip." Which form the experi-

---

[8] Not including the mainly visual alcoholic hallucinosis and the mainly auditory and tactile hallucinations of schizophrenics.

[9] The proof of the (sensory) pudding is in the (motor) eating.

ence takes is dependent on the individual and social expectations, set and setting, and other variables most of which can be controlled especially through the assistance of an experienced and sympathetic guide. Not all schizophrenias end with a psychological deficiency; there are individuals in whom the schizophrenic episode brings about a positive change in the total personality resulting in increasingly gifted ways of thinking, hypermnesia, and an increased urge for activity. Quite a few writers, scientists and poets display superior performance after a schizophrenic episode with some of them manifesting true creativity for the first time after the schizophrenic experience.

But, it is perhaps insufficiently known that even average, artistically untrained schizophrenics are able to produce aesthetically pleasing, and sometimes unusual and fantastic, art. These individuals lose their artistic abilities after recovery and are again "average." Only the gifted individual can use the change implied in the shift between creative and schizophrenic states in his artistic production. . . .

Within our model, schizophrenic hyperarousal occupies a central position between creatively aroused and mystically exalted states. Schizophrenic hyperarousal has, therefore, a very special meaning by being on the continuum between the creative and the religious, both of which fuse and transcend the fleeting moments of our species to evolutive history.

While the "burnt out" chronic schizophrenics crowding the wards of State Mental Hospitals may be regarded as a "genetic load," the price we pay for the exquisite luxuries of creative brilliance and mystical exaltation, the hyperaroused schizophrenic in his fertile, manneristic period is the metaphorical representative of the mythical realm.

# PSYCHOTHERAPY
# AND LIBERATION

## ALAN W. WATTS

If we look deeply into such ways of life as Buddhism and
Taoism, Vedanta and Yoga, we do not find either philosophy
or religion as these are understood in the West. We find
something more nearly resembling psychotherapy. . . .

The main resemblance between these Eastern ways of life
and Western psychotherapy is in the concern of both with
bringing about changes of consciousness, changes in our ways
of feeling our own existence and our relation to human society
and the natural world. The psychotherapist has, for the most
part, been interested in changing the consciousness of pecul-
iarly disturbed individuals. The disciplines of Buddhism and
Taoism are, however, concerned with changing the consciousness of normal, socially adjusted people. But it is increasingly
apparent to psychotherapists that the normal state of consciousness in our culture is both the context and the breeding
ground of mental disease. A complex of societies of vast material wealth bent on mutual destruction is anything but a
condition of social health. . . .

Seeing this, the psychotherapist must realize that his science, or art, is misnamed, for he is dealing with something
far more extensive than a psyche and its private troubles.
This is just what so many psychotherapists are recognizing
and what, at the same time, makes the Eastern ways of libera-

tion so pertinent to their work. For they are dealing with people whose distress arises from what may be termed *maya*, to use the Hindu-Buddhist word whose exact meaning is not merely "illusion" but the entire world-conception of a culture, considered as illusion in the strict etymological sense of a play (Latin, *ludere*). The aim of a way of liberation is not the destruction of *maya* but seeing it for what it is, or seeing through it. Play is not to be taken seriously, or, in other words, ideas of the world and of oneself which are social conventions and institutions are not to be confused with reality. The rules of communication are not necessarily the rules of the universe, and man is not the role or identity which society thrusts upon him. For when a man no longer confuses himself with the definition of himself that others have given him, he is at once universal and unique. He is universal by virtue of the inseparability of his organism from the cosmos. He is unique in that he is just *this* organism and not any stereotype of role, class, or identity assumed for the convenience of social communication. . . .

It is of course a common misapprehension that the change of personal consciousness effected in the Eastern ways of liberation is "depersonalization" in the sense of regression to a primitive or infantile type of awareness. Indeed, Freud designated the longing for return to the oceanic consciousness of the womb as the *nirvana*-principle, and his followers have persistently confused all ideas of transcending the ego with mere loss of "ego strength." This attitude flows, perhaps, from the imperialism of Western Europe in the nineteenth century, when it became convenient to regard Indians and Chinese as backward and benighted heathens desperately in need of improvement by colonization.

It cannot be stressed too strongly that liberation does not involve the loss or destruction of such conventional concepts as the ego; it means seeing through them—in the same way that we can use the idea of the equator without confusing it with a physical mark upon the surface of the earth. Instead of falling below the ego, liberation surpasses it. . . .

However various [the] doctrines [of the ways of liberation] and however different their formal techniques, all seem to culminate in the same state or mode of consciousness in which the duality of the ego and the world is overcome. Call it "cosmic consciousness" or "mystical experience," or what you will, it seems to me to be the felt realization of the physical world as a field. But because language is divisive rather than relational, not only is the feeling hard to describe but our attempted descriptions may also seem to be opposed. Buddhism emphasizes the unreality of the ego, whereas Vedanta emphasizes the unity of the field. Thus in describing liberation the former seems to be saying simply that the egocentric viewpoint evaporates, and the latter that we discover our true self to be the Self of the universe. However pundits may argue the fine points, it comes to the same thing in practical experience.

There is, then, nothing occult or supernatural in this state of consciousness, and yet the traditional methods for attaining it are complex, divergent, obscure, and, for the most part, extremely arduous. Confronted with such a tangle, one asks what is common to these methods, what is their essential ingredient, and if this can be found the result will be a practical and theoretical simplification of the whole problem. . . .

We must start from the well-recognized fact that all the ways of liberation, Buddhism, Vedanta, Yoga, and Taoism,[1] assert that our ordinary egocentric consciousness is a limited and impoverished consciousness without foundation in "reality." Whether its basis is physical or social, biological or cultural, remains to be seen, but there is no doubt that release from this particular limitation is the aim of all four ways. In every case the method involves some form of meditation which may take the form of concentrated attention upon some particular object, problem, or aspect of consciousness, or simply of the relaxed and detached observation of whatever comes into mind. It may take the form of trying to suppress all verbal thinking, or the form of a dialectic in which the most rigorous thinking is carried to its full conclusions. It may be an attempt to be directly aware of the perceiving

[1] Perhaps I should also include Islamic Sufism and aspects of Jainism, but these are subjects which I have not studied to anything like the same extent.

self, or it may follow out the idea that the self is not anything that can be known, not the body, not the sensations, not the thoughts, not even consciousness. In some instances the student is simply asked to find out, exhaustively and relentlessly, *why* he wants liberation, or *who* it is that wants to be liberated. Methods vary not only among the differing schools and teachers, but also in accordance with the needs and temperaments of their disciples. . . .

With their differing methods, Vedanta, Buddhism, and Taoism all involve the realization that life ceases to seem problematic when it is understood that the ego is a social fiction. Sickness and death may be painful, indeed, but what makes them problematic is that they are shameful to the ego. This is the same shame that we feel when caught out of role, as when a bishop is discovered picking his nose or a policeman weeping. For the ego is the role, the "act," that one's inmost self is permanent, that it is in control of the organism, and that while it "has" experiences it is not involved in them. Pain and death expose this pretense, and this is why suffering is almost always attended by a feeling of guilt, a feeling that is all the more difficult to explain when the pretense is unconscious. Hence the obscure but powerful feeling that one *ought* not to suffer or die. . . .

The state of consciousness which follows upon liberation from the ego fiction is quite easily intelligible in neuropsychiatric terms. One of the important physical facts that socialization represses is that all our sensory experiences are states of the nervous system. The field of vision, which we take to be outside the organism, is in fact inside it because it is a translation of the external world into the form of the eye and the optical nerves. What we see is therefore a state of the organism, a state of ourselves. Yet to say even this is to say too much. There is not the external world, and then the state of the nervous system, and then something which sees that state. The seeing is precisely that particular state of the nervous system, a state which for that moment *is* an integral part of the organism. Similarly, one does not hear a sound. The sound is the hearing, apart from which it is simply a vibration in the air. The states of the nervous system need not, as we suppose, be watched by something else, by a little man inside the head who registers them all. Wouldn't he have to have *another* nervous system, and another little man inside *his* head, and so ad infinitum? When we get an infinite regression of this kind we should always suspect that we have made an unnecessary step in our reasoning. It is the same kind of oscillation that happens when the earpiece of a telephone is placed against the mouthpiece. It "howls."

So, too, when we posit what is in effect a second nervous system watching the first, we are turning the nervous system back upon itself, and thereupon our thoughts oscillate. We become an infinite series of echoes, of selves behind selves behind selves. Now indeed there is a sense in which the cortex is a second nervous system over and above the primary system of the thalamus. Oversimplifying things considerably, we could say that the cortex works as an elaborate feedback system for the thalamus by means of which the organism can to some extent be aware of itself. Because of the cortex, the nervous system can know that it knows; it can *re*cord and *re*cognize its own states. But this is just one "echo," not an infinite series. Furthermore, the cortex is just another neural pattern, and its states are neural patterns; it is not something other than neural pattern as the ego agent is supposed to be, in the organism but not of it.

How can the cortex observe and control the cortex? Perhaps there will come a day when the human brain will fold back on itself again and develop a higher cortex, but until then the only feedback which the cortex has about its own states comes through other people. (I am speaking here of the cortex as a whole. One can of course remember remembering.) * Thus the ego which observes and controls the cortex is a complex of social information relayed back into the cortex—Mead's "generalized other." But this is social misinformation when it is made to appear that the information of which the ego consists is something other than states of the cortex itself, and therefore ought to be controlling the cor-

* Since this was written, the development of biofeedback has provided another means by which the cortex can "observe" itself. See "Meditation and Biofeedback" in this book. [J.W.]

tex. The ego is the unconscious pretense that the organism contains a higher system than the cortex; it is the confusion of a system of interpersonal information with a new, and imaginary, fold in the brain—or with something quite other than a neural pattern, a mind, soul, or self. When, therefore, I feel that "I" am knowing or controlling myself—my cortex —I should recognize that I am actually being controlled by other people's words and gestures masquerading as my inner or better self. Not to see this brings about utter confusion, as when I try to force myself to stop feeling in ways that are socially objectionable.

If all this is true, it becomes obvious that the ego feeling is pure hypnosis. Society is persuading the individual to do what it wants by making it appear that its commands are the individual's inmost self. What we want is what you want. And this is a double-bind, as when a mother says to her child, who is longing to slush around in a mud puddle, "Now darling, you don't *want* to get into that mud!" This is misinformation, and this—if anything—is the "Great Social Lie."

Let us suppose, then, that the false reflex of "I seeing my sights" or "I feeling my feelings" is stopped, by such methods as the ways of liberation employ. Will it not thereupon become clear that all our perceptions of the external world are states of the organism? The division between "I" and "my sights" is projected outwardly into the sharp division between the organism and what it sees. Just such a change of perception as this would explain the feeling, so usual at the moment of liberation (*satori*), that the external world is oneself and that external actions are one's own doing. Perception will then be known for what it is, a field relationship as distinct from an encounter.[2] It is hardly too much to say that

---

[2] I am reasonably satisfied that something approximating this change of perception, the realization that sensations are states of the organism itself, is brought about by lysergic acid (LSD-25). Many drugs suspend inhibitions that are useful, but it seems that LSD suspends an inhibition which is of very doubtful value, and thus its use as a therapeutic might be explored further on the hypothesis that this is the main feature of its action. Elsewhere . . . I have discussed more fully the partial resemblances between the LSD experience and "cosmic consciousness."

such a change of perception would give far better ground for social solidarity than the normal trick of misinformation and hypnosis.

There is one further question which should be raised at this point, a question that repeatedly comes up in any discussion of the usefulness of the ways of liberation to the psychotherapist. Despite Freud's own basic prudishness, the whole history of psychotherapy is bound up with a movement toward sexual freedom in western culture. This seems to be in sharp conflict with the fact that the ways of liberation so largely enjoin celibacy and the monastic or eremitic life upon their followers. Many texts could be cited to show that sexual passion is held to be a major obstacle to liberation.

To understand this, we must first go back to the social context of liberation in ancient India. In the normal course of things, no one entered upon these disciplines until the latter part of his life. In the various *ashramas* or stages of life the liberative stage of "forest dweller" (*vanaprastha*) came only after completion of the stage of "householder" (*grihastha*). No one was expected to seek liberation until he had raised a family and handed over his occupation to his sons. It was assumed that liberation was not only freedom from social convention but also from social responsibility. Mahayana Buddhism was to modify this idea radically, and we shall see that the answer to our problem lies here rather than in the disciplines that remain inseparable from Hindu culture—Vedanta and Yoga. But it is significant that Jung, too, regards the individuation process of his psychotherapy as a task for the second half of life, as a preparation for death.

In all ancient precontraceptive societies sexual activity is obviously inseparable from procreation, and thus from several points of view it seemed unsuitable for a man in the stage of *vanaprastha* to become a father. In an age when life expectancy was far shorter than it is today, there was slight chance that he would live to raise his children to maturity. Furthermore, there was a potential conflict between the duty of socializing the children and liberating himself. It must also be remembered that primitive physiology associates the seminal emission with a "loss" of vital fluid comparable to a loss of blood, confusing the relaxation of detumescence with impaired vitality. Hence the widespread but quite fallacious notion that "Every animal is sad after intercourse [*Omne animal triste post coitum*]." But, apart from all these considerations, the main reason for insisting upon the repression of sexual desire was that this offered a major challenge to the reality of the ego, as if to say, "If you can thwart your biological nature, you really do exist!"

This is such a drastic method of challenging the ego that, as with certain potent drugs, one is justified in using them only if fairly certain that they will work. Indeed, all the methods of liberation were supposed to work and therefore to be *temporary* disciplines. The Buddhist discipline is often likened to a raft for crossing from the shore of *samsara* to the shore of *nirvana,* and the texts say again and again that when the farther shore is reached the raft should be left behind. In Mahayana Buddhism, as we have seen, the liberated Bodhisattva returns from the forest or hermitage into society and the world. . . .

The common design of all these methods is now clear: they challenge the student to demonstrate the power and independence of his presumed ego, and to the extent that he believes this possible he falls into a trap. As the trap closes, his feeling of helplessness becomes more and more critical, just because his habitual sense of being able to act from his own center has been so completely challenged. While the least identification with the observing ego remains, he seems to be being reduced more and more to an inert and passive witness. His thoughts, feelings, and experiences appear to be a mutually conditioning series of events in which he cannot genuinely intervene, since it always turns out that intervention was motivated, not by the ego, but by one or more of the observed events. Thoughts and feelings are conditioned by other thoughts and feelings, and the ego is cut down to a mute observer. Finally, as in the exercise of trying to concentrate only on the present, even its power to observe is challenged. Or perhaps its very passivity is challenged by the invitation to *be* passive, or simply to watch and accept what happens. But then, how is one to accept what happens when, among the things that are happening, there are feelings of resistance to life, of nonacceptance; or if it turns out that one is really accepting life in order to be one-up on it?

This is the point where, in the imagery of Zen, the student is likened to a mosquito biting an iron bull, or to a man who has swallowed a ball of red-hot iron which he can neither spit out nor gulp down. Press the point, and there is suddenly a "flip" of consciousness. There is no ego left with which one can identify. As a result the sense of self shifts from the independent observer to everything that is "observed." It feels that one *is* all that one knows, that one is doing all that is seen to happen, for the conflict of subject and object has entirely disappeared. This may at first be disconcerting and confusing, because there seems to be no independent point from which to act upon events and control them. It is like the moment in which one first learns to ride a bicycle or to swim: the new skill seems to be happening by itself. "Look, Mama, no hands!" But as the shock of unfamiliarity wears off, it becomes possible to conduct one's affairs in this new dimension of consciousness without the least difficulty.

In the language of psychotherapy, what we have here is the end of alienation, both of the individual from himself and of the individual from nature. The new state of affairs could also be described as self-acceptance or as psychological integration. . . .

# ZEN BUDDHISM:
# A PSYCHOLOGICAL REVIEW

### EDWARD W. MAUPIN

Zen, a sect of Mahayana Buddhism, originated in China and has played an important role in Japanese culture since its introduction there in the thirteenth century. It has traditionally sought to bring about in its students a direct experience of the enlightenment which characterized the Buddha. What makes this of interest to psychologists is that enlightenment is considered to be essentially a psychological problem to be worked out by the student. Appeals to divine intervention or intensive study of scriptures are felt to be irrelevant.

Zen involves a variety of training techniques designed to guide the student to a turning point, *satori,* which appears to be a major shift in the mode of experiencing oneself and the world, and which is an important step on the way to enlightenment. Since the individual, with satori, is described as living an increasingly effective and satisfying life, Zen is of interest in terms of psychotherapy. . . .

The experience of satori is the central core of Zen. Everything else is considered secondary to it. Since it must be experienced in order to be fully understood, I have given primary attention to the authors who have had it. Where pertinent issues are raised, and especially where these bear on psychotherapy, I have turned to the secondhand sources.

From *Psychedelic Review,* No. 5, 1965. Reprinted by permission of *Psychedelic Review* and the author.

## The Ordinary Adult Mind and Satori

Zen literature makes no particular distinction between types of psychopathology. As a therapy it seems designed for people who are normally mature and have achieved a fair degree of self-control. Existential problems are seen as resulting from the way the ordinary adult experiences himself and his world —from the terms in which the problems are couched. For an answer, a radical shift in the mode of experience, satori, is proposed. The term "satori" seems to be used in two ways in Zen literature. One is to refer to an experience of insight, lasting only a short time, which may recur more than once. Another, vaguer usage refers to the changes in one's outlook and ability to function which are brought about as a result of the insight. A part of the confusion seems to stem from the timelessness of the experience, a feeling of immortality, which leads the person having it to deny that it comes and goes. It is an insight into the nature of things as they have always been.

Satori is not a trance. Consciousness is not lost, nor does it impair the ability to use ordinary cognitive functions as required. It is not a quietistic retreat. All of these possible outcomes of the training procedures are considered byways to be guarded against with the help of the Zen master. Satori is described as an added mode of experience, comparable to the opening of a third eye. It is considered impossible to express in rational language.

This raises the problem of irrationality in Zen literature, which warrants a short digression. The confusing, non-logical quality seems to stem from three main sources. First, there is the ordinary difficulty in describing any state of consciousness. Under the proper circumstances we can specify the content of consciousness—what fantasies, thoughts or sensations are present—but the formal qualities are much more difficult to communicate. One recourse is to speak in analogies and hope that the hearer has had such experience that the analogy seems familiar. We find one Zen master counseling his students to keep a kind of "doubt" which arises in the course of meditation "neither too fine nor too coarse." Both the term "doubt" and the sensory terms with which he qualifies it are analogies which become meaningful only when the student reaches that stage. This first source of unclarity in Zen literature, then, is one which often plagues the attempt to communicate subjective experience.

A second source is the teaching method of Zen. The problem to which the Zen master addresses himself is to have the student get beyond concepts of satori to the experience itself. The student may come with a question about some important aspect of Buddhism, the training, or his own problems in reaching satori. But a direct, conceptual answer would only be *about* the topic; it would not bring the student to see the thing itself. There is a deep feeling in Zen that conceptual knowledge can come only so close to its object. In satori one no longer mediates experience through concepts. So the Zen master may make an apparently illogical retort which may jolt the student into seeing the thing for himself.

The third source of unclarity seems to be a genuinely illogical quality of satori itself. Certain aspects of this new mode of experience, such as the feeling of oneness, seem genuinely inexpressible in a language posited on a subject-object dichotomy, conventional time, space, and so on.

Although descriptions of satori are given with a caution that they are only inadequate analogies, there are certain uniformities in the way people compare it with the ordinary mode of experience. The first contrast is between intellection and intuition. Suzuki writes that man tends to mistake his conceptual tools for reality. "He forgets that concepts are his own creations and by no means exhaust reality. Zen is fully conscious of this and all its *mondo* are directed towards casting off the false mask of conceptualization" (1949a, p. 28).

Chang (1959, p. 141) outlines other characteristics of the ordinary mind. It must break reality into discrete entities and can only deal with a few things at a time. It is rigid and fixed, unable to deal with all possible aspects of a thing, and it tends to "cling" to the object thus separated and objectified. The term "clinging" hints at personal motivation to maintain the stability achieved by this kind of structuring. It will be noted that the conceptual mode is under attack not because it is useless in general, but because, improperly used, it separates the individual from another, more direct contact with his experience. It is this loss of immediate experience which plunges the individual into existential problems.

> The intellect is primarily intended to have us get on well with a world dualistically conceived; but as to its probing into ultimate reality it is an inadequate instrument. (Suzuki, 1949a, p. 112.)

> . . . human consciousness weaves a time-continuum and regards it as reality. When this is accomplished, the procedure is now reversed, and we begin to build up our experience on the screen of time. Serialism comes first now and we find our lives miserably bound up by it. The absolute present is pushed away back, we are no more conscious of it. We regret the past and worry about the future. Our crying is not pure crying, nor is our laughing pure laughing. There is always something else mixed up with it, that is the present has lost its innocence and absoluteness. The future and the past overlay the present and suffocate it. (*Ibid.*, pp. 72–73.)

The loss of immediate experience refers in part to the tendency to live in a fantasy world (which treats objects and events in terms of a personal—and necessarily cognitive—network of goals, plans, wishes and fears). Also included is the tendency to impose too quickly the conventional structures like time, space, the subject-object dichotomy, and self-other value systems. It should be noted, too, that the psychological unconscious, as repository of repressed derivatives of unacceptable wishes, is included in this conceptual filter. Suzuki is inclined to think of this as merely a lower stratum of the same kind of conceptual mind, "probably accumulated ever since we began to become conscious of our own existence" (1949a, p. 95).

Contrasted with this is "intuition," which Dr. Akihira Kondo, a Japanese psychoanalyst, interprets as "the function of the human mind for perceiving totality" (1953). Suzuki speaks of it in terms of the more traditional *prajna*:

> Prajna is the experience a man has when he feels in its most fundamental sense the infinite totality of things, that is psychologically speaking, when the finite ego,

breaking its hard crust, refers itself to the infinite which
envelops everything that is finite and limited and therefore transitory. We may take this experience as being
somewhat akin to a totalistic intuition of something that
transcends all our particularized, specified experiences.
(Fromm *et al.*, 1960, p. 74.)

Intimately connected with the conceptual mode of experience is the experience of self. The individual mistakes the
self which he can take as an object of consciousness for his
real self. Like other objects of consciousness it must be separated out, and this, in particular, leads the individual into a
frantic scramble to defend, maintain, and bolster himself.
Herrigel writes:

> By learning to discriminate himself more and more
> from everything that is not himself, that does not belong
> to him, man experiences the tension between the ego and
> non-ego as an opposition. The more consciously he con-
> fronts everything not himself as an object, the more the
> ego places itself outside—outside what is "opposite" to
> it. The result is a continuous division of being into the
> two realms of subjective and objective. (1960, p. 19.)

> Man feels and experiences himself as an ego. Ego-
> hood leads to selfishness and self-assertion in the face of
> everything that is not-self, and hence to hardness of
> heart. He feels himself and makes himself the center, if
> not consciously, then in secret. (*Ibid.*, p. 19.)

It will be seen from this that the experience of a separate
self is felt to stand in a causal relationship to other aspects
of the clinging, conceptual mind. But from the standpoint of
satori this self is a fiction.[1]

Satori, in contrast, is the intuitive seeing into the real self,

---

[1] Regarding this fictional aspect, compare Sartre: "The ego is
not the owner of consciousness, it is the object of consciousness.
To be sure we constitute spontaneously our states and actions as
productions of the ego. But our states and actions are also objects.
We never have a direct intuition of the spontaneity of an instantaneous consciousness as produced by the ego. That would be impossible. It is only on the level of meanings and psychological
hypotheses that we can conceive of such a production—and this
error is possible only because on this level the ego and consciousness are indicated emptily" (1957, p. 97).

the true author of one's behavior, which is at the same time a part of the whole flux of the universe.[2] This contact, however, does not mean reflexive awareness of the real self—which would then only replace the old self as an object of conscious thought. One's experience is felt to take place directly through the real self unmediated by conscious thought, and without consciousness of the process. "It is rather a state of mind in which there is no specific consciousness of its own workings" (Suzuki, 1949b, p. 105). One is content to let behavior bring out a self which cannot be fully conceptualized. One trusts this self enough to suspend conscious reflective control over it.

It is this getting out of the way of the unfolding of the real self which is the "therapeutic" effect of satori:

> Zen in its essence is the art of seeing into the nature of one's being, and it points the way from bondage to freedom. . . . We can say that Zen liberates all the energies properly and naturally stored in each of us, which are in ordinary circumstances cramped and distorted so that they find no adequate channel for activity. . . . It is the object of Zen, therefore, to save us from going crazy or being crippled. This is what I mean by freedom, giving free play to all the creative and benevolent impulses inherently lying in our hearts. Generally, we are blind to this fact, that we are in possession of all the necessary faculties that will make us happy and loving towards one another. (Suzuki, 1956, pp. 3 ff.)

Although one may make forays into the cognitive world as various situations require, there is direct contact with experi-

[2] The concept is a difficult one. Logically if we reject the conceptualized "I" as the author of one's behavior, then there remains a real self which actually acts. Groddeck's description of the "it" has been advanced as an insight parallel to what is experienced as the real self in Zen. "The it of a particular man starts—if we must start somewhere—with fertilization. It embraces all the powers which govern the formation and further development of individual man. The outstanding fact of this being is that without a brain it fulfills the most difficult functions of life, and indeed that the brain —and with it the power of thought and later of consciousness and the ego itself—are created by the it. The it is the deepest nature and force in man. It accomplishes everything that happens with and through and in man" (Weisz, 1960).

ence, unmediated by concepts. This means the transcension of existential problems.

> For satori stands firmly on the Absolute Present, Eternal Now, where time and space are coalesced and yet begin to get differentiated. They lie there dormant as it were with all their futurities and possibilities; they are both there rolled up with all their achievements and unfoldments. It is the privilege of satori to be sitting in the Absolute Present quietly surveying the past and contemplating the future. (Suzuki, 1949a, p. 61.)

> "This very 'moment' is not subject to birth-and-death and therefore there is no going beyond it as long as we live this present moment. Here is absolute tranquility which is no other than this present moment. Bliss lies in the timelessness of this present moment. There is here no particular recipient of this bliss and, therefore, every one of us is blessed with eternal bliss. (*Ibid.*, p. 111. Quoted from the ancient monk, Yeno.)

It is important to note that ordinary perception and conceptualization are not impaired in satori. Rather, while intuiting totality, the individual sees objects more objectively than before, less distorted by personal motives. Cognitive skills remain available as required.

Thus far we have discussed satori as though it were more or less a constant state of mind after a certain point in Zen training. Actually, the first experience of satori probably lasts only a short time. Further training is directed toward expanding the situations in which such a state of mind may be maintained. Enlightenment, a nearly impossible ideal, is felt to be a constant experience of satori. Nevertheless, at times following satori, the individual may deepen the experience to a point of complete union. Relaxing conceptual consciousness and falling back on unreflected intuition are felt to have important effects on the range of stimuli to which one can respond. Zen-trained artists and soldiers especially have made use of this state of mind to heighten their effectiveness.

## Training

We turn now to the techniques which are used to lead the student toward the experience of satori. It must be emphasized that satori is felt to be an awakening to something which was always there, not the product of some particular technique. What procedures are used will depend on what the Zen master feels his student needs to awaken him to this kind of experience. Thus specific methods will vary far more than the present review can convey. Generally, however, the student sets aside a portion of the day for sitting motionless and engaging in some time of concentration exercise. The object of concentration varies considerably and may be changed as the student progresses. The aim is to suspend the ordinary flow of thoughts without falling into a stupor. The achievement of undistracted concentration is the first means of coming to grips with the purely conceptual mode of experience.

The bodily position used is of some importance. It must be relaxed and comfortable, yet not supine and likely to induce sleep. Ordinarily the crossed-legged half- or full-lotus positions are used by the Japanese. The eyes are kept partly open, again to avoid sleep or stupor.

Three subjects of concentration deserve special mention: breathing, the *hua t'ou* and the *koan*. Concentration on breathing seems to be the simplest of these and is frequently used to develop the ability to concentrate. *Hua t'ou* is a Chinese word which means "ante-thought." It describes the state of mind of a person who approaches himself with the question "Who is this who calls on the name of Buddha?" (Luk, 1960.) As such, it appears to define a particular attitude of detached observation toward one's mental contents, whose subjective origin is kept in mind. It is also an attempt to grasp the mind originating these contents. The hua t'ou overlaps with the koan, a statement which is impossible of rational comprehension but understandable to the person who has experienced satori. Any of a number of traditional exchanges between masters and monks may be taken as the object of concentration. The idea is not to run through the words themselves, but to penetrate to their meaning, the state of mind which they express. Not all Zen sects use the koan exercise. Where used, it seems to deepen the intellectual crisis preceding satori and to produce a deeper and more vivid satori experience. De Martino (Fromm *et al.*, 1960) suggests that the koan serves to crystallize and focus the desperate personal need to break through to an answer which is necessary for satori. As he describes it, the attempt to solve the koan becomes almost a surrogate for the struggle to solve one's life. In the wealth of subjective reports it is generally possible to distinguish two main stages in the course of training before satori. There is an initial phase in which concentration, difficult at first, eventually becomes more successful.

Relaxation and a kind of pleasant "self-immersion" begin to follow. At this point internal distractions, often of an anxiety-arousing kind, come to the fore. Herrigel (1956) indicates that the only way to render this disturbance inoperative is "to look at it equably and at last grow weary of looking" (p. 55).

Eventually a second phase begins (Herrigel, 1956). This is a state "in which nothing definite is thought, planned, striven for, desired or expected, which aims in no particular direction and yet knows itself capable alike of the possible and the impossible, so unswerving is its power . . ." (pp. 55–56). Concentration seems to be accompanied by a sense of calm stillness, of energy and vitality, and a feeling of invulnerability (Chang, 1959; Kondo, 1952, 1958). Sato (1959) and his students, who undertook a special "accelerated" course of training from a Zen master, reached this point after about five days. Both Chang and Herrigel suggest that the phase begins with a "jolt" or "shock," but this is not invariably mentioned.

This state of mind is traditionally described with the analogy of a mirror, which reflects many things, yet is itself unchanged by them. It seems likely that this phase of meditation, in particular, increases receptivity to previously excluded experience. But the ability to deal with it in a detached, non-anxious fashion is also facilitated. This state of mind is similar to a phenomenon reported by patients in psychoanalysis. Associations are experienced as derivatives of one's own mental processes, regardless of the reality of the objects represented. An observing attitude can be maintained until anxiety or other effects become too intense (cf. Sterba, 1930). Sato (1958), too, feels this state of mind may have its counterpart in the free association method of psychoanalysis, but emphasizes the fact that Western therapy usually works with words, whereas the Zen student in this stage does not dissect what he is experiencing with ideational operations. "In Zen, the ideas, if they appear, are allowed to pass uncared about. They need not be grasped or verbalized" (p. 217).

Obviously, there are dangers. Traditional Zen literature considered this middle phase to be one in which the monk was in danger of possession by demons (Luk, 1960). There are handbooks, unfortunately not translated, which warn the student against the many experiences in this phase to which he might be tempted to "cling." While the Zen master does not attempt to interpret the emerging material, he is apparently active in guarding the student against acting out, unconscious projection, and loss of awareness of its subjective origin. He also acts to curb temptations to go into a stupor, toy with paranormal psychic functions, indulge in ecstasies or quietistic retreat. All of these are considered blind alleys. Such dangers must be taken into account in any proposed application of Zen or its procedures. They do not seem to occur during the early portions of training, but later supervision may be critical. Herrigel (1956) does not report having had florid reactions at this stage, and there are apt to be gross individual differences. Where they occur they are considered to be manifestations of the dualistic mind attempting to defend a fictitious ego.

What follows seems to be a very long period of struggle until the intellectual approach is exhausted. Kondo (1952), Herrigel (1956) and Suzuki (1956) describe nearly identical experiences when, having reached a state of inner stillness, the student is given a koan to solve. Time after time he reaches an intellectual solution which is rejected by the Zen master. With increasing despair he concentrates more and more on the koan until his concentration is no longer voluntary; the problem cannot be put aside. Where the hua t'ou is used, the feeling of doubt which emerges is carefully maintained until something like a crisis is reached. This crisis is still, rather than turbulent. Intellectual skills seem worthless for the problem, and one can only wait. Death images like "walking in darkness" or "enclosed in a black lacquer casket" are used to describe the state of mind. In the midst of it, the student "lets go" of his egoistic self, "throws himself into the abyss," and satori follows.

## Interpretations of Satori

Erich Fromm, who has conferred extensively with Suzuki, concludes that satori is not a pathological phenomenon. He interprets Zen statements about the limitations of ordinary consciousness in terms of his own explanations of estrangement and alienation. Social learning and individual conflicts tend to produce a "filter" through which only a part of one's experience may pass to be represented in consciousness. He understands satori to be the result of breaking through this filter: "the immediate unreflected grasp of reality, without effective contamination and intellectualization" (Fromm et al., 1960, p. 133). In a sense it is a repetition of the direct grasp of the child, but on a new level, in the context of the full development of adult reason, objectivity and individuality. If one defines the unconscious to include all the aspects of experience which are filtered out, and if one carries the psychoanalytic goal of "making the unconscious conscious" to its ultimate extreme, then the goal of psychoanalysis approximates the Zen goal of enlightenment. The methods obviously differ. To Fromm, the difference is that Zen makes a frontal attack on the alienated mode of experience by means of sitting, koans, and the authority of the Zen master, while psychoanalysis trains consciousness to get hold of the unconscious by directing attention, step by step, to individual distortions and personal fictions in the perception of experience.

Schachtel (1959) appears to be in essential agreement, seeing the nature of satori as a breaking away from conventionalized and structured experience. He has traced the role of this mode of experience in adult amnesia for childhood experiences and brings forward the death-imagery surrounding the pre-satori state as evidence of the defensive purposes for which the conventionalized mode is used.

Fingarette (1958) has undertaken a fairly comprehensive mapping of mystic states into psychoanalytic ego psychology. His material is taken mainly from the Eastern literature of mysticism, including that of Zen. He feels that interpretations which emphasize pathological regression fail to take into account the "significant marks of insight" associated with the great mystics. Patients who have made progress in psychoanalysis describe their changed experience in terms which are sometimes comparable to mystic paradoxes. The mystics may be describing a singularly integrated mode of ego-syntonic functioning. Selflessness cannot refer to an actual loss of the subject-object distinction as it occurs in hallucinations and paranoid delusions, because the social behavior of mystics is often highly realistic and effective. Rather it refers, he feels, to that normal unselfconscious characteristic of experience which is non-anxious and motivated by neutralized drives functioning within the conflict-free portions of the ego.

> The introspected, self-conscious "I" is not in fact a perception of one's total person; it is some particular part affect, idea or action of the person as perceived by the person in a context where the dynamically dominant affect is some form of anxiety. Consciousness of self is not an awareness of some self-identical entity; it is, rather, any consciousness colored by intrapsychic conflict and anxiety. (*Ibid.,* p. 16.)

"Freedom from striving," "acceptance," and "desirelessness" seem to refer, not to a flaccid absence of motivation, but the absence of inner conflict. Similarly, "no-mind" refers to the absence of compulsive thoughts about thoughts. "Dwelling in voidness" refers to complete openness to experience, unblocked by preconceived ideas of overly-rigid maintenance of logical forms.

Fingarette suggests that such integrated functioning indicates that the mystic has undertaken a prior phase similar to psychotherapy in which he has achieved a deep personality reorganization by facing his underlying problems and gaining insight into them. The regressive phenomena—trances, hallucinations, and so forth—reported in the literature of mysticism appear to belong to an earlier phase of self-exploration rather than to the mystical state itself.

## The Feeling of Oneness

In satori, one experiences the universe as a totality of being, of which oneself and all other objects are manifestations. This is the aspect of satori which is most inexpressible, yet known so directly that it is irrefutable with logical argument.

William James (1928) considered mystic states to be characterized by a breaking through of the subliminal or subconscious mind into consciousness. He noted that union, ineffability, certainty, and passive reception were found in most such descriptions. While the experience carries strong authority for the individual himself, other people must evaluate it in terms of the empirical functioning of the individual after the experience. Mere contact with the subconscious, then, does not guarantee that the experience is psychologically constructive. Certainly the material which he reviews ranges between extremes of sickness and health. He does not carry his thinking about the subconscious far enough to try to account for those incursions which are apt to be pathological and those which are not.

Psychoanalytic interpretations of oneness begin with Freud's (1935) comparison of the oceanic feeling with the primal experience of unity of the satisfied infant with the maternal breast. This interpretation, in terms of oral fantasies, is followed by many subsequent psychoanalytic writers.

Bertram Lewin (1950) has explored the oral basis of the feeling of oneness as it occurs during the early phases of manic or hypomanic episodes and in the writings of two Christian mystics. Psychoanalytic material suggests that the earliest feeding experiences of the infant involve not only the wish to devour, but also the wishes to be devoured and to sleep. The well-fed and predormescent infant apparently feels itself merged with and devoured by the breast, and later sleep comes to have this meaning. This is the matrix of subjective experience from which spring ideas of sleep, death, nirvana, immortality, heaven and the oceanic feeling. The continuing oral meaning of sleep among normal adults may be inferred from hypnagogic phenomena observed by Isakower (1938). Typically, the sleeper may feel something being pushed into his mouth (to devour) and feel that something is enveloping him (to be devoured).

In the hypomanic episodes studied by Lewin, the wishes to be devoured and to sleep may break through as deeply regressive phenomena leading, at times, to ecstatic experiences of union. In ecstasies the breast is often condensed psychologically with the superego, a deathless one with which the ego identifies so as to participate in its immortality. Along with the active, devouring fantasies there is the sense of yielding, and ultimately joining it in sleep or a sleep-like state. The hypomanic episode may follow and serve to deny and ward off these wishes.

Lewin makes an interesting contribution by treating the feelings of inexpressibility and certainty as elements of manifest content. He points out that the mystics and his patients have sometimes given excellent descriptions. The indescribability is subjective and points to the nonverbal latent content, the union at the breast which is being relived. Similarly the noetic quality reflects the realness of the breast experience:

> This experience is what one knows because it is primal, immediate, and unquestioned experience. It was not learned by seeing or hearsay, but represents the primitive narcissistic trust in subjective experience. (1950, pp. 149–50.)

Fingarette (1958) concedes that the feeling of oneness may be considered a fantasy of the primal unity, but occurring in the context of a highly integrated and flexible ego, and made possible by this flexibility. Acceptable residues of infantile fantasy and partial instinct gratification can be maintained without making experience anti-realistic. Thus the selflessness of anxiety-free experience would, through regression in the service of the ego, be deepened and colored by the selflessness of the primal fantasy. The sense of joy and power derived from conflict-free functioning would have ecstatic overtones of fantasies of primal gratification and omnipotence.

The feeling of oneness and its accompanying inexpressibility, certainty, and passivity may also occur quite unexpectedly to non-religious and apparently quite healthy people. James notes several recorded instances. One such person describes a preceding state of mind which may be characteristic.

> "My mind, deeply under the influence of the ideas, images, and emotions called up by the reading and talk, was calm and peaceful. I was in a state of quiet, almost passive enjoyment, not actually thinking, but letting ideas, images, and emotions flow of themselves, as it were, through my mind." (Quoted by James, 1902, p. 399.)

This particular writer was a Canadian psychiatrist, Dr. R. M. Bucke. His experience began with a flash of light. He felt joy and assurance, and an "intellectual illumination." This was a "clear conception in outline of the meaning and drift of the universe," a whole to which he belonged. He saw that "all is life," man is eternal and the soul immortal, and all things work together for good (Bucke, 1923).

Coming as a complete surprise, this experience made a deep impact on Bucke. He evidently spent the rest of his life documenting similar cases and evolving a theory regarding them. He interpreted these experiences as manifestations of "cosmic intelligence," a coming evolutionary stage in human intelligence beyond "simple" and "self" consciousness. His episode lasted only about a half hour, but he noted a number of effects persisting for many years after: loss of fear of death and the sense of sin, "elevated moral character," and the certainty of immortality. He observed that episodes of cosmic consciousness occur among earnest people of "strong moral nature" and usually between the ages of thirty and forty.

If we assume, as Fromm does (1960), that Bucke had satori, then his account gives us important information. His sense of immortality seems to demonstrate the effect of culture on satori. Satori has overtones of immortality, but not of the soul after death. Rather, in the Zen accounts, it seems to be the present moment which is immortal and the universe to which one belongs. His comments about age and previous character of people experiencing genuine cosmic consciousness may be important contributions to understanding satori. Finally, Bucke never experienced cosmic consciousness again. Zen students may experience full satori several times and at other times abandon self-consciousness for various purposes. This may emphasize the importance of the social context in which satori occurs. It would seem that Bucke did not know what to do with the experience he had had.

James also noted that the experience of oneness sometimes occurs under chloroform. More recently Watts (1960) and Van Dusen (1961) have compared experiences under LSD with what they understand to be the nature of satori. If we apply James' criteria, it seems clear that some LSD experiences exhibit the marks of mystical experience similar to satori. This writer feels, though, that the prior training of Zen students may lead to more thorough integration of the experience into their daily life. . . .

The inspirational phase of creative work may also be accompanied by similar experience for some artists. Anton Ehrenzweig treats this in a highly stimulating review of a book by Joanna Fields (Ehrenzweig, 1957). The problem of the artist, he says, is to maintain an ego organization flexible enough to gain periodic contact with the less differentiated images outside ordinary consciousness. These images rescue art from stultification by the clichés of surface consciousness. In the "creative surrender" the subject-object distinction may be temporarily abandoned in an oceanic fusion between inner and outer world. Since the ordinary feeling of self is abandoned in this state of consciousness, this surrender may be experienced in sado-masochistic terms as death and rebirth. The effective tone of this experience tends to vary from catastrophic fear to a blissful, almost austere stillness according to the flexibility of the ego and how easily the reversal in ego functioning may be brought about.

Ehrenzweig makes an extremely interesting comparison between the ways Schreber and Rilke dealt with the undifferentiated imagery stemming from regressed ego states. Both men apparently experienced bisexual fantasies of procreation in states of regressed consciousness which antedated distinctions between sexes and between bodily orifices. Schreber, in order to fend off the ego-disruptive effect of such imagery, imposed the precise verbal structuring of surface consciousness on his fantasy. The result was an obscene paranoid delusion. Rilke submitted to the undifferentiated state more voluntarily. And he was not compelled to articulate his fantasy fully in order to stave off disorganization, but kept its undifferentiated ambiguity in his poetry.[3]

This line of reasoning may help to explain differences in the experience of oneness as it is reported by different mystics. The "surface" consciousness is faced with the problem of rendering the experience into its own terms. In ordinary consciousness the undifferentiated experience undergoes a kind of "structural repression," the extent of which varies with the tolerance of the ego. A person raised in a culture

[3] Rilke has a rare sensitivity to this level of experience. His *Sonnets to Orpheus* celebrate and record an experience of intense inspiration. In the portions quoted below, he describes the stillness of the creative state and distinguishes it from other states.

> A tree ascending there. O pure transcension!
> O Orpheus sings! O tall tree in the ear!
> All noise suspended, yet in that suspension
> what new beginnings, beckoning, change, appear!
> (Rilke, 1949, Sonnet I, 1. 1–4)

> A god can do it. But can a man expect
> to penetrate the narrow lyre and follow?
> His sense is discord. Temples for Apollo
> are not found where two heart-ways intersect.
> For song, as taught by you, is not desire,
> not wooing of something finally attained;
> song is existence. For the god unstrained.
> But when shall we *exist*? And he require
> the earth and heavens to exist for us?
> It's more than being in love, boy, though your ringing
> voice may have flung your dumb mouth open thus:
> learn to forget those fleeting ecstasies.
> Far other is the breath of real singing.
> An aimless breath. A stirring in the god.
> A breeze.
> (*ibid.*, Sonnet III)

which recognizes a personal deity is likely to turn to such terms to explain his experience. Individuals may also differ in their need to impose structure, so that, even in cultures where "God" is available, some people will not explain their feeling of oneness in these terms. Finally, the feeling of indescribability may be a residual awareness of the artificial structuring which has been imposed.

We have come now to a very complex situation. The experience of oneness, with its attendant feelings of ineffability, certainty, and passive reception, may occur in many different situations—under the onslaught of deeply regressive oral wishes and of certain drugs, in quiet, reflective states of healthy people, and as a fairly voluntary act of some artists, Zen students and certain other mystics. Union may be experienced in terms of a highly personalized deity or of an impersonal universe. In affective tone the experience may vary from extreme ecstasy to austere stillness. It should be noted that the satori of Zen is clearly of the impersonal, non-ecstatic variety. Ecstasies, like trances, hallucinations, and similar phenomena are considered blind alleys, simply other manifestations of the egoistic mind defending itself.

Two main lines of explanation have been advanced. One is the classical psychoanalytic explanation in terms of a fantasy of the primal union of the infant with the maternal breast. One line of evidence supporting this view is the oral content given by psychoanalytic patients who have had this experience and the oral terms in which certain Christian mystics have expressed themselves. This genetic explanation refers the feelings of indescribability and certainty to the preverbal nature of the situation which is being "relived."

The other explanation is a structural one. The radical change in the state of consciousness is considered to represent, in psychoanalytic terms, a structural regression of the ego. This is more in line with Zen thinking, which construes satori as a breaking through of one state of ("conceptualizing") consciousness to another. Fingarette uses both explanations, and interprets mystic states as the function of a flexible ego, able to regress safely and voluntarily and, from a position of strength, able to entertain residues of oral fantasies without loss of reality. The Zen writers might take issue with this reference to fantasy. From a structural point of view, oneness and undifferentiation may be considered a characteristic mode of organization of a particular ego state. The Zen writers, quite consistent with this, attribute oneness to the state of mind which is no longer conceptual: an awareness of reality no longer encumbered by concepts or fantasies.

It is clear that the two explanations may easily be combined, but the genetic one offers little means for distinguishing psychologically destructive instances from constructive ones. The structural explanation is able to take into account both forms.

We turn now to the theory of regression in the service of the ego, both to consider how well satori fits this model and for the additional information which the theory may give.

## Regression in the Service of the Ego

Schafer (1958) has organized an excellent review of the psychoanalytic concept of regression in the service of the ego. Satori seems to fit into this class of psychologically adaptive regressions for several reasons. First, discussions of satori repeatedly emphasize flexibility in the use of ego functions. One thinks when the situation requires it, and the intellectual mode may be abandoned when it is unnecessary. Secondly, other types of regressions which might be less adaptive—hallucinations, trances, ecstasies—are consistently rejected as spurious by the Zen master. Thirdly, the states of mind which become possible as a result of satori are clearly used for adaptive purposes. Zen was closely involved in the training of the samurai class in traditional Japanese society (cf. Reischauer & Fairbank, 1958, pp. 547–49): more effective action, rather than monastic withdrawal, was the goal. Finally, the implied increase in energy, and decrease in conflict, inhibiting self-consciousness, and anxiety suggest that satori promotes adaptation.

Since the concept seems relevant, we may use it to increase our understanding of Zen and its training procedures. Schafer has also reviewed some general factors which tend to hamper or facilitate the ability to regress for adaptive purposes. Conditions that interfere seem to center around the unconscious significances or the regressive process. Such meanings as passivity and femininity, sinful and defiant transgression, or magically potent destructiveness have been cited.

The ability to regress is fostered by a sense of self able to tolerate momentary blurring of boundaries, a well-developed set of affect signals to guard against getting too close to unassimilable contents, relative mastery of early traumata, moderateness of superego pressures, adequate trust and mutuality in relationships, personal and effective communication to other people, and self-awareness.

We might expect the hampering conditions to become issues in the period of Zen training which precedes satori. It is noteworthy that the Zen literature itself focuses mainly on issues involving the sense of self and the techniques used to defend it.

The sequence of Zen training might easily be conceptualized as a series of "regressed" states, each of which develops functions on which succeeding states must depend. For example, the first phase eventually deepens to a kind of relaxed drowsiness in which primary-process derivatives appear. The ability to deal with them in an accepting fashion enables the student to get through to the next phase in which much more "regressed" elements are apparent. Feelings of omnipotence appear to color this stage of "mirror-like" detachment. The nonstriving quality of this state is apparently its chief safeguard against maladaptive reactions, even though further impulse derivatives are probably emerging. This non-striving is probably a lesson of the previous phase. Satori, in turn, grows out of the second phase, and is probably based on certain safeguards which were developed there. . . .

## REFERENCES

BUCKE, R. M. *Cosmic Consciousness: A Study in the Evolution of the Human Mind*, 4th ed. (New York: E. P. Dutton & Co., 1923).

CHANG CHEN-CHI, *The Practice of Zen* (New York: Harper, 1959).

EHRENZWEIG, A. "The Creative Surrender: A comment on 'Joanna Field's' book, *An Experiment in Leisure,*" *American Imago, 14,* 193–210, 1957.

FREUD, S. *Civilization and Its Discontents,* 1930 (London: Hogarth Press, 1955).

FROMM, E., SUZUKI, D. T., and DE MARTINO, R. *Zen Buddhism and Psychoanalysis* (New York: Harper, 1960).

HERRIGEL, E., *Zen in the Art of Archery* (New York: Pantheon, 1956).

——, *The Method of Zen* (New York: Pantheon, 1960).

ISAKOWER, O. "A Contribution to the Pathopsychology of Phenomena Associated with Falling Asleep," *International Journal of Psychoanalysis, 19,* 331–45, 1938.

JAMES, W. *The Varieties of Religious Experience,* 1902 (New York: Longmans, Green, 1928).

KONDO, A. "Intuition in Zen Buddhism," *American Journal of Psychoanalysis, 12,* 10–14, 1952.

——, "Morita Therapy: A Japanese Therapy for Neurosis," *American Journal of Psychoanalysis, 13,* 31–37, 1953.

——, "Zen in Psychotherapy: The Virtue of Sitting," *Chicago Review, 12:2,* 57–64, 1958.

LEWIN, B. D. *The Psychoanalysis of Elation* (New York: W. W. Norton, 1950).

LUK, C. *Ch'an and Zen Teaching* (London: Rider, 1960).

REISCHAUER, E. O. and FAIRBANK, J. K. *East Asia: The Great Tradition* (Boston: Houghton-Mifflin, 1958).

SATO, K. "Psychotherapeutic Implications of Zen," *Psychologia, 1,* 213–18, 1958.

——, "How to Get Zen Enlightenment: On Master Ighiguru's Five Days Intensive Course for Its Attainment," *Psychologia, 2,* 107–18, 1959.

SCHACHTEL, E. G. *Metamorphosis* (New York: Basic Books, 1959).

SCHAFER, R. "Regression in the Service of the Ego: The Relevance of a Psychoanalytic Concept for Personality Assessment," in G. Lindzey (ed.), *Assessment of Human Motives* (New York: Rinehart, 1958).

STERBA, R. "The Fate of the Ego in Analytic Therapy," *International Journal of Psychoanalysis, 11,* 12–23, 1930.

SUZUKI, D. T. *Living by Zen* (Tokyo: Sanseido Press, 1949 [a]).

——, *The Zen Doctrine of No-Mind* (London: Rider & Co., 1949 [b]).

——, *Zen Buddhism* (Garden City: Doubleday & Co., 1956).

VAN DUSEN, W. "LSD and the Enlightenment of Zen," *Psychologia, 4,* 11–16, 1961.

WATTS, A. *This Is It, and Other Essays on Zen and Spiritual Experience* (New York: Pantheon, 1960).

# THE PSYCHOLOGY OF
# MYSTICISM

### U. A. ASRANI

## Mysticism and Religion

Mysticism has been called the vital core of religion, its personal or subjective form. It has also been described as religion minus its ritual and its theology. Even the ethical systems developed by religion do not fall within the scope of mysticism so long as they signify merely compliance with the moral codes imposed by the Scriptures, or by society. Ethics becomes a facet of the mystical life only when it is inspired by an inner urge toward the mystical transformation or transcendence of personality.

Religion itself cannot be justifiably defined in relation to any particular dogma, such as monotheism, pantheism, or atheism. Hence many writers prefer to define the religious attitude either through reference to some transcendental Being, Power or Substratum, or to the basic human needs of security and protection from fear. Thus among many aboriginal tribes, religion is a symbolic projection of social cohesion and function. Mysticism, however, which is the personal aspect of religion par excellence, appears to be just as universal a human need—one which has resulted in a method of dispelling frustration, fear and mental conflict, and of gaining peace, equanimity and joy. That is why it has appeared in all ages and among all peoples, and why there is a general similarity in the statements of all mystics, no matter what the cultural background. However, it should be noted that any purely transcendental definition of religion tends to minimize

From *Main Currents in Modern Thought*, Vol. 25, No. 3, January–February 1969. Reprinted by permission.

the role of mystical experience, and even excludes such prominent schools as the Buddhist and the Jain. Even Patanjali's Ashtanga Yoga, a widely revered method, gives a very subordinate position to Ishwara, or a personal God.

Still, if we must beware, in the interests of mysticism, of too lofty a definition of religion, so must we also be wary of one that is too broad, such, for example, as Bertrand Russell's claim that any creed which is dogmatically held is religion. A definition of this kind could easily include nationalism, fascism or communism. Embracing an ideology with fervor or even with self-denying passion is still not religion. It is apparent that the Communist definition is based on economic and political theory, without reference to the overpowering and persistent human need which has made religion, and the mystical tradition, survive throughout history, in spite of rationalism, bigotry, scientific discovery, or the influence of logical positivism.

Therefore, although there are many other definitions of mysticism which may be offered, we prefer something of this kind: Mysticism is an inward search for unity, whereby the narrow bonds of egotism are dissolved.

After this brief introduction, we should like to describe some of the more famous techniques which have been practiced with success in the East for many centuries.

## Jnana Yoga

In his book *Personality,* Gardner Murphy writes that a psychotic uses three types of relatively tolerable defense against frustration, in addition to the unhealthy response of displaced aggression. These three means are: 1. making a mental picture of oneself, as superior to the frustrating circumstances; 2. making a mental picture of the world so that it no longer poses any threat; 3. making such a picture of the relation between the world and the self as would give confidence that the self can conquer the threat of the world. Murphy also states that a "normal" person uses similar defenses, but in a subtler form (1). Now, even a slight acquaintance with the three principal maxims of Vedanta philosophy, on which

Jnana Yoga is based, reveals that they present the votary with all three means to escape the frustrations of life. These three tenets are: 1. Brahman, the Infinite Substratum of the universe, is real; 2. the world is unreal; 3. the Jiva (the self) is identical with Brahman. These principles are logically supported by the Vedanta philosophy, which has been held in time-honored respect in India. Thus, Jnana can be regarded as a method of positive autosuggestion, if nothing more. Faced with the seemingly haphazard and inequitable circumstances of human existence, the practitioner of Jnana Yoga renames the world and life therein as a Sport (*Lila*) of the Infinite Brahman, and thus accepts life's losses as well as its gains in a spirit of sportsmanship. Hence the method of Jnana Yoga provides a mechanism for what psychologists call "identification" or "rationalization."

The Nirvikalpa Samadhi, or the relaxation of the process of thinking-feeling, as well as of relinquishing the ego,* convinces the student of Jnana Yoga that the world—or at least our world-image, which is colored by our emotion—can be rolled up like a map. What is more, the highly enjoyable, tensionless state of mind which is experienced in Samadhi and which persists for some time thereafter, induces a state of equanimity which is resistant to tensions and conflicts. The result may be that the practitioner retires to live a life of quietude (which some might call escapism), or, if he is temperamentally inclined toward an activist role, he may succeed in conjoining a state of inner peace with a busy and active life. He then lives what the Christians call a "unitive life," and the Hindus refer to as a state of Jivana Mukta—liberated in life. Such a life is both realized and thoroughly realistic; it has no need for any of the mechanisms of philosophic projection or rationalization, for it has achieved perfect nonattachment, freedom from egotism, and complete integration.

* Sankara's explanation of the technique of Jnana Yoga Sadhana implies that the Samadhi in question is relaxation (2).

## Buddhist Mysticism and Ashtanga Yoga

Buddhist methods utilize Mindfulness or Attentiveness—Samyaka Smritti, the seventh step of the Eightfold Path (3) (4). In this step, every item of life is viewed attentively, but as an unconcerned witness; it is a preparation for the eighth step of meditation or Jnana. Buddhism uses this technique of attentiveness in place of the autosuggestion of Vedantic metaphysics, or the mechanisms of identification which Jnana Yoga adopts. But it should be noted that this idea of the unconcerned witness is itself based on the Samkhya philosophy, which is also the philosophy of Patanjali's Ashtanga Yoga, and its final step of Viveka Khyati. The concept involves a belief that the self—the Purusha—is untainted by any changes in nature, including the mind (5)(6)(7).

Hartman first pointed out that in building up motor and perceptional patterns in infancy, attention energies are required. With continued practice, these patterns become automatic. Gill and Brenman have suggested that we should de-automatize by reinvesting actions and percepts with attention (8). This is exactly what the Buddhist Samyaka Smritti does. Such a deautomatization prepares the ground for a new type of consciousness, different from that to which we are accustomed; it gives, in a sense, access to the consciousness of a child in the midst of adult life.

Buddhism has its stages of Jnana; the Ashtanga Yoga has its Asamprajnat Samadhi state, which is comatose, yet conscious. These states may be different in depth and reached by differing mechanisms, but they have the same psychological effects on the mind of the practitioner. The Buddhist state of Shunya (Voidness) may or may not be akin to the Nirvikalpa Samadhi of Jnana Yoga, for the mystical practices which were associated with the Ashtanga Yoga were also known in Buddhist circles.

Buddhism recognizes three Lokas or spheres of consciousness of life: First, Kama Loka, which is the ordinary sphere of desires; second, the Rupavacara Chitta or realm of form (corresponding to the Savikalpa Samadhi of Jnana Yoga), in which there are five stages. The last of these stages is characterized by Concentration and Indifference (Upakkha), and leads to the third Loka, the Arupavacara Chitta, or formless sphere. There are four stages in this: "Dwelling on Infinity of Space," "Dwelling on Infinity of Consciousness," "Dwelling on Nothingness (Shunya)," and finally, a state of the subtlest perception. Thus, instead of the consciousness expanding philosophy of the Vedanta used by Jnana Yoga, the Buddhist mysticism uses "cosmic consciousness" as such—the infinity of space, the infinity of consciousness—in order to reach the stage of Shunya (9).

In Buddhist mysticism we also find a Summit State, called that of an Arahat or Boddhisattwa (10) which corresponds with the Jnana Yogic Sahaj, Jivana Mukta, or Sthita Prjna State. Patanjali's *Yoga Sutras* likewise mention a Dharma Megha Samadhi (11), which appears to be like the Sahaj Samadhi or the Sahaj Awastha of the Jnana Yoga, that is, again the same Jivana Mukta state. Attentiveness, the seventh step of the Buddhist path, also prepares the Buddhist votary for concentrated attention to the immediate work in hand, every moment of the day, and this is a prominent feature of this same Jivana Mukta state.

In Jnana Yoga, the individual self is regarded as identical with Brahman, hence, as a thing-in-itself, it is unreal. According to the Buddhist An-Atta Doctrine (12), the individual self does not exist at all; it is only a moving stream of momentary experiences. In Samkhya and Yoga, the individual self is the Purusha—the unconcerned witness of nature or the world (prakritti). In all these systems, therefore, an axe is laid at the root of egotism, which indicates the self as being related to the world. In all, equally, attachment to the world and its things is diminished, since it is held to be maya (illusory or unreal), or merely a sequence of transitory states, or a materiality (prakritti) which does not touch the self (Purusha).

The Ashtanga Yoga holds that without a physiological preparation, the purification of mental currents is not possible to achieve fully. Hence it prescribes, in the first part of its discipline (in the same way that Hatha Yoga does) some very unusual and difficult poses (Asanas) and breathing exercises (pranayamas). The Hatha Yoga adds to them its Mudras, Bandhas, etc. These—particularly the easier and less risky exercises—have been utilized to some extent by the Buddhist, Jain and Jnana Yoga systems also. But very probably they did not desire to give prominence to the body, lest body consciousness or egotism, and the miraculous powers which some of the Ashtanga and Hatha Yogic methods yield, may retard the development of unselfishness or egolessness, the central object of mysticism. What is more, they probably always regarded the body-mind to be one unit, which can be approached at either end or both simultaneously; they have been alert to prevent the practice of mysticism from becoming mechanical or to rely solely upon physiological means.

Recent research at Lonavla in India (13) indicates that Asanas produce a rhythm in the neuro-muscular mechanism, thus improving muscle tone with which our emotions and even perceptions are related. Asanas also correct the "Postural Substrate," of which our muscular, visceral and glandular systems are an integral part. Similarly, some Mudras (hand gestures) give conscious control over semivoluntary muscles; others, along with Bandhas, benefit the glandular system. Pranayamas are widely known to decrease the domination of egotistic thought, and to give emotional stability.

Jnana Yogis, on the other hand, assert that most of our physiological troubles are due to faulty mental attitudes, a point of view to some extent substantiated by psychosomatic medicine. The nature of the human mind is complex, and while mental states are affected by body chemistry and so on, the problem of egotism, which is a unique development of human personality, is much more subtle. A healthy body is not enough to produce a state of mental health. The techniques we have been describing are all designed, in their various ways, to effect a transformation in inner attitudes from a selfish egocentrism to a benign and loving universality. The final goal is in every case the same.

## Bhakti Yoga, Christian Mysticism, Sufism

In other schools of mysticism, importance is laid upon the love of God (or, as in the case of Sufism, to the Immanent Haq). Self-surrender to this love of God reaches such a pitch as to produce ecstasies and visions, and these are so rapturous and so convincing that they swallow up all worldly loves and attachments. However powerful, this experience is but preliminary in the search for true enlightenment. God is substituted for worldly attachment, but it is quite possible that a sect, a prophet, a guru, or even a psychotherapist could serve as surrogate for God. Devotional mysticism is characterized by fervent and intense emotion rather than by a calm and dispassionate mind; there are obvious dangers of fanaticism if the devotee retains a residue of opinion in the midst of his self-surrender.

However, a number of the Bhakti or devotional schools also recognize a higher state of realization akin to the Jivana Mukta stage (14). The highest stage of Bhakti, "Atma Nivedana," signifies complete merging in, or identity with, God. Some Bhaktas like Kabir, as well as some of the Christian mystics and Sufis, have shown by their writings that they have passed beyond the stage of attachment to God, beyond the concept of separateness to that of complete unity with God and so with all. The Haquiquat stage of the Sufis has been interpreted as embodying the Jivana Mukta type of unitive life.

The mystical disciplines of the emotional kind yield a trance-like state (Bhava Samadhi) in which, after concentration on the personal God and his vision (Sa-Vikalpa Samadhi), a state of complete merging, quiet or silence ultimately supervenes. This last stage of their Samadhi amounts, like the Nirvikalpa Samadhi of the Jnana Yogis, to a complete relaxation of thoughts and emotions, and a relinquishment of the ego.

The effectiveness of non-analytic and non-intellectual concentration or attentiveness has been verified by A. J. Deikman of the Austin Riggs Center of Psychological Research in

Stockbridge, Massachusetts. A group of adults, well educated and intelligent professionals, were asked to concentrate on a vase. Many of them reported a pleasurable and rewarding experience, which even resulted in a sort of personal attachment to the vase. One person felt as if his body was nothing, and that the vase was radiating heat. Another, a lady, passed for a few moments into a complete silence, wherein she was wholly unconscious of purposely produced disturbing sound (15). This was concentration on a mere vase; one might easily imagine that if the object had been a picture of Jesus, and she a devout Christian, she might well have had the kind of religious vision which so many Christian mystics have reported. It is obvious that suggestion and expectation exert a powerful influence on the mind. All that we have so far been able to discover about mystical states seems to indicate that all such phenomena as ecstasies, visions, celestial voices, and so on, are products of changes of consciousness.

## Karma Yoga

Another kind of yoga is based on the hypothesis that the Jivana Mukta state is one of mental balance or equipoise. If this is so, it follows that it can be acquired by practice alone, i.e., through normal life activities, called Karma in India. Just as various acts of physical and mechanical balance—cycling, swimming, dancing, or the Asanas of Hatha Yoga like the Mayur Asana (horizontal peacock pose)—can be learned by practice, so also mental equipoise can be similarly acquired. This yoga holds that no metaphysical scaffolding is essential beyond the surrender of the fruits of one's action to God (16). Neither is the achievement of Samadhi necessary; the joy of equipoised living is a sufficient incentive. The practice of unselfishness or non-attachment is the technique; whether it succeeds by itself alone, without any support from Bhakti, Jnana or Ashtanga methods, is a matter which may be experimentally tested. Most Indian mystics combine Karma Yoga with other disciplines.

The reverse of Karma Yoga is Quietism. The Karma Yogi contends that the goal of all mystical discipline is not a constant enjoyment of visions, ecstasies or Samadhis; it is a state of unruffled equipoise based on selflessness or non-attachment. Quietism or escapism discloses an attachment to mystical experience itself, hence it retains elements of the personal. Besides, no purification of the mind is possible without first exposing that which lies hidden in the unconscious layers of the psyche. Active life, with its varied situations, gives the votary excellent opportunities for observing the causes of inner conflict and so helps him to achieve that tensionless, conflictless state which is his goal. Quietism provides no such opportunities. He who would withdraw from the world must prove that he has an alternative method of equal utility for exploring the sources of his own weaknesses. He must also indicate the utility of his constant absorption in mystical union, on personal, social or evolutionary grounds. For it must be pointed out that the *Gandapadya, Ashtavakra Gita* and the *Yoga Vasistha,* as well as the *Bhavavad Gita,* have stated positively that continuous absorption in Samadhi is not the goal.

## Other Forms of Yoga

The repetition of sacred syllables, known as Mantra or Shabda Yoga, is a method in use in many schools, and is especially emphasized in Northern Buddhism. A mantra (which means literally a "tool for thinking") is a blending of sound, rhythm and idea clothed in devotion-inspiring symbol; as such it is an undoubted aid in meditation. The sacred word OM, (pranava) whose power and universality have been recognized since the most ancient times, might be called the quintessence of all mantras, the seed or germ syllable: "This imperishable sound is the whole of this visible universe. . . . What has become, what is becoming, what will become—verily, all of this is the sound OM. And what is beyond these three states of the world of time—that too, verily, is the sound OM." (*Mandukya Upanishad,* 1.)

It should be emphasized that the value of mantras as a psychological tool depends upon the ability of the practitioner to use them as a means of liberation. Empty, mechanical repetition is no more effective than is the use of any other device without proper knowledge and fully attentive awareness. It is said that the shabda or sound of the mantra is not a physical sound but a spiritual one, which cannot be uttered by the mouth but by the mind. The effectiveness of mantras in yoga, therefore, depends upon the ability of the user to become aware of their meaning and methods of operation. During the course of the spiritual venture inward, the emphasis shifts from the outer world to the inner. It is said that the skillful practitioner of yoga can make the states of consciousness come and go according to his will.

Tantric Yoga, being based upon the Tantric idea that man, in general, must rise through and by means of nature, not by the rejection of nature, does not exclude the body in its method. "The Sadhaka [Tantric student]," writes Sir John Woodroffe, "is taught not to think that we are one with the Divine in Liberation only, but here and now, in every act we do." (17) Tantric Yoga is particularly concerned with the awakening and control of the various psychophysical centers in the body, known as chakras (wheels). According to Western conceptions, the brain is the exclusive seat of consciousness, but yogic experience shows that brain-consciousness is only one among a number of forms of consciousness which can be localized or centered in various parts of the body. The chakras are the centers of consciousness and of psychic energies. Tantric Yoga, which has perhaps been more misunderstood than any other form of yoga, is designed to give conscious knowledge of all the psychophysical centers available to man, and bring them under his control.

Kundalini Yoga, which is part of the Tantric system, refers to those practices which are specifically directed to the arousal of the Kundalini (Serpent Power) in the human body and to the purification of the elements of the body which takes place upon that event. This yoga is mentioned in the Yoga-Upanishads which refer to the centers or chakras, and also in some of the Puranas. Other references are to be found in the works of some of the Sufi fraternities, and in treatises on Hatha Yoga. However, this form of yoga is particularly associated with the Tantras or Agamas. The awakening of

Kundalini, which is said to be "sleeping" because at rest in the Muladhara (root) Chakra in ordinary man, is achieved by will power, with the aid of the most rigorously controlled practices of bodily purification, certain Asanas and Mudras. The effect of the rousing of this force is said to exalt the physical consciousness through the ascending planes, finally to ultimate union with the Supreme Self, or Kaivalya Mukti.

## The Jivana Mukti State

We have mentioned this state several times, in referring to the aims and achievements of the various types of yoga; it has also been called by various other names, such as the Sahaj State, or the Sthita Prajna, or the Arahat, Vita Raga or Haquiquat State, or the Unitive Life. We should now like to specify some of the characteristics of this state, as they have been described by many practitioners of the different forms of yoga.

This state of waking consciousness is one in which thinking and action are not disjointed. When thinking is necessarily involved in action, concentration and attentiveness follow everything undertaken, including even such physiological activities as eating and drinking. But when thinking is not necessary for action, the mind is relaxed or disengaged, and lapses into a condition of harmony and equipoise. The man begins to live in the living present, and to be free of wishful thinking, brooding over the past or worrying about the future. It is a state characterized by self-confidence and self-reliance in action, but non-attachment and relaxation after work is over; most particularly, there is no lingering possessiveness about the results of one's work.

In addition, there is freedom from anxiety and other mental tensions—a freedom which extends even to a loss of philosophical inquisitiveness, which some might regard as a deprivation! Yet metaphysical problems seem to dissolve into a larger perspective, and the mind is not impelled to speculation. The relinquishment of ego values, of which we have already spoken, makes the appreciation of other values almost spontaneous, and the fresh eye with which the world is viewed opens up whole ranges of aesthetic appreciation hitherto unknown.

In other words, the Jivana Mukta state produces an inner environment wherein the integration of personality can take place. There results a natural, warm, loving and spontaneous attitude of openness to life and to others, without fear or condemnation.

## Conclusions

It will be noted that we have been concentrating upon the psychological results of the various methods of achieving mystical experience prescribed by different forms of yoga, without reference to their religious or spiritual implications. Heretofore, most Western psychologists and psychiatrists have tended to dismiss the content of mysticism as hallucinatory and neurotic, probably because most accounts tended to individual interpretations couched in non-scientific language, and imbued with an atmosphere of belief rather than of objective inquiry. For this reason, much significant and important material has been disregarded, and a major technique for the reconstruction of personality has been ignored. However, there are now many third-force or death psychologists who are beginning to respect the human potential which is being revealed through modern psychotherapy, and who are no longer so closed to the immense amount of data which has been accumulated by Indian students over the past hundreds of years. Even by modern scientific standards, much of this material is exceedingly well-documented, and deserves objective and unprejudiced evaluation.

However, it must be admitted that the psychological aspects of mysticism which we have been discussing are not the only results of the practice, and some of these results are difficult for Westerners to accept. For example, many yogis are reputed to possess paranormal powers of various kinds. An impartial inquiry by reputable parapsychologists on a larger scale than has so far been attempted would place these phenomena in proper perspective. It should be said at once, however, that all genuine yogis minimize such paranormal powers, dismissing them as a mere byproduct or adjunct of the heightened consciousness which is the aim of their search. Such powers or siddhis result from increasing control over the mechanisms of consciousness; if they are sought for themselves their practice is often fraught with serious dangers.

Then there is the fact that many yogis of high attainment become famous seers and gurus, accepting pupils and giving instruction of a philosophical or metaphysical nature. Almost every mystic who has experienced the depths of peace and joy encountered in Samadhi has desired that other human beings should similarly attain; the result has been the large literature of mysticism which has sought in various ways to describe the indescribable and ineffable. The view of reality which the mystic has gained is for him overpowering, bearing its own witness, and therefore he frequently is impelled to teach or talk about it. However, the philosophical utterances which result are undoubtedly colored by the inherited or acquired views of his culture, and must be judged upon their intrinsic merits, not upon their method of revelation. Some mystical schools are pantheistic, some are theistic, some are atheistic; some believe in reincarnation, others in a final resurrection. It is obvious that whatever degree of reality is encountered in the mystical experience, the results must filter through ordinary brain-consciousness, if they are to have application in daily life and human affairs. Again, it is important that the significant facts be distinguished from the halo of belief and emotion with which devotees surround them.

One of the tasks of importance to be undertaken in this whole area is the development of a theory which will be acceptable to modern science. This has proven a major stumbling block to the general acceptance of the findings of parapsychological research, and the data of yoga or mysticism are even more difficult to fit into existing physical theory. The proposals of Gardner Murphy and others that a psychological field theory could account for the presence of energies different from those with which we are most familiar is certainly worthy of serious attention. The operation of such energies in the growth and development of living creatures is now widely documented. What is more, even in atomic physics, recent advances indicate that language and logic, with their rigid analytical categories, are incapable of expressing the entire field of experimentally observed facts. These are indications within modern science itself that analytic techniques are not capable of dealing with some of the subtler phenomena of nature, much less with the consciousness of man. Too much reliance upon language and logic in our efforts to understand reality may land us in a set of negative assertions, like the "Neti-Neti" of the Upanishads. Reality is, and will continue to be, larger than life; if we foolishly believe we can capture it in the cages of language and logic—no matter how skillfully we construct our technical devices—we are doomed to disappointment.

A spirit of open inquiry and search for truth, in the context of discovery and innovation which characterize the last decades of the 20th century, should allow us to recognize the benefits which the practice of mysticism is able to confer. Now, more than at any time in history, men need to find ways to overcome the divisive and contumacious mental attitudes indicative of an ego-centered life. If ample evidence suggests that the transforming experience of the Jivana Mukti state provides a viable method for achieving inner peace and unity, surely the method deserves the attention of thoughtful men and women.

REFERENCES

1. MURPHY, GARDNER, *Personality*, pp. 401, 584.
2. SANKARA, *Laghu Vakya Vritti*, Verses 5, 9–17.
3. LOUNSBERY, G. C., *Buddhist Meditations in the Southern School*, pp. 19–22.
4. GRIMM, GEORGE, *The Doctrine of the Buddha*.
5. CONZE, E., *Buddhistic Thought in India*, p. 9.
6. HUMPHREYS, C., *The Way of Action*, p. 29.
7. KAVIRAJ, PT. GOPINATH, *Kalyan Yoga Number*, pp. 54–56.
8. BUCKE, R. M., Mem. Society, *Newsletter*, April 1967, p. 25.
9. KASHYABA, BIKKHU J., *Abhidhamma Philosophy*, pp. 28–34.
10. DAYAL, HAR, *Buddhist Doctrine in Buddhist Sans. Literature*, pp. 9–18.
11. PATANJALI, *Yoga Sutras*, IV, 28.
12. MUKERJI, R., *The Theory and Art of Mysticism*, pp. 477, 487.

13. KUVALAYANANDA and VINEKAR, *Yogic Therapy.*
14. DAS GUPTA, S. N., *History of Indian Philosophy,* Vol. IV, pp. 88, 418, 428, 445.
15. *Journal of Nerv. and Ment. Dis.,* Vol: 1364, 1963.
16. *The Bhagavad Gita.*
17. WOODROFFE, *Shakti and Shakta,* 3d ed., Madras, p. 587.

# THE ECSTASY OF BREAKING-THROUGH IN THE EXPERIENCE OF MEDITATION

## LAMA ANAGARIKA GOVINDA

Just as the *Ḍākinīs* represent the inspirational impulses of consciousness, leading to knowledge and understanding, so the *Herukas* (the male qualities of the Buddha-nature) represent the active aspect of *karuṇā,* of unlimited compassion, in the ecstatic act of breaking through the confines of egohood to the universal state of the all-comprising essentiality. In this aspect all hindrances are annihilated: the own illusory "I" as well as all ideas of selfhood and separateness—in short, all intellectual thought and ratiocination. Intuitive knowledge and spontaneous feeling merge here into an inseparable unity— as inseparable as the union of *Ḍākinī* and *Heruka* in the aspect of *yab-yum,* which only emphasizes in visible form, what is present in every process of enlightenment and in each symbol of Buddhahood, even though it may be put into the form of the male aspect only.

. . . Just as every new discovery of science not only contributes to the wealth of data and the widening of our field of knowledge, but leads to further discoveries and to a reappraisal of former data, in the same way each new experience of meditation opens new horizons and creates new methods of practice and realization. The human mind cannot stop at any point on its way towards knowledge. Standstill

From *The Foundations of Tibetan Mysticism*, by Lama Anagarika Govinda, 1960. Reprinted by permission of Rider & Co., London.

means death, rigidity and decay. This is the law of all life and of all consciousness. It is the law of the spirit, from which life and consciousness flow.

Just as in mathematical thought each dimension necessarily demands another, higher one, until we are forced to the conclusion that there must be an infinite series of dimensions—in the same way each further extension of our spiritual horizon hints at new, undreamed of dimensions of consciousness.

The fact that each experience points beyond itself and can therefore not be defined or limited as something that exists in itself, but only in relationship to other experiences; this fact is circumscribed in the concept of *"śūnyatā,"* the emptiness of all determinations, the non-absoluteness, the infinite relationship of all experience. And this "super-relativity" contains at the same time the unifying element of a living universe, because infinite relationship becomes all-relationship and therewith a metaphysical magnitude, which can neither be described as "being" nor as "non-being," neither as movement nor as non-movement.

Here we have reached the boundary of thought, the end of all that is thinkable and conceivable. Like movement, which in its ultimate extreme, in its highest form, cannot be distinguished from perfect rest and immobility, thus relativity in the highest sense of universal relationship is indistinguishable from the "absolute." "The eternally constant can only be represented in the changeable; the eternally changeable only in the constant, the whole, the present moment." (Novalis.)

For this reason *śūnyatā* and *iathatā* (suchness) are identical in their nature. The former characterizes the negative, the latter the positive side of the same reality. The realization of the former starts from the experience of transitoriness, momentariness, temporal and spatial relativity—the latter from the experience of timelessness, of completeness, of the whole, the absolute. This, however, does not mean that *śūnyatā* exhausts itself in the quality of relativity, nor that *tathatā* is to be identified with the absolute. We use these expressions only as a bridge leading from the Western to the Eastern, or, more correctly, from the logical-philosophical to the intuitive-metaphysical mode of thinking.

D. T. Suzuki is therefore right when he denounces the intellectual shallowness which tries to equate the modern conception of relativity with that of *śūnyatā* on purely logical grounds. "Emptiness is the result of an intuition and not the outcome of reasoning. The idea of Emptiness grows out of experience, and in order to give it a logical foundation the premise is found in relativity. But, speaking strictly logically, there is a gap between relativity and Emptiness. Relativity does not make us jump over the gap; as long as we stay with relativity we are within a circle; to realize that we are in a circle and that therefore we must get out of it in order to see its entire aspect presupposes our once having gone beyond it.[1]

This leap over the chasm, which yawns between our intellectual surface-consciousness and the intuitive supra-personal depth-consciousness, is represented in the ecstatic dance of the "blood-drinking deities," embraced by *Ḍākinīs*. The inspirational impulse of the *Ḍākinīs* drives us from the protected, but narrowly fenced circle of our illusory personality and our habitual thought, until we burst the boundaries of this circle and of our egohood in the ecstatic thrust towards the realization of totality. In this ecstatic thrust, all bonds, all worldly fetters, all prejudices and illusions are destroyed, all conventional concepts are swept away, all craving and clinging is cut off at the root, past and future are extinguished, the power of *karma* is broken, and the Great Void is experienced as the eternal present and ultimate Reality and Suchness. . . .

## *Māyā* as the Creative Principle and the Dimensions of Consciousness

We are not concerned here with a subjective idealism, based on logical speculations, concepts and categories, but with a doctrine which is founded upon the reality of the mind and its deepest experiences.

[1] Suzuki, D. T. *Essays in Zen Buddhism,* Vol. III (London: Rider & Co., 1953), p. 241.

If we call *māyā* a reality of a lower degree, we do this because illusion rests on the wrong interpretation of a partial aspect of reality. Compared with the highest or "absolute" reality, all forms, in which this reality appears to us, are illusory, because they are only partial aspects, and as such incomplete, torn out of their organic connections and deprived of their universal relationship. The only reality, which we could call "absolute," is that of the all-embracing whole. Each partial aspect must therefore constitute a lesser degree of reality—the less universal, the more illusory and impermanent.

To a point-like consciousness the continuity of a line is inconceivable. For such a consciousness there exists only a continual and apparently unrelated origination and passing-away of points.

To a linear consciousness—we could call it a one-dimensional consciousness, in contrast to the non-dimensional point-like consciousness—the continuity of a plane would be inconceivable, because it can only move in one direction and only comprehend a linear relationship of points following each other.

To a two-dimensional consciousness the continuity of a plane, i.e., the simultaneous existence of points, straight lines, curves, and designs of all kinds are conceivable, but not the spatial relationship of planes, as they form for instance the surface of a cube.

In three-dimensional space-consciousness, however, the relationship of several planes is co-ordinated to form the concept of a body, in which the simultaneous existence of different planes, lines and points can be conceived and grasped in their totality.

Thus the consciousness of a higher dimension consists in the co-ordinated and simultaneous perception of several systems of relationship or directions of movement, in a wider, more comprehensive unity, without destroying the individual characteristics of the integrated lower dimensions. The reality of a lower dimension is therefore not annihilated by a higher one, but only "relativized" or put into another perspective of values.

If we perceive and co-ordinate the different phases in the

movement of a point proceeding in one direction, we arrive at the perception of a straight line.

If we perceive and co-ordinate the different phases in the movement of a straight line, traveling in a direction not yet contained in it, we arrive at the conception of a plane.

If we perceive and co-ordinate the different phases in the movement of a plane, in a direction not yet contained in its dimension, we arrive at the perception of a body.

If we perceive and co-ordinate the different phases in the movement of a body, we arrive at the perception and understanding of its nature, i.e., we become conscious of its inherent laws and mode of existence.

If we perceive and co-ordinate organically the inner movement (growth, development; emotional, mental, and spiritual movement, etc.) of a conscious being, we become aware of its individuality, its psychic character.

If we perceive the manifold forms of existence, through which an individual has to pass, and observe how these forms arise, according to various conditions, and depending on a multitude of inherent factors, we arrive at the perception and understanding of the law of action and re-action, the law of *karma*.

If we observe the various phases of a karmic chain reaction in their relationship to other sequences of karmic action and reaction, as this is said to have been observed by the Buddha, we become conscious of a supra-individual karmic interrelatedness, comprising nations, races, civilizations, humanity, planets, solar systems and finally the whole universe. In short, we arrive at the perception of a cosmic world order, an infinite mutual relationship of all things, beings and events, until we finally realize the universality of consciousness in the *Dharmakāya*, when attaining Enlightenment.

Seen from the consciousness of the *Dharmakāya*, all separate forms of appearance are *māyā*. *Māyā* in the deepest sense, however, is reality in its creative aspect, or the creative aspect of reality. Thus *māyā* becomes the *cause* of illusion, but it is not illusion itself, as long as it is seen as a whole, in its continuity, its creative function, or as infinite power of transformation and universal relationship.

As soon, however, as we stop at any of its creations and try to limit it to a state of "being" or self-confined existence, we fall a prey to illusion, by taking the effect for the cause, the shadow for the substance, the partial aspect for ultimate reality, the momentary for something that exists in itself.

It is the power of *māyā* which produces the illusory forms of appearance of our mundane reality. *Māyā* itself, however, is not illusion. He who masters this power, has got the tool of liberation in his hand, the magic power of *yoga*, the power of creation, transformation and reintegration.

"The power of our inner vision produces in Yoga forms and worlds, which, while we become aware of them, can fill us with such a feeling of incredible reality, that compared with it, the reality-content of our sensuous and mental everyday world fades away and evaporates. Here we experience (as in the enjoyment of love) something that means nothing to our thought and that yet is true; that reality has degrees or steps. That the way of the Divine outwardly and inwardly, towards fullness of form and towards inner awareness, is graded, and that Yoga is the power to ascend and to descend these steps. . . ."[2]

Those who think that form is unimportant, will miss the spirit as well, while those who cling to form lose the very spirit which they tried to preserve. Form and movement are the secret of life and the key to immortality. Those who only see the transitoriness of things and reject the world because of its transitory character, see only the change on the surface of things, but have not yet discovered that the form of change, the manner in which change takes place, reveals the spirit that inspires all form, the reality that informs all phenomena. With our physical eye we see only change. Only our spiritual eye is capable of seeing stability in transformation. Transformation is the *form* in which the spirit moves: it is life itself. Whenever material form cannot follow the movement of the spirit, decay appears. Death is the protest of the spirit against the unwillingness of the formed to accept transformation: the protest against stagnation.

---

[2] Zimmer, Heinrich, *Ewiges Indien* (Zurich: Orell Füssli Verlag, 1930), p. 151.

In the *Prajñāpāramitā-Sūtra* all phenomena are regarded as being *śūnyatā* according to their true nature—and *śūnyatā* as not being different from form, feeling, perception, mental formations and consciousness; i.e., *śūnyatā* is here equated with *māyā*. And just as *śūnyatā* is not only emptiness from all designations of a limited self-nature, but also an expression of ultimate reality, in the same way *māyā* is not only the negative, the veiling, the phenomenal form, but also the dynamic principle, which produces all forms of appearance and which never reveals itself in the single, completed end-product, but only in the process of becoming, in the living flow, in infinite movement.

*Māyā*, as something that has become, that is frozen and rigid in form and concept, is illusion, because it has been torn from its living connections and limited in time and space. The individuality and corporeality of the unenlightened human being, trying to maintain and preserve its illusory selfhood, is *māyā* in this negative sense.

Also the body of an Enlightened One is *māyā*, but not in the negative sense, because it is the conscious creation of a mind that is free from illusion, unlimited, and no more bound to an "ego."

Only for the unenlightened worldling, who is still enmeshed in ignorance and delusion, the visible form or personality of a Buddha is *māyā* in the ordinary sense of the word. Therefore the *Mahāyāna-Śraddhotpāda-Śāstra;* says "The harmonizing activities of the *Tathāgatas*, that are no activity in the worldly sense, are of two kinds. The first can be perceived by the minds of common people . . . and is known as *Nirmāṇakāya* . . . the second kind can only be perceived by the purified minds . . . it is the *Dharmakāya* in its aspect of Spirit and Principle. It is the *Sambhogakāya*, which possesses a vast and boundless potentiality.

"That of the *Dharmakāya* which can be perceived by the minds of common people, is only a shadow of it, and takes on different aspects, according as it is considered from the different viewpoints of the six different realms of existence. Their crude perception of it does not include any conception of its possibilities for happiness and enjoyment; they see only its reflection in the *Nirmāṇakāya*.

"But as the Bodhisattvas advance along the stages (on their way towards Enlightenment) their minds become purified, their conceptions of it (the *Dharmakāya*) more profound and mysterious, their harmonizing activities more transcendental, until, when they have attained the highest stage they will be able to realize intuitively its reality. In that final realization all traces of their individual selfness . . . will have faded away and only a realization of one undifferentiated Buddhahood will remain."[3]

## The Fearlessness of the *Bodhisattva*-Path

The certainty "that nothing can happen to us that does not belong to us in our innermost being" is the foundation of the fearlessness, which *Avalokiteśvara* proclaims, which is expressed in *Amoghasiddhi*'s gesture (*abhaya mudrā*) and embodied in the nature of *Maitreya*, the Great Loving One, the Buddha to come, whose human incarnation will reflect the qualities of *Amoghasiddhi*.

Fearlessness is the quality of all *Bodhisattvas* and of all those who tread the *Bodhisattva*-Path. For them life has lost its horrors and suffering its sting, for they imbue this earthly existence with new meaning, instead of despising and cursing it for its imperfections, as so many do, who in the teachings of the Buddha try to find a pretext for their own negative conception of the world. Is the smiling countenance of the Buddha, which is millionfold reflected by countless images in all Buddhist countries, the expression of an attitude that is inimical to life, as modern intellectual representatives of Buddhism (especially in the West) so often try to make out?

To condemn life as evil, before having exhausted its possibilities for a higher development, before having penetrated to an understanding of its universal aspect, and before having realized the highest qualities of consciousness in the attain-

[3] Translated by Bhikshu Wai-tao and Dwight Goddard in *A Buddhist Bible* (Vermont: Thetford, 1938), p. 383 f.

ment of enlightenment, the noblest fruit and ultimate fulfilment of all existence, such an attitude is not only presumptuous and unreasonable, but utterly foolish. It can only be compared to the attitude of an ignorant man who, after examining an unripe fruit, declares it uneatable and throws it away, instead of giving it time to mature.

Only one who has reached that supra-individual state of Perfect Enlightenment can renounce "individuality." Those, however, who only suppress their sense-activities and natural functions of life, before they even have tried to make the right use of them, will not become saints but merely petrefacts. A saintliness, which is built merely on negative virtues, merely on avoidance and escape, may impress the crowd and may be taken as proof of self-control and spiritual strength; however, it will lead only to spiritual self-annihilation, but not to Enlightenment. It is the way of stagnation, of spiritual death. It is the liberation from suffering at the price of life and of the potential spark of Illumination within us.

The discovery of this spark is the beginning of the *Bodhisattva*-Path, which achieves the liberation from suffering and from the fetters of egohood not by a negation of life, but by service to our fellow beings, while striving towards Perfect Enlightenment. . . .

Before we pass judgment on the meaning of life and the real nature of the universe, we should ask ourselves: "Who is it after all, who assumes here the role of a judge?" Is not the judging, discriminating mind itself a part and product of that world which he condemns? If we deem our mind capable of judgment, then we have already conceded to the world a spiritual value, namely the faculty of producing a consciousness that goes beyond the mere necessities and limitations of a transient life. If this, however, is the case, we have no reason to doubt the further possibilities of development of such a consciousness or of a deeper kind of consciousness, which lies at the very root of the universe, and of which we only know a small superficial section.

If, on the other hand, we take the view that consciousness is not a product of the world, but that the world is a product of consciousness (which is the view of the *Mahāyāna* in general), it becomes obvious that we live in exactly the type of world which we have created and therefore deserved, and that the remedy cannot be an "escape" from the "world" but only a change of "mind." Such a change, however, can only take place, if we know the innermost nature of this mind and its power. A mind which is capable of interpreting the rays of heavenly bodies, millions of light-years distant, is not less wonderful than the nature of light itself. How much greater is the miracle of that inner light, which dwells in the depths of our consciousness!

The Buddha and many of his great disciples have given us an insight into this deeper (universal) consciousness. This fact in itself is of greater value than all scientific and philosophical theories, because it shows to humanity the way of the future. Thus there can be only *one* problem for us: to awaken within ourselves this deeper consciousness and to penetrate to that state, which the Buddha called the "Awakening" or "Enlightenment." This is the *Bodhisattva-Mārga*, the way to the realization of Buddhahood within ourselves.

That such a realization should no more be possible in our present world, as has been maintained in certain circles of Buddhist orthodoxy, or that the attainment of perfect enlightenment (*samyak-sambodhi*) could only be possible for a single individual within a period of thousands of years, so that it would be utterly senseless to strive after such an aim, this indeed is nothing but an admission of spiritual bankruptcy and dogmatic ossification. A religion, whose ideal is only a matter of the past or of the most distant future, has no living value for the present.

The main fault in such a view lies in the separation of the Buddha's teaching from the living personality of the Teacher, on account of which his doctrine becomes dehumanized, and is sterilized and converted into a pseudoscientific system of pure negations and abstractions. In such a system meditation merely turns into a morbid, analytical, dissecting attitude, in which everything is taken to pieces and finally disintegrates into putrid matter or empty functions of a senseless mechanism.

If we would examine a masterwork of art, say a painting, with a microscope and come to the conclusion that it is nothing but some sort of fibrous matter combined with some colored substance, and that all this can again be reduced to mere elementary vibrations—this would not bring us one step nearer to the phenomenon of beauty or to the understanding of its significance, its meaning or its message; it would only reveal the senselessness of such a philosophy of "nothing-but-ism" and its methods of "objective" analysis. (In reality it is neither "objective," i.e., unprejudiced, nor an analysis of the thing in question, because it is an intentional arbitrary suppression of all non-material factors, without which the particular form and composition of matter could not exist.)

Nevertheless there are people who in this way try to investigate the nature of life, of corporeality and of psychic and physical functions. We only need to remember in this connection those passages in post-canonical Buddhist literature, in which the analysis of the body and its functions proceeds on the basis of a naïve realism (which from the start anticipates the conclusions which are to be proved by a seemingly objective analysis), without the slightest attempt to see the inner connections of spiritual and physical functions or to understand the underlying unity of physiological, vital, psychological and spiritual phenomena.

As long as we look upon the body and its organs as if it were a "bag filled with various kinds of grain or pulses," arbitrarily or accidentally thrown together, we not only by-pass the real problem, but we deceive ourselves. It is a similar self-deception to create an artificial aversion against the body by the contemplation of corpses in various states of decay. As long as we feel aversion against the body, we have not overcome it. We overcome it only if we grow beyond it. And we can only grow beyond it, if we can *see* beyond it, i.e., if we can see the body in connection with its antecedents, the forces that built it up and keep it going, the world in which it moves, in short, in connection with the whole, in its universal perspective. The analysis gets its meaning only from the synthesis; without it it degenerates into a meaningless process of disintegration. "We then have merely the parts in our hand, while missing their spiritual connection," the very essence and *conditio sine qua non,* due to which they constitute a living organism.

All this does not mean, however, that we should close our eyes to the unpleasant aspects of existence. The masters of the *Vajrayāna* often used cemeteries and cremation-grounds for practicing meditation—not, however, in order to produce aversion against life, but in order to get acquainted with all its aspects and, last but not least, because in these places, which were avoided by others, they could devote themselves undisturbed to their *sādhanā.*

For the beginner such places and the particular meditations connected with them, are a way towards fearlessness, towards the overcoming of aversion and the attainment of equanimity. Even the Buddha relates, that during his spiritual training, he frequented lonely and uncanny places in order to overcome fear.

The contemplation of corpses and similar exercises, which may appear extreme to the layman, have a meaning only when they lead to that fearlessness which enables the *Sādhaka* to come face to face with reality and to see things in their true nature, without attachment and without aversion. He who fights desire by creating aversion and disgust, only replaces one evil by another. We do not feel aversion against dead leaves or dried flowers. And we do not enjoy flowers less because we know that they are transient. On the contrary: the knowledge of their impermanence makes their flowering all the more precious to us—just as the fleetness of the moment and of human life gives each of them their special value. To make this perishable body the abode of the Imperishable, the temple of the Mind—just as the flower makes its impermanent form the abode of timeless beauty—this is the task of man according to the teaching of the Adamantine Vehicle.

In a similar way we should look upon our spiritual and intellectual functions. Then the ego loses its importance automatically and naturally, without any effort on our part, in trying to destroy it by force (which would only strengthen its illusory reality) and without trying to deny its relative existence (which would only lead to hypocrisy or self-deception). As long as every act of ours tends towards our self-preservation, and as long as every thought circles round our own personal interests, all our protestations against the existence of an "ego" are meaningless. In fact it would be truer in that case to admit that we still possess an ego, or rather that we are possessed by it (as a drunkard is possessed by some persistent hallucination) and that we in our present state can only hope and try to get rid of it in course of time.

The surest way to this end is to see ourselves in the proper perspective to the rest of the world, i.e., in the universal perspective, which has been opened to us by the teachings of the Enlightened Ones, illustrated by their lives and emphasized by the teachers of the Great Vehicle. As long as we see life only through the pinpoint of our ordinary human consciousness, it seems to make no sense, while, if we would see the "whole picture" of the universe, as mirrored in the mind of an Enlightened One, we would discover its meaning. And this meaning, or what we might call "ultimate reality," would probably no more be expressible in human words, except in symbols like *"samyak-sambodhi,"* or *"nirvāṇa,"* or *"prajñā-pāramitā,"* etc., which cannot be explained and which the Buddha refused to define—insisting that we should experience it for ourselves! The meaning of this our life and of the universe that it reveals, lies in the fact of consciousness itself, but nowhere outside ourselves.

Whether life in itself has a meaning or not: it is up to us to *give* it a meaning. In the hands of an inspired artist a worthless lump of clay turns into a priceless work of art. Why should we not likewise try to make something worthwhile out of the common clay of our lives, instead of lamenting about its worthlessness? Our life and the world, in which we live, have as much meaning as we choose to give them.

"Man is exactly as immortal as his ideal and exactly as real as the energy with which he serves it." These words of Count Keyserling point in the right direction. The problems of value and reality are matters of attitude and creative realization, not of conceptual objectivity.

The Buddhas, therefore, or the state of Buddhahood, represent the highest reality, and those who want to realize it, have to follow the example of the Buddhas: the *Bodhisattva*-Path, in which there is no place for escapism, no running away from discomfort and suffering, but, on the contrary, the recognition, the understanding and acceptance of the fact that perfect enlightenment cannot be attained without the readiness to take upon oneself the suffering of the world. It is exactly this point in which the Buddha went beyond the teachings of the *Vedas* and *Upaniṣads* and through which his doctrine, instead of merely becoming one more sect of Hinduism, grew into a world religion.

To take upon oneself the suffering of the world, does not mean that one should seek suffering, or that one should glorify it, or inflict it upon oneself as penance, like certain ascetics among Hindus and Christians. This is an extreme, which should be avoided as much as the overemphasis of our own well-being. The Buddhist attitude flows from the inner urge to identify oneself with all living and suffering beings.

This attitude does not only prevent us from laying too much stress on our own suffering—which would only strengthen our ego-consciousness—but it actually helps us to overcome it and to minimize our own suffering.

Did not the Buddha himself point out this way to *Kisā Gautamī*,[4] when he made her realize that death was a universal affliction and that she was not alone in her grief?—He who accepts suffering in this spirit, has already won half the battle—if not the whole!

The Buddha did not teach a merely negative avoidance of suffering, otherwise he would have chosen the short cut to liberation, which was within his reach in the times of Buddha

---

[4] A young mother, whose only child had died so suddenly, that she could not believe in its death, came to the Buddha with the dead child in her arms and asked him for a remedy. The Buddha, who realized her state of mind, answered: "Go into the town and bring me some mustard seeds from a house where nobody has ever died." The young woman did as she was told, but could not find a single house which had not been visited by death. Thereupon she realized that she was not alone in her grief, returned to the Buddha, gave up the body of her child and found her inner peace.

*Dīpaṅkara,* and would have saved himself from the sufferings of innumerable rebirths. But he knew that only by going through the purifying fires of suffering can one attain highest enlightenment and become fit to serve the world.

His way was not to escape suffering, but to *conquer* it (this is why the Buddhas are called *"Jinas"* or "Conquerors"), to *overcome* suffering by facing it bravely and seeing it not only as a personal affliction but in its totality, as the common fate of all living beings.

It is in this spirit that the *Bodhisattva's* vow is taken by all those who want to follow the sacred path of the Buddhas:

"I take upon myself the burden of all suffering, I am determined to endure it. I do not turn back, I do not flee, neither do I tremble. I fear not, I yield not, neither do I hesitate.—And why?—Because the deliverance of all beings is my vow. . . .

"I am working for the establishment of the incomparable realm of knowledge among all beings. I am not only concerned with my own salvation. All these beings must be rescued by me from the ocean of *saṁsāra* by the vessel of perfect knowledge."[5]

The attainment of this state of salvation implies the overcoming of all narrow individual limitations and the recognition of super-individual realities within one's own mind. It is the most universal experience the human mind can attain, and from the very outset it demands a universal attitude; for he who strives for his own salvation, or merely with a view of getting rid of suffering in the shortest possible way, without regard for his fellow beings, has already deprived himself of the most essential means for the realization of his aim.

Whether it is objectively possible to liberate the whole world is beside the point—firstly, because there is no such thing as an "objective world" for the Buddhist, since we can only speak of the world of our experience, which cannot be separated from the experiencing subject; secondly, the state

[5] From the *Vajradhuaja Sūtra,* quoted in *Sāntideva's Sikṣāsamuccaya,* XVI.

of enlightenment is no temporal state, but an experience of a higher dimension, beyond the realm of time.

Therefore, even if Buddha *Śākyamuni*'s enlightenment took place at a certain point in the history of mankind, yet we cannot identify the process of enlightenment with this point in time. Just as, according to the Buddha's own words, his consciousness penetrated countless world periods of the past, in the same way it penetrated countless world periods of the future; in other words, the infinity of time, irrespective whether we call it past or future, became for him the immediate present.

What appears to us as the gradually unfolding consequences of this event in temporal sequence, is what was present in the Buddha's mind as an accomplished reality. Expressed in the language of our mundane consciousness, the universality of the Buddha-Mind created such a far-reaching effect, that its presence can be felt until the present day, and that the torch of liberating wisdom, which he lit two and a half millenniums ago, still radiates and will continue to radiate, as long as there are beings who yearn for light.

It is in the very nature of enlightenment that it tolerates no exclusiveness (which, indeed, is the root of all suffering), neither on the way towards its realization, nor after its attainment—because it radiates without limits and without exhausting itself, allowing others to participate in it—like the sun which gives its light without restriction to all who have eyes to see and sensitiveness to feel its warmth, or organs to absorb its life-giving forces.

And just as the sun, while illuminating the universe impartially, acts in different ways upon different beings, in accordance with their own receptivity and qualities, so the Enlightened One—though he embraces all living beings without distinction in his mind—knows that not all can be liberated at the same time, but that the seed of enlightenment, which he is sowing, will bear fruit sooner or later according to the readiness or maturity of each individual.

But since to an Enlightened One time is as illusory as space, he anticipates in the supreme experience of enlightenment the liberation of all. This is the universality of Buddhahood and the fulfilment of the *Bodhisattva*-vow through the "Wisdom which accomplishes all works," the Wisdom of *Amoghasiddhi.*

This All-Accomplishing Wisdom consists in the synthesis of heart and mind, in the union of all-embracing love and deepest knowledge, in the complete self-surrender to the highest ideal of human striving, which finds the force for its realization in the fearless acceptance of life's sufferings. For fearlessness is the gesture of *Amoghasiddhi.*

He who, inspired by this attitude, takes upon himself the *Bodhisattva*-vow at the feet of the Buddha, in the eternal presence of all the Enlightened Ones, may remember Tagore's deep-felt words:

> *Let me not pray to be sheltered from dangers*
> *    but to be fearless in facing them.*
> *Let me not beg for the stilling of my pain*
> *    but for the heart to conquer it.*
> *Let me not look for allies in life's battlefield*
> *    but to my own strength.*
> *Let me not crave in anxious fear to be saved*
> *    but hope for patience to win my freedom.* [272–280]

# DRUGS AND MYSTICISM

## WALTER N. PAHNKE

The claim has been made that the experience facilitated by psychedelic (or mind-opening) drugs such as LSD, psilocybin, and mescaline can be similar or identical to the experience described by the mystics of all ages, cultures, and religions. This paper will attempt to examine and explain this possibility.

There is a long and continuing history of the religious use of plants which contain psychedelic substances. Scholars such as Osmond, Schultes, and Wasson have made valuable contributions to this intriguing field. In some instances, such natural products were ingested by a priest, shaman, or witch doctor to induce a trance for revelatory purposes; sometimes they were taken by groups of people who participated in sacred ceremonies. For example, the dried heads of the peyote cactus, whose chief active ingredient is mescaline, were used by the Aztecs at least as early as 300 B.C. and are currently being employed by over 50,000 Indians of the North American Native Church as a vital part of their religious ceremonies. Both *ololiuqui,* a variety of morning glory seed, and certain kinds of Mexican mushrooms (called *teonanacatl,*

From the *International Journal of Parapsychology,* Vol. VIII, No. 2, Spring 1966. Also appeared in slightly different form as "The Contributions of the Psychology of Religion to the Therapeutic Use of Psychedelic Substances" in *The Uses of LSD in Psychotherapy and Alcoholism,* edited by Harold Abramson, copyright 1967 by Bobbs-Merrill Company. Reprinted by permission of the American Society for Psychical Research, the Bobbs-Merrill Company, and Walter Pahnke.

"flesh of the gods") were also used for divinatory and religious purposes by the Aztecs. These practices have continued to the present among remote Indian tribes in the mountains of Oaxaca Province in Mexico. Modern psychopharmacological research has shown the active chemicals to be psilocybin in the case of the mushrooms, and several compounds closely related to LSD in the case of *ololiuqui. Amanita muscaria,* the mushroom which has been used for unknown centuries by Siberian shamans to induce religious trances, does not contain psilocybin. The most important psychologically active compound from this mushroom has not yet been isolated, but promising work is in progress. Other naturally occurring plants, which are used by various South American Indian tribes in a religious manner for prophecy, divination, clairvoyance, tribal initiation of male adolescents, or sacred feasts, are: cohoba snuff, made from the pulverized seeds of *Piptadenia;* the drink *vinho de Jurumens,* made from the seeds of *Mimosa hostilis;* and the drink *caapi,* made from *Banisteriopsis.* These last three products contain various indolic compounds which are all closely related to psilocybin, both structurally and in their psychic effects (e.g., bufotenine, dimethyltryptamine, and harmine, respectively). Both LSD and psilocybin contain the indolic ring, and mescaline may be metabolized to an indole in the body.

## An Experimental Examination
## of the Claim that Psychedelic Drug Experience
## May Resemble Mystical Experience

Some of the researchers who have experimented with synthesized mescaline, LSD, or psilocybin have remarked upon the similarity between drug-induced and spontaneous mystical experiences because of the frequency with which some of their subjects have used mystical and religious language to describe their experiences. This data interested the author in a careful examination and evaluation of such claims. An empirical study, designed to investigate in a systematic and scientific way the similarities and differences between experiences described by mystics and those facilitated by psychedelic drugs, was undertaken [by the author in 1963]. First, a phenomenological typology of the mystical state of consciousness was carefully defined, after a study of the writings of the mystics themselves and of scholars who have tried to characterize mystical experience. (For example, William James was an invaluable pioneer in this area.) Then, some drug experiences were empirically studied, not by collecting such experiences wherever an interesting or striking one might have been found and analyzed after the fact, but by conducting a double-blind, controlled experiment with subjects whose religious background and experience, as well as personality, had been measured *before* their drug experiences. The preparation of the subjects, the setting under which the drug was administered, and the collection of data about the experience were made as uniform as possible. The experimenter himself devised the experiment, collected the data, and evaluated the results without ever having had a personal experience with any of these drugs.

A nine-category typology of the mystical state of consciousness was defined as a basis for measurement of the phenomena of the psychedelic drug experiences. Among the numerous scholars of mysticism, the work of W. T. Stace* was found to be the most helpful guide for the construction of this typology. His conclusion—that in the mystical experience there are certain fundamental characteristics which are universal and not restricted to any particular religion or culture (although particular cultural, historical, or religious conditions may influence both the interpretation and description of these basic phenomena)—was taken as a presupposition. Whether or not the mystical experience is "religious" depends upon one's definition of religion and was not the problem investigated. Our typology defined the universal phenomena of the mystical experience, whether considered "religious" or not.

* See Appendix

The nine categories of our phenomenological typology may be summarized as follows:

## CATEGORY I: Unity

Unity, the most important characteristic of the mystical experience, is divided into internal and external types, which are different ways of experiencing an undifferentiated unity. The major difference is that the internal type finds unity through an "inner world" *within* the experiencer, while the external type finds unity through the external world *outside* the experiencer.

The essential elements of *internal unity* are loss of usual sense impressions and loss of self without becoming unconscious. The multiplicity of usual external and internal sense impressions (including time and space), and the empirical ego or usual sense of individuality, fade or melt away while consciousness remains. In the most complete experience this consciousness is a pure awareness beyond empirical content, with no external or internal distinctions. In spite of the loss of sense impressions and dissolution of the usual personal identity or self, the awareness of oneness or unity is still experienced and remembered. One is not unconscious but is rather very much aware of an undifferentiated unity.

*External unity* is perceived outwardly with the physical senses through the external world. A sense of underlying oneness is felt behind the empirical multiplicity. The subject or observer feels that the usual separation between himself and an external object (inanimate or animate) is no longer present in a basic sense; yet the subject still knows that on another level, at the same time, he and the objects are separate. Another way of expressing this same phenomenon is that the essences of objects are experienced intuitively and felt to be the same at the deepest level. The subject feels a sense of oneness with these objects because he "sees" that at the most basic level all are a part of the same undifferentiated unity. The capsule statement "all is One" is a good summary of external unity. In the most complete experience a cosmic dimension is felt, so that the experiencer feels in a deep sense that he is a part of everything that is.

## CATEGORY II: Transcendence of Time and Space

This category refers to loss of the usual sense of time and space. This means clock time but may also be one's personal sense of his past, present, and future. Transcendence of space means that a person loses his usual orientation as to where he is during the experience in terms of the usual three-dimensional perception of his environment. Experiences of timelessness and spacelessness may also be described as experiences of "eternity" or "infinity."

## CATEGORY III: Deeply Felt Positive Mood

The most universal elements (and, therefore, the ones which are most essential to the definition of this category) are joy, blessedness, and peace. The unique character of these feelings in relation to the mystical experience is the intensity which elevates them to the highest levels of human experience, and they are highly valued by the experiencers. Tears may be associated with any of these elements because of the overpowering nature of the experience. Such feelings may occur either at the peak of the experience or during the "ecstatic afterglow," when the peak has passed but while its effects and memory are still quite vivid and intense. Love may also be an element of deeply felt positive mood, but it does not have the same universality as joy, blessedness, and peace.

## CATEGORY IV: Sense of Sacredness

This category refers to the sense of sacredness which is evoked by the mystical experience. The sacred is here broadly defined as that which a person feels to be of special value and capable of being profaned. The basic characteristic of sacredness is a non-rational, intuitive, hushed, palpitant response of awe and wonder in the presence of inspiring realities. No religious "beliefs" or traditional theological terminology need necessarily be involved, even though there may be a sense of reverence or a feeling that what is experienced is holy or divine.

## CATEGORY V: Objectivity and Reality

This category has two interrelated elements: (1) insightful knowledge or illumination felt at an intuitive, non-rational level and gained by direct experience; and (2) the authoritative nature of the experience, or the certainty that such knowledge is truly real, in contrast to the feeling that the experience is a subjective delusion. These two elements are connected because the knowledge through experience of ultimate reality (in the sense of being able to "know" and "see" what is really *real*) carries its own sense of certainty. The experience of "ultimate" reality is an awareness of another dimension unlike the "ordinary" reality (the reality of usual, everyday consciousness); yet the knowledge of "ultimate" reality is quite real to the experiencer. Such insightful knowledge does not necessarily mean an increase in facts, but rather in intuitive illumination. What becomes "known" (rather than merely intellectually assented to) is intuitively felt to be authoritative, requires no proof at a rational level, and produces an inward feeling of objective truth. The content of this knowledge may be divided into two main types: (a) insights into being and existence in general, and (b) insights into one's personal, finite self.

## CATEGORY VI: Paradoxicality

Accurate descriptions and even rational interpretations of the mystical experience tend to be logically contradictory when strictly analyzed. For example, in the experience of internal unity there is a loss of all empirical content in an *empty* unity which is at the same time *full* and complete. This loss includes the loss of the sense of self and the dissolution of individuality; yet something of the individual entity remains to experience the unity. The "I" both exists and does not exist. Another example is the separateness from, and at the same time unity with, objects in the experience of external unity (essentially a paradoxical transcendence of space).

## CATEGORY VII: Alleged Ineffability

In spite of attempts to relate or write about the mystical experience, mystics insist either that words fail to describe it adequately or that the experience is beyond words. Perhaps the reason is an embarrassment with language because of the paradoxical nature of the essential phenomena.

## CATEGORY VIII: Transiency

Transiency refers to duration and means the temporary nature of the mystical experience in contrast to the relative permanence of the level of usual experience. There is a transient appearance of the special and unusual levels or dimensions of consciousness as defined by our typology, their eventual disappearance, and a return to the more usual. The characteristic of transiency indicates that the mystical state of consciousness is not sustained indefinitely.

## CATEGORY IX:
## Persisting Positive Changes in Attitude and Behavior

Because our typology is of a healthful, life-enhancing mysticism, this category describes the positive, lasting effects of the experience and the resulting changes in attitude. These changes are divided into four groups: (1) toward self; (2) toward others; (3) toward life; and (4) toward the mystical experience itself.

(1) Increased integration of personality is the basic inward change in the personal self. Undesirable traits may be faced in such a way that they may be dealt with and finally reduced or eliminated. As a result of personal integration, one's sense of inner authority may be strengthened, and the

vigor and dynamic quality of a person's life may be increased. Creativity and greater efficiency of achievement may be released. An inner optimistic tone may result, with a consequent increase in feelings of happiness, joy and peace. (2) Changes in attitude and behavior toward others include more sensitivity, more tolerance, more real love, and more authenticity as a person by virtue of being more open and more one's true self with others. (3) Changes toward life in a positive direction include philosophy of life, sense of values, sense of meaning and purpose, vocational commitment, need for service to others, and new appreciation of life and the whole of creation. Life may seem richer. The sense of reverence may be increased, and more time may be spent in devotional life and meditation. (4) Positive change in attitude toward the mystical experience itself means that it is regarded as valuable and that what has been learned is thought to be useful. The experience is remembered as a high point and an attempt is made to recapture it or, if possible, to gain new experiences as a source of growth and strength. The mystical experiences of others are more readily appreciated and understood.

The purpose of the experiment in which psilocybin was administered in a religious context was to gather empirical data about the state of consciousness experienced. In a private chapel on Good Friday, twenty Christian theological students, ten of whom had been given psilocybin one and one-half hours earlier, listened over loudspeakers to a two-and-one-half-hour religious service which was in actual progress in another part of the building and which consisted of organ music, four solos, readings, prayers, and personal meditation. The assumption was made that the condition most conducive to a mystical experience should be an atmosphere broadly comparable to that achieved by tribes who actually use natural psychedelic substances in religious ceremonies. The particular content and procedure of the ceremony had to be applicable (i.e., familiar and meaningful) to the participants. Attitude toward the experience, both before and during, was taken into serious consideration in the experimental design. Preparation was meant to maximize positive expectation, trust, confidence, and reduction of fear. The setting was planned to utilize this preparation through group support and rapport; through friendship and an open, trusting atmosphere; and through prior knowledge of the procedure of the experiment in order to eliminate, if possible, feelings of manipulation which might arise.

In the weeks before the experiment, each subject participated in five hours of various preparation and screening procedures which included psychological tests, medical history, physical examination, questionnaire evaluation of previous religious experience, intensive interview, and group interaction. The twenty subjects were graduate student volunteers, all of whom were from middle-class Protestant backgrounds and from one denominational seminary in the free-church tradition. None of the subjects had taken psilocybin or related substances before this experiment. The volunteers were divided into five groups of four students each on the basis of compatibility and friendship. Two leaders, who knew from past experience the positive and negative possibilities of the psilocybin reaction, met with their groups to encourage trust, confidence, group support, and fear reduction. The method of reaction to the experience was emphasized (i.e., to relax and cooperate with, rather than to fight against, the effects of the drug). Throughout the preparation, an effort was made to avoid suggesting the characteristics of the typology of mysticism. The leaders were not familiar with the typology which had been devised.

Double-blind technique was employed in the experiment, so that neither the experimenter nor any of the participants (leaders or subjects) knew the specific contents of the capsules, which were identical in appearance. Half of the subjects and one of the leaders in each group received psilocybin (30 mg for each of the ten experimental subjects and 15 mg for five of the leaders). Without prior knowledge of the drug used, or of its effects, the remaining ten subjects and the other five leaders each received 200 mg of nicotinic acid, a vitamin which causes transient feelings of warmth and tingling of the skin, in order to maximize suggestion for the control group.

Data were collected during the experiment and at various times up to six months afterwards. On the experimental day, tape recordings were made both of individual reactions immediately after the religious service and of the group discussions which followed. Each subject wrote an account of his experience as soon after the experiment as was convenient. Within a week all subjects had completed a 147-item questionnaire which had been designed to measure the various phenomena of the typology of mysticism on a qualitative, numerical scale. The results of this questionnaire were used as a basis for a one-and-one-half-hour, tape-recorded interview which immediately followed. Six months later each subject was interviewed again after completion of a follow-up questionnaire in three parts with a similar scale. Part I was open-ended; the participant was asked to list any changes which he felt were a result of his Good Friday experience and to rate the degree of benefit or harm of each change. Part II (52 items) was a condensed and somewhat more explicit repetition of items from the post-drug questionnaire. Part III (93 items) was designed to measure both positive and negative attitudinal and behavioral changes which had lasted for six months and were due to the experience. The individual descriptive accounts and Part I of the follow-up questionnaire were content-analyzed with a qualitative, numerical scale by judges who were independent of the experiment and who knew only that they were to analyze twenty accounts written by persons who had attended a religious service.

Prior to the experiment, the twenty subjects had been matched in ten pairs on the basis of data from the pre-drug questionnaires, interviews, and psychological tests. Past religious experience, religious background, and general psychological make-up were used for the pairings, in that order of importance. The experiment was designed so that by random distribution one subject from each pair received psilocybin and one received the control substance, nicotinic acid. This division into an experimental and control group was for the purpose of statistical evaluation of the scores from each of the three methods of measurement which used a numerical scale: the post-drug questionnaire, the follow-up questionnaire, and the content analysis of the written accounts.

A summary of percentage scores and significance levels reached by the ten experimentals and ten controls, for each category or sub-category of the typology of mysticism, is presented in Table I. The score from each of the three methods of measurement was calculated as the percentage of the maximum possible score if the top of the rating scale for each item had been scored. The percentages from each

TABLE I

Summary of Percentage Scores and Significance Levels Reached
by the Experimental versus the Control Group for
Categories Measuring the Typology of Mystical Experience

| CATEGORY | % OF MAXIMUM POSSIBLE SCORE FOR 10 Ss | | |
|---|---|---|---|
| | Exp. | Cont. | P* |
| 1. Unity | 62 | 7 | .001 |
| A. Internal | 70 | 8 | .001 |
| B. External | 38 | 2 | .008 |
| 2. Transcendence of Time and Space | 84 | 6 | .001 |
| 3. Deeply Felt Positive Mood | 57 | 23 | .020 |
| A. Joy, Blessedness and Peace | 51 | 13 | .020 |
| B. Love | 57 | 33 | .055 |
| 4. Sacredness | 53 | 28 | .020 |
| 5. Objectivity and Reality | 63 | 18 | .011 |
| 6. Paradoxicality | 61 | 13 | .001 |
| 7. Alleged Ineffability | 66 | 18 | .001 |
| 8. Transiency | 79 | 8 | .001 |
| 9. Persisting Positive Changes in Attitude and Behavior | 51 | 8 | .001 |
| A. Toward Self | 57 | 3 | .001 |
| B. Toward Others | 40 | 20 | .002 |
| C. Toward Life | 54 | 6 | .011 |
| D. Toward the Experience | 57 | 31 | .055 |

\* Probability that the difference between Experimental and Control Scores was Due to Chance.

method of measurement were then averaged together. A comparison of the scores of the experimental and control subject in each pair was used to calculate the significance level of the differences observed by means of the non-parametric Sign Test. As can be seen from Table I, for the combined scores from the three methods of measurement, p was less than .020 in all categories except deeply felt positive mood (love) and persisting positive changes in attitude and behavior toward the experience, where p was still less than .055.

Although this evidence indicates that the experimentals as a group achieved to a statistically significant degree a higher score in each of the nine categories than did the controls, the degree of completeness or intensity must be examined.

In terms of our typology of mysticism, ideally the most "complete" mystical experience should have demonstrated the phenomena of all the categories in a maximal way. The evidence (particularly from the content analysis and also supported by impressions from the interviews) showed that such perfect completeness in all categories was not experienced by all the subjects in the experimental group. In the data the various categories and sub-categories can be divided into three groups in regard to the degree of intensity or completeness, as shown in Table II. Criteria were the percentage levels and the consistency among different methods of measurement. The closest approximation to a complete and intense degree of experience was found for the categories of internal unity, transcendence of time and space, transiency, paradoxicality, and persisting positive changes in attitude and behavior toward self and life. The evidence indicated that the second group had almost but not quite the same degree of completeness or intensity as the first group. The second group consisted of external unity, objectivity and reality, joy, and alleged ineffability. There was a relatively greater lack of completeness for sense of sacredness, love, and persisting positive changes in attitude and behavior toward others and toward the experience. Each of these last eight categories or sub-categories was termed incomplete to a more or less degree for the experimentals, but was definitely present to some extent when compared with the controls. When analyzed most

TABLE II

Relative Completeness\* of Various Categories in Which there Was a
Statistically Significant Difference between Experimental and
Control Groups

| (1) | (2) | (3) |
|---|---|---|
| *Closest approximation to the most complete and intense expression* | *Almost, but not quite as complete or intense as (1)* | *Least complete or intense, though still a definite difference from the control group* |
| Internal Unity | External Unity | Sense of Sacredness |
| Transcendence of Time and Space | Objectivity and Reality | Deeply Felt Positive Mood (Love) |
| Transiency | Alleged Ineffability | Persisting Positive Changes in Attitude and Behavior toward others and the Experience |
| Paradoxicality | Deeply Felt Positive Mood (Joy, Blessedness, and Peace) | |
| Persisting Positive Changes in Attitude and Behavior toward Self and Life | | |

\* Based on qualitative score levels and agreement among the three methods of measurement in comparing the scores of the experimental versus the control group.

rigorously and measured against all possible categories of the typology of mysticism, the experience of the experimental subjects was considered incomplete in this strictest sense. Usually such incompleteness was demonstrated by results of the content analyses.

The control subjects did not experience many phenomena of the mystical typology, and even then only to a low degree of completeness. The phenomena for which the scores of the controls were closest to (although still always less than) the experimentals were: blessedness and peace, sense of sacredness, love, and persisting positive changes in attitude and behavior toward others and toward the experience.

The design of the experiment suggested an explanation for the fact that the control subjects should have experienced any phenomena at all. The meaningful religious setting of the experiment would have been expected to encourage a response of blessedness, peace, and sacredness. In the case of love and persisting changes toward others and toward the experience, observation by the controls of the profound experience of the experimentals and interaction between the two groups on an interpersonal level appeared, from both post-experimental interviews, to have been the main basis for the controls' experience of these phenomena.

The experience of the experimental subjects was certainly more like mystical experience than that of the controls, who had the same expectation and suggestion from the preparation and setting. The most striking difference between the experimentals and controls was the ingestion of thirty milligrams of psilocybin, which it was concluded was the facilitating agent responsible for the difference in phenomena experienced.

After an admittedly short follow-up period of only six months, life-enhancing and -enriching effects similar to some of those claimed by mystics were shown by the higher scores of the experimental subjects when compared to the controls. In addition, after four hours of follow-up interviews with each subject, the experimenter was left with the impression that the experience had made a profound impact (especially in terms of religious feeling and thinking) on the lives of eight out of ten of the subjects who had been given psilocybin. Although the psilocybin experience was quite unique and different from the "ordinary" reality of their everyday lives, these subjects felt that this experience had motivated them to appreciate more deeply the meaning of their lives, to gain more depth and authenticity in ordinary living, and to re-think their philosophies of life and values. The data did not suggest that any "ultimate" reality encountered had made "ordinary" reality no longer important or meaningful. The fact that the experience took place in the context of a religious service, with the use of symbols which were familiar and meaningful to the participants, appeared to provide a useful framework within which to derive meaning and integration from the experience, both at the time and later.

The relationship and relative importance of psychological preparation, setting, and drug were important questions raised by our results. A meaningful religious preparation, expectation, and environment appeared to be conducive to positive drug experiences, although the precise qualitative and quantitative role of each factor was not determined. For example, everything possible was done to maximize suggestion, but suggestion alone cannot account for the results because of the different experience of the control group. The hypothesis that suggestibility was heightened by psilocybin could not be ruled out on the basis of our experiment. An effort was made to avoid suggesting the phenomena of the typology of mysticism, and the service itself made no such direct suggestion.

## Implications for the Psychology of Religion

The results of our experiment would indicate that psilocybin (and LSD and mescaline by analogy) are important tools for the study of the mystical state of consciousness. Experiences which previously have been possible only for a small minority of people, and which have been difficult to study because of their unpredictability and rarity, are now reproducible under suitable conditions. The mystical experience has been called by many names which are suggestive of areas which are paranormal and not usually considered easily available for investigation (e.g., an experience of transcendence, ecstasy, conversion, or cosmic consciousness); but this is a realm of human experience which should not be rejected as outside the realm of serious scientific study, especially if it can be shown that a practical benefit can result. Our data would suggest that such an overwhelming experience, in which a person existentially encounters basic values such as the meaning of his life (past, present, and future), deep and meaningful interpersonal relationships, and insight into the possibility of personal behavior change, can possibly be therapeutic if approached and worked with in a sensitive and adequate way.

Possibilities for further research with these drugs in the psychology of religion can be divided into two different kinds in relation to the aim: (1) theoretical understanding of the phenomena and psychology of mysticism, and (2) experimental investigation of possible social application in a religious context.

The first or theoretical kind of research would be to approach the mystical state of consciousness as closely as possible under controlled experimental conditions and to measure the effect of variables such as the dose of the drug, the preparation and personality of the subject, the setting of the experiment, and the expectation of the experimenter. The work described above was a first step in the measurement of these variables, but more research is needed. The results should be proved to be reproducible by the same and by different experimenters under similar conditions. Such work could lead to a better understanding of mysticism from a physiological, biochemical, psychological, and therapeutic perspective.

Several experimental approaches can be envisioned for the second kind of research, to determine the best method for useful application in a religious context. One suggestion would be the establishment of a research center where carefully controlled drug experiments could be done by a trained research staff which would consist of psychiatrists, clinical psychologists, and professional religious personnel. Subjects, ideally, would spend at least a week at the center to facilitate thorough screening, preparation, and observation of their reactions, both during and after drug experiments. Another suggestion would be the study of the effect of mystical experience on small natural groups of from four to six people who would meet periodically, both prior to and after a drug experience, for serious personal and religious discussion, study and worship. The reactions of a varied range of subjects with different interests could be studied, but perhaps a good place to start would be with persons professionally interested in religion, such as ministers, priests, rabbis, theologians, and psychologists of religion.

Such research may have important implications for religion. The universal and basic human experience which we have called mystical is recorded from all cultures and ages of human history, but mysticism has never been adequately studied and understood from a physiological, biochemical, sociological, psychological, and theological perspective.

Perhaps there is more of a biochemical basis to such "natural" experiences than has been previously supposed. Certainly many ascetics who have had mystical experiences have engaged in such practices as breathing and postural exercises, sleep deprivation, fasting, flagellation with subsequent infection, sustained meditation, and sensory deprivation in caves or monastic cells. All of these techniques have an effect on body chemistry. There is a definite interplay between physiological and psychological processes in the human being. Some of the indolic substances in the body do not differ greatly from the psychedelic drugs.

Many persons concerned with religion are disturbed by drug-facilitated mystical experiences because of their apparent ease of production, with the implication that they are "unearned" and therefore "undeserved." Perhaps the Puritan and Calvinistic element of our Western culture—especially in the United States, where most of the controversy about psychedelic drugs has centered—may be a factor in this uneasiness. Although a drug experience might seem unearned when compared with the rigorous discipline which many mystics describe as necessary, our evidence has suggested that careful preparation and expectation play an important part, not only in the type of experience attained but in later fruits for life. Positive mystical experience with psychedelic drugs is by no means automatic. It would seem that the "drug effect" is a delicate combination of psychological set and setting in which the drug itself is the trigger or facilitating agent—i.e., in which the drug is a *necessary* but not *sufficient* condition. Perhaps the hardest "work" comes after the experience, which in itself may only provide the motivation for future efforts to integrate and appreciate what has been learned. Unless such an experience is integrated into the on-going life of the individual, only a memory remains rather than the growth of an unfolding renewal process which may be awakened by the mystical experience. If the person has a religious framework and discipline within which to work, the integrative process is encouraged and stimulated. Many persons may not need the drug-facilitated mystical experience, but there are others who would never be aware of the undeveloped potentials within themselves, or be inspired to work in this direction, without such an experience. "Gratuitous grace" is an appropriate theological term, because the psychedelic mystical experience can lead to a profound sense of inspiration, reverential awe, and humility, perhaps partially as a result of the realization that the experience *is* a gift and not particularly earned or deserved.

Mysticism and *inner* experience have been stressed much more by Eastern religions than by Western. Perhaps Western culture is as far off balance in the opposite direction—with its manipulation of the *external* world, as exemplified by the emphasis on material wealth, control of nature, and admiration of science. Mysticism has been accused of fostering escapism from the problems of society, indifference to social conditions, and disinterest in social change. While the possibility of such excesses must always be remembered, our study has suggested the beneficial potential of mystical experience in stimulating the ability to feel and experience deeply and genuinely with the full harmony of both emotion and intellect. Such wholeness may have been neglected in modern Western society.

The subjects in our experiment who were given psilocybin found the religious service more meaningful, both at the time and later, than did the control subjects. This finding raises the possibility that psychedelic drug experiences in a religious setting may be able to illuminate the dynamics and significance of worship. Increased understanding of the psychological mechanism involved might lead to more meaningful worship experiences for those who have not had the drug experience. The analogy with the efficacy of the sacraments is one example of what would have to be considered for a better psychological understanding of what goes on during worship. Such considerations raise the question of the place of the emotional factor, compared to the cognitive, in religious worship. An even more basic question is the validity of religious experience of the mystical type, in terms of religious truth. Reactions to such religious implications will vary with theological position and presuppositions, but one value of our study can be to stimulate thoughtful examination of the problems.

Although our experimental results indicated predominantly positive and beneficial subjective effects, possible dangers must not be underestimated and should be thoroughly evaluated by specific research designed to discover the causes and methods of prevention of physical or psychological harm, both short-term and long-term. While physiological addiction has not been reported with psychedelic substances, psychological dependence might be expected if the experience were continually repeated. The intense subjective pleasure and enjoyment of the experience for its own sake could lead to escapism and withdrawal from the world. An experience which is capable of changing motivation and values might cut the nerve of achievement. Widespread apathy toward productive work and accomplishment could cripple a society. Another possible danger might be suicide or prolonged psychosis in very unstable or depressed individuals who are not ready for the intense emotional discharge. If it can be determined that any of these forms of harm occur in certain types of individuals, research could be directed toward the development of pre-test methods to screen out such persons. Our evidence would suggest that research on conditions and methods of administration of the drugs might minimize the chance of harmful reactions. Spectacular immediate advance must be sacrificed for ultimate progress by careful, yet daring and imaginative, research under adequate medical supervision.

The ethical implications also cannot be ignored. Any research which uses human volunteers must examine its motives and methods to make certain that human beings are not being manipulated like objects for purposes which they do not understand or share. But in research with powerful mental chemicals which may influence the most cherished human functions and values, the ethical problem is even more acute. The mystical experience, historically, has filled man with wondrous awe and has been able to change his style of life and values; but it must not be assumed that greater control of such powerful phenomena will automatically result in wise and constructive use. Potential abuse is just as likely.

Those who undertake such research carry a heavy responsibility.

This is not to say that research should be stopped because of the fear of these various risks in an extremely complex and challenging area which has great promise for the psychology of religion. But while research is progressing on the theoretical or primary level and before projects for testing useful social applications in a religious context become widespread, serious and thoughtful examination of the sociological, ethical, and theological implications is needed without delay.

Not the least of these implications is the fear that research which probes the psyche of man and involves his spiritual values may be a sacrilegious transgression by science. If the exploration of certain phenomena should be prohibited, should the mystical experiences made possible by psychedelic drugs be one of the taboo areas? Such restrictions raise several relevant questions. Who is wise enough to decide in advance that such research will cause more harm than good? If such restrictions are applied, where will they end and will they not impede knowledge of unforeseen possibilities? This attitude on the part of religion is not new. Galileo and Servetus encountered it hundreds of years ago. The issue should not be whether or not to undertake such research, but rather how to do so in a way which sensitively takes into consideration the contribution, significance, and values of religion. A better scientific understanding of the mechanisms and application of mysticism has the potential for a greater appreciation and respect for heretofore rarely explored areas of human consciousness. If these areas have relevance for man's spiritual life, this should be a cause for rejoicing, not alarm. If the values nurtured by religion are fundamental for an understanding of the nature of man, then careful and sensitive scientific research into the experiential side of man's existence has the potential for illumination of these values. The importance of such research should be emphasized, especially because of its possible significance for religion and theology. . . .

Many unknown conscious and unconscious factors operate in the mystical experience. Much investigation is needed in this area, and drugs like psilocybin can be a powerful tool. Experimental facilitation of mystical experiences under controlled conditions can be an important method of approach to a better understanding of mysticism. Better understanding can lead to appreciation of the role and place of such experiences in the history and practice of religion. . . .

# LSD AND MYSTICAL
# EXPERIENCES

## G. RAY JORDAN, JR.

With the publication of Aldous Huxley's *The Doors of Perception* and *Heaven and Hell*, and of R. C. Zaehner's *Mysticism, Sacred and Profane*, attention has again been given to the similarities between certain kinds of drug-induced experiences and mystical experiences.[1] The student of world religions has long known of the sacramental use of such special agents as alcohol, plants, mushrooms, etc., to facilitate contact with the gods or make available spiritual knowledge or powers—as in the ancient Aryan use of *soma* and the still-practiced peyote sacrament of certain North American Indians. In spite of a long recognition of the use of such agents to facilitate or produce states of consciousness considered to be of the highest religious significance, psychologists of religion have given very little attention to the phenomena involved. Even psychologists in general had until recently studied very little the patterns and significance of a wide range of drug-induced states of consciousness. The last fifteen years have brought a tremendous increase in psychiatric and psychological research in drug experiences. But psychologists of religion have as yet shown relatively little concern with some

From the *Journal of Bible and Religion*, XXXI, 2, April 1963. Copyright © 1963 American Academy of Religion. Reprinted by permission.

[1] *The Doors of Perception* (New York: Harper & Brothers, 1954); *Heaven and Hell* (New York: Harper & Brothers, 1956); *Mysticism, Sacred and Profane* (New York: Oxford Galaxy Books, 1961 [1957]).

of the very interesting aspects of these practices which might help shed light on certain varieties of religious experience.

After a brief introduction to the known physical effects of hallucinogenic drugs—principally, LSD-25 or, more simply, LSD—this article summarizes the characteristics of a variety of drug-induced experiences. These experiences are then confronted with various types of mystical experiences which in the author's opinion are of the same nature. In the course of the comparative confrontation several suggestions are made regarding the value of hallucinogenic drugs as potential aids to psychological studies of religion. The general standpoint of the article is that of the history and psychology of religions. In addition to data from others' reports—historical and experimental—the writer has been able to draw on his own experiences as a voluntary, normal subject in experimentations with lysergic acid diethylamide (LSD).

# I

Of the recently studied drugs which often facilitate mystical-like experiences the most accessible and most used has been LSD, and perhaps secondarily, mescaline.[2] The latter appears naturally in the peyote plant but can be synthetically produced. LSD is derived from a fungus which sometimes develops in rye. It is far less expensive to use and far more powerful than mescaline. Four to five thousand times as much mescaline as LSD is required to obtain similar effects in a subject. Generally speaking, the effects are very similar in similar subjects. As one researcher expressed it to me, psychologically there seems to be more similarity between the mescaline experience(s) and the LSD experience(s) of one subject who has had both than between the experiences of several subjects all of whom have had only one of the drugs.[3] An excellent account of both somatic and

[2] Most recently, psilocybin, the active hallucinogenic agent in certain mushrooms, has been extensively used in research.

[3] Sidney Cohen, "Lysergic Acid Diethylamide: Side Effects and Complications," *The Journal of Nervous and Mental Disease*, CXXX, 1 (January 1960), 36; Janiger, Oscar, "The Use of

typical psychological effects associated with LSD is given by
Oscar Janiger.[4] The following summary draws on Janiger's
article and several other published sources as well as conver-
sations and personal experiences. Most of the effects we shall
be concerned with may be described, phenomenologically,
as "psychological," i.e., they are accessible to us chiefly
through the subject's own descriptions. But first a few observations about certain physical effects of the drug are in order.

The exact nature of LSD's biochemical influence is not yet
known with certainty, but it is clear that neither that drug nor
mescaline is addicting in the sense that usage makes the user
physically dependent on it. And so far the evidence indicates
a high probability against psychological dependence. At the
time of usage, however, there are typical physiological effects which include marked changes in autonomic responses
such as sweating, salivation, respiration, pulse, blood pressure, body temperature, and pupillary and vasomotor functions. These changes begin about half an hour after the drug
has been taken orally and tend to persist through the height
of the drug's effects. Peak effects usually occur three to four
hours after oral ingestion, but certain effects of a "psychological" nature may continue through a period of eight to ten
hours or even longer. It is interesting to note that according
to Janiger, "the initial degree of autonomic involvement does
not seem to offer any clue as to the intensity or nature of the
on-coming psychological reaction." The psychological reactions are of primary interest for the present study.

In the following paragraphs summaries are given of experiences reported by normal LSD subjects. These are composite
descriptions taken from many different sessions and subjects. Probably no single subject will have experienced all the
varieties, certainly not in one session. The more experiments
a subject has participated in, the more varied his experiences
are likely to be. For example, a friend of the author who is
very skillful with verbal descriptions thought that on the

Hallucinogenic Agents in Psychiatry," *The California Clinician*,
LV, 7–8 (July–August 1959), p. 256.
    [4] Janiger, *op. cit.*, p. 252.

basis of his first two or three LSD sessions he could map and describe fairly accurately what was going on. Subsequent experiences opened entirely different vistas for him which language seemed far less adequate to describe.

Let us examine fairly common effects as well as typical variations reported by normal LSD subjects. First and very generally, the world of experience seems very different. Sometimes the difference can be specifically described in terms of visual, feeling, and/or thought processes, described to some extent but perhaps never completely and in some instances hardly at all. Before my first experience with LSD, I had read several accounts of others' experiences and talked with two or three former LSD subjects. I thought I had a fairly good idea of what to expect. In some respects my expectations were fulfilled, but there was in that experience and all subsequent sessions a certain pervading yet indefinable quality, atmosphere or perspective which persisted with greater or less intensity so long as LSD-influenced experiences continued. Since my last LSD session I have several times faintly experienced the world again in this indefinable, nonspecific way. (The instances are sufficiently frequent that I have not kept count, but they are by no means commonplace.) Although vague and indefinable, this pervasive "LSD quality" is recognizable by anybody who has once encountered it. The report of those LSD subjects I have conversed with concurs with my own observations that although each session is unique, each one after the first is also like a re-entry to familiar, though lost, country.

When it is said that the world one experiences seems very different this does not mean that it is necessarily an entirely different world from the one normally experienced. There are those who under the influence of LSD meet creatures, objects and/or dimensions which have no place or part in the world of ordinary life. And for many more LSD subjects a shutting of the eyes will reveal a realm that seems to have very little to do with the everyday world. The vague, general difference introduced by LSD pervades these different realms, but it also pervades the realm which was ordinary before LSD.

Throughout my first LSD session I could best express what was going on with the declaration, "It's more of the same, only more so"—by which I meant that it was much like my experiences before taking LSD except that there was an entirely new intensity or new dimension to everything. My own view is that this general LSD-quality may be much like what Rudolph Otto describes as the "numinous," provided we remember that for Otto the numinous is demonic as well as divine and may be present in less-developed cases of the weird, the uncanny, the fascinatingly strange, as well as in the mystic's exalted communion or union with God.[5]

One of the regular features of LSD experiences which is also characteristic of Otto's numinous is the element of fascination. Whatever the content of his experiences, the LSD subject typically finds them filled with such significance that his whole interest and being cannot be drawn away from them. Often, new meanings in the form of valid insights into one's life situation emerge. Occasionally, in a patient with psychotic disturbances or in a normal subject with psychotic tendencies, a systematized delusional system may be elaborated under LSD. But it is not meanings of this variety, meanings which can be more or less adequately verbalized or symbolized, which constitute the basic ground of fascination. Rather, *any* object or item of experience may become, and usually does become, fraught with boundless, indefinable significance.[6] The fascination may be total interest, pure and simple, or it may be total interest colored by such emotions as elation, joy, anxiety, or fear.

A more definable effect which appears regularly is the modification of the LSD subject's sense of time. Perhaps most

[5] Rudolph Otto, *The Idea of the Holy* (New York: Oxford Galaxy Books, 1958 [1950]).

[6] The usage of "significance" here and below cannot be further defined than the context of the analysis indicates. It is not a question of some element or aspect (idea, word, perception, etc.) of experience being significant of something else. Significance or meaning is inherent in the whole moment of experience and cannot be defined or *adequately* indicated by any sort of cognitive or intellectual abstraction which stands outside the moment of experience, for at such a moment there is no separation of any sort.

commonly, a brief duration of clock time seems to him to have been of great duration. It is not that time drags; rather, so much seems to be going on and with such intensity that one thinks it must have taken hours or sometimes years for it to have happened, when by the clock it was only a few minutes. Closely associated with this time modification is an oft-present timelessness which is known immediately as reality and not as merely metaphor. The eternal now spoken of in various mystical traditions *is* the true nature of all existence.

Various modifications of visual perceptions are common. Colors become brighter. Contrasts of light and dark are sharply accentuated. Sometimes a certain color actually in the visual field will become predominant and cast its tone over everything. Often the color that so predominates seems to be closely in accord with the emotions of the moment, but of equal frequence, according to my observations, an exterior change in lighting, such as the passage of a cloud over the sun, affects interior emotions. Sometimes correlated with changes in color, contrasts, and lighting, and sometimes not so correlated, forms of objects and their lines change either subtly or grossly. Surfaces may move, as, for example, when the wall takes a breath. What has been a gestalt very easily becomes ground, and vice versa. Such new ways of seeing the world often do not terminate with the ending of the LSD session. The intensity of color and objectivity of movement do not continue, although they may return more faintly in everyday life. What does remain, if one chooses to attend to it, is a new sensitivity to all visual relationships. Ever since my first LSD session I have had a new, continuing visual appreciation of all art forms, an appreciation which I did not have before.

All the visual modifications mentioned so far occur in fairly close association with the normal objective world. One can always point to certain visual elements recognizable by a normally perceiving person which are the bases for all changes. Sometimes, however, hallucinations appear which are not just modifications of the world of public perceptions. There may be colored geometric patterns of great beauty, continually changing. There may be people or objects or fantastic creatures which appear "out there," objectively confronting one.

Spatial distances and relationships may vary greatly. Such changes, which one sees clearly "out there," are often correlated with inner feelings of "distance" or "attraction," but not always. On one occasion—my first LSD session—I experienced a very unpleasant spatial modification in connection with a paranoiac moment of suspicion. Certain events taking place in the doctor's waiting room where I was seated reminded me of the concern of an ill-informed friend who had warned me against getting "hooked" on a drug which might prove addictive. For a few seconds I thought that I had been tricked and might turn into an addict. During those few seconds all the objects and spaces in my whole visual field receded away from me so that everything about me was small and far away—as though I were looking through the wrong end of a telescope. But reflecting reasonably upon what I actually knew about LSD from authoritative sources, I recognized the absurdity of the idea of entrapment, the anxiety faded, and spatial relationships became normal.

## II

A type of phenomenon regularly reported by LSD subjects is alteration of self. Many different kinds of alteration may occur. Sometimes one's self-image will change simply in terms of self-confidence, views about one's abilities, or the sense of one's importance in life. In other instances the very structure of self will radically change.

The radical self-modifications which I have experienced can best be described in terms of four major varieties. (1) I have realized that quite literally everything is Self, everything in the whole field of experience—both what is usually known as self and all that usually is not self (people, objects, sky, earth, etc.). This Self which is everything is not the same as the ego-self. It is not that I, Ray Jordan, am everything, but that there is a more fundamental Self which is everything, including Ray Jordan. Since this realization, the Upanishadic statements that the Self (*Atman*) is All have a far clearer meaning to me than before. However, I cannot today do a better job of logically explaining the Upanishads than I could before. On the contrary, even now all logical arguments for or against the Upanishadic statements remain clearly beside the point. (2) A second radical modification of self has retained the usual ego-self—the "I" or "me" of everyday life—but has extended the boundaries of its identity. Certain people and objects physically separate from me have become quite literally me. Apart from these particular people and objects, everything and everybody else has remained "other," "not me"— more or less as they are "not me" under non-LSD conditions. The particular objects or people which were part of me have changed as the perimeters of self have fluctuated. (3) I have remained more or less the self I usually am, but I have become intensely aware of the relative nature of this self in relation to others. I have perceived that the self is not an independent entity completely separable from other selves. "I" and "other" have become correlate existences, neither of which could be isolated but both of which continually interacted interdependently. Accompanying this type of self-awareness and the preceding one, there has invariably been a tremendously strong sense of empathy with those about me at the time. (4) Distinguishable from all the above changes there has also occurred a complete disappearance of self in any and every sense—whether that of ego-self, universal Self, or other selves. Consciousness has continued, and perhaps more clearly than ever, with all the activities of body, mind, feeling, other humans, cars, sun, sky, earth, etc., continuing on in a complex, boundless flow neither chaotic nor orderly. At such a moment reality (or Reality) simply is being as it is, and this "beingness" has been of the deepest significance, beyond both chaos and particular patterns.

It is important to remember that the four radical transformations of self I have tried to describe were immediate, nonconceptual realizations and not sudden, conceptualized insights. While under the influence of LSD one may have many ideational insights, or he may have none. He may intentionally think or endeavor to conceptualize, or he may not. Although I have made great effort to think about what was going on, or had just gone on while still in LSD sessions, the modifications described above were not originally discoveries of thought, and I have never been satisfied with any of my attempts to describe them verbally.

A very common experience reported by many LSD subjects is a changed perspective toward conventional social forms. The conventionalities of everyday interpersonal behavior appear to be ridiculous and superficial. Many times such interchanges as "How are you?", "I am fine," "I am so glad to see you," are even seen to be hypocritical.

With one or two exceptions the selections of typical LSD experiences referred to thus far have not included obviously psychotic-like features. Yet one term which has been used to classify LSD, mescaline, and similar drugs is "psychotomimetic." Literature on LSD experiments with normal subjects is full of accounts of psychotic-like responses. Increased anxiety, confusion, paranoiac suspicion, withdrawal from any actions or communication, may dominate the experiences of a particular subject. Psychotomimetic responses generally seem to be characterized by contraction and withdrawal. The subject does not go along with the experience, does not relax into it or accept whatever may come. He fights it and tries to control or suppress the various events in accordance with his ideas of order and reason. If the dosage is weak enough or if certain inner defenses are strong enough, he may succeed in shutting out all effects. But such success is often accompanied by withdrawal from all communication and/or restless uneasiness and anxiety.[7] On the other hand, instead of suppressing or over-controlling the experience, one may "go with it," accepting whatever comes. Yet it is as impossible to advise another how to do this as it is to tell another how to balance a bicycle. "Going with it" does not necessarily banish immediately all threatening and terrifying events, although it does make such events positively interesting and exhilarating.

If one has some problems which he has not faced—of either a preconscious or unconscious sort—these are likely to pre-

---

[7] J. N. Sherwood, M. J. Stolaroff and W. W. Harman, "The Psychedelic Experience—A New Concept in Psychotherapy" (unpublished paper, International Foundation for Advanced Study, Menlo Park, California), 2.

sent themselves in some form or other at the time he is relaxing into the LSD experience. If he does not try to evade or suppress the insights regarding his self and his life situation, the act of experiencing is likely to become more fluid, exhilarating, and unifying, and this may lead to exalted experiences of union with God or Reality. An example of this latter development is given in an autobiographical account by Wilson Van Dusen, Chief Clinical Psychologist at Mendocino State Hospital. After describing how in his first three LSD sessions he had been stripped of all with which he ordinarily identified himself—professional role, physical body, and internal images—Van Dusen says that in the fourth session, he was in bed withdrawn into his primal me-ness:

> If this [primal me-ness] went I would die because it was all that was left of me. In this black void there was just me, I prayed accepting this death. God was walking on me and I cried with joy. My own voice seemed to speak of His coming, but I didn't believe it. Suddenly and totally unexpectedly the zenith of the void was lit up with the blinding presence of the One. How did I know it? All I can say was that there was no possibility of doubt. Down beneath *me,* above the *One.* Suddenly the light from above fused into the me below. Then I knew there was only God and from the beginning of time I was destined to reappear as a psychologist. Sadly I was thrown out of paradise to return as a most upset man. How could I be God and man at the same time? My conventional concept of myself had been shattered in a few minutes.[8]

Van Dusen goes on to tell how later he learned "the most bitter lesson of all," that "the One beyond time and space and the One of the commonplace were the same." He reports that after his initial experiences of God and paradise there was a strong desire to know them again with the aid of LSD. "At first there is a dependence as though only this drug can bring back the vision of paradise, but with the opening up of the commonplace the need of the drug draws to a close." Van Dusen also indicates that unitive experiences such as his must

[8] Wilson Van Dusen, "LSD and the Enlightenment of Zen," *Psychologia,* IV, 1 (March 1961), 13f.

be distinguished from the feelings of the schizophrenic who thinks he is God. The schizophrenic experiences an ego-inflation which cuts off communication and isolates him from the commonplace. In Van Dusen's experience it was clear that all other people are also of divine nature, with the result that "one inclines to a more humble respect of others."[9]

## III

In the preceding sections types of experiences reported by LSD subjects are surveyed. The variety is bewilderingly complex—extending from schizophrenic-like delusions to enhanced perceptions of visual relationships; from paranoiac withdrawal to expansive recognition of the living interrelatedness of all beings in everyday life; from chaotic anxieties to a liberating experience of "union with God" which carries over into the commonplace. Can any way be found to explain the apparent unpredictability of LSD experiences? It may seem a truism to say that the great variations are due to a multiplicity of complex factors, but I think that in theorizing about the dynamics of LSD experiences, it is most necessary to assert continually a multi-factor view of causation. With many others who write on LSD, Sherwood, Stolaroff, and Harman insist that results from such drugs as this one and mescaline "are dependent not only upon dosage, but upon the intention of the subject as he submits himself to the experience, the kind of preparation he has had prior to the taking of the material, the setting of the session, and the help of the therapist who has himself explored deeply in these unfamiliar regions of the mind. Because of this dependence, reports and opinions in the literature vary widely."[10]

In spite of such clear statements about the complexity of the matter, much of the literature still suggests, if not declares outright, that LSD itself causes more or less directly paranoiac states, schizophrenic responses, visual modifications, mystical realizations, etc. If one thing is certain from all the differing

[9] *Ibid.*, pp. 14f.
[10] Sherwood *et al.*, *op. cit.*, p. 1.

reports, it is that the effects of LSD are not a matter of simple linear causality. To put it crudely, LSD does not "secrete" or directly cause the "secretion" of either schizophrenia or mystical enlightenment. This is not to deny that LSD is an important factor in facilitating or precipitating the experiences described. The point is that LSD per se does not determine the particular nature or significance of the experiences. Of crucial positive importance are the personality of the subject with his current attitudes and problems, the physical setting of the sessions, and the interpersonal relations of doctor and subject, together with other factors that are at present unknown.

Sherwood *et al.* introduce some order into the situation by classifying LSD experiences according to three major "stages." In the "evasive" stage the subject endeavors to evade the impact of the experience either by rigidly controlling it or by suppressing it. It is here that most of the extreme psychotomimetic effects occur. In the second or "symbolic" stage, there emerge all of the hallucinatory visual effects which usually are related to insights into the subject's own personality or into general ideals of a philosophical or religious nature. In the third stage of "immediate perception," the subject relinquishes his habitual concepts about himself and the world and confronts an entirely new reality, or perceives reality in an entirely new way. It is here that experiences like Van Dusen's realization of God in the commonplace occur. For Sherwood *et al.* the evidence strongly suggests that as various subjects move into this third stage there may be "a universal central perception, apparently independent of subjects' previous philosophical or theological inclinations. . . ."[11] These investigators point out that similar insights are found in many religious traditions. The examples they use make it clear that they have in mind what are usually called mystical forms of religion.

[11] *Ibid.*, pp. 2–4, 13.

## IV

Are LSD experiences like mystical experiences? As there are many varieties of LSD experiences, so there are many varieties of experiences called "mystical." J. B. Pratt points out that at least two dozen different definitions of mysticism can easily be found, "each differing in something besides words from all the rest, and every one representing some fairly common usage."[12] In so far as either mystical or LSD experiences can be described, selected varieties of the one are undoubtedly like selected varieties of the other. In the present exploratory study reference can be made to only a few major types of mystical experiences. For convenience, these types are tentatively classified under five headings:

(1) One feels unified with the world around him, a world that is perceived as shiningly new and of profound significance. Thomas Traherne tells of such an experience in which everything seemed to exist and move for him alone and "to stand in Eden, or be built in Heaven."[13] Huxley's first experience with mescaline seems to have been somewhat of the same order.[14] R. C. Zaehner has given several examples of this type, both involving and not involving drugs, although several of his selections have negative or "demonic" aspects.[15]

(2) One beholds visionary creatures, which psychologically would be termed "hallucinations," and with which one may or may not feel united. Famous examples of this from the literature of mysticism are found in the writings of Ezekiel, William Blake, and Emanuel Swedenborg. Some biblical scholars have alleged that because similar images were present in the myths and art forms of Near Eastern cultures, the visions of Ezekiel were fabrications of his conscious mind. Should such scholars once see, "really out there," LSD-

---

[12] J. B. Pratt, *The Religious Consciousness* (New York: Macmillan, 1920), p. 337.

[13] As quoted in Aldous Huxley, *The Perennial Philosophy* (New York: Harper & Brothers, 1945), pp. 75f.

[14] Huxley, *The Doors of Perception*, pp. 18–22.

[15] Zaehner, *op. cit.*, chaps. 3, 4.

induced visions, they might revise this opinion. The particular forms present in one's cultural environment may be the very ones which emerge as living "realities" in visionary experiences.

My present impression is that statistically speaking, most mystical-like LSD experiences could be classified under the preceding two headings. In *Heaven and Hell*, Huxley seems to think that drug-induced experiences are "visionary."[16] The examples of mystical-like drug experiences which R. C. Zaehner selects mostly fall under the first two categories, although Zaehner might recognize the next type as possible in connection with drugs.

(3) As Plotinus succinctly puts it, you are "self-gathered in the purity of your being, nothing now remaining that can shatter that inner unity, . . . wholly true to your essential nature. . . ."[17] Preceding this inner unity there has been a withdrawal from sense operations, ordinary mental operations, and imagination. This withdrawal is a major aspect of what is often called "purgation" by Western mystics and seems to parallel very closely Van Dusen's withdrawal into his "primal me-ness" as well as experiences described in conversation by two or three other LSD subjects.

(4) One's essential nature or self is united with God or Brahman or whatever it may be called. According to many writers this is *the* mystical experience. Various descriptions of this type may be found in the writings of such mystics as St. John of the Cross, Suso, Eckhart, Jalalu'l-Din Rumi, Sankara, and Ramakrishna. Two different types of experiences may be involved which seem similar, descriptively speaking. In the one, which Zaehner calls "the normal type of Christian mystical experience," the essential self and God remain separate realities even though the self may be "permeated through and through with the divine substance."[18] In the other, there is a union with God, Brahman, or Reality which obliterates the distinction between the individual and the universal or

16 Huxley, *Heaven and Hell*, pp. 16f., 43, 56.

17 *Plotinus: The Ethical Treatises*, I.6.9., trans. Mackenna (Boston: C. T. Branford, n.d.).

18 Zaehner, *op. cit.*, pp. 22, 33.

divine. Sankara's affirmation that the liberated man *is* Brahman might be considered an example, as might various affirmations of identity with God made by Christian mystics. Zaehner recognizes that such claims to identity have been made by Christians but he explains them away as poetic figures of speech, or as accurate descriptions of what the mystic feels but which must be corrected in the light of orthodox doctrine.[19] He further interprets non-Christian experiences of absolute unity as instances of our fourth category. It is interesting to note that Martin Buber similarly explains mystics' experiences of absolute oneness as either unity of self or mis-evaluations of ecstatic union with God in which self and God nonetheless remain distinct.[20]

On the basis of my own LSD experiences and of careful comparison with various mystics' descriptions, I am convinced that there may be both the experiences describable only in terms of a trans-individual universal oneness *and* experiences of "union with God" in which the individual self is not lost. Thorough discussion of this point is beyond the scope of the present analysis. As a matter of fact, such discussion would probably be difficult and obscure for those who have not had at least a glimpse of the experiences in question. The mystics have always claimed that one cannot hope really to understand their verbal and symbolic reports unless he also has had similar experiences. Drugs like LSD could be of tremendous aid to the non-mystical psychologist of religion who seeks greater understanding of the data of mystical religious experiences. Several sessions as an LSD subject under proper medical supervision and with thoughtful advanced preparation might well lead the psychologist of religion to approach his data with more flexible assumptions as to what can occur in human experiences and with clearer evaluation of the mystic's problems of communication and interpretation. Probably several sessions would be needed to make him fully aware of the variety of effects that can occur.

(5) A final type of mystical apprehension has been well

---

[19] *Ibid.*, pp. 29, 32.

[20] Martin Buber, *I and Thou* (Edinburgh: T. and T. Clark, 1937), pp. 86f.

described by Martin Buber: "To look away from the world, or to stare at it, does not help a man to reach God; but he who sees the world in Him stands in His presence . . . to eliminate or leave behind nothing at all, to include the whole world in the *Thou*, to give the world its due and its truth, to include nothing beside God but everything in Him—this is full and complete relation."[21] In this case the mystery of the divine Being is not beyond nature and the phenomenal world, as Zaehner says it must be;[22] rather, asserts Buber, "it has made its dwelling here where everything happens as it happens."[23] After experiencing purgation and union with God, as in our fourth category, Van Dusen learned "the most bitter lesson of all," that "the One beyond time and space and the One of the commonplace were the same." Van Dusen thinks that this sort of realization is not just one experience among others, "but is rather the very heart of human experience."[24] In light of Buber's theory of knowledge, I think that Buber would agree.[25] This "very heart of human experience" is probably the "universal central perception" of which Sherwood *et al.* speak and which, in their observation, has not led their subjects away from everyday life but has given them "added meaning and zest in their life in this world."[26]

Though the mode of experiencing in our last category keeps one responsively and responsibly involved in everyday life,[27] many other varieties of mysticism are often compared to certain psychotic states. Zaehner even suggests that most "natural" (as distinguished from "supernatural") mystical experiences are forms of "madness." He points out that both natural mystical experiences and drug experiences heighten "the susceptibilities" and hence "will make the good man better and

[21] *Ibid.*, p. 79.

[22] Zaehner, *op. cit.*, pp. 22, 33.

[23] Buber, *Between Man and Man* (Boston: Beacon Paperbacks, 1955 [1948]), p. 14.

[24] Van Dusen, *op. cit.*, p. 16.

[25] See Maurice S. Friedman, *Martin Buber: The Life of Dialogue* (New York: Harper Torchbooks, 1960 [1955]), pp. 161–75.

[26] Sherwood *et al., op. cit.*, pp. 14f.

[27] Cf. Buber, *I and Thou*, p. 87; *Between Man and Man*, pp. 14–17.

the bad man worse."[28] What he does not take into account is the persistent claim of many researchers that drugs like LSD more often than not seem to precipitate therapeutic insights even when the experiences are hellish for the subject.[29] This thrust toward healing insights even in the midst of, or because of, psychotic-like reactions which are similar to or identical with certain types of religious experience suggests that such hallucinogenic drugs as LSD can be potent research aids for exploring Anton Boisen's hypothesis that the frequent association of the mystical and the pathological in the history of religions is not accidental. For Zaehner, as for many, the term "madness" seems to carry principally negative connotations. Boisen, on the other hand, contends that "the correct contrast is not between the pathological and the normal in religious experience but between spiritual defeat and spiritual victory, and the more severe disturbances serve to isolate and throw into clear relief certain of the significant variables."[30]

If thoughtful approaches to co-operative research could be worked out by the joint endeavor of psychiatrists, psychologists, and psychologists of religion, investigations with hallucinogenic drugs might clarify and extend the implications of Boisen's hypothesis. Such clarification and extension might be the most important contribution psychology of religion could make to the sick world of today, particularly if it is true that at least certain mental disorders are not simply "diseases" but have, more importantly, a positive, therapeutic significance in man's spiritual quest.

[28] Zaehner, *op. cit.*, chaps. 4, 5; p. 104.

[29] See, for example, Ditman and Whittlesey, report summarized in *Medical Science,* III, 12 (June 25, 1958), 746f.; Sherwood *et al., op. cit.;* Van Dusen, *op. cit.*, pp. 14f.

[30] Anton T. Boisen, *The Exploration of the Inner World* (New York: Harper Torchbooks, 1962 [1936]), p. 79.

# TRANSCENDENTAL MEDITATION

## STUDENTS INTERNATIONAL MEDITATION SOCIETY and DEMETRI P. KANELLAKOS

## I

The purpose of transcendental meditation is to help every individual expand his mind, develop his creative intelligence and make use of his full potential in studies, career and recreation.

Transcendental meditation is a natural technique which allows the conscious mind to experience increasingly more subtle states of thought until the source of thought, the unlimited reservoir of energy and creative intelligence, is reached. This simple practice expands the capacity of the conscious mind, and a man is able to use his full potential in all fields of thought and action.

It is natural for every man to want to develop his potential and evolve his life. This development is easy and automatic when one knows how to make contact with the source of thought which lies deep within. This basic source, which is one's own Self or Being, is transcendental in nature, nonchanging and absolute, as distinguished from one's field of activity, which is of relative and changing nature.

The first portion of this article is reprinted from the *Outline of Basic and Advanced Courses in Transcendental Meditation* by permission of the Students International Meditation Society, National Headquarters, 1015 Gayley Avenue, Los Angeles, California 90024. The second portion is adapted from a lecture by Demetri P. Kanellakos on "The Science of Creative Intelligence," delivered at Stanford University in Palo Alto, California, in January 1970, and reprinted by permission of Mr. Kanellakos.

Every man has the ability to include within his consciousness the transcendental field as well as the subjective and objective aspects of life. The whole range of relative creation and the field of absolute Being lie within the scope of human consciousness. And when a man makes conscious contact with Being he is encompassing within his individual life the basis of all life. Thus, his full potential is the unlimited potential of absolute Being. A man begins to reflect and enjoy that unlimited potential in his own activity and begins to experience, in his own terms, a better life.

The full range of man's life in terms of absolute and relative may be made clearer through the example of the life of a tree. The relative aspects of a tree are the trunk, branches, leaves, flowers and fruit, which are obvious, together with the root, which is less obvious. Investigating more closely, we find that although the basis of the outer tree is the inner root, the root itself has no independent, absolute status. It is dependent completely upon the field of nourishment which lies beyond the root. This field is the basis of both the inner and outer aspects of the tree and provides the essential constituent of its life. The whole tree is made of this essential constituent, and if any part of the tree begins to lose contact with this field of nourishment, problems arise. However, as long as contact is maintained the tree enjoys full growth and life. Thus, we find the tree to be an individual expression of its own unlimited field of nourishment; the tree appears to be bound to the relative aspects of the inner root and outer limbs, but its very basis, from which it draws its own life strength, is beyond these limitations in a transcendental absolute field.

Similarly, individual human life has the same outer and inner relative aspects together with the aspect of transcendental absolute nature. The outer aspect of a man's life is his body and environment; the inner aspect of his personality is his mind, and his transcendental aspect is Being or the field of pure consciousness which is the essential constituent of man and the basis of all his experience and activity.

## Skill in Action

For an individual to expand his mind, develop his potential and thereby experience increasing progress and fulfillment in his life, it is necessary for him to be in contact with transcendental pure consciousness, his own essential nature. Success in action, or skill in action, demands that *before* engaging in activity the mind be brought to this stable field of unlimited energy and creative intelligence. This is necessary in the same way that an archer must first pull the arrow back on the bow before shooting it ahead. As the arrow is drawn back fully it gains maximum power and direction for going forward. If the arrow is not pulled back first, the attempt will lack skill and fall short of success.

The two phases of man's existence, as we have seen, are absolute and relative, and it is skill in action which brings these two together, enabling all values of life to be lived. Otherwise, on the one hand, the absolute remains transcendental, outside the field of activity and as if of no practical value; on the other hand, the field of relative life is left strained because one's experience and activity remain without basis and, therefore, weak in an ever-changing, unstable phase. If, in this one-sided situation, a man's activity continues to require more energy and intelligence from him, it is inevitable that stress and tension will develop. This lack of *available* potential is what restricts man's progress and enjoyment of life. That is why it is skill in action which integrates the stable absolute of transcendental nature with the changing relative field of experience. Both are brought together on the level of the mind, just as in the life of the tree the field of nourishment and the outer sphere of the tree are brought together by the instrumentality of the root, which draws nourishment from one side and supplies it to the other.

The practice of transcendental meditation is skill in action because by expanding the mind to the source of thought it puts an individual in direct contact with his own infinite reservoir of energy and creative intelligence, and thereby prepares him for successful action. Coming out of meditation, having more of his full potential available, a meditator naturally begins to experience increased happiness and success in his activity of daily life.

Anyone can begin to practice skill in action by devoting a few minutes in the morning and evening to transcendental meditation. The process is effortless, requiring no particular ability on the part of the meditator other than the natural ability to think. During meditation he automatically experiences more subtle states of thought until his mind gains the state of Being. The process is increasingly pleasant as the mind consciously transcends to the state of pure consciousness.

Transcendental meditation is easy and natural in that it makes use of the tendency of the mind to shift attention always in the direction of more satisfying fields of experience. We find that the natural tendency of the mind is to go automatically to a field of greater happiness; no one has to be taught to want to enjoy more in life, to be more, to accomplish more, to experience more . . . Therefore, transcendental meditation involves no control or effort, no concentration or contemplation. These methods tend to restrict the attention and hold the mind to gross levels of perception, whereas in transcendental meditation the mind is allowed to expand and experience subtler states of thought in the direction of the source of thought until the source is reached.

## Physiology of an Evolving Man

It has been found that different states of consciousness are reflected through different states of the nervous system, the machinery we use to experience our life. Waking, dreaming and deep sleep—the relative states of consciousness—have their corresponding physiological states in the body, and there is, as well, a corresponding physiological state when the mind transcends to the state of pure consciousness. Therefore, the different states of consciousness that an individual experiences can be accounted for by changes in the state of the nervous system. Man enjoys the variety of his own existence through changes in his machinery of experience. In reality, he remains absolute in the pure consciousness of his essential nature even while different relative states of consciousness are experienced. This same principle may be found in the example of one bright sun shining everywhere, remaining one even while its many and varied reflections are produced through changes in the reflecting substance; for instance, as cloudy water becomes clear the reflection is closer to the reality of the sun itself.

As the mind transcends during meditation, natural physiological changes occur in the body corresponding to changes in mental activity and the level of experience. Profound rest is brought to the system. The mind and body gain a state of *"restful alertness"* which, on the physical level, corresponds to the state of pure consciousness. For this state to be lived always, or in other words, for full potential to be readily available in all activity, it is essential that the nervous system be refined to reflect or maintain transcendental Being even while fully engaged in activity.

An evolved man enjoys the stability of Being in the midst of dynamic activity. To accomplish this state involves culturing the nervous system, the seat of consciousness, in such a way that it becomes capable of reflecting Being along with the other states of consciousness. The process of refining the system to this normal and integrated state of life is simple and natural, yet delicate, taking its own time. Alternating two brief periods of transcendental meditation with daily activity brings this infusion of Being into the nature of the active mind and through it into all aspects of one's experience in the relative field.

## II

It has recently been more widely recognized, particularly in the West, that in a similar way the human nervous system acquires what we may call the transcendental state as a consequence of meditative "exercises," and especially during transcendental meditation. It has been found that physiological processes take place during the time the human nervous system is in the meditative state. These physiological and biochemical processes apparently relieve the strains and stresses accumulated on the nervous system itself more efficiently than during either dreaming or sleeping. Subtler levels of the nervous system (or the mind) are touched and brought into conscious use (hence the expansion of mind).

Some of the physiological changes that take place during a half-hour of practicing of transcendental meditation or other meditative exercise successfully performed, such as some practices of Yoga and Zen meditation, are, for example: 1) a reduction of the metabolic rate by up to 25–30 per cent; 2) a reduction of the total oxygen consumption by up to 20 per cent; 3) a reduction of the breathing rate to 4–6 breaths per minute from 12–14 per minute; 4) an increase of the amount of alpha waves (8–12Hz) of the brain; 5) the appearance of theta waves (5–8Hz) in the brain; 6) a reduction of the blood pressure by an average 20 or so per cent in hypersensitive patients; 7) a great increase (more than five times) of the skin resistance; 8) changes in the pH and sodium bicarbonate of blood; 9) reduction of the uropepsin output; 10) a decrease of the cardial output (heart blood flow) by about 25 per cent; 11) a marked decrease (up to 50 per cent) of the lactate ion in the blood; and others.

Some of the results of transcendental meditation are 1) increased energy and efficiency in performing any kind of work a person performed before he began to meditate; 2) increased calmness and decreased physical and mental tensions; 3) increases in creativity, productivity, inventiveness, discrimination, intuitiveness and concentration (getting better grades in school, for example); 4) loss of a desire for or a complete elimination of hallucinogenic or depressant drugs such as LSD, marijuana, amphetamines, tobacco, coffee or alcohol; 5) attenuation of such symptoms as bad body posture, insomnia, high blood pressure; and 6) better mobilization of body resources to combat various strenuous circumstances such as in accidents, sensory monotony, confined places, cases of injury and others. Such results can be experienced by anyone who practices transcendental meditation regularly and correctly.

The changes that accompany both the meditative state and

the living style during wakefulness come about rapidly, easily, naturally and quite automatically. No mood need be created by wearing beads, special headgear or clothes, or performing any ceremonies or adhering to any strange practices. All these activities tend to inhibit overall and natural progress. It is reported, for example, that persons who have practiced transcendental meditation a few minutes in the morning and evening for a few months or years produce some of the physiological changes observed on Zen masters of more than twenty years of ascetic meditation. The mind (i.e., dynamic thinking), however, is more effective or powerful in bringing about a change in consciousness, i.e. from the waking state to that of the transcendental state, than the manipulation of the body (i.e. postures or physical exercise) even though the two interact. Transcendental meditation is a dynamic technique on the natural thinking (not intellectual) level. It can be taught very easily by a trained teacher in a few hours over a period of four days.

Man therefore can exist in at least four major states of consciousness: those of deep sleep, dreaming, wakefulness and transcendental. The time we spend in deep sleep is apparently used to rejuvenate the body by the emission of certain growth hormones, and to remove body fatigue so we can function physiologically during wakefulness. The time we spend during dreaming is apparently used to remove psychological strains and stresses from our minds so that we can function better mentally and psychologically during wakefulness. The well-known sleep and dreaming deprivation experiments on men and animals support this view.

Similarly, the time spent during meditation is used to rejuvenate both the body and the mind at deeper and finer levels, i.e. to rejuvenate our machinery of experiencing the central nervous system itself. If a person is deprived of his daily meditation time, then he feels not as sharp, not as clear, not as fulfilled. He is not as energetic and he strains more in whatever he does. In a few words, he experiences suffering. Transcendental meditation, which takes the practitioner to the fourth major state of human existence, comes to fill this vital need of our time. The technique is as ancient as mankind, universal in its application and anyone who wishes can add this new physiological rhythm to his existence. This new physiological rhythm would then work together with the other physiological rhythms (such as the heartbeat, the breathing, the circadian rhythm, etc.) which are controlled by the autonomic nervous system.

# THE EXPERIMENTAL INDUCTION OF RELIGIOUS-TYPE EXPERIENCES

JEAN HOUSTON and
ROBERT E. L. MASTERS

Of all the hard facts of science, I know of none more solid and fundamental than the fact that if you inhibit thought (and persevere) you come at length to a region of consciousness below or behind thought, and different from ordinary thought in its nature and character—a consciousness of quasi-universal quality, and a realization of an altogether vaster self than that to which we are accustomed. And since the ordinary consciousness, with which we are concerned in ordinary life, is before all things founded on the little local self, and is in fact self-conscious in the little local sense, it follows that to pass out of that is to die to the ordinary self and the ordinary world.

It is to die in the ordinary sense, but in another sense, it is to wake up and find that the "I," one's real, most intimate self, pervades the universe and all other beings —that the mountains and the sea and the stars are a part of one's body and that one's soul is in touch with the souls of all creatures. . . .

So great, so splendid is this experience, that it may be said that all minor questions and doubts fall away in face of it; and certain it is that in thousands and thousands of cases the fact of its having come even once to a man has

Unpublished paper, first presented by Jean Houston at Brandeis University, October 30, 1968. Printed here by permission of the authors. The non-drug work described in this paper was supported by funds of the Erickson Educational Foundation, New York, and Baton Rouge, Louisiana.

completely revolutionized his subsequent life and outlook on the world.[1]

The foregoing statement, made over half a century ago by
the poet-scientist Edward Carpenter, seems very timely today
—because, of course, it is timeless. It describes a reality of the
human psyche that does not change with events and environ-
ments as do the forms of our madnesses and our lesser aber-
rations. The experience is real and essentially unchanging;
and, as he observes, it can be psychotherapeutic, growth-
promoting, radically transformative of human personality.
What Carpenter intends by "inhibiting thought" is one, but
not the only, means to achieve similar awarenesses with similar results.

In recent years, as everyone now knows, it has been discovered that psychedelic drugs can facilitate religious-type
experiences which have a therapeutic effect; and, indeed, that
psychedelic psychotherapy tends to be most effective precisely when religious-type experiences of some profundity do
occur. This conclusion stems not just out of our research but
out of the experience of a large number of investigators and
psychotherapists who have worked with the LSD-type drugs
throughout the world. For example, Dr. Ruth Fox, the medical director of the National Council on Alcohol, stated with
reference to LSD therapy of chronic alcoholics:

"In this transcendental (drug-state) experience there may
be a recognition of 'cosmic consciousness.' Not every patient
experiences this complete feeling of 'being at one with the
universe.' It seems that the closer one comes to it, however,
the more effective and lasting is the change in personality."[2]

To this it should be added that the therapeutic and transformative religious-type experiences take various forms, of
which "being at one with the universe" is only one, but a
frequent, example.

In view of the foregoing, it should be evident why work

[1] Carpenter, E., *The Drama of Love and Death* (New York:
H. Allen, 1912).
[2] Quoted by Clark, W. H., "Religious Aspects of Psychedelic
Drugs," *California Law Review*, Vol. 56:86, 1968, p. 92.

with psychedelic drugs has had the following effects, among others:

It has made viable once more a previously near-moribund psychology of religious experience; and it has excited great interest in the therapeutic and self-actualizing potentials of religious-type experiences and the states of consciousness in which they happen in their most potent forms. . . .

Like many other LSD researchers, we did not set out to investigate religious or mystical experiences. But we very soon found ourselves obliged to undertake serious and extensive studies in the psychology of religious experience. We had to do this if we hoped to understand what was happening with subjects whose reports of profound mystical union with God did not seem to be adequately explained by such notions as somatopsychic depersonalization or ego dissolution, both labels that have within conventional psychiatry the function of describing severe psychopathology. Some of the claims of encounter with God, Ground of Being, Ultimate Reality, seemed to be accompanied by profound and beneficent personality changes. This does not usually occur as a product of a transient psychosis; but it has been reported throughout history in cases of religious experience.

In a possible LSD session that proceeds, in eight hours or so, through the principal drug-state levels of consciousness, the subject may experience, first of all, a great variety of sensory awarenesses unlike anything that he has known before. This appears to have a deconditioning function, freeing the subject from the confines of his usual categories and contexts. After that, the walls of the unconscious may be breached, psychodynamic processes magnified and revealed, and important insights be achieved. Next, the life-historical materials might emerge in symbolic and allegorical terms, seen with the eyes closed as eidetic images. The same sequence of materials also may be experienced at the same time in other sensory-image modes with a total involvement in dramatic sequences leading to symbolic resolution of personal conflicts and other problems. Finally, the person "descends" to that level of awareness apprehended as Essence, Noumenon,

Ground of Being. It is on this level that there occur the profound and sometimes transformative experiences of encounter
or mystical union with God—experiences adjudged by some
leading authorities, such as the late W. T. Stace, to be phenomenologically indistinguishable from religious and mystical
experiences traditionally accepted as authentic. When such
experience results in a drastic and positive change in behavior, including an enrichment of the spiritual life, we have
further evidence of a classical sort for authenticity.

This paper will not be concerned primarily with psychedelic drugs or those religious-type experiences occurring in
the drug-state. There now is an extensive literature devoted
to that subject, including our own book, *The Varieties of
Psychedelic Experience*,[3] especially the concluding chapters.
And it should, therefore, be of greater interest to report on
some new non-drug research which we have been conducting
and continue to conduct at our laboratory in New York City.
However, for the benefit of those still unfamiliar with the
drug-state experiences one case will be described here briefly.

The research subject—and all of our work has been in research and not in psychotherapy—was a successful executive
in his early fifties. As is the case with all of our subjects, he
should be considered "normal," with no problems beyond
those confronting even the best-adjusted members of our species. He is intensely interested in art.

This subject's experience followed, in general, the pattern
of "descent" that has been described, except that, having no
urgent psychological problems, there was little concern with
his own personal history and, instead, a somewhat greater
than usual amount of philosophical discussion. His attention
then was focused upon Eastern art, as he selected several
illustrated books on that subject from among a broad selec-
tion of art and other books that were available to him. The
religious art occupied him especially, and he mentioned that
he thought a particular picture would be extremely important
for him, if only he could find it. He was then handed a picture
of a Japanese Buddha, and at once he sighed ecstatically,

[3] New York: Holt, Rinehart & Winston, 1966.

started to weep and then closed his eyes. What followed next, he describes in a report written several days later.

> . . . I experienced a shattering thunderbolt of ecstacy and my body dissolved into the flow of matter or energy of which the universe is made. I was swept into the core of existence from which all things arise and into which all things converge. Here there is no distinction between subject and object, space and time, or anything else. Here everything simply *is* and there is no beginning and no ending—only becoming.
>
> The aspect of this place is quite simple, although I cannot recall details too well. There is a flow into the center and a flow out from the center, but no form. The color is neutral, both warm and cool, and there is a soft light emanating from underneath, giving off a faint glow. I do not remember if there was any sound, but there was total integration so there would be no distinction between sound and no sound. All one is aware of is pure ecstacy and love.
>
> There was no dominant element or directing force. Everything flowed from itself by its own energy. If there is any god or creative power, it exists only as a man-made concept.
>
> In form, the ultimate reality seemed at times to have four corners, but this may have been a transitional stage of vision prior to reaching the center. I recall describing the core as a sphere composed of an infinite number of small spheres revolving in a spiral toward a center which itself is infinite, and that each of the small spheres is composed of still smaller spheres also revolving toward an infinite center and so on. How this concept came to me I do not know, as I do not have a clear recollection of such an image. It may be that at the ultimate point one is within the core and can no longer observe.
>
> There is no sensation as such at the core—only a state of utter, ineffable bliss. Here, as in the earlier phases, one is aware of a tremendous surge of compassion and a powerful desire to share one's rapture with others. As the self dissolves, the other becomes one with all else and so there is no selfishness. Nor is there any element of conflict—because all are one.
>
> I am aware of having made a loud exclamation at the moment of revelation and having spoken at some times during my deepest experience, but I do not remember any words except that at the end I said, "all is indeed

one," as I discovered this truth. I have no idea whether I was seconds or hours in this state.

As I felt myself reappearing from the profound rapture of the core, I questioned, momentarily, the value of returning. For an instant (or was it an hour?) I was tempted to remain in the place of infinite beauty, but I began to think of the interest that life in the world holds —music, books, art, people—a different kind of pleasure than the other, and I let myself rise to the surface of consciousness. What would have happened if my joy in the world were not quite so strong and I had yielded to that temptation?

As is characteristic of both psychedelic and traditional mystics, the subject accompanied his account with apologies for his feeble effort to describe an essentially ineffable experience.

Some years later, this man still regards the experience just described as having been the most profound and most beautiful of his life. Lacking urgent problems and major personality deficits, he was not changed by his experience in any ways sharply apparent to himself or others. Yet he feels that there were profound, although subtle, changes. On the whole, as is typical of subjects of this kind, he felt that the experience basically confirmed his life-pattern. As he notes, he contained the experience well within what he regards as his atheistic framework. He did not become messianic about drugs, although he has subsequently made such efforts as he could to promote legitimate research and a sober, informed view of LSD in both its social and its scientific contexts. He retains his feeling that "all are one," and believes himself to be more compassionate than he was previously. He has not sought further LSD experiences.

During our years of psychedelic drug research, we observed experiences equally profound, and a great many others ranging down from this qualitative level to experiences superficial and of types such as are presently associated with the faddist mysticism and religion thriving in the current drug subculture. When there was need for it, the profound experiences changed person and behavior in important ways, resolving psychological conflicts in some cases, but in others giving new philosophical concepts and values, improving perception, reawakening affection for a marriage partner or bringing about various other significant, beneficent changes. And these changes seemed much more dependent upon the person's reaching deep levels of consciousness and having religious-type experiences than they were upon occurrences of the kinds considered therapeutically important within the frameworks of psychoanalytic and most other psychotherapies now in use. For the sick, such experiences tended to be healing; but they also appeared to contribute to the growth and self-realization of the comparatively healthy individual. Moreover, it appeared that psychedelic experience could bring about an enhanced creativity, as we have discussed at some length, with case histories, in our recent book, *Psychedelic Art.*[4]

Our work with psychedelics was increasingly concerned with growth- and creativity-enhancing experiences, with mapping the phenomenology of the religious-type experiences, and with exploring the nature and functions of eidetic imagery. Then, several years ago, and long before we would have wished to discontinue the research, our work and almost all other work with psychedelics was terminated by legislation intended to cope—but not really coping—with the growing social problem of unsupervised self-experimentation with the drugs. The hysteria generated by psychedelic drugs presumably needs no detailed description. But it is extremely unfortunate that a major victim of that public reaction was the research and almost all therapeutic use as well. Presently, there is no research whatever with normal people, and it has been said that there will be none; and the therapeutic use is confined to just a handful of small, federally controlled projects.

Thus, the recent interest of young people in finding ways of "turning on without drugs" has had its parallel among some former LSD researchers bent upon finding means to continue to explore avenues of highly promising investigation opened up by the psychedelic drugs and then so abruptly closed by the bans upon drug work. Our own current research project is one result of the search for adequate alternatives to the psychedelics. Although (as of this writing) the

4 New York: Grove Press, 1968.

project has been of short duration, it has already yielded some results of interest, including the creation of devices and techniques that do alter consciousness and do give continuity to our work.

Two of these devices are called by us, respectively, the Altered States of Consciousness Induction Device—which abbreviates to A.S.C.I.D., or ASCID—and the Audio-Visual Environment, which comes down to A.V.E., or AVE, a famous salutation of the Angel Gabriel to the Virgin Mary that has the twin meanings of hail and farewell! When one is dealing daily in visions and ecstacies it is best to keep a sense of humor in the armamentarium.

The ASCID was developed by us initially as a facilitator of visual or eidetic imagery. It is essentially a metal swing or pendulum in which the subject stands upright, supported by broad bands of canvas and wearing blindfold goggles. The device containing the subject moves in side-to-side, forward-and-backward, and rotating motions generated by the subject's body. Typically, in from two minutes to twenty, an altered state of consciousness or trance state results. Trance depth ranges from light to profound somnambulistic, but in almost all cases the subject experiences eidetic imagery, imagery in other sense modalities, and other phenomena characteristic of trance and psychedelic drug states. The trance is different from a hypnotic trance, especially in that the usual hypnotist-subject relationship does not obtain and the experience of the subject occurs with a high degree of autonomy and spontaneity—he goes, if you will, on his own trip. He is responsive, in most cases, to suggestions given him by the experimenter; but he is unusually free of dependency upon the suggestions and also feels very free to reject them. Subjects experienced in both hypnotic and ASCID trance states feel that the trances are distinctly different in basic ways; but a language adequate to a precise differentiation between types of trance states is presently lacking.

The Audio-Visual Environment is also productive of altered states of consciousness, of hypnoid and trance states, and of responses to the stimuli indicative of the altered state. This program consists of dissolving 2 × 2-inch slides, projected by two projectors, accompanied by a co-ordinated taped sound sequence, principally electronic music. The program is exactly repeatable since the sound tape controls at programmed intervals both the changing of the slides and the (flexible: 1 to 20 seconds) duration of the slide dissolves—a rather sophisticated, computerized system that is difficult to describe. Present audio-visual programs consist of from 120 to 160 slides and are from 30 to 45 minutes duration.

The slides, each one an individual oil painting, painted with transparent colors on 2 × 2-inch pieces of glass, are mostly abstract and intended either to suggest emotional and projective responses or to facilitate and encourage free projection—a "seeing into" the abstraction.

Slides are projected over the whole surface of an 8 × 8-foot semicircular rear projection screen, behind which the subject is sitting. This gives the effect of an "environment," of almost being *in* the painting pictured. Sound comes to the subject through a headphone or from speakers at each side of him. We work usually with a single subject but have utilized the program effectively with small groups of simultaneous viewers.

Responses to the program often are intense and include marked time distortion, empathy, anxiety, euphoria, body image changes, religious and erotic feelings and imagery, pronounced muscular relaxation, heightened suggestibility and, in some cases, trance states that continue after the program has ended and which then may be utilized for further experimentation. This is not "the movies," and it is not just another "light show," but it suggests film and multimedia possibilities that we may have to contend with in the near future. And it also may disclose in a magnified form alterations of consciousness with heightened suggestibility that already occur in milder forms with multimedia, television viewing and films. Many workers with altered states of consciousness believe that prolonged television viewing, especially, induces hypnoid states with increased suggestibility, especially to certain types of highly emotogenic imagery and propaganda messages. It is, of course, of very great importance to understand these media potentials.

We are continuing to refine our own program and make it more effective. There are important possibilities for induction and study of altered states of consciousness and also, possibly, for diagnosis and therapy—in addition to the implications and applications possible in the fields of communications and entertainment. As a vehicle for experimental induction of religious-type experiences, the audio-visual program has not achieved anything spectacular. But even the tapping of such deep psychical levels as are involved in such experiences seems a distinct possibility for the not-too-distant future.

On the other hand, the Altered States of Consciousness Induction Device already has been the setting for a number of religious-type experiences, both spontaneous and in varying degrees suggested.

For example, one subject with whom we have been working is a rather well-known theologian. His experiences in the device have been extremely intense, ecstatic and visionary. They have also had the fruitful effect of enriching his creative as well as his spiritual life. A writing block of long-standing has been dissolved, and in a period of just three months he has produced a series of papers that he thinks to be among the best he has yet written. We have read some of these, and they are, in fact, outstanding examples of a highly lucid presentation of difficult, complex ideas. He also reports several other benefits—improved relations with his family, better teaching and a continuing sense of growth—but these claims are less subject to verification than the dissolution of a creative block and subsequent high-level creative productivity.

It should be remarked that the subject was not given suggestions of improvement in any of these areas—no suggestions about the writing block, the better teaching, or any of the rest of it. If the effects he describes are attributable to the session, there might be many reasons for that. But one should not exclude as a possible cause the experiencing of deep psychical levels where, as with psychedelic drugs, there appears to be activated an entelechy or healing, self-actualizing force, including a creative thrust. This last is not surprising, and more and more we observe the similarities when not identities of the components of the creative process and the religious-type experiences. The artist, if he follows his road far enough, becomes a mystic—or, sometimes, a madman.

In the Altered States of Consciousness Induction Device, our subject-theologian entered quickly and deeply into what is presumably a trance state. He reported descending through darkness, then water, then fire, until he reached a vision of the Platonic forms. Speaking ecstatically, he declared that "It is as if my mind were united to the mind of God. I am expanding, expanding . . . and I can read secrets of the universe and glimpse the forms of things . . . Beautiful forms, mathematical forms, geometrical forms. They are all alive, colorful and brilliant. This is the Source of the Forms, the World of the Divine Ideas, the Creative Source. It is the *Fons et origo*." He continued his description, sighing, joyously weeping, moaning and sometimes writhing as if the experience were almost more than he was able to endure. Still he kept describing his experience: "It is the unity unified, it is the experience of the Unity, the *Nous,* the *Logos* of the soul, as if all unified in me!"

In his subsequent written account of this session, which lasted an hour and a half and throughout was similarly visionary and ecstatic, the subject wrote, in part:

> My experience of the world of forms was one of the two most profound and beautiful experiences of the session. The forms were luminescent—like mathematical or geometrical figures—but not abstract. They were spirit made concrete and were unbelievably dynamic, like the seeds of life. Their texture was crystal and they reflected the brilliant and glorious light of the sun. I felt that this was the world that Plato saw and that Augustine referred to as the *rationes seminales*.
> . . . Then I experienced many sides of matter—as dark and consuming non-being, as the infinite multiplicity. Ultimately I saw matter grounded in God—as the infinite womb of forms . . . Then I experienced the world of life—the infinite variety of living cells, the vast expanse of the night skies with millions of stars, the sands and the sea. I was asked what this might mean in my personal life, and I saw my home—all the plants and trees, my children and my wife and other persons whom I know. All formed a vast symphony of life—and I saw

the various levels of life all flowing from the Source and back to the Source.

After that I witnessed the generation of *Logos* from the Ground—this was the deepest experience I have yet had—and I saw it as light emanating out of the abyss. And I felt that my mind shared in this great mystery— that I had touched the depths and secret of my own mind.

. . . Then I had a long and extremely satisfying ex- perience of the integral and emanating aspect of all crea- tion as participating in the infinite life of the Source. And I was gradually restored to wakefulness by the instruc- tions of the guide.

What are we to say of experiences like this, occurring in a modern laboratory setting, and of the experimenter who helps make them possible? Is the experimenter priest, shaman or scientist primarily? What may be his responsibilities? After having witnessed, first with psychedelic drugs and more re- cently under other conditions, the most intense and subjec- tively valid mystical unions and encounters with God in various types of transcendental experiences, we have often pondered especially our moral position. The experimenter must ask himself if the Presence of God, so intensely experi- enced by the subject, is delusion or reality—and if reality, what kind—or what? If God is truly present in some religious experiences, but not present in those that occur during our experiments, then we are assisting in the production of an inauthentic religious experience that nonetheless can power- fully and beneficially transform the deluded individual and awaken in him, or intensify, a dedicated spiritual life. Similar questions arise with regard to the other varieties of profound religious-type experiences that we may induce or enable to occur. It is our feeling that these experiments and explorations are permissible given the experimenter's open-mindedness, re- spect for the subject and the subject's experience, and dedica- tion to the pursuit of knowledge. Given these attitudes and aims, there seems no reason why the experimenter should not venture upon terrain he shares with traditional gurus of the East and spiritual directors of the West. If man comes equipped with a spiritual core that can be made conscious to the end of health and enrichment, then it should be desirable to join in the effort to study that core and to make it more readily available to consciousness. If religious and mystical experiences are *only* regressive and nothing more than products of the activation of brain mechanisms and chemicals, then that harsh fact had best be made plain and adjustment made to it. We do shudder at the prospect, say, of implanted electrodes being used to trigger mystical experiences on the one hand, and to titillate various pleasure centers in the brain on the other. But should such a thing be possible, the brain researchers will discover it regardless of our own efforts. While remaining open to such a possibility, we must admit a bias in hoping that it does not occur. But, even if it did, what would be demonstrated is only the rather well-known fact that man is a psychoneuro-physiological being; and stimulating his "spiritual centers" by mechanical means would no more be a substitute for traditional religious experience than stimulating certain pleasure centers would be an adequate substitute for the union of two persons.

With regard to the cases already described, it probably would be more accurate to say that we helped *enable* the experience to occur, rather than that we *induced* it. Each of the individuals in question brought to his session a degree of development and an orientation that made possible the depth and richness of the experience on the one hand, the formal characteristics of the experience, on the other. And throughout our work it has been our observation that the profound and possibly authentic experiences occur only with those persons who could be considered well prepared for such experience. In therapy, it may be, the situation is different, and intensity of need, desperation and long-suffering can partly satisfy the prerequisite conditions.

In the absence of the subject's preparation, whether by spiritual growth-seeking or by need, can a religious-type experience occur? And can one *induce* a religious-type experience or, rather, at the most help to enable such experience? We have explored these questions in numerous experiments of widely differing kinds by utilizing trance and inferred hypnoidal states variously induced.

One experiment was typically conducted in the Altered States of Consciousness Induction Device. The subject, in the altered state induced by that device, was led to experience a variety of changes in his body image. He experienced various of the *Alice in Wonderland*-type body image changes which so often occur spontaneously in psychedelic drug states: extreme shrinkage and growth, becoming heavier and lighter, alterations in the felt body density and substance. Finally, it was brought to his attention that, as he now knew, he could experience his body in just about any way at all.

The subject then was instructed that he would experience his body as breaking down into minute, moving particles. Everything else in the environment, in the world, was also breaking down into basic particles. The world would then consist of a vast sea of particles of matter and the subject would just merge with that sea, losing all sense of his body and becoming one with the whole. He would just experience that oneness. Then he was further instructed to let go of his self concept, his I, and to let that also merge with and drift out into the vast and endless sea of being. "No more ego, no more self, just pure being, extending outward, and outward, and one with all that is." The subject was told to experience this body and ego dissolution for as long as he wished, and that then the body and ego would gradually coalesce, and that when this had happened he would so indicate by an involuntary nodding of his head.

With deep trance subjects this invariably produced an interval of from two or three to ten minutes during which the subject was out of rapport with the experimenter. These subjects later reported the impression that there had been a loss of personal identity, a sense of union with "the one," and, apparently, a period of unconsciousness. Ecstatic, oceanic, blissful, and other mystical-type states were described by almost all subjects, whatever the trance depth. Afterwards, there was extreme relaxation and joyousness or euphoria.

In another experiment, the subject, in trance, was instructed to image with the eyes closed a series of progressively deepening personal or "self symbols." When finally a symbol is imaged that the subject feels to be the deepest and most comprehensive he is able to achieve, he then is instructed to observe this symbol as it becomes smaller and smaller, until it is no larger than a pinpoint. Then, should he feel that he is prepared to do that, he can permit the symbol to become extinguished altogether. Then he will die, remain in the symbolic death state for as long as he wishes, and then he will be reborn. When he has experienced rebirth and is ready to do so, he then will communicate to the experimenters all that has happened.

This experience, with the deep trance subjects, also produces periods of time during which rapport is lost and the subject has a sense of having been unconscious or of having lost all sense of personal identity. Two of our subjects, in lighter trance states, reported later that death was "like being in a deep, black hole where there was nothing," and "blackness, emptiness, just nothing." One subject became anxious as the self symbol dwindled, tried to reverse the process, could not, and finally "just let it go out, accepting that I would die, but knowing that I would be reborn." All subjects described this experiment as leading to the deepest trance they had yet experienced.

A somnambulistic subject, following "rebirth," reported "awakening" to find herself "being pushed along by some force . . . I came out feet first . . . such a weird sensation . . . and you're wide open, permeable, diaphanous, whatever you want to call it, and as if you could be imprinted . . . And you are emerging in such a happy way . . . you're the one who's happy at being there and nobody has to stand around to welcome you with open arms . . . because it's not that they are going to give you something, it's that you are bringing something."

This same subject described the experience of "dying" as slowly dissolving, fading out emotionally, visually, physically, intellectually. "You have to die emotionally first, because you can't go if the emotion to stay is there. I guess next you stop seeing, and then your body goes, and your mind, your intellect is the last thing to go . . . After that there was nothing until the sensation of being pushed . . . the sensation first, and then the idea, I'm being born . . ."

How potent may such an *induced* and *suggested* experience be? and how religious? We have, of course, witnessed some very different responses to the death and rebirth experiment. For example, a group experiment involving eight trance subjects, all given simultaneous suggestions, yielded experiences fairly well typified by the following excerpts from accounts provided by three of the subjects, all of them female college students, ages twenty-one to twenty-five.

One subject's self symbol emerged as "a circle which soon changed form and became a curved sea shell, the kind you can listen to. I watched it become filled with spirit which created itself anew as flesh . . . I understood the symbol immediately: the round receptivity of a shell, its emptiness to spirit. The significance of the shell's transformation into flesh —into softness and sensitivity, was obvious. As the symbol became smaller, there was a heightening of intensity and emotion. I experienced fear of the death process which was grasped as a loss of so much of self that destruction and creation appeared terrifyingly one . . . Everything appeared possible and impossible at once . . . I was filled with an unquenchable desire and fear before the death-rebirth event.

> I remember being in the throes of death and not knowing what my outcome would be. This not-knowing was central to my choice to surrender to death. As I experienced myself rising from the depth of death, I knew that the gift of life was before me and I reached out for it. I was filled with an ecstatic relief and acceptance that seemed to embrace my whole being. Then I felt as if my spirit were being quickened and reformed and was pulsing within. After that, an intense passivity and sense of being filled. I became aware of the tears on my cheek which had come during the struggle.
> When I was told I might open my eyes, I saw the face [of the experimenter] before me. I saw it in a real but different way. His reality was no longer contained in what he looked like or what he was saying. He was man, depth, possibility, sensitivity, desire. The rest of my surroundings were considerably whole in themselves, and I looked and related to them as a Self that stood in the world, grasped its own beingness and could take hold of other beings as they were.

The self symbol of a second subject was a triangle. As it disappeared she felt her body growing smaller and smaller, then lost all awareness of it. She felt curiously suspended or frozen and wondered if she really wanted to "come back." "But then," she says, "I was suddenly aware that all I had to do was want to be reborn—the instant this occurred was simultaneous with the wish and also the fulfillment of the wish. I was swept back by what I can only describe as a sweep of light across a textural surface like a canvas; and I leaned back and slowly, inevitably smiled.

> When we were told that we could open our eyes, I was quietly astounded! I felt as if my eyes were large dark pools looking at stars on the clearest of nights.
> Afterwards I felt very good and happy for about four days. After that I felt like my old self again and am back to drinking lots of fattening beer. What I remember most is the imagery in my mind, the sound of voices, and remembering the feeling of being at least momentarily reborn. It didn't last, but it was a real experience and a real feeling."

A third subject's symbol was that of a circle filled with white fire. She writes that "The circle became smaller and smaller, drawing my vision of it to a tiny velvet line. It finally disappeared and I felt myself go totally silent in waiting. Then there was a tremendous slow-motion kind of explosion and upsurge and outgo of energy all around and from the point where the light disappeared. It was incredible. Then the circle grew and grew to infinite proportions within me, and all the sound was white. It was a silent Beethoven symphony throbbing all over the place. All the colors in the world were transformed in the whiteness and alive glow of this fire . . . I grew huge and transparent, filled and permeated with the light and the fire. And I thought: My God is a God of Love and He lives within me.

"When I opened my eyes the whole room was living brown, then as I shifted my vision from the wood to the books and the ceiling, I was part of all there was, yet wholly myself. Beautiful is all I can say."

Once again, how potent may such experiences be? and how religious may they be? In one case, as related, there were mood and behavior changes of a positive nature lasting just four days. Certain insights into possibilities of mind presumably are going to be retained. In some other instances, changes were longer or shorter lasting. Some evaluated the experience as deeply religious; others found it a moving or beautiful experience, but were hesitant to term it "religious."

What we did observe in these experiences was that, once again, the depth and the intensity—if these are subject to evaluation—were largely dependent upon what we have called the *preparation,* the readiness or need of the individual for a religious-type experience.

The specifically suggested and directed religious-type experiences have not been, in our work to date, as potent as the most powerful of those which happen spontaneously. But does that mean anything more than that techniques for inducing such experiences need to be refined? The answer may come with further work.

Certain elements which might intensify the experiences have been omitted. A church setting, for instance, and specific suggestions involving confrontation or union with God. In co-operation with a clergyman or priest such experiments might be conducted and probably ought to be conducted.

One effect of experiments already performed has been a temporary heightening of perception—such as that described by the subjects when first they opened their eyes after the "rebirth" experience. This "cleansing of the doors of perception" is one major aim of our research program and we have achieved it for varying periods of time by a variety of experimental techniques. Psychedelic experiences also enable some persons to "see once again," as with a child's eyes. Whether the adult whose eyes have been thus opened can maintain the freshness of his perceptions depends, in the main, upon his willingness to make the effort to do so.

There are other traditionally sought-after experiences that are not really too difficult to give to the experimental subject. He can be enabled, for example, like Blake:

*To see a World in a Grain of Sand,*
*And a Heaven in a Wild Flower,*
*Hold Infinity in the palm of your hand*
*And Eternity in an hour.*

Or, to give but one additional example, he may go into "visionary worlds" which, if explored with sufficient dedication, might well prove as inexhaustible as those described by a Swedenborg or the medieval Sufi mystics.

These and similar experiences, however gratifying, are less important for that reason than for what they teach us about our own capacities—about all of the faculties we have but do not use, about the impoverished awareness we impose upon ourselves. Man not only uses just a small fraction of his brain cells, but also—and this could be subject to quick change—just a few of his demonstrable capacities.

It is impossible to state what man's mental limitations are. The degree to which awareness might be expanded, the extent of acceleration of thought processes, potentials for control of perception, for self-healing, for escaping the tyranny of time. The extent to which creativity might be enhanced, or capacity to learn, or to remember. That all of these, and far more, are possibilities of the human being has long been known. But contemporary man, with all his new knowledge, with all his new instruments, makes very little effort to transcend his limitations or to develop latencies known about for centuries.

In our context of experiment and exploration, of seeking out and mapping regions of the mind, the induction of religious-type experiences represents an effort to achieve access to the farthest and deepest reaches of the psyche. And we take that path because, repeatedly in our work, the deepest psychical probes have taken us "down" to what is apprehended by the person as Ground of Being, Ultimate Reality, or God. But, all along the way to this Ground are observed human faculties and areas of experience of potential or certain value. Thus, it may be said that whatever the truth of the depths, the way down is surely one of progressive revelation.

# MEDITATION AND BIOFEEDBACK

## DURAND KIEFER

## Summary

From one subject's experience of ten years of daily meditation, with many special meditation sessions of twelve hours a day for four to thirteen days, plus a day and a half of instrumented meditation in a sensory isolation laboratory, and several weeks of daily meditation for two to four hours with EEG alpha-wave feedback, it was found that meditation and feedback are experientially complementary and mutually reinforcing. *Both* are "autoregulation of internal states." Therefore, it is proposed that they be programmed together in psychophysiological laboratories in such a way as to hasten common achievement of meditation's ancient promise of the heaven of voluntary cerebration.

## Introduction

Although meditation and EEG feedback, taken as religious and scientific techniques, respectively, are found to have much in common experientially, there has been so far one very important difference, which, hopefully, will be soon resolved in the laboratory. The experiential emphasis in religion (used in its deepest sense) is subjective; it is a so-called in-

Prepared for the first meeting of the Biofeedback Society at Santa Monica, California, in October 1969. Printed by permission of Durand Kiefer.

ternal or self-examination practice, which, when carried to its extreme, results in the experiential dissolution of the subject-object dichotomy and the total disappearance of consciousness of self (self-consciousness). Religious knowledge is knowledge *of* rather than about. To know, in religious language, is simply to experience in order to use intuitively or spontaneously (sometimes called spiritually).

The experiential emphasis in most science today is still objective; it depends upon "trained observation" of external phenomena for its knowledge *about,* in order to be able to explain or describe its "subject" phenomena. This still seems to apply to most feedback research as well as other scientific investigations of meditation. Carried to its extreme, however, the objective method as an approach comes to the same conclusion as the subjective method (Jeans, Eddington, Schroedinger, Planck, Bronowski), *vis:* Subjectivity and objectivity are indistinguishable. "We cannot get behind consciousness," as Max Planck put it.

In addition, there are special obstacles to the objective method in the study of meditation, which is a "subjective" phenomena, and, *unless* studied quantitatively by instrumentation, depends upon verbal recall-reports of subjective states for its "objectivity."

And finally, the ultimately successful meditation, by reports of the masters of the practice, results in an experience that is intrinsically ineffable—or indescribable, probably because its seat is extra-lingual; that is, it occurs only when the learned responses of the nervous system, such as language, are largely or wholly deactivated. Or deautomatized, in Deikman's term.

Thus it would appear that if a scientist is to improve his knowledge of meditation, he must either spend much time in meditation himself or depend upon instrumental read-out of physiological phenomenon during meditation of others. A combination of both will probably prove most effective. Incidentally, since it has been shown that deautomization of motor behavior can be accomplished not only by meditation but also by sensory isolation, deep relaxation, and probably by hypnosis, it is exciting to anticipate results when several of these techniques are combined with meditation in a laboratory instrumentation study of deautomization. And even more exciting when this is done with two or more subjects in various arrangements of a common feedback circuit which may include such novel aural reinforcement as taped music and visual reinforcement as oscilloscopes with juxtaposed optimum performance profiles.

## Procedure

Because of the limitations of the objective approach to a subjective phenomenon cited above, the serious study of meditation begun full time by the writer in 1959 has been conducted mainly in the literature and the convenient laboratory of his own consciousness. The initial meditation method chosen was Krishnamurti's very subtle and very difficult intensive self-examination. Although after two years of daily sessions of it, from one to six hours each, some startling discoveries were made, they were insufficient reinforcement for the long difficult hours between these rewards, and help was sought at the nearest weekly meditation meetings of the Quakers. This led to five months in 1961 and 1962 at the Quaker seminary called Pendle Hill, near Philadelphia, where a Zen Buddhist monk, also a student, wordlessly taught *zazen* (sitting meditation) for two hours one evening each week. Almost all of the meditation practiced since has been one of the four basic exercises of elementary *zazen*—counting breaths, "watching" breaths, *shikantaza,* or holding the koan, *Mu;* the latter practice indistinguishable, as taught by the Zen Master Yasutani Hakuun, from the Hindu practice of *japam,* as taught by Eknath Easwaren. *Japam,* in turn, is repetition of the Holy Name in Christian terminology.

This practice of *zazen* has included at least nine months, intermittently, as a student at Zenshinji monastery at Tassajara, and at some sixteen scattered Zen *sesshins,* as they are called, where *zazen* is practiced in groups of twenty to forty under the close supervision of a team consisting of a Japanese Zen Master and his helpers—usually one or two Japanese Zen monks and one or two American adepts. The student group lives together in the same building(s) for seven days, in silence and real individual solitude, the sexes segregated for sleep, and practices *zazen* and *kinhin,* a kind of walking meditation, for ten to twelve hours of each seventeen-hour day, for from four to six and a half days. At the latest of these six-and-a-half-day *sesshins* the writer continued the *zazen* schedule alone for an additional six and a half days under the supervision of the Zen Master, and with the occasional surreptitious help of a portable EEG alpha-feedback device rented from its designer and builder, Hugh McDonald of Stanford University hypnosis laboratory.

Previous EEG alpha-feedback experience consisted of about ten days of three or four hours a day on equipment in [Dr. Joseph] Kamiya's lab at Langley-Porter [Neuropsychiatric Institute in San Francisco] in the fall of 1967, again for about twenty-five days at this laboratory in the fall of 1968, and a few hours each on the equipments of the University of Pennsylvania and of Stanford University. The Langley-Porter experience included an alpha-feedback "24-hour marathon" attempt that was abandoned for lack of alpha and surfeit of fatigue after eighteen continuous hours. A total of about twenty-five hours of *zazen* has been spent on [the portable alpha feedback device].

One four-hour and one seven-hour session of instrumented floating meditation in a sensory-isolation environment, then called sensory-deprivation, was undertaken in the research laboratory "womb-tank" of the V. A. Hospital at Oklahoma City in 1963 or 1964.

Short periods of three days to three months each have been spent in practicing the meditation techniques taught by various institutions such as Self-Realization Fellowship at Encinitas [California], the Western Vedanta Society at Trabujo Monastery near Santa Ana, the Ananda Ashrams at La Crescenta and Pohassett, Joel Goldsmith's Infinite Way Center in Honolulu, Questhaven Retreat in Escondido (two months), Graf Durckheim's Hara meditation center at Todtmoos-Rutte, Germany (three months), the Catholic Camaldolese Hermitage at Lucia in the Big Sur (two weeks), Subramunya's Himalayan Academy at Virginia City, Nevada, and Christian Yoga Center in San Francisco, Eknath Easwaran's

326 THE HIGHEST STATE OF CONSCIOUSNESS

Mantra Yoga Meditation Center in Berkeley, some Hatha Yoga and Tai Chi Chuan lessons at Stillpoint Foundation near Los Gatos, several five-to-ten-day workshops with Charlotte Selvers, a couple of Ron Hubbard's Scientology classes, a couple of weekend seminars in meditation at Esalen Big Sur, and so forth—a fair sampling of the long catalogue of meditation techniques taught around the world. There has been no experience with the use of any of the consciousness-altering drugs, however, except for two trials of about ten minutes each to learn that it is impossible for the writer to meditate after using even very small amounts of either alcohol or marijuana.

## Results

The startling discovery produced by the Krishnamurti self-examination meditation after two years of daily practice was that the self and the examiner, or observer, are identical, so that when observation is fully achieved there is literally nothing subjective to observe. The mind is simply still, at last at peace, and consciousness is clear, total, and ecstatic. As later noted in the Zen Buddhist literature, self, ego, psyche, personality, mind—all are non-existent, a normally persistent illusion momentarily dispelled. These moments of realization, however, endured only two or three minutes before automatic conceptualizing reestablished itself, and they were too infrequent to compensate for the amount of hard work that went into creating them.

The weekly hour of meditation in Quaker meetings for five or six weeks resulted only in some warm friendships with these wistful people and dismay at their custom of interrupting their meditation to confess aloud the thinking they are doing instead. The same experience resulted from the half-hour of daily group meditation at Pendle Hill for five months where the vocal witness, as they call it, was usually more eloquent, but no more enlightening, than in their more provincial meetings for worship.

The results of some eight years of daily *zazen*, alone or in group meetings for the purpose, are too difficult to appraise, partly because any change in consciousness that may have occurred as a consequence was too gradual to be subjectively noted, and partly because the daily practice was interspersed with several weekly *sesshins* each year, which usually produced such notable transient changes in consciousness that any persistent change might be attributed to them also. These changes were usually in the direction of greater clarity, tranquility, and general understanding or acceptance. On three occasions in consecutive years, the realization of a god-like omniscience and infallibility was so abrupt and so distinct as to approach the condition called *satori*, or *kensho*, in the Zen Buddhist literature. The condition did not endure the presiding Zen Master's benevolent assaults upon it, however, in each instance, so it was not an authentic enlightenment in the Zen sense. The day following every *sesshin* was distinctly euphoric, but no more so than that following two or three days of EEG alpha conditioning for three to four hours each day, with a meditative mood maintained between conditioning sessions. And alpha conditioning is painless, while pain, both physical and psychological, is a necessary condition of the Zen *sesshin*.

Every hour spent in meditation with EEG alpha feedback has produced some degree of euphoria, and when several hours have been consecutive, the sense of well-being and general serenity of the sort called grace in the Christian terminology, has become very marked and persisted for twenty-four to forty-eight hours afterward, as noted previously. This is with percent-time alpha ranging from 75 to 95 in the final hour, with frequent bursts of high amplitude sine-waves of a few seconds duration each. A steady frequency tone, or a blue light whose intensity varied with alpha amplitude, or both, combined with reported percent-time score every five minutes, was the reinforcement. On one occasion when tone-off was the reinforcement for a few hours, the alpha-enhancement performance was about the same as with the usual tone-on reinforcement.

It is still too early to determine results of meditation with [the] battery-powered alpha-feedback equipment, in which the reinforcement signal is steady in volume but varies in frequency in direct proportion to the amplitude of the alpha. The twenty-five hours to date have shown insufficient consistency in both the performance of the equipment and in the subjective response to it. This is attributed to learning errors in operating the novel device, so far.*

The first four hours in the Oklahoma City sensory isolation tank resulted in about three and a half hours of intermittent sleep after a tiring journey to get there. But the following day's seven consecutive hours produced several remarkable results. One was an almost perfectly quiet but alert mind, in which nothing moved, while consciousness remained clear and highly euphoric for long periods totaling about four and a half hours out of seven. As a seven-channel EEG recording was made of this meditation, it would be interesting, in the light of subsequent alpha-conditioning experience, to know the character of the EEG traces. A corollary result was a cumulative ecstasy that was so profound at the end of seven hours that it was very difficult to accept the termination of the experience. . . . Another result was a real and deep affection for the experimenter, J. T. Shurley, when in his presence following the experiment. This was probably both because of his role as provider of the experience, and because of the over-all reinforcement of his constant benevolent attention, even though remote, in the otherwise extreme isolation of the experimental setting.

The principal result of the broad sampling of various meditation techniques was to deepen an appreciation of meditation in general as a tranquilizer and an intuition-developer, and particularly of the Zen Buddhist *zazen* in this respect.

## Conclusions

It is characteristic of the subjective method of experiments in consciousness-alteration that much more data is

---

* Current portable subject-operated EEG alphawave feedback devices with electrodes located on scalp muscles (such as the frontalis, or forehead) have a potential of conditioning muscle-neuron rhythmic firing to satisfy the reinforcement-signal criteria of the device, with the result that muscle-tension headaches rather than alpha training can result.

stored in memory for use in analyzing the experiment than it is practicable to include in a brief report of the results of the experiment. Thus, the following conclusions and their implications, while drawn from the experiences reported here, are based upon many more considerations than are immediately apparent in the results reported.

It is difficult but possible to dispel the almost universal human illusion of bifurcated consciousness—of the observer and the observed, of self and other, by retraining attention, through "passive volition," as Elmer Green calls it, to "lock on" to the unitive principle: consciousness, observation, existence, occurrence, experience itself.

This effortless, exquisite, aimless, "dispersed attention," in William James's phrase, is apparently what so many young people seek these days as "expanded awareness," although a single experience of it is but a first step on a long hard road to the Master's habitude.

It is difficult but possible, however, by the same means (for it is to the same end) to free the human organism of its apparently autonomic cerebration and restore it to the bliss of voluntary cerebration of which the saints and sages have sung for centuries.

And it is much less difficult to do this with a combination of physiological feedback and meditation than with meditation alone. For although cerebration does often appear to have evolved in man to an autonomic function, or nearly so, physiological feedback has now demonstrated that many autonomic functions can be regulated by passive volition.

Thus we can now hope that the freeing of our consciousness from what Ernest Cassirer has called the symbolic net may soon prove much less difficult than ever before. Perhaps within another decade the number of alpha-masters, theta-masters, and delta-masters living among us may exceed the number of Zen-masters, Yoga-masters, and Sufi-masters who have lived since time began. For statistically the number of fully enlightened meditators throughout history has been thoroughly discouraging. Yet, if we accept the testimony of the mere hundreds who have achieved the trained-transcendant state, in Deikman's phrase, there is no other way for humans to solve the ancient problem of evil. For it is the illusion of the alien ego—the separation from God, as they see it—that is the very root and stem of the experience of evil.

Surprisingly, in this insistence on the unitary consciousness as the only redemption of the human condition, the mystics have the support of some of the most respected physical scientists of our time: James Jeans, Arthur Eddington, Erwin Schroedinger, Max Planck, Bronowski, de Broglie. All have testified, also, that "consciousness is absolutely fundamental," as Schroedinger put it.

They were speaking, of course, of that absolute, eternal infinity where the unimaginably minute atomic construct of the physicist is indistinguishable from the unimaginably immense egoless void, or oceanic experience, of the transcendental mystic. Or in a word, of that infinite field of energy or spirit in which we live and move and have our being.

To thoroughly investigate physiologically the corner of that field that is the intelligent living organism with the most sophisticated instrumentation of which *homo instrumentalus* is capable, is the greatest adventure into infinite space that we have so far undertaken, moon landings and planet probes notwithstanding. For if the reports of the earliest pioneers in this field, the heroes that we know as the Old Man, the Buddha, the Christ, and the Prophet, are at last verified in our experiential-physiology laboratories, it will be found that inner and outer space are infinitely coextensive and timeless, with no boundaries or limits distinguishable in any direction.

A famous physicist is said to have observed that physics is a branch of chemistry, chemistry a branch of biology, and biology a branch of philosophy. Perhaps this is why our natural scientists are called doctors of philosophy. But the poetry of philosophy, and especially the philosophy of science, has fallen on lean times in this weapons culture of ours, and seldom seems to inspire our research.

In the physiological exploration of so-called transcendental consciousness there lies the greatest hope in centuries for rebirth of a philosophical inspiration that must finally eventuate in that union of true science and true religion of which gentlemen and scholars have dreamed since Plato's time.

# TRANCE DANCE

## ERIKA BOURGUIGNON

. . . From the point of view of the scientific observer rather than that of the participant and believer, we may speak of trance in somewhat different terms. We may define it as a state of altered consciousness; that is, a state in which one or several psychological and physiological changes occur: a change in the perception of time and form, of colors and brightness, of sound and movement, of tastes and odors, a change in the feel of one's own body, in sensations of pain, or heat or cold, of touch; a change in memory or in notions of one's own identity. Such changes may last for shorter or longer periods, may be of greater or lesser intensity, may be frequent or rare or even a single event in the life of the individual. They may be fleeting experiences given little or no cultural interpretation or value, they may be terrifying events of major proportions. Or they may be prized and cultivated, intentionally induced, as a means toward a supreme experience of the self or of the powers of the universe.

The reader will recognize in these comments some of the effects attributed to hallucinogenic drugs. The whole field of altered states of consciousness has in recent years acquired a popular fascination and an aura of familiarity. But drugs are only one of many ways to achieve such states. They have been sought, or feared and avoided, given cultural explanations and treated ritually in many hundreds of societies for thousands of years. The "psychedelic movement" and the "psychedelic experience" in contemporary America represent only a special, local variant of a major theme in human cultural history.

While trance states can be—and often are—induced by drugs, in the ritual context these methods are especially typical of South American Indians and of some North Asiatic peoples. Where drugs are used the aim will be to have visions, to communicate with spirits, to gain special powers, to send one's soul on errands to find lost objects or to bring back the abducted souls of sick persons. Indeed, the Siberian or South American shaman sends his soul "on a journey"—and we are not very far from the hippy term, "to take a trip." Elsewhere, particularly in Africa and among descendants of Africans in the Americas, drugs are rarely used for this purpose. Nor are dissociational states generally utilized to attain visions or insights. Instead, they are part of public ceremonial occasions in which dissociated individuals are believed to be possessed by certain spirits and act out the behavior of these spirits. Typically, musical rhythms associated with a given spirit or group of spirits are played, and the trancers dance the characteristic steps and movements of the spirits. They may be dressed to fit the part, often in elaborate costumes, but significantly, while impersonating the spirits, they generally do not wear masks. Masks, representing other groups of spirits, involve a different type of impersonation and are associated with other occasions, other dances and other dancers. . . .

Like the mask, the possession trance phenomenon is intimately related to the dance. Indeed this is the kind of trance state (or dissociational state) most frequently linked to the dance. Non-possession trance, particularly the drug-induced variety, is essentially a passive, subjective and private experience, even when it occurs to several persons at the same time or to one person in the presence of others. The effect of the drug is likely to alter the perception of sound, of music and rhythm, and to limit more or less severely the controlled, co-ordinated and disciplined execution of patterns of motion. This in itself would tend to make dance performance unlikely. Possession trance, with its emphasis on impersonation, is an objectively demonstrated, active, public phenomenon.

It requires an audience not only to validate the experience but, in most cases, to bring it about in the first place. Furthermore, possession trance may at times be more significant for the group that observes it than for the individual who experiences it; this is particularly true when, as is frequently the case, the experience is not remembered by the subject. The dance and the accompanying music may be used to initiate dissociation, or, in the language of the believers, to "invite" the spirits; or the dance may be the characteristic motion of the spirit. Or again—where the spirits are to be dispatched, forcing the trancer to dance to exhaustion, to unconsciousness—the dance may be the preferred method of exorcising or removing the possessing, interfering, alien spirit.

Dance, music, handclapping, singing, costuming, the presence of an expectant and participating audience, a ritual setting at an appropriate place and time—all these are ideally suited to produce both induction of dissociation and the therapeutic results of the ritual. Expectation and suggestion are obviously of great importance in bringing these about. The music, with its increasing frequency and intensity, facilitates rhythmical movement and itself has a clear psychological effect: it may help to release the dancer of part of his responsibility for his movements and actions. But it may have a physiological effect on the brain as well, helping to induce dissociation. The dance itself will contribute to an alteration of breathing patterns; it may bring about hyperventilation and—if prolonged—partial exhaustion, both of which again facilitate dissociation. Another significant factor, however, is to be found in the frequent whirling and turning, of circular and rotational movements. These tend to affect the sense of balance and equilibrium, thus leading to dizziness. Disturbances of balance are likely to be experienced, involving a loss of control over the body and thus over the self. They may indicate the impending loss of consciousness. If, furthermore, a disturbance in the sense of balance is believed to be a preliminary to possession, to being "mounted" by a spirit as it is so frequently phrased, this in itself will contribute to the likelihood of the occurrence of trance.

Thus there are many types of ritualized, patterned forms

of trance; there are many types of beliefs in possession by spirits. In fact, several such types of trance and spirit-possession belief may co-exist in the same society or in different segments of the same society. When trance is interpreted as due to spirit possession and when spirit possession finds its expression in states of trance, then we are also likely to find a linkage between trance and dance. Non-possession trance more rarely uses the dance as its vehicle of expression and it is least likely to do so when hallucinogenic drugs are employed. Where spirit possession trance occurs, the trancer impersonates the spirit, but he is unlikely to utilize masks among his accessories.

Ritualized, formalized dissociational states are found worldwide, are given a great variety of cultural interpretations and are embedded into many different institutions, customs, traditions and practices, most of which are religious in nature. The very wide distribution of these states among the peoples of the world would suggest that they are very ancient. We cannot trace their origins in the nearly two million years of human evolutionary history and to speculate about these origins would be rather pointless. . . .

However, if we are more modest in our aims and look back to the span of five thousand years of recorded history, we meet many ancient examples of ecstatic dance involving experiences of dissociation and, often quite explicitly, a statement of belief in supernatural possession or union with the Divine. Our own Western tradition has its deepest roots in the Mediterranean world of Jew and Greek, and we find what we are looking for in both of these traditions. For example, we are told in the Bible (I Samuel 10) that Saul traveled with a company of ecstatic prophets. "And David danced before the Lord with all his might." (II Samuel 6). He leaped and danced ecstatically before the Ark while he and his men played on such instruments as harps and psaltries, timbrels, cornets and cymbals, as the King James Version lists them. Ecstatic and dissociated behavior, visions and voices, appear throughout the Bible, both in the Old and New Testaments. The dancing sects and dancing epidemics of the Middle Ages, and the dancing processions of present-day Belgium and Luxemburg, are all reminders of these Biblical traditions and practices. So were the ecstatic dances of the Hasidim among the Jews of Eastern Europe which inspired the choreography of *Fiddler on the Roof*. In all these dances there is a heightened sense of participation in the mystic powers of the Divine. All of our examples refer to group dances, to forms of collective mysticism. There is no acting out here of the characters of diverse specific spirits, of impersonation or role playing, for there is only one Spirit and all share in His power.

The impersonating, acting-out type of possession trance, however, appears to have played a significant part in the other ancestral cultural stream: the religious life of ancient Greece. The cults of Dionysos and of the Corybantes are only sketchily known to us from a few fragmentary references in the remnants of Greek literature and iconography. However, we know that the cult of Dionysos, which gave rise to the theater in its classic form, also involved periodic trances of the god's followers. There is every reason to believe that Euripides' play *The Bacchae* contains a strong element of historic truth in its representation of the frenzied, dissociated states of the Maenads. Greek painting and sculpture offer examples of the movements and faces of the Maenads in no uncertain terms. The few references we have to Corybantic rituals tell us about dances and music specific for each spirit that is invoked and of the use of these spirit rituals in the treatment of "mania" or madness. . . .

We do not know with any certainty whether the ancient Greek cults have any connection with diverse other ecstatic dancing practices in the Mediterranean basin in later times: tarantism and related patterns in Apulia, Sardinia, Spain and Provence; the *zar* cult of North East Africa; the *stambuli* or *bori* cults of Tunisia, Algeria and Morocco and several others. Still, the occasions for contact for groups of diverse cultural backgrounds throughout this region were many. Christianity is known to have incorporated various Greek and other pagan elements and thus to have helped in their diffusion. Nevertheless, however fascinating such speculations about possible contacts might be, we risk being led to unfounded and hence useless conclusions by this sort of guesswork. We can learn more by looking at the concrete examples of contemporary peoples whom we can study at firsthand, observing their activities and finding out from their own statements what these activities represent to them.

We can say with some assurance that the ecstatic dance, the dance connected in some way with the phenomena of trance, is very widespread and undoubtedly a very ancient element of ritual. It appears in many forms and takes on many cultural styles, including a variety of styles of dance. It is also linked to a great variety of beliefs and of social and ritual practices. However, to put some order into our materials, we may distinguish two basic types of ecstatic dance: that used as a vehicle for achieving mystic states and that used in the ritual enactment of a role. . . .

## Visionary Trance

The dance as employed in order to bring about mystic states is typically a group phenomenon. In private, individual attempts to achieve such states the dance appears to be rarely used and other methods are given preference. The dance is found in this context in various aspects of Jewish, Christian and Moslem traditions. We have found it in ancient Israel in the accounts of Saul and David; we have found it in the recent past among the Hasidim. An interesting secular adaptation of such ecstatic dancing is to be seen in the Hora, the ecstatic, whirling, circle dance of the Israeli pioneers. It is secular in the sense that no supernaturalism is involved in this intense experience of personal abandon. Rather, it is a kinesthetic reaffirmation of the group, of belongingness, indeed of the primacy of the group over the individual. The Hora is a device for the experience of intensification of group identity, of zeal and of devotion. This is quite explicitly stated in some of the texts of the highly rhythmical, monotonously repeated songs that accompany and structure the dance:

*Hora', ali', ali'!*           (Hora, rise! rise!
*Esh hidli'ki belibi'!*        light a fire in my heart!)

In Christianity we have found ecstatic dancing in the dancing sects and dancing manias of the Middle Ages and in the dancing processions of today. There is a trend toward this type of behavior also in the singing, clapping and stomping to be seen in some American Pentecostal Churches—white as well as Negro—together with other ecstatic manifestations such as speaking in tongues (glossolalia), faith healing, and even falling and losing consciousness temporarily. A tent revival in the Middle West or South is a good place to observe these practices.

Among Christian sects to whom the ecstatic group dance was an essential part of worship we must mention the Shakers who flourished in the United States in the 19th century. Similarly, pronounced patterns of ecstatic group dancing associated with receiving the Holy Spirit are found among various Christian churches in the West Indies, groups that have their basis—at least in part—in the traditions of Methodism. Among them are groups who are known as Spiritual Baptists in Trinidad and on the island of St. Vincent, and related groups in Jamaica and Haiti as well. Some of them, as those in St. Vincent and in Haiti are also known (in a bit of terminological confusion) as Shakers, as are certain American Indian Christian churches of the Northwestern United States.

My associate, Jeannette H. Henney, studied the trance behavior of the St. Vincent Shakers in great detail. After describing how single individuals might go into trance during the hours-long hymn singing and sermonizing, during which rhythm is kept by handclapping and foot stamping but where no instruments are used, she tells us about a second, group level of dissociation: "Not only are the sounds of breathing kept to a precise tempo, but the motion patterns are depersonalized and unified, so that each person . . . is reproducing the same movement." . . . "Each person was bent over at the waist, knees were bent, and they all bobbed up and down simultaneously, keeping the rhythm." Afterwards, the trancers "were not singing or humming, [but] they were producing gasps, groans, sighs, and shouts in profusion. [They] . . . appeared to be bewildered and perhaps breathless from exertion. The scene was one of confusion."[1]

[The] so-called "whirling dervishes" [of Turkey] have a very wide distribution, and such orders or brotherhoods are found in a great arc from the Atlantic Coast of North Africa to Malaya and Indonesia. Their mystic practices involve the repetition—sometimes hundreds of times—of the prayer formula of the *dhikr*. These repetitions are performed in unison by a group of men chanting in response to a leader; the responses are accompanied by typical rotational, rhythmic motions of the torso (if not by actual dancing and whirling) and by a characteristically patterned intake and release of breath. The rhythm of the chant and the movement are accelerated, first slowly, then more and more rapidly. Many, if not all, of the participants may reach mystic states and go into trance.

The goal of all these practices is that of attaining Unity with the Divine, to achieve a state of strengthened hope, a feeling of release, of salvation, of sacred euphoria. It makes you "feel good" or "feel happy" as they say in American Negro churches of a Fundamentalist or Pentecostal sort. The experience is a very personal, even intimate, one. But it is accomplished in a group setting, often through a shared effort with others—whether of prayer and devotion, of rhythmic singing and dancing or other spiritual exercises, and perhaps usually a combination of several of these. During the period of dissociation there is a narrowing and intensification of the field of awareness, and afterwards there is a memory of a sublime and often inexpressible joy and satisfaction. The experience may be terminated by a brief period of unconsciousness, as in the falling to the ground so typical of American tent revivals.

Some Messianic movements, as well as established religions, have made use of the ecstatic dance as a method of achieving

[1] Jeannette Henney, "Trance Behavior Among the Shakers of St. Vincent," *Working Paper No. 8, Cross-Cultural Studies of Dissociational States* (Columbus, Ohio, 1967), pp. 6, 9.

individual and collective mystical experiences. For example, in the late 19th century, a movement that came to be known as the Ghost Dance swept through the Western Indian tribes of the United States. . . .

## Trance, Dance and Social Change

While the field we have surveyed is broad, it actually constitutes only a segment of a much broader area of experience, activity and belief. What, then, is the relationship between the dance on the one hand and states of altered consciousness, be they trance or possession trance, on the other? Dance, as we have indicated, appears to have two principal points of contact with such states: one, as a means of inducing them and two, as a means of acting out the prescribed behavior during such states. In the visionary trances the former appears to be primarily the case, while in states of possession trance both appear to be equally relevant and important. In particular, the behavior of the spirit who is supposed to possess the trancer may involve characteristic choreographic features.

It becomes clear that the expectations of the group among whom these phenomena take place—the spectators as well as the trancers themselves, their beliefs concerning the persons in the trance—are highly relevant to the actual behavior that will be exhibited. These expectations and beliefs *structure* the behavior of the trancers; they act much like the commands the hypnotist gives to his subjects. All of this indicates how variable trance behavior is, how much it is modified and patterned by specific traditions. It indicates the significance of cultural learning as it affects this often spectacular and extraordinary—presumably often superhuman or at least nonhuman—behavior of dissociated individuals. It must be stressed, therefore, that whatever idiosyncratic, individual innovations and embellishments may occur in any given ritual situation, such trances and possession trances are above all culturally stylized performances and experiences.

We may look at the whole matter from yet another point of view: we may consider the ecstatic dance as a psychokinetic experience of the dancer and as an aesthetic-religious experience of the spectators. Since it is both, any attempt at a full analysis of what is taking place must take both of these aspects of the situation into account.

The dancer undergoes physiological and psychological changes as a result of several factors in the situation: the activity of the dance itself with its stylized, usually rhythmic movements; exertion and often hyperventilation are involved; there is a modification of various types of sensory experiences such as balance and spatial orientation; an intensification and a narrowing of attention both occur; there is an awareness of the goals of the dance and of the expectations connected with this awareness; patterns of previously observed and previously experienced alterations of consciousness and of behavior during trance play their role. A significant factor is the knowledge concerning the identity of the entities to be impersonated and of their special characteristics. At the same time, there is a release from the normal expectations concerning one's own identity; an awareness of the spectators and of their expectations; the effects of the music and of other sensory stimuli such as the smell of incense or of fumes, heat, light, noise, crowd effects.

The duration of the induction phase of the trance may vary from a few minutes to several hours. This will depend both on the traditional programming of the performance and on the degree of habituation of the trancer, among a variety of other factors. The trance itself may have an impact on the individual subject or performer for a variety of physiological and psychological reasons, although some of these are as yet poorly understood; some of the trance activities may be violent seizures or prolonged trembling, cataleptic states of prolonged duration, etc. It has been argued that these involve subcortical areas of the brain and bring about significant modification of brain functioning somewhat analogous to what is supposed to happen under electro-shock treatment.

Analogies have also been made between trance experience and religious conversion on the one hand, and brainwashing on the other; bringing about as they do an alteration of attitudes, memory functions, world view or self-concept. Whether these results are to be ascribed to physiological, psychological, social-psychological factors or several of these in interaction remains to be seen. It may be, for example, that trance permits the acting out of prohibited and repressed impulses or provides an opportunity of being, for once, someone else— perhaps someone important—and does so in a sacred and sheltered setting. This may then be a type of social-psychological process that makes a difference to the individual in his interaction with others and with himself, rather than neurological or physiological or biochemical changes in the brain.

For the spectator other factors come into play. There is the heightened excitement and expectation aroused by the performance; the possibility of interacting with trancers and most likely with the spirits themselves, of gaining help from them through advice or curing or blessings. There is the added assurance of the reality of the spirits and the truth of the religious teachings which are so graphically demonstrated by the very presence of the spirits among the people in the case of possession trance, and of the possibility of establishing contact with them in the case of visionary trance. And this demonstration is as strong or stronger for the trancers themselves. There is thus the religious as well as the practical and aesthetic satisfaction in attending such a performance. For the audience there is also the vicarious experience of the powers and emotions demonstrated by the trancers. The experience of the performers and that of the spectators are thus complementary and one would be meaningless without the other. In many societies those who are spectators at one time may be performers at another and vice versa. For children particularly the performances represent important learning experiences where it is possible to see how trancers, or spirits, behave.

For a full study of the ecstatic dance, for an understanding of its functions and meanings, we must not stop here. We must attempt to see how the ecstatic dance fits into the larger fabric of the society we are observing. How similar or how different are individual performances? How much individuality or stereotype is there to be found? Who are the participants in the ritual, performers and spectators alike; do they belong to the same or different segments of society? Do they represent the entire society or only some particular section of it—men or women, persons of high or low status, minorities of race or caste or ethnic group, natives or foreigners, and so on? Do the beliefs acted out in these performances represent those of the society as a whole or do they express only one among several, perhaps competing, views of the world? Are these beliefs and rituals, as well as their practitioners, a force for conservatism, for stability or for change? Do they help to maintain the social system or to change it, or is their principal effect to help individuals to live with the changes that are, in fact, occurring?

In its cultural context the ecstatic dance may be said to express some aspects of the life of a society in symbolic terms. But it also fulfills a function in the maintenance or modification of a society. The ecstatic dance seems to play no role in the formal religious life of this country. And yet any observer of contemporary teen-age dancing and music will be struck by the intense, dissociated, ecstatic character of this activity. The young people appear to be utterly involved, utterly oblivious to the external world, except for the music, the beat. The motions of the dance are expressive rather than communicative. . . . The satisfaction seems to be not only of solitary sex but also of a masochistic experience in contact with the music. The high level of noise, the loudness of the sounds, heat, crowding, the effects of lighting and smoke all contribute to the setting. As one teen-ager described it to me, there is a loss of self: "After a while," she said, "I'm no longer there. There is only the dancing and the music. And I couldn't stop as long as the music lasts, even if I wanted to." The ecstatic dance here appears to be a means of releasing individual tensions, of providing pleasure and pain. If it is sex, it does not involve love, a relationship to another human being. Clearly, we are far away from the romance of cheek to cheek dancing of former years! The singleness, the isolation of the individual in the crowd, stands out as the most striking aspect of this type of dancing.

Suppose we compare the ecstatic dancing of traditional societies with that of teen-age America; suppose we ask what all this tells us about the society and what it does for the society. In traditional societies ecstatic dancing links the individual, and through him frequently the group, with the forces of the universe. Teen-age dancing is entirely secular and leads to no such religious intensification. It concerns only the individual and not the group. Traditional, ecstatic dancing serves purposes of worship, of therapy, or relief for the individual and the group and sometimes for the world as a whole. Teen-age dancing is an end in itself. The traditional society is group oriented; the actions of the individual reflect and further the ends of the group. American society seems to rely largely on anonymous crowds in which the individual tries to find a place by seeking satisfaction for himself and by establishing a more or less imaginary connection with figures of power or symbols of authority. The musician plays this role for the dancers. One other theme is expressed here in addition to sex and violence, loneliness and self-centeredness, anonymity and the search for an identity link-up: that is the revolt of the youngsters against the generation of their parents whom they perceive as fettering and handicapping them.

Such an analysis can lead us far afield and would require a searching view of contemporary American society. Rather than seeing this ecstatic rock dancing of the young as a passing fad, we should see it as expressive of several important themes in American society and we should ask what its implications are for the changes that are now occurring in this society. Perhaps it is not necessary to state again that the ecstatic dance cannot be seen meaningfully in isolation, in purely aesthetic or culture-historical terms. It represents a vital form of human expression in the context of particular, larger, cultural wholes. It must be seen in each instance within that cultural whole, and yet we must be aware that it represents not merely a particular local invention, but a local utilization of a universal human capacity which has been used in many societies throughout human history.

# TRANSPERSONAL
# POTENTIALITIES
# OF DEEP HYPNOSIS

## CHARLES T. TART

. . . There's a great failure to recognize that hypnosis is one of the most flexible states of consciousness known. The subject is extremely sensitive to what you expect from him. So if you have a theory of hypnosis, you can pretty well prove it on your subjects because they'll pick it up and do the right thing. If you're a psychoanalyst, you can always find "regression in the service of the ego" and "primary drives" coming out in hypnosis. If you don't believe in that, you may never see that sort of thing in your laboratory. So, it's too easy to prove particular theories without realizing that basically you have a very flexible kind of state of consciousness. And although there's a lot of lip service to a more permissive kind of approach—you know, "I'm here to help you with experiences" and so forth—the old authoritarian game is still there fairly heavily because basically "I'm the professor and you're the student. And you don't know what you're doing, kid, so now we'll do the experiment my way" and so forth. There are emerging trends in hypnosis, though, which I think are going to make the whole thing a more humanistic sort of experience and a more transcendental kind of experience. What I want to do to illustrate this is show a single slide of some research I've been doing that shows how hypnosis can move into a kind of transcendental area. This results from some very intensive work with a single subject that I've been working with for over a year. I might add that this is a particularly gifted subject; you can't expect this from just anyone.

The kind of climate I create in my laboratory for hypnosis is basically, "Look, I do know more than you, but I'm not an authority in the sense that I can program your every bit of behavior. I'm more a guide when it comes to hypnosis. I know how to do certain things that are going to change the state of your mind, but unless you constantly tell me where you're at I'm in the dark; I'm just pushing my line of things." So this is a subject who's quite verbal in telling me what's going on and making suggestions as to how to continue to go about things and so forth, and who's been able to reach some extremely profound states of hypnosis. This guy has also done some meditation on his own and had some psychedelic drug trips in the past, so he has a vocabulary for talking about the sorts of things that happen. I should also explain that hypnosis has a dimension you might call depth or profundity. Subjects in my lab have been taught in this kind of permissive relationship to scale the depth of their hypnotic state and do it kind of intuitively.[1] You don't say, "Now think about all of the things you're experiencing and come up with some complex intellectual concept to describe it," but rather, "Some part of your mind kind of knows where you're at at every moment. Give me an intuitive answer." I won't go into that in detail, but this sort of turns out to be a beautiful kind of way of figuring out where people are at in hypnosis; it relates to all sorts of other things they do.

Now, this is a subject who goes extremely deep, and I'm just briefly going to describe some of the sorts of things he experiences to show you, I think, where hypnosis can go and how it can lead into this area that I think could best be described as sort of a transcendental level of hypnosis.

Ordinary hypnosis on this kind of scale would be the region

[1] Tart, C. "Self-report Scales of Hypnotic Depth," *Intern. J. Clinical Exp. Hyp., 18,* 1970, 105–25.

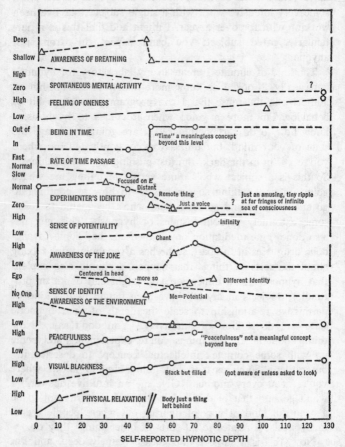

FIG. 1. *The relationship of the intensity of various experiences to self-reported hypnotic depth. (Values marked with a triangle were obtained in the interview before the hypnotic session; values marked with a circle, during the hypnotic session.)*

of zero to about 25 on the horizontal axis; as you go down to 30 or 40 on the depth scale, that would be called *deep* hypnosis. When you get down to about 50, that's usually been called extremely profound hypnosis, and, by and large, you don't get any reports from people of what goes on there, which I think is largely a function of the fact that Westerners don't have the vocabulary to talk about what's going on. This fellow has an exceptionally good vocabulary.

I would ask him about his many experiences in hypnosis in various projects in my laboratory (plotted with triangles on the chart) and also run him into some very deep hypnosis (plotted with circle). I'd tell him to go deeper and tell me what was going on and ask him about these various things, like "Do you have more or less of that last thing you were experiencing? What's happening with it?" This is an attempt to plot the inner relationships of all these various sorts of things that were going on.

The first thing plotted at the bottom of the chart is physical relaxation. You can see that this steadily gets higher, except that by the time you get to about 20 on this scale his body feels absolutely relaxed, and after that he says "No, I can't tell you how relaxed I am because my body has reached its limit. It's absolutely relaxed." And in point of fact, by the time you get down to the level of about 50 notice it's not "my body" but "This body is just a thing that's not really of any importance. How can I tell you how relaxed it is? It's not that important."

I ask him what he's seeing. At the very beginning he sees a little light and it starts getting blacker. As he goes deeper he sees more and more blackness until he reaches a point very early where it's absolutely black—his eyes are closed, of course. Then it continues to get blacker as he goes deeper and deeper into hypnosis but it's a funny kind of blackness. It's a blackness that's "filled," which sounds like a paradoxical statement but I think some of you who have had psychedelics will realize the kind of thing he's talking about. There are no definite shapes, but it's a blackness that seems full somehow. This kind of plateaus off at around 60 on this scale so that this blackness is simply totally filled but it's absolutely black.

The third line plots feeling of peacefulness. He doesn't feel terribly peaceful when he first starts out in hypnosis, but this fairly rapidly goes up and by the time he gets to around 70 once again peacefulness is no longer a meaningful concept. As you'll see later his whole sense of identity is changed. You know, "I can talk about me being peaceful, but if I don't feel *me* any more how can I talk about whether me is peaceful or not peaceful," or something like that.

His awareness of what's going on around him, the environment, starts out at a normal level; he hears the noises in the hall outside and so forth. It fairly rapidly decreases and, once again, around 50 it reaches a low. As far as he's concerned he might be in the world's best sensory deprivation chamber. There is no physical world environment. He can hear my voice but there's absolutely nothing going on otherwise.

I asked him about his sense of identity at various points. "Who are you?" "What's your identity?" That sort of thing. He starts out as himself, ego, and then his sense of identity tends to become less distributed through his body and more just his head; just sort of a thinking part. And that becomes a little more so and then that begins a kind of dropping out until his ordinary identity—let's call him John Smith—steadily decreases and as he goes deeper into hypnosis John Smith no longer exists. But there is a change taking place in who he is. He becomes more and more identified with a new identity, and that identity is *potential*. He's not anybody in particular; he's potential. He could be this, he could be that. He's aware of identifying with this flux of potentiality that could evolve into many sorts of things.

The "awareness of the joke" is a hard one to explain. This runs along at zero, he's not aware of the joke, and suddenly around 50 to 60 or 70 he becomes quite aware of the joke and then it fades out. The joke will be recognized by many of you who have had psychedelic drugs. You're starting to get high and somewhere along in there you suddenly realize from some higher part of "yourself" how ridiculous it is to attempt to get high! I mean really, what's the point of trying to find out where it's at, to get high and all that sort of thing? Here's this poor pitiful little ego that doesn't know it's already there trying to get up there! It's kind of funny. But he goes beyond that. The joke fades out after a while as he continues to go further into hypnosis (if it's still "hypnosis").

I talked about a sense of potentiality in the identity thing. Here, looking at it in a sort of different way, he eventually becomes aware of an infinite amount of potential. Anything is possible. Absolutely anything could be experienced in the kind of existence he's in.

The experimenter's identity is interesting. I'm just me at the lightest levels of hypnosis; as he goes into what we would call ordinary deep hypnosis he becomes more and more focused on me. I'm the only thing that he really pays strict attention to. But then I start becoming distant and kind of a remote thing and then I lose my identity altogether. I'm no longer Charlie Tart; I'm just a voice: just something that keeps talking. And it not only stays that way but finally he says, as he exists in infinite consciousness, the whole sea of being and so forth, that way out on the edge somewhere here's this little ripple. It keeps asking silly questions like "How do you feel now?" A total depersonalization of who I am but he sort of feels kindly toward this voice. The voice has to ask questions so he'll be nice to me and so forth. Although it's a drag to have to answer them!

Time is an interesting thing. A lot of times in hypnosis you get people's sense of time slowing down. Here time seems to go slower and slower up to this quite deep hypnosis range of about 40, but then a very interesting thing happens. He suddenly says he can't tell me whether time is going slower or faster because at that point his nature of being in time changes. He's in time here which is slowing, and then he goes out of time and time is a meaningless concept. Beyond this point, queries about his time going fast or slow are stupid questions. They just don't mean anything. He no longer feels that he's in the kind of space-time framework we talk about.

A feeling of oneness with the universe continues to go up. I don't know whether it plateaus off at a very deep level or not.

If I ask you "What are you thinking about?" you'll undoubt-edly tell me something going through your mind. We keep the old machine whirling around all the time computing everything that comes along. This spontaneous mental ac-tivity continues to decrease as he goes deeper in hypnosis and beyond the deep range he's simply not having any spon-taneous thought. If I don't tell him "Think about this" or "Answer this question" there's nothing going on in his mind. It's absolutely quiet.

One other thing, his awareness of his breathing; he feels as if his breathing gets deeper and deeper as he goes into hyp-nosis until there's a point when his breathing suddenly feels as if it becomes quite shallow. He's virtually not aware of it any more unless this little voice at the edges of consciousness says "How's your breathing?"

Now, the point I want to make about this is that up to 40 or so on the graph we're talking about hypnosis, and we're talking about a rather neutral kind of hypnosis. I haven't suggested particular things. These are just the kinds of things he usually experiences as he's going into deep hypnosis. In a higher range, roughly 50 to 70, a lot of these kinds of phe-nomena change fairly suddenly. There's some step function: some of these things start going up or down rather suddenly. And I think what we have here is a transition to a new state of consciousness. In many ways it sounds like what's tradi-tionally been called the Void. I'm a little leery of using that word because the Void is a great thing to be in, and you get a lot of prestige and all that sort of spiritual one-upmanship. But it kind of sounds like the Void. His identity is poten-tiality, he's aware of everything and nothing, his mind is absolutely quiet, he's out of time, out of space and so forth. But this is the sort of thing that happens to him.

Now I should again emphasize that this is an extremely good subject. This is not something that the average hypnotic sub-ject could just move right into, although probably more sub-jects could move into it if they were given special training. The main thing that I want to emphasize is that I think this illustrates first the humanistic potential of hypnosis, where the experimenter-subject relationship changes: I'm no longer the boss shaping his consciousness to do what I think he ought to do, I'm just sort of the guide and he's the one who does this sort of thing. But even more it illustrates some of the transcendental potentialities of hypnosis: how you can use this to move to relatively profound states of consciousness; you can use it to explore consciousness; and we can open up a number of things that ordinarily you don't think of in connection with hypnosis where the usual association is the big authority figure who says "sleep." . . .

# THE "CORE-RELIGIOUS," OR "TRANSCENDENT," EXPERIENCE

## ABRAHAM MASLOW

The very beginning, the intrinsic core, the essence, the universal nucleus of every known high religion (unless Confucianism is also called a religion) has been the private, lonely, personal illumination, revelation, or ecstasy of some acutely sensitive prophet or seer. The high religions call themselves revealed religions and each of them tends to rest its validity, its function, and its right to exist on the codification and the communication of this original mystic experience or revelation from the lonely prophet to the mass of human beings in general.

But it has recently begun to appear that these "revelations" or mystical illuminations can be subsumed under the head of the "peak-experiences" or "ecstasies" or "transcendent" experiences which are now being eagerly investigated by many psychologists. That is to say, it is very likely, indeed almost certain, that these older reports, phrased in terms of supernatural revelation, were, in fact, perfectly natural, human peak-experiences of the kind that can easily be examined today, which, however, were phrased in terms of whatever conceptual, cultural, and linguistic framework the particular seer had available in his time (Laski, *Ecstasy*).

From *Religions, Values and Peak-Experiences,* by Abraham Maslow. Copyright 1964 by Ohio State University Press, Columbus, Ohio. Reprinted by permission of Kappa Delta Pi, an honor society in education.

In a word, we can study today what happened in the past and was then explainable in supernatural terms only. By so doing, we are enabled to examine religion in all its facets and in all its meanings in a way that makes it a part of science rather than something outside and exclusive of it.

Also this kind of study leads us to another very plausible hypothesis: to the extent that all mystical or peak-experiences are the same in their essence and have always been the same, all religions are the same in their essence and always have been the same. They should, therefore, come to agree in principle on teaching that which is common to all of them, i.e., whatever it is that peak-experiences teach in common (whatever is *different* about these illuminations can fairly be taken to be localisms both in time and space, and are, therefore, peripheral, expendable, not essential). This something common, this something which is left over after we peel away all the localisms, all the accidents of particular languages or particular philosophies, all the ethnocentric phrasings, all those elements which are *not* common, we may call the "core-religious experience" or the "transcendent experience."

To understand this better, we must differentiate the prophets in general from the organizers or legalists in general as (abstracted) types. . . . The characteristic prophet is a lonely man who has discovered his truth about the world, the cosmos, ethics, God, and his own identity from within, from his own personal experiences, from what he would consider to be a revelation. Usually, perhaps always, the prophets of the high religions have had these experiences when they were alone.

Characteristically the abstraction-type of the legalist-ecclesiastic is the conserving organization man, an officer and arm of the organization, who is loyal to the structure of the organization which has been built up on the basis of the prophet's original revelation in order to make the revelation available to the masses. From everything we know about organizations, we may very well expect that people will become loyal to it, as well as to the original prophet and to his vision; or at least they will become loyal to the organization's version of the prophet's vision. I may go so far as to say that characteristically (and I mean not only the religious organizations but also parallel organizations like the Communist Party or like revolutionary groups) these organizations can be seen as a kind of punch card or IBM version of an original revelation or mystical experience or peak-experience to make it suitable for group use and for administrative convenience.

It will be helpful here to talk about a pilot investigation, still in its beginnings, of the people I have called non-peakers. In my first investigations . . . I used this word because I thought some people had peak-experiences and others did not. But as I gathered information, and as I became more skillful in asking questions, I found that a higher and higher percentage of my subjects began to report peak-experiences. . . . I finally fell into the habit of expecting everyone to have peak-experiences and of being rather surprised if I ran across somebody who could report none at all. Because of this experience, I finally began to use the word "non-peaker" to describe, not the person who is unable to have peak-experiences, but rather the person who is afraid of them, who suppresses them, who denies them, who turns away from them, or who "forgets" them. My preliminary investigations of the reasons for these negative reactions to peak-experiences have led me to some (unconfirmed) impressions about why certain kinds of people renounce their peak-experiences.

Any person whose character structure (or Weltanschauung, or way of life) forces him to try to be extremely or completely rational or "materialistic" or mechanistic tends to become a non-peaker. That is, such a view of life tends to make the person regard his peak- and transcendent experiences as a kind of insanity, a complete loss of control, a sense of being overwhelmed by irrational emotions, etc. The person who is afraid of going insane and who is, therefore, desperately hanging on to stability, control, reality, etc., seems to be frightened by peak-experiences and tends to fight them off. For the compulsive-obsessive person, who organizes his life around the denying and the controlling of emotion, the fear of being overwhelmed by an emotion (which is interpreted as a loss of control) is enough for him to mobilize all his stamping-out and defensive activities against the peak-experience. I have one instance of a very convinced Marxian who denied—that is, who turned away from—a legitimate peak-experience, finally classifying it as some kind of peculiar but unimportant thing that had happened but that had best be forgotten because this experience conflicted with her whole materialistic mechanistic philosophy of life. I have found a few non-peakers who were ultra-scientific, that is, who espoused the nineteenth-century conception of science as an unemotional or anti-emotional activity which was ruled entirely by logic and rationality and who thought anything which was not logical and rational had no respectable place in life. . . . Finally, I should add that, in some cases, I could not come to any explanation for non-peaking.

If you will permit me to use this developing but not yet validated vocabulary, I may then say simply that the relationship between the prophet and the ecclesiastic, between the lonely mystic and the (perfectly extreme) religious-organization man may often be a relationship between peaker and non-peaker. Much theology, much verbal religion through history and throughout the world, can be considered to be the more or less vain efforts to put into communicable words and formulae, and into symbolic rituals and ceremonies, the original mystical experience of the original prophets. In a word, organized religion can be thought of as an effort to communicate peak-experiences to non-peakers, to teach them, to apply them, etc. Often, to make it more difficult, this job falls into the hands of non-peakers. On the whole we now would expect that this would be a vain effort, at least so far as much of mankind is concerned. The peak-experiences and their experiential reality ordinarily are not transmittable to non-peakers, at least not by words alone, and certainly not by non-peakers. What happens to many people, especially the ignorant, the uneducated, the naïve, is that they simply concretize all of the symbols, all of the words, all of the statues, all of the ceremonies, and by a process of functional autonomy make *them*, rather than the original revelation, into the sacred things and sacred activities. That is to say, this is simply a form of the idolatry (or fetishism) which has been the curse of every large religion. In idolatry the essential original meaning gets so lost in concretizations that these finally become hostile to the original mystical experiences, to mystics, and to prophets in general, that is, to the very people that we might call from our present point of view the truly religious people. Most religions have wound up denying and being antagonistic to the very ground upon which they were originally based. . . .

What I have been saying is that the evidence from the peak-experiences permits us to talk about the essential, the intrinsic, the basic, the most fundamental religious or transcendent experience as a totally private and personal one which can hardly be shared (except with other "peakers"). As a consequence, all the paraphernalia of organized religion —buildings and specialized personnel, rituals, dogmas, ceremonials, and the like—are to the "peaker" secondary, peripheral, and of doubtful value in relation to the intrinsic and essential religious or transcendent experience. Perhaps they may even be very harmful in various ways. From the point of view of the peak-experiencer, each person has his own private religion, which he develops out of his own private revelations in which are revealed to him his own private myths and symbols, rituals and ceremonials, which may be of the profoundest meaning to him personally and yet completely idiosyncratic, i.e., of no meaning to anyone else. But to say it even more simply, each "peaker" discovers, develops, and retains his own religion.

In addition, what seems to be emerging from this new source of data is that this essential core-religious experience may be embedded either in a theistic, supernatural context or in a non-theistic context. This private religious experience is shared by all the great world religions including the atheistic ones like Buddhism, Taoism, Humanism, or Confucianism. As a matter of fact, I can go so far as to say that this intrinsic core-experience is a meeting ground not only, let us say, for Christians and Jews and Mohammedans but also for priests and atheists, for Communists and anti-Communists, for conservatives and liberals, for artists and scientists, for men and for women, and for different constitutional types, that is to say, for athletes and for poets, for thinkers and for doers.

I say this because our findings indicate that all or almost all people have or can have peak-experiences. Both men and women have peak-experiences, and all kinds of constitutional types have peak-experiences, but, although the content of the peak-experiences is approximately as I have described for all human beings the situation or the trigger which sets off peak-experience, for instance in males and females, can be quite different. These experiences can come from different sources, but their content may be considered to be very similar. To sum it up, from this point of view, the two religions of mankind tend to be the peakers and the non-peakers, that is to say, those who have private, personal, transcendent, core-religious experiences easily and often and who accept them and make use of them, and, on the other hand, those who have never had them or who repress or suppress them and who, therefore, cannot make use of them for their personal therapy, personal growth, or personal fulfillment. . . .

## Religious Aspects of Peak-Experiences

Practically everything that happens in the peak-experiences, naturalistic though they are, could be listed under the headings of religious happenings, or indeed have been in the past considered to be only religious experiences.

1. For instance, it is quite characteristic in peak-experiences that the whole universe is perceived as an integrated and unified whole. This is not as simple a happening as one might imagine from the bare words themselves. To have a clear perception (rather than a purely abstract and verbal philosophical acceptance) that the universe is all of a piece and that one has his place in it—one is a part of it, one belongs in it—can be so profound and shaking an experience that it can change the person's character and his Weltanschauung forever after. In my own experience I have two subjects who, because of such an experience, were totally, immediately, and permanently cured of (in one case) chronic anxiety neurosis and, in the other case, of strong obsessional thoughts of suicide.

This, of course, is a basic meaning of religious faith for many people. People who might otherwise lose their "faith" will hang onto it because it gives a meaningfulness to the universe, a unity, a single philosophical explanation which makes it all hang together. Many orthodoxly religious people would be so frightened by giving up the notion that the universe has integration, unity, and, therefore, meaningfulness (which is given to it by the fact that it was all created by God or ruled by God or *is* God) that the only alternative for them would be to see the universe as a totally unintegrated chaos.

2. In the cognition that comes in peak-experiences, characteristically the percept is exclusively and fully attended to. That is, there is tremendous concentration of a kind which does not normally occur. There is the truest and most total kind of visual perceiving or listening or feeling. Part of what this involves is a peculiar change which can best be described as non-evaluating, non-comparing, or non-judging cognition. That is to say, figure and ground are less sharply differentiated. Important and unimportant are also less sharply differentiated, i.e., there is a tendency for things to become equally important rather than to be ranged in a hierarchy from very important to quite unimportant. For instance, the mother examining in loving ecstasy her new-born infant may be enthralled by every single part of him, one part as much as another one, one little toenail as much as another little toenail, and be struck into a kind of religious awe in this way. This same kind of total, non-comparing acceptance of everything, as if everything were equally important, holds also for the perception of people. Thus it comes about that in peak-experience cognition a person is most easily seen per se, in himself, by himself, uniquely and idiosyncratically as if he were the sole member of his class. Of course, this is a very common aspect not only of religious experience but of most theologies as well, i.e., the person is unique, the person is sacred, one person in principle is worth as much as any other person, everyone is a child of God, etc.

3. The cognition of being (B-cognition) that occurs in peak-experiences tends to perceive external objects, the

world, and individual people as more detached from human concerns. Normally we perceive everything as relevant to human concerns and more particularly to our own private selfish concerns. In the peak-experiences, we become more detached, more objective, and are more able to perceive the world as if it were independent not only of the perceiver but even of human beings in general. The perceiver can more readily look upon nature as if it were there in itself and for itself, not simply as if it were a human playground put there for human purposes. He can more easily refrain from projecting human purposes upon it. In a word, he can see it in its own Being (as an end in itself) rather than as something to be used or something to be afraid of or something to wish for or to be reacted to in some other personal, human, self-centered way. That is to say, B-cognition, because it makes human irrelevance more possible, enables us thereby to see more truly the nature of the object in itself. This is a little like talking about god-like perception, superhuman perception. The peak-experience seems to lift us to greater than normal heights so that we can see and perceive in a higher than usual way. We become larger, greater, stronger, bigger, taller people and tend to perceive accordingly.

4. To say this in a different way, perception in the peak-experiences can be relatively ego-transcending, self-forgetful, egoless, unselfish. It can come closer to being unmotivated, impersonal, desireless, detached, not needing or wishing. Which is to say, that it becomes more object-centered than ego-centered. The perceptual experience can be more organized around the object itself as a centering point rather than being based upon the selfish ego. This means in turn that objects and people are more readily perceived as having independent reality of their own.

5. The peak-experience is felt as a self-validating, self-justifying moment which carries its own intrinsic value with it. It is felt to be a highly valuable—even uniquely valuable—experience, so great an experience sometimes that even to attempt to justify it takes away from its dignity and worth. As a matter of fact, so many people find this so great and high

an experience that it justifies not only itself but even living itself. Peak-experiences can make life worthwhile by their occasional occurrence. They give meaning to life itself. They prove it to be worthwhile. To say this in a negative way, I would guess that peak-experiences help to prevent suicide.

6. Recognizing these experiences as end-experiences rather than as means-experiences makes another point. For one thing, it proves to the experiencer that there are ends in the world, that there are things or objects or experiences to yearn for which are worthwhile in themselves. This in itself is a refutation of the proposition that life and living is meaningless. In other words, peak-experiences are one part of the operational definition of the statement that "life is worthwhile" or "life is meaningful."

7. In the peak-experience there is a very characteristic disorientation in time and space, or even the lack of consciousness of time and space. Phrased positively, this is like experiencing universality and eternity. Certainly we have here, in a very operational sense, a real and scientific meaning of "under the aspect of eternity." This kind of timelessness and spacelessness contrasts very sharply with normal experience. The person in the peak-experiences may feel a day passing as if it were minutes or also a minute so intensely lived that it might feel like a day or a year or an eternity even. He may also lose his consciousness of being located in a particular place.

8. The world seen in the peak-experiences is seen only as beautiful, good, desirable, worthwhile, etc. and is never experienced as evil or undesirable. The world is accepted. People will say that then they understand it. Most important of all for comparison with religious thinking is that somehow they become reconciled to evil. Evil itself is accepted and understood and seen in its proper place in the whole, as belonging there, as unavoidable, as necessary, and, therefore, as proper. Of course, the way in which I (and Laski also) gathered peak-experiences was by asking for reports of ecstasies and raptures, of the most blissful and perfect moments of

life. Then, of course, life *would* look beautiful. And then all the foregoing might seem like discovering something that had been put in a priori. But observe that what I am talking about is the perception of evil, of pain, of disease, of death. In the peak-experiences, not only is the world seen as acceptable and beautiful, but, and this is what I am stressing, the bad things about life are accepted more totally than they are at other times. It is as if the peak-experience reconciled people to the presence of evil in the world.

9. Of course, this is another way of becoming "god-like." The gods who can contemplate and encompass the whole of being and who, therefore, understand it must see it as good, just, inevitable, and must see "evil" as a product of limited or selfish vision and understanding. If we could be god-like in this sense, then we, too, out of universal understanding would never blame or condemn or be disappointed or shocked. Our only possible emotions would be pity, charity, kindliness, perhaps sadness or amusement. But this is precisely the way in which self-actualizing people do at times react to the world, and in which all of us react in our peak-experiences.

10. Perhaps my most important finding was the discovery of what I am calling B-values or the intrinsic values of Being. When I asked the question, "How does the world look different in peak-experiences?" the hundreds of answers that I got could be boiled down to a quintessential list of characteristics which, though they overlap very much with one another can still be considered as separate for the sake of research. What is important for us in this context is that this list of the described characteristics of the world as it is perceived in our most perspicuous moments is about the same as what people through the ages have called eternal verities, or the spiritual values, or the highest values, or the religious values. What this says is that facts and values are not totally different from each other; under certain circumstances, they fuse. Most religions have either explicitly or by implication affirmed some relationship or even an overlapping or fusion between facts and values. For instance, people not only existed but they

were also sacred. The world was not only merely existent but it was also sacred.

11. B-cognition in the peak-experience is much more passive and receptive, much more humble, than normal perception is. It is much more ready to listen and much more able to hear.

12. In the peak-experience, such emotions as wonder, awe, reverence, humility, surrender, and even worship before the greatness of the experience are often reported. This may go so far as to involve thoughts of death in a peculiar way. Peak-experiences can be so wonderful that they can parallel the experience of dying, that is of an eager and happy dying. It is a kind of reconciliation and acceptance of death. Scientists have never considered as a scientific problem the question of the "good death"; but here in these experiences, we discover a parallel to what has been considered to be the religious attitude toward death, i.e., humility or dignity before it, willingness to accept it, possibly even a happiness with it.

13. In peak-experiences, the dichotomies, polarities, and conflicts of life tend to be transcended or resolved. That is to say, there tends to be a moving toward the perception of unity and integration in the world. The person himself tends to move toward fusion, integration, and unity and away from splitting, conflicts, and oppositions.

14. In the peak-experiences, there tends to be a loss, even though transient, of fear, anxiety, inhibition, of defense and control, of perplexity, confusion, conflict, of delay and restraint. The profound fear of disintegration, of insanity, of death, all tend to disappear for the moment. Perhaps this amounts to saying that fear disappears.

15. Peak-experiences sometimes have immediate effects or aftereffects upon the person. Sometimes their aftereffects are so profound and so great as to remind us of the profound religious conversions which forever after changed the person. Lesser effects could be called therapeutic. These can range from very great to minimal or even to no effects at all. This

is an easy concept for religious people to accept, accustomed as they are to thinking in terms of conversions, of great illuminations, of great moments of insight, etc.

16. I have likened the peak-experience in a metaphor to a visit to a personally defined heaven from which the person then returns to earth. This is like giving a naturalistic meaning to the concept of heaven. Of course, it is quite different from the conception of heaven as a place somewhere into which one physically steps after life on this earth is over. The conception of heaven that emerges from the peak-experiences is one which exists all the time all around us, always available to step into for a little while at least.

17. In peak-experiences, there is a tendency to move more closely to a perfect identity, or uniqueness, or to the idiosyncracy of the person or to his real self, to have become more a real person.

18. The person feels himself more than at other times to be responsible, active, the creative center of his own activities and of his own perceptions, more self-determined, more a free agent, with more "free will" than at other times.

19. But it has also been discovered that precisely those persons who have the clearest and strongest identity are exactly the ones who are most able to transcend the ego or the self and to become selfless, who are at least relatively selfless and relatively egoless.

20. The peak-experiencer becomes more loving and more accepting, and so he becomes more spontaneous and honest and innocent.

21. He becomes less an object, less a thing, less a thing of the world living under the laws of the physical world, and he becomes more a psyche, more a person, more subject to the psychological laws, especially the laws of what people have called the "higher life."

22. Because he becomes more unmotivated, that is to say, closer to non-striving, non-needing, non-wishing, he asks less

for himself in such moments. He is less selfish. (We must remember that the gods have been considered generally to have no needs or wants, no deficiencies, no lacks, and to be gratified in all things. In this sense, the unmotivated human being becomes more god-like.)

23. People during and after peak-experiences characteristically feel lucky, fortunate, graced. A common reaction is "I don't deserve this." A common consequence is a feeling of gratitude, in religious persons, to their God, in others, to fate or to nature or to just good fortune. It is interesting in the present context that this can go over into worship, giving thanks, adoring, giving praise, oblation, and other reactions which fit very easily into orthodox religious frameworks. In that context we are accustomed to this sort of thing—that is, to the feeling of gratitude or all-embracing love for everybody and for everything, leading to an impulse to do something good for the world, an eagerness to repay, even a sense of obligation and dedication.

24. The dichotomy or polarity between humility and pride tends to be resolved in the peak-experiences and also in self-actualizing persons. Such people resolve the dichotomy between pride and humility by fusing them into a single complex superordinate unity, that is by being proud (in a certain sense) and also humble (in a certain sense). Pride (fused with humility) is not hubris nor is it paranoia; humility (fused with pride) is not masochism.

25. What has been called the "unitive consciousness" is often given in peak-experiences, i.e., a sense of the sacred glimpsed *in* and *through* the particular instance of the momentary, the secular, the worldly. . . .

# IN SEARCH OF THE
# MIRACULOUS

## P. D. OUSPENSKY

. . . Very often, almost at every talk, [Gurdjieff] returned to the absence of unity in man.

"One of man's important mistakes," he said, "one which must be remembered, is his illusion in regard to his I.

"Man such as we know him, the 'man-machine,' the man who cannot 'do,' and with whom and through whom everything 'happens,' cannot have a permanent and single I. His I changes as quickly as his thoughts, feelings, and moods, and he makes a profound mistake in considering himself always one and the same person; in reality he is *always a different person,* not the one he was a moment ago.

"*Man has no permanent and unchangeable I.* Every thought, every mood, every desire, every sensation, says 'I.' And in each case it seems to be taken for granted that this I belongs to the *Whole,* to the whole man, and that a thought, a desire, or an aversion is expressed by this Whole. In actual fact there is no foundation whatever for this assumption. Man's every thought and desire appears and lives quite separately and independently of the Whole. And the Whole never expresses itself, for the simple reason that it exists, as such, only physically as a thing, and in the abstract as a concept. Man has no individual I. But there are, instead, hundreds and thousands of separate small I's, very often entirely unknown to one another, never coming into contact, or, on the contrary, hostile to each other, mutually exclusive and incompatible. Each minute, each moment, man is saying or thinking 'I.' And each time his I is different. Just now it was a thought, now it is a desire, now a sensation, now another thought, and so on, endlessly. *Man is a plurality.* Man's name is legion.

"The alternation of I's, their continual obvious struggle for supremacy, is controlled by accidental external influences. Warmth, sunshine, fine weather, immediately call up a whole group of I's. Cold, fog, rain, call up another group of I's, other associations, other feelings, other actions. There is nothing in man able to control this change of I's, chiefly because man does not notice, or know of it; he lives always in the last I. Some I's, of course, are stronger than others. But it is not their own conscious strength; they have been created by the strength of accidents or mechanical external stimuli. Education, imitation, reading, the hypnotism of religion, caste, and traditions, or the glamour of new slogans, create very strong I's in man's personality, which dominate whole series of other, weaker, I's. But their strength is the strength of the 'rolls' in the centers. And all I's making up a man's personality have the same origin as these 'rolls'; they are the results of external influences; and both are set in motion and controlled by fresh external influences.

"Man has no individuality. He has no single, big I. Man is divided into a multiplicity of small I's.

"And each separate small I is able to call itself by the name of the Whole, to act in the name of the Whole, to agree or disagree, to give promises, to make decisions, with which another I or the Whole will have to deal. This explains why people so often make decisions and so seldom carry them out. A man decides to get up early beginning from the following day. One I, or a group of I's, decide this. But getting up is the business of another I who entirely disagrees with the decision and may even know absolutely nothing about it. Of course the man will again go on sleeping in the morning and in the evening he will again decide to get up early. In some cases this may assume very unpleasant consequences for a man. A small accidental I may promise something, not to itself, but to someone else at a certain moment simply out of vanity or for amusement. Then it disappears, but the man, that is, the whole combination of other I's who are quite innocent of this, may have to pay for it all his life. It is the tragedy of the human being that any small I has the right to sign checks and promissory notes and the man, that is, the Whole, has to meet them. People's whole lives often consist in paying off the promissory notes of small accidental I's. . . .

On one occasion while talking with G. I asked him whether he considered it possible to attain "cosmic consciousness," not for a brief moment only but for a longer period. I understood the expression "cosmic consciousness" in the sense of a higher consciousness possible for man in the sense in which I had previously written about it in my book *Tertium Organum.*

"I do not know what you call 'cosmic consciousness,'" said G., "it is a vague and indefinite term; anyone can call anything he likes by it. In most cases what is called 'cosmic consciousness' is simply fantasy, associative daydreaming connected with intensified work of the emotional center. Sometimes it comes near to ecstasy but most often it is merely a subjective emotional experience on the level of dreams. But even apart from all this before we can speak of 'cosmic consciousness' we must define in general *what consciousness is.*

"How do you define consciousness?"

*"Consciousness* is considered to be indefinable," I said, "and indeed, how can it be defined if it is an inner quality? With the ordinary means at our disposal it is impossible to prove the presence of consciousness in another man. We know it only in ourselves."

"All this is rubbish," said G., "the usual scientific sophistry. It is time you got rid of it. Only one thing is true in what you have said: that you *can know* consciousness only in yourself. Observe that I say you *can know,* for you can know it only when you have it. And when you have not got it, you can know that you have not got it, not at that very moment, but afterwards. I mean that when it comes again you can see that it has been absent a long time, and you can find or remember the moment when it disappeared and when it reappeared. You can also define the moments when you are nearer to consciousness and further away from consciousness. But by observing in yourself the appearance and the disappearance of consciousness you will inevitably see one fact which you neither see nor acknowledge now, and that is that moments of consciousness are very short and are separated by long intervals of completely unconscious, mechanical working of the machine. You will then see that you can think, feel, act, speak, work, *without being conscious of it*. And if you learn to see in yourselves the moments of consciousness and the long periods of mechanicalness, you will as infallibly see in other people when they are conscious of what they are doing and when they are not.

"Your principal mistake consists in thinking that you *always have consciousness*, and in general, either that consciousness is *always present* or that it is *never present*. In reality consciousness is a property which is continually changing. Now it is present, now it is not present. And there are different degrees and different levels of consciousness. Both consciousness and the different degrees of consciousness must be understood in oneself by sensation, by taste. No definitions can help you in this case and no definitions are possible so long as you do not understand *what* you have to define. And science and philosophy cannot define consciousness because they want to define it where it does not exist. It is necessary to distinguish *consciousness* from the *possibility of consciousness*. We have only the possibility of consciousness and rare flashes of it. Therefore we cannot define what consciousness is."

I cannot say that what was said about consciousness became clear to me at once. But one of the subsequent talks explained to me the principles on which these arguments were based.

On one occasion at the beginning of a meeting G. put a

question to which all those present had to answer in turn. The question was: "What is the most important thing that we notice during self-observation?"

Some of those present said that during attempts at self-observation, what they had felt particularly strongly was an incessant flow of thoughts which they had found impossible to stop. Others spoke of the difficulty of distinguishing the work of one center from the work of another. I had evidently not altogether understood the question, or I answered my own thoughts, because I said that what struck me most was the connectedness of one thing with another in the system, the wholeness of the system, as if it were an "organism," and the entirely new significance of the word *to know* which included not only the idea of knowing this thing or that, but the connection between this thing and everything else.

G. was obviously dissatisfied with our replies. I had already begun to understand him in such circumstances and I saw that he expected from us indications of something definite that we had either missed or failed to understand.

"Not one of you has noticed the most important thing that I have pointed out to you," he said. "That is to say, not one of you has noticed that *you do not remember yourselves*." (He gave particular emphasis to these words.) "You do not feel *yourselves;* you are not conscious of *yourselves*. With you, 'it observes' just as 'it speaks,' 'it thinks,' 'it laughs.' You do not feel: *I* observe, *I* notice, *I* see. Everything still 'is noticed,' 'is seen.' . . . In order really to observe oneself one must first of all *remember himself.* . . .

At one of the following lectures G. returned to the question of consciousness.

"Neither the psychical nor the physical functions of man can be understood," he said, "unless the fact has been grasped that they can both work in different states of consciousness.

"In all there are four states of consciousness possible for *man*." (He emphasized the word "man.") "But ordinary man, that is, man number one, number two, and number three, lives in the two lowest states of consciousness only. The two higher states of consciousness are inaccessible to him, and although he may have flashes of these states, he is unable to understand them and he judges them from the point of view of those states in which it is usual for him to be.

"The two usual, that is, the lowest, states of consciousness are first, *sleep,* in other words a passive state in which man spends a third and very often a half of his life. And second, the state in which men spend the other part of their lives, in which they walk the streets, write books, talk on lofty subjects, take part in politics, kill one another, which they regard as active and call 'clear consciousness' or the 'waking state of consciousness.' The term 'clear consciousness' or 'waking state of consciousness' seems to have been given in jest, especially when you realize what *clear consciousness* ought in reality to be and what the state in which man lives and acts really is.

"The third state of consciousness is *self-remembering* or self-consciousness or consciousness of one's being. It is usual to consider that we have this state of consciousness or that we can have it if we want it. Our science and philosophy have overlooked the fact that *we do not possess* this state of consciousness and that we cannot create it in ourselves by desire or decision alone.

"The fourth state of consciousness is called the *objective state of consciousness.* In this state a man can see things *as they are.* Flashes of this state of consciousness also occur in man. In the religions of all nations there are indications of the possibility of a state of consciousness of this kind which is called 'enlightenment' and various other names but which cannot be described in words. But the only right way to objective consciousness is through the development of self-consciousness. If an ordinary man is artificially brought into a state of objective consciousness and afterwards brought back to his usual state he will remember nothing and he will think that for a time he had lost consciousness. But in the state of self-consciousness a man can have flashes of objective consciousness and remember them.

"The fourth state of consciousness in man means an altogether different state of being; it is the result of inner growth and of long and difficult work on oneself.

"But the third state of consciousness constitutes the natural right of man *as he is,* and if man does not possess it, it is only because of the wrong conditions of his life. It can be said without any exaggeration that at the present time the third state of consciousness occurs in man only in the form of very rare flashes and that it can be made more or less permanent in him only by means of special training.

"For most people, even for educated and thinking people, the chief obstacle in the way of acquiring self-consciousness consists in the fact that they think *they possess it,* that is, that they possess self-consciousness and everything connected with it; individuality in the sense of a permanent and unchangeable I, will, ability *to do,* and so on. It is evident that a man will not be interested if you tell him that he can acquire by long and difficult work something which, in his opinion, he already has. On the contrary he will think either that you are mad or that you want to deceive him with a view to 'personal gain.

"The two higher states of consciousness—'self-consciousness' and 'objective consciousness'—are connected with the functioning of the *higher centers* in man.

"In addition to those centers of which we have so far spoken there are two other centers in man, the 'higher emotional' and the 'higher thinking.' These centers are in us; they are fully developed and are working all the time, but their work fails to reach our ordinary consciousness. The cause of this lies in the special properties of our so-called 'clear consciousness.'

"In order to understand what the difference between states of consciousness is, let us return to the first state of consciousness which is sleep. This is an entirely subjective state of consciousness. A man is immersed in dreams, whether he remembers them or not does not matter. Even if some real impressions reach him, such as sounds, voices, warmth, cold, the sensation of his own body, they arouse in him only fantastic subjective images. Then a man wakes up. At first glance this is a quite different state of consciousness. He can move, he can talk with other people, he can make calculations ahead, he can see danger and avoid it, and so on. It stands to reason that he is in a better position than when he was asleep. But if we go a little more deeply into things, if we take a look into his inner world, into his thoughts, into the causes of his actions, we shall see that he is in almost the same state as when he is asleep. And it is even worse, because in sleep he is passive, that is, he cannot do anything. In the waking state, however, he can do something all the time and the results of all his actions will be reflected upon him or upon those around him. *And yet he does not remember himself.* He is a machine, everything with him *happens.* He cannot stop the flow of his thoughts, he cannot control his imagination, his emotions, his attention. He lives in a subjective world of 'I love,' 'I do not love,' 'I like,' 'I do not like,' 'I want,' 'I do not want,' that is, of what he thinks he likes, of what he thinks he does not like, of what he thinks he wants, of what he thinks he does not want. He does not see the real world. The real world is hidden from him by the wall of imagination. *He lives in sleep.* He is asleep. What is called 'clear consciousness' is sleep and a far more dangerous sleep than sleep at night in bed.

"Let us take some event in the life of humanity. For instance, war. There is a war going on at the present moment. What does it signify? It signifies that several millions of sleeping people are trying to destroy several millions of other sleeping people. They would not do this, of course, if they were to wake up. Everything that takes place is owing to this sleep.

"Both states of consciousness, sleep and the waking state, are equally subjective. Only by beginning to *remember himself* does a man really awaken. And then all surrounding life acquires for him a different aspect and a different meaning. He sees that it is *the life of sleeping people,* a life in sleep. All that men say, all that they do, they say and do in sleep. All this can have no value whatever. Only awakening and what leads to awakening has a value in reality.

"How many times have I been asked here whether wars can be stopped? Certainly they can. For this it is only necessary that people should awaken. It seems a small thing. It is, however, the most difficult thing there can be because this sleep is induced and maintained by the whole of surrounding life, by all surrounding conditions.

"How can one awaken? How can one escape this sleep?

These questions are the most important, the most vital that can ever confront a man. But before this it is necessary to be convinced of the very fact of sleep. But it is possible to be convinced of this only by trying to awaken. When a man understands that he does not remember himself and that to remember himself means to awaken to some extent, and when at the same time he sees by experience how difficult it is to remember himself, he will understand that he cannot awaken simply by having the desire to do so. It can be said still more precisely that a man cannot awaken *by himself*. But if, let us say, twenty people make an agreement that whoever of them awakens first shall wake the rest, they already have some chance. Even this, however, is insufficient because all the twenty can go to sleep at the same time and dream that they are waking up. Therefore more still is necessary. They must be looked after by a man who is not asleep or who does not fall asleep as easily as they do, or who goes to sleep consciously when this is possible, when it will do no harm either to himself or to others. They must find such a man *and hire him* to wake them and not allow them to fall asleep again. Without this it is impossible to awaken. This is what must be understood.

"It is possible to think for a thousand years; it is possible to write whole libraries of books, to create theories by the million, and all this in sleep, without any possibility of awakening. On the contrary, these books and these theories, written and created in sleep, will merely send other people to sleep, and so on.

"There is nothing new in the idea of sleep. People have been told almost since the creation of the world that they are asleep and that they must awaken. How many times is this said in the Gospels, for instance? 'Awake,' 'watch,' 'sleep not.' Christ's disciples even slept when he was praying in the Garden of Gethsemane for the last time. It is all there. But do men understand it? Men take it simply as a form of speech, as an expression, as a metaphor. They completely fail to understand that it must be taken literally. And again it is easy to understand why. In order to understand this literally it is necessary to awaken a little, or at least to try to awaken. I tell you seriously that I have been asked several times why nothing is said about sleep in the Gospels. Although it is there spoken of almost on every page. This simply shows that people read the Gospels in sleep. So long as a man sleeps profoundly and is wholly immersed in dreams he cannot even think about the fact that he is asleep. If he were to think that he was asleep, he would wake up. So everything goes on. And men have not the slightest idea what they are losing because of this sleep. As I have already said, as he is organized, that is, being such as nature has created him, man can be a self-conscious being. Such he is created and such he is born. But he is born among sleeping people, and, of course, he falls asleep among them just at the very time when he should have begun to be conscious of himself. Everything has a hand in this: the involuntary imitation of older people on the part of the child, voluntary and involuntary suggestion, and what is called 'education.' Every attempt to awaken on the child's part is instantly stopped. This is inevitable. And a great many efforts and a great deal of help are necessary in order to awaken later when thousands of sleep-compelling habits have been accumulated. And this very seldom happens. In most cases, a man when still a child already loses the possibility of awakening; he lives in sleep all his life and he dies in sleep. Furthermore, many people die long before their physical death. But of such cases we will speak later on.

"Now turn your attention to what I have pointed out to you before. A fully developed man, which I call 'man in the full sense of the word,' should possess four states of consciousness. Ordinary man, that is, man number one, number two, and number three, lives in two states of consciousness only. He knows, or at least he can know, of the existence of the fourth state of consciousness. All these 'mystical states' and so on are wrong definitions but when they are not deceptions or imitations they are flashes of what we call an objective state of consciousness.

"But man does not know of the third state of consciousness or even suspect it. Nor can he suspect it because if you were to explain to him what the third state of consciousness is, that is to say, in what it consists, he would say that it was his usual state. He considers himself to be a conscious being governing his own life. Facts that contradict that, he considers to be accidental or temporary, which will change by themselves. By considering that he possesses self-consciousness, as it were by nature, a man will not of course try to approach or obtain it. And yet without self-consciousness, or the third state, the fourth, except in rare flashes, is impossible. Knowledge, however, the real *objective* knowledge towards which man, as he asserts, is struggling, is possible only in the fourth state of consciousness, that is, it is conditional upon the full possession of the fourth state of consciousness. Knowledge which is acquired in the ordinary state of consciousness is intermixed with dreams. There you have a complete picture of the being of man number one, two, and three."

" 'Conscience' is again a term that needs explanation.

"In ordinary life the concept 'conscience' is taken too simply. As if we had a conscience. Actually the concept 'conscience' in the sphere of the emotions is equivalent to the concept 'consciousness' in the sphere of the intellect. And as we have no consciousness we have no conscience.

"*Consciousness* is a state in which a man *knows all at once* everything that he in general knows and in which he can see how little he does know and how many contradictions there are in what he knows.

"*Conscience* is a state in which a man *feels all at once* everything that he in general feels, or can feel. And as everyone has within him thousands of contradictory feelings which vary from a deeply hidden realization of his own nothingness and fears of all kinds to the most stupid kind of self-conceit, self-confidence, self-satisfaction, and self-praise, to feel all this *together* would not only be painful but literally unbearable.

"If a man whose entire inner world is composed of contradictions were suddenly to feel all these contradictions simultaneously within himself, if he were to feel all at once that he loves everything he hates and hates everything he loves; that he lies when he tells the truth and that he tells the truth when he lies; and if he could feel the shame and horror of it all, this would be the state which is called 'conscience.'

A man cannot live in this state; he must either destroy contradictions or destroy conscience. He cannot destroy conscience, but if he cannot destroy it he can put it to sleep, that is, he can separate by impenetrable barriers one feeling of self from another, never see them together, never feel their incompatibility, the absurdity of one existing alongside another.

"But fortunately for man, that is, for his peace and for his sleep, this state of conscience is very rare. From early childhood 'buffers' begin to grow and strengthen in him, taking from him the possibility of seeing his inner contradictions and therefore, for him, there is no danger whatever of a sudden awakening. Awakening is possible only for those who seek it and want it, for those who are ready to struggle with themselves and work on themselves for a very long time and very persistently in order to attain it. For this it is necessary to destroy 'buffers,' that is, to go out to meet all those inner sufferings which are connected with the sensations of contradictions. Moreover the destruction of 'buffers' in itself requires very long work and a man must agree to this work realizing that the result of his work will be every possible discomfort and suffering from the awakening of his conscience.

"But conscience is the fire which alone can fuse all the powders in the glass retort which was mentioned before and create the unity which a man lacks in that state in which he begins to study himself.

"The concept 'conscience' has nothing in common with the concept 'morality.'

"Conscience is a general and a *permanent* phenomenon. Conscience is the same for all men and conscience is possible only in the absence of 'buffers.' From the point of view of understanding the different categories of man we may say that there exists the conscience of a man in whom there are no contradictions. This conscience is not suffering; on the contrary it is joy of a totally new character which we are unable to understand. But even a momentary awakening of conscience in a man who has thousands of different I's is bound to involve suffering. And if these moments of conscience become longer and if a man does not fear them but on the contrary co-operates with them and tries to keep and prolong them, an element of very subtle joy, a foretaste of the future 'clear consciousness' will gradually enter into these moments.

"There is nothing general in the concept of 'morality.' Morality consists of buffers. There is no general morality. What is moral in China is immoral in Europe and what is moral in Europe is immoral in China. What is moral in Petersburg is immoral in the Caucasus. And what is moral in the Caucasus is immoral in Petersburg. What is moral in one class of society is immoral in another and vice versa. Morality is always and everywhere an artificial phenomenon. It consists of various 'taboos,' that is, restrictions, and various demands, sometimes sensible in their basis and sometimes having lost all meaning or never even having had any meaning, and having been created on a false basis, on a soil of superstition and false fears.

"Morality consists of 'buffers.' And since 'buffers' are of various kinds, and as the conditions of life in different countries and in different ages or among different classes of society vary considerably, so the morality created by them is also very dissimilar and contradictory. A morality common to all does not exist. It is even impossible to say that there exists any general idea of morality, for instance, in Europe. It is said sometimes that the general morality for Europe is 'Christian morality.' But first of all the idea of 'Christian morality' itself admits of very many different interpretations and many different crimes have been justified by 'Christian morality.' And in the second place modern Europe has very little in common with 'Christian morality,' no matter how we understand this morality.

"In any case, if 'Christian morality' brought Europe to the war which is now going on, then it would be as well to be as far as possible from such morality."

"Many people say that they do not understand the moral side of your teaching," said one of us. "And others say that your teaching has no morality at all."

"Of course not," said G. "People are very fond of talking about morality. But morality is merely self-suggestion. *What is necessary is conscience.* We do not teach morality. We teach how to find conscience. People are not pleased when we say this. They say that we have no *love*. Simply because we do not encourage weakness and hypocrisy but, on the contrary, take off all masks. He who desires the truth will not speak of love or of Christianity because he knows how far he is from these. Christian teaching is for Christians. And Christians are those who live, that is, who do everything, according to Christ's precepts. Can they who talk of love and morality live according to Christ's precepts? Of course they cannot; but there will always be talk of this kind, there will always be people to whom words are more precious than anything else. But this is a true sign! He who speaks like this is an empty man; it is not worth while wasting time on him.

"Morality and conscience are quite different things. One conscience can never contradict another conscience. One morality can always very easily contradict and completely deny another. A man with 'buffers' may be very moral. And 'buffers' can be very different, that is, two very moral men may consider each other very immoral. As a rule it is almost inevitably so. The more 'moral' a man is, the more 'immoral' does he think other moral people.

"The idea of morality is connected with the idea of good and evil conduct. But the idea of good and evil is always different for different people, always subjective in man number one, number two, and number three, and is connected only with a given moment or a given situation. A subjective man can have no general concept of good and evil. For a subjective man evil is everything that is opposed to his desires or interests or to his conception of good.

"One may say that evil does not exist for subjective man at all, that there exist only different conceptions of good. *Nobody ever does anything deliberately in the interests of evil, for the sake of evil.* Everybody acts in the interests of good, *as he understands it*. But everybody understands it in a different way. Consequently men drown, slay, and kill one another *in the interests of good*. The reason is again just the same, men's ignorance and the deep sleep in which they live.

"This is so obvious that it even seems strange that people have never thought of it before. However, the fact remains that they fail to understand this and everyone considers *his good* as the only good and all the rest as evil. It is naïve and useless to hope that men will ever understand this and that they will evolve a general and identical idea of good."

"But do not good and evil exist in themselves apart from man?" asked someone present.

"They do," said G., "only this is very far away from us and it is not worth your while even to try to understand this at present. Simply remember one thing. The only possible permanent idea of good and evil for man is connected with the idea of evolution; not with mechanical evolution, of course, but with the idea of man's development through conscious efforts, the change of his being, the creation of unity in him, and the formation of a permanent I. . . ."

# INTRODUCTION TO THE
## *TAO TE CHING*

### ARTHUR WALEY

### Quietism

. . . There was another sect [of Taoism] that . . . met with
equally severe condemnation. Han Fei Tzu speaks of people
who "walk apart from the crowd, priding themselves on being
different from other men. They preach the doctrine of Quietism, but their exposition of it is couched in baffling and
mysterious terms. I submit to your Majesty [the king of
Ch'in] that this Quietness is of no practical value to any one
and that the language in which it is couched is not founded
on any real principle . . . I submit that man's duty in life is
to serve his prince and nourish his parents, neither of which
things can be done by Quietness. I further submit that it is
man's duty, in all that he teaches, to promote loyalty and good
faith and the Legal Constitution. This cannot be done in
terms that are vague and mysterious. The doctrine of the
Quietists is a false one, likely to lead the people astray."

How did this doctrine arise? We have seen the gradual
inward-turning of Chinese thought, its preoccupation with
self and the perfection of self. We have seen how out of the
ritual preparation of the sacrificer for the reception of the
descending spirit grew the idea of a cleansing of the heart
which should make it a fit home for the soul. Such cleansing

consisted above all in a "stilling" of outward activities, of
appetites and emotions; but also in a "returning"; for the soul
was looked upon as having become as it were silted up by
successive deposits of daily toil and perturbation, and the
business of the "self-perfecter" was to work his way back
through these layers till "man as he was meant to be" was
reached. Through this "stillness," this complete cessation of
outside impressions, and through the withdrawal of the senses
to an entirely interior point of focus, arose the species of
self-hypnosis which in China is called *Tso-wang*, "sitting with
blank mind," in India Yoga, *dhyāna* and other names; in
Japan, Zen. A definite technique was invented [or borrowed
from Yoga] for producing this state of trance. The main feature of this technique was, as in India, breath-manipulation—
the breathing must be soft and light as that of an infant, or,
as later Quietists said, of a child in the womb. There were
also strange exercises of the limbs, stretchings and postures
much like the *āsanas* connected with Indian yoga; but some
Quietists regarded these as too physical and concrete a
method for the attainment of a spiritual end.

The process of Quietism, then, consisted in a traveling back
through the successive layers of consciousness to the point
when one arrived at Pure Consciousness, where one no longer
saw "things perceived," but "that whereby we perceive." For
never to have known "that whereby we know" is to cast away
a treasure that is ours. Soon on the "way back" one comes to
the point where language, created to meet the demands of
ordinary, upper consciousness, no longer applies. The adept
who has reached this point has learned, as the Quietists expressed it in their own secret language, "to get into the bird
cage without setting the birds off singing."

Here a question arises, which is indeed one which Quietists
have been called upon to answer in diverse parts of the world
and at many widely separated periods of history. Granted
that consciousness can actually be modified by yoga, self-
hypnotism, Zen, Quietness or whatever else one chooses to
call it, what evidence is there that the new consciousness has
any advantage over the old? The Quietist, whether Chinese,

Indian, German or Spanish, has always made the same reply: by such practices three things are attained—truth, happiness and power.

From the theoretical point of view there is of course no reason to believe that the statements of Tao are truer than those of ordinary knowledge; no more reason, in fact, than to believe that the music we hear when our radio is adjusted to 360 is any "truer" than the music we hear when it is adjusted to 1600. But in actual practice the visions of the Quietists do not present themselves to him merely as more or less agreeable alternatives to everyday existence. They are accompanied by a sense of finality, by a feeling that "all the problems which all the schools of philosophers under Heaven cannot settle this way or that have been settled this way or that." Moreover, the state to which the Quietist attains is not merely pleasurable rather than painful. It is "absolute joy," utterly transcending any form of earthly enjoyment. And finally, it gives as the Indians say *siddhi*, as the Chinese say *tê*, a power over the outside world undreamed of by those who pit themselves against matter while still in its thralls. Nor is this aspect of Quietism confined, as is sometimes supposed, to its eastern branches. *"Sin trabajo sujetarás las gentes y te servirán las cosas,"* says St. John of the Cross in his Aphorisms, *"si te olvidares de ellas y de ti mismo."*[1] It is this last claim of Quietism—the belief that the practicant becomes possessed not merely of a power over living things (which we should call hypnotism) but also of a power to move and transform matter—that the world has been least disposed to accept. "Try it (*yung chih*) and find out for yourself," has been the Quietist's usual answer to the challenge "show us, and we will believe."

We know that many different schools of Quietism existed in China in the fourth and third centuries before Christ. Of their literature only a small part survives. Earliest in date was what I shall call the School of Ch'i. Its doctrine was called *hsin shu* "The Art of the Mind." By "mind" is meant not the

[1] Literally "without labor you shall subject the peoples and things shall be subject to you, if you forget both them and yourself."

brain or the heart, but "a mind within the mind" that bears to the economy of man the same relation as the sun bears to the sky. It is the ruler of the body, whose component parts are its ministers. It must remain serene and immovable like a monarch upon his throne. It is a *shên*, a divinity, that will only take up its abode where all is garnished and swept.[2] The place that man prepares for it is called its temple (*kung*). "Throw open the gates, put self aside, bide in silence, and the radiance of the spirit shall come in and make its home." And a little later: "Only where all is clean will the spirit abide. All men desire to know, but they do not enquire into that whereby one knows." And again: "What a man desires to know is *that* (i.e. the external world). But his means of knowing is *this* (i.e. himself). How can he know *that*? Only by the perfection of *this*."

Closely associated with the "art of the mind" is the art of nurturing the *ch'i*,[3] the life-spirit. Fear, pettiness, meanness—all those qualities that pollute the "temple of the mind" —are due to a shrinkage of the life-spirit. The valiant, the magnanimous, the strong of will are those whose *ch'i* pervades the whole body, down to the very toes and finger-tips. A great well of energy must be stored within, "a fountain that never dries," giving strength and firmness to every sinew and joint. "Store it within; make of it a well-spring, flood-like, even and level. Make of it a very store pool of *ch'i*.

*Never till that pool runs dry shall the Four Limbs fail;*
*Nor till the well is exhausted shall the traffic of the Nine Ap-*
      *ertures cease.*
*Thereby[4] shall you be enabled to explore Heaven and Earth,*
*Reach the Four Oceans that bound the world;*
*Within, have no thoughts that perplex,*

[2] The fact that the *shên* is here in a transitional state, half outside divinity, half a "soul" makes me think that this system is earlier than that of the better-known Taoists, to whom Tao was never a thing that came from outside.

[3] *Ch'i* may always be translated breath, if we add the proviso that to the Chinese "breath" was a kind of soul.

[4] By an accumulation of *ch'i*. I see no reason to doubt that the passages here quoted refer, in a cryptic way, to practices of breath manipulation. . . .

*Without, suffer no evil or calamity.*
*Inside, the mind shall be whole;*
*Whole too the bodily frame.*

All this is the work of the life-breath (*ling-ch'i*) that is within the "mind." For it can "come and go where it will. Be so small that nothing could go inside it; so large that nothing exists beyond it. He alone loses it who harms it by perturbation."

What is the nature of the perturbations that cause the loss of this "mind within the mind?" These are defined as "grief and joy, delight and anger, desire and greed for gain. Put all these away, and your mind ('heart' would fit this particular context better) will return to its purity. For such is the mind that only peace and stillness are good for it. Do not fret, do not let yourself be perturbed and the Accord[5] will come unsought. It is close at hand, stands indeed at our very side; yet is intangible, a thing that by reaching for cannot be got. Remote it seems as the farthest limits of the Infinite. Yet it is not far off; every day we use its power. For Tao (i.e. the Way of the Vital Spirit) fills our whole frames, yet man cannot keep track of it. It goes, yet has not departed. It comes, yet is not here. It is muted, makes no note that can be heard, yet of a sudden we find that it is there in the mind. It is dim and dark, showing no outward form, yet in a great stream it flowed into us at our birth."

The branch of Confucianism founded by Mencius was profoundly influenced by the Ch'i-country Taoism which centered round the Art of the Mind and the tending of the Vital Spirit. In this there is nothing surprising, for Mencius spent much of his life in the country of Ch'i, now part of Shantung. Indeed, the passages in which Mencius deals with the acquisition of the Unmoved Mind and with the use of man's "well-spring" of natal breath are unintelligible unless we relate them to the much fuller exposition of the same theories in Kuan Tzŭ. Mencius, as we know, learnt the art of maintaining an "unmoved mind" at the age of forty, that is to say on his ar-

[5] Harmony between the mind and the universe, which gives power over outside things.

rival in the country of Ch'i, which happened about 330 B.C. When asked about the method that he employed, he replied that he had cultivated the art of using his "flood-like breath-spirit," obviously an allusion to the system described by Kuan Tzŭ. Mencius however gives his own turn to this doctrine. With him the "flood-like spirit" is something that is produced cumulatively by the constant exercise of moral sense (*i*). But it can only come into existence as an accessory of such exercise. Its growth cannot be aided by any special discipline or regime. It is clear that Mencius is here combatting the ideas of the yoga practitioners who performed particular exercises in order to "expel the old (i.e. the used breath-spirit) and draw in the new." Those who try to force the growth of the spirit by means other than the possession of a tranquil conscience he compares to the foolish man of Sung who, grieved that his crops came up so slowly, tried to help them by pulling at the stalks.

## Taoism

In the Ch'i system of Quietism the central conception is that of the "mind within the mind," the sanctuary . . . of the spirit. Tao is the way that those must walk who would "achieve without doing." But Tao is not only a means, a doctrine, a principle. It is the ultimate reality in which all attributes are united, "it is heavy as a stone, light as a feather"; it is the unity underlying plurality. "It is that by losing of which men die; by getting of which men live. Whatever is done without it, fails; whatever is done by means of it, succeeds. It has neither root nor stalk, leaf nor flower. Yet upon it depends the generation and the growth of the ten thousand things, each after its kind."

The Quietists who developed this idea of Tao as the unchanging unity underlying a shifting plurality, and at the same time the impetus giving rise to every form of life and motion, were called Taoists. . . .

The first great principle of Taoism is the relativity of all attributes. Nothing is in itself either long or short. If we call a thing long, we merely mean longer than something else that we take as a standard. What we take as our standard depends upon what we are used to, upon the general scale of size to which we belong. The fact that we endow our standard with absoluteness and objectivity, that we say "No one could regard this as anything but long!" is merely due to lack of imagination. There are birds that fly hundreds of miles without stopping. Someone mentioned this to the cicada and the wren, who agreed that such a thing was out of the question. "You and I know very well," they said, "that the furthest one can ever get by the most tremendous effort is that elm there; and even this we can't be sure of doing every time. Often we find ourselves sinking back to earth, and have to give up the attempt as hopeless. All these stories about flying hundreds of miles at a stretch are pure nonsense."

To those, then, who have rather more imagination than the cicada and the wren, all attributes whatsoever, whether they imply color, height, beauty, ugliness, goodness, badness—any quality that can be thought of—are relative. And this applies, clearly, not only to the long and short, the high and low, but also to the "inside" and "outside." The earlier Quietists regarded the soul as something that came from outside to dwell in the body. But to the Taoists, Tao was something that was at the same time within and without; for in Tao all opposites are blended, all contrasts harmonized. . . .

The main controversy of Chinese philosophy in the 4th century B.C. had centered round the rival claims of life and death, of the Ancestors as against the living "sons and grandsons." To the Taoist such debates were meaningless. Looked at from Anywhere, the world is full of insecurities and contradictions; looked at from Nowhere, it is a changeless, uniform whole. In this identity of opposites all antinomies, not merely high and low, long and short, but life and death themselves merge.

When Chuang Tzǔ's wife died, the logician Hui Tzǔ came to the house to join in the rites of mourning. To his astonishment he found Chuang Tzǔ sitting with an inverted bowl on his knees, drumming upon it and singing a song.[6] "After

[6] Both his attitude and his occupation were the reverse of what the rites of mourning demand.

all," said Hui Tzǔ, "she lived with you, brought up your children, grew old along with you. That you should not mourn for her is bad enough; but to let your friends find you drumming and singing—that is really going too far!" "You misjudge me," said Chuang Tzǔ. "When she died, I was in despair, as any man well might be. But soon, pondering on what had happened, I told myself that in death no strange new fate befalls us. In the beginning we lack not life only, but form. Not form only, but spirit. We are blended in the one great featureless, indistinguishable mass. Then a time came when the mass evolved spirit, spirit evolved form, form evolved life. And now life in its turn has evolved death. For not nature only but man's being has its seasons, its sequence of spring and autumn, summer and winter. If someone is tired and has gone to lie down, we do not pursue him with shouting and bawling. She whom I have lost has lain down to sleep for a while in the Great Inner Room. To break in upon her rest with the noise of lamentation would but show that I knew nothing of nature's Sovereign Law."

This attitude towards death, exemplified again and again in Chuang Tzǔ, is but part of a general attitude towards the universal laws of nature, which is one not merely of resignation nor even of acquiescence, but a lyrical, almost ecstatic acceptance which has inspired some of the most moving passages in Taoist literature. That we should question nature's right to make and unmake, that we should hanker after some role that nature did not intend us to play is not merely futile, not merely damaging to that tranquility of the "spirit" which is the essence of Taoism, but involves, in view of our utter helplessness, a sort of fatuity at once comic and disgraceful. If the bronze in the founder's crucible were suddenly to jump up and say "I don't want to be a tripod, a plowshare or a bell. I must be the sword 'Without Flaw,'" the bronzecaster would think it was indeed reprobate metal that had found its way into his stock.

To be in harmony with, not in rebellion against the fundamental laws of the universe is the first step, then, on the way to Tao. For Tao is itself the always-so, the fixed, the unconditioned, that which "is of itself" and for no cause "so." In the individual it is the Uncarved Block, the consciousness on which no impression has been "notched," in the universe it is the Primal Unity underlying apparent multiplicity. Nearest then to Tao is the infant. Mencius, in whose system Conscience, sensitiveness to right and wrong, replaces the notion of Tao, says that the "morally great man" is one who has kept through later years his "infant heart." The idea is one that pervades the literature of the third century. But weakness and softness in general, not only as embodied in the infant, are symbols of Tao. Such ideas as that to yield is to conquer, whereas to grasp is to lose—are indeed already inherent in the premoralistic phase of thought. For example by retreating from a country that one has it in one's power to lay waste, one extorts a blessing from the soil-gods and ancestral spirits of that country. Whereas by any act of aggression one ranges against one a host of unseen powers. Older too than Taoism is the idea that pride invites a fall, that the axe falls first on the tallest tree. But it was Taoism that first welded these ideas together into a system in which the unassertive, the inconspicuous, the lowly, the imperfect, the incomplete become symbols of the Primal Stuff that underlies the kaleidoscope of the apparent universe. It is as representatives of the "imperfect" and the "incomplete" that hunchbacks and cripples play so large a part in Taoist literature. To be perfect is to invite diminution; to climb is to invite a fall. Tao, like water, "takes the low ground." We have already met with the conception of the soul as a well that never runs dry. In Taoism water, as the emblem of the unassertive, and the "low ground," as the home of water, become favorite images. . . . Kuan Tzŭ devotes a particularly eloquent passage to water as pattern and example to the "ten thousand things," that is to say to everything in the universe, and to the low ground as "dwelling place of Tao." It is by absorbing the water spirit . . . that vegetation lives, "that the root gets its girth, the flower its symmetries, the fruit its measure." "The valley spirit," says another Taoist work, meaning what Kuan Tzŭ means by "water spirit," "never dies. It is named the Mysterious Female, and the Doorway of the Mysterious Female is the base from which

Heaven and Earth sprang. It is there within us all the while; draw upon it as you will, it never runs dry."

The valleys, then, are "nearer to Tao" than the hills; and in the whole of creation it is the negative, passive, "female" element alone that has access to Tao, which can only be mirrored "in a still pool." Quietism consists in the cultivation of this "stillness." In its extreme forms, consciousness continues but the functions of the outward senses are entirely suspended and the mind moves only within itself. Between this and the normal state of consciousness there are innumerable stages, and though definite yoga, with complete suspension of the outward senses, was certainly practiced by initiate Taoists, I do not think that anything more than a very relative Quiet was known to the numerous non-Taoist schools of thought that adopted Quietism as a mystical background to their teaching. There is no reason for example to suppose that Mencius's "stilling of the mind" reached an actual *samādhi*, a complete gathering in of the consciousness into itself. But it led him to make a distinction between two kinds of knowledge, the one the result of mental activity, the other passive and as we should say "intuitive"; and it is the second kind that he calls "good knowledge." Indeed, the whole of education consists, Mencius says, in recapturing intuitive faculties that in the stress of life have been allowed to go astray. With him these faculties are moral; whereas the Quiet of the Taoists produces a secondary "virtue" (*tê*) a power "that could shift Heaven and Earth," a transcendental knowledge in which each of the "ten thousand things" is separately mirrored "as the hairs of the brow and head are mirrored in a clear pool." For "to a mind that is 'still' the whole universe surrenders."

How the "power" works is a question upon which the Taoist writers throw very little light. According to one explanation it is a question of equilibrium. The perfect poise that Quietism gives to the mind can for example communicate itself to the hand, and so to whatever the hand holds. The case is cited of a philosopher who possessed this "poise" to such a degree that he could land huge fish from a deep pool with a line consisting of a single filament of raw silk. A line snaps at the point where most strain is put upon it. But if, owing to the perfect equilibrium of the fisherman's hand, no such point exists, the slenderest thread can bear the greatest imaginable weight without breaking. The Taoists indeed saw in many arts and crafts the utilization of a power akin to if not identical with that of Tao. The wheelwright, the carpenter, the butcher, the bowman, the swimmer, achieve their skill not by accumulating facts concerning their art, nor by the energetic use either of muscles or outward senses; but through utilizing the fundamental kinship which, underneath apparent distinctions and diversities, unites their own Primal Stuff to the Primal Stuff of the medium in which they work. Like Tao itself every "art" is in the last resort incommunicable. Some forms of mysticism have laid stress on an oral tradition, not communicable in books; we are indeed often told that the whole Wisdom of the East is enshrined in such a tradition. Taoism went much further. Not only are books the mere discarded husk or shell of wisdom, but words themselves, expressing as they do only such things as belong to the normal state of consciousness, are irrelevant to the deeper experience of Tao, the "wordless doctrine." If then the Taoist speaks and still more if he writes, he does so merely to arouse interest in his doctrines, and not in any hope of communicating what another cannot be made to feel any more than you can feel the pain in my finger.

# DEATH AND RENEWAL

## RICHARD WILHELM

As the Chinese conceive the world the appearance of everything that exists is conditioned by a pair of polar opposites, light and shadow, positive and negative, *Yang* and *Yin*. These extend also into the metaphysical realm as the opposites, life and death. It is not accidental that one of the oldest Chinese documents we have includes among the good fortunes promised to man the finding of a death that will crown life, *his* death, while among the misfortunes which threaten him the worst is an untimely death, a death which dismembers life instead of completing it. So we see that even death, the dark side which accompanies the light, is not merely negative and opposed to life but that, by its presence and its form, it also conditions the light of the living side. That the ancients accounted no man lucky until he was dead was not merely caution or superstition; rather it is a fact that life receives meaning from what lies beyond it, from that dark something toward which we advance.

In order to face this directly a certain courage is required, for no one has the right to speak of death who still fears it. We must develop in ourselves an habitual readiness to meet without fear whatever comes upon us and to encounter directly whatever the future may bring.

Let us ask, therefore, what China can tell us of death. From the very beginning the problem was approached somewhat differently there than in Europe. For in Europe life and death were formerly regarded as two time periods of unequal

From *Spring* 1962, pp. 20–44. Copyright © 1962, Analytical Psychology Club of New York, Inc. Reprinted by permission.

length, opposed to each other. The Western concept has been that life, lasting seventy, eighty, or even a hundred years, takes its rise in time and is, despite its brevity, of the greatest importance, since whether a man will go to heaven or hell for eternity—that is, for time without end—depends upon its outcome. This conception—which apparently originated in Persia and was then, along with certain Platonic influences, borrowed by Christianity—is generally felt to be unsatisfactory in present-day Europe, although on the whole we have nothing with which to replace it. The first half of this concept—namely, the brevity of life on earth—we accept as real but we are doubtful about the second half, about what follows. In the East the idea of reality is somewhat differently apportioned between these two halves. Life, the half which seems so important to us, is robbed, as it were, of its garish sunlight. It is less real than with us. For in the end reality in the East still signifies only appearance, only one reality within the polarity mentioned above. As a result, although on one side life has less body, on the other side the shadowy world of death is not so purely negative; instead, the darkness of night is drawn into the great context including life and death. This is carried so far that life and death belong to the same extent in the world of appearance, and being transcends them both.

There is a natural and quite general idea in the East that anything which begins in time also ends in time. But similarly whatever ends also begins again. The life which comes to an end in time will begin in time again. The idea of a circulation is expressed here, a circulation which—just as it contains day and night in equal measures—also contains death and life. Such a circular movement is familiar to us throughout all of organic nature. When the leaves fall in the autumn and the sap withdraws from the ends of the branches, we are sure that this ending will be followed by a new beginning; when the sun comes back and springtime recurs, the sap will rise once more and new leaves will bud out where the old ones dropped off.

## The Confucian Interpretation

Starting from this general concept of life and death which is current in the Far East, we will speak now of some of the attempts to find solutions that give meaning to human life. First, the Confucian interpretation. Naturally Confucius must have reflected upon these matters, too, but he took care not to say much about them. When a young man questioned him about death, he replied: "You hardly know life yet. How can you know death? Wait till you die; then you will experience it yourself." Another time when a young man asked him if the dead were conscious, he replied: "If I should say that they have consciousness, then it is to be feared that respectful sons and obedient descendants would use up everything for the burial of the dead and leave too little for the living. But should I say that the dead have no consciousness, then it is to be feared that undutiful sons might leave their parents unburied." The point of view of Confucius is that men should be left in a state of doubt and tension about these matters lest their behavior be conditioned by dogmatic creeds and conceptions, for a personal sense of value and dignity is the inner imperative that leads men to act rightly. Therefore, in general, Confucius refused to answer such questions. He did not wish to set up any dogma but wanted men's moral behavior to be shaped quite freely, independent of both those great enemies of mankind, fear and hope.

However, we cannot say that Confucianism had no views about death; quite clear conceptions of it are to be found there. It is entirely due to our ignorance that for centuries we have tended to see Confucius as nothing but a rationalist, leading the millions of Chinese for thousands of years with a worthy, bourgeois, and somewhat humdrum code of morals. This image of Confucius is always reappearing and seems well-nigh indestructible. It derives entirely from the fact that a misunderstanding of Confucius was imported to Europe at the time of the Enlightenment, and that this false picture, highly honored in its day, has, like the Enlightenment itself, lost esteem with the changing times.

But what are the views of Confucianism about death? They are to be found in those commentaries to the *Book of Changes* which go back to Confucius and his school. Here we find the idea that a polarity exists which can be designated as heaven and earth, or light and darkness. Of these two principles, it is said:

> "Looking upward we contemplate . . . the signs in the heavens; looking downward, we examine the lines of the earth. Thus we know the circumstances of the dark and the light. Going back to the beginnings of things and pursuing them to the end, we come to know the lessons of birth and death. The union of seed and power produces all things; the escape of the animus (and the sinking of the anima to the depths) brings about change (*Verfall*, literally, decline, decay).[1] Through this we come to know the conditions of outgoing and returning spirits."[2]

The union of seed (the image, the concept) and power (the material, the form) produces animated substance. On the other hand something quite different happens, too: consciousness arises, and this arising consciousness contains, preformed, as it were, the primal image of the human being. The life of the psyche originates the moment when this preformed consciousness, this spiritual thing, unites with nature (that is, with power or energy)—not in such a way that they mix but so that they constitute a polar tension which calls forth a kind of rotation. Thus the psychic life moves continually between these two poles, the poles of consciousness and of power. This motion attracts the elements and shapes them into forms that correspond with its nature. Therefore this duality is a basic characteristic of life as a whole. As I have said elsewhere, at the moment when the infant gives his first cry the two principles—which till now slumbered united in the mother's womb—separate and never find each other again during the whole

---

[1] Here the terms, anima and animus, are used in a metaphysical rather than a psychological sense: anima denotes the corporeal soul and animus the immanent spirit. (Edit. note)

[2] *The I Ching or Book of Changes,* the Richard Wilhelm translation rendered from German into English by Cary F. Baynes (New York: Pantheon Books, 1950). Bollingen Series XIX, Vol. 1, p. 316.

course of life. From then on consciousness is the observer, the knower. Deeper down, consciousness is the experiencer, too, and, in the deepest depths, the feeler. Beyond that the motion reaches to the realm below, to the realm of organic power or energy. But the organic is only indirectly accessible to consciousness, and is by no means a compliant tool. Rather, it is something against which the spirit (which is higher but less powerful) must fight. From this we can understand why consciousness and power separate again. "The animus escapes and the anima sinks to the depths." That is death. And in the moment of death the two principles take on another aspect. During life they constituted what appeared to be a seeming unity in the body. That which we call a person (*persona*, meaning really a mask) is in Chinese the body. The body is the bond unifying the different psychic powers that act within a man. But inside this bond they always act as separate powers, and only the wise man, who stations himself at the center of their movement, succeeds in establishing harmony between them. At death the body disintegrates and therewith the appearance of unity also ceases. At one place in the *Book of Documents*[3] the death of a prince is described as "a soaring upward and a sinking downward." The two principles are so constituted that one, the corporeal soul, the anima (*Po*), sinks down and the other, the immanent spirit, the animus (*Hun*), mounts up. After the elements divide, what sinks falls into a condition of dissolution. For along with the body the anima also disintegrates. But this dissolution does not mean simply annihilation: just as the constituent parts of the body do not disappear at death but undergo reorganization and may even retain organic connections which are taken over by the new organism, so this Chinese point of view supposes that another kind of entity may be constituted from these corporeal souls. For they are not completely dissolved, and, even though they sink down with the matter in which they previously governed and are naturally no longer personalities, nevertheless they still may be thought of as capacities, tendencies, or forces. Along with the corporeal elements, these psychic elements

[3] *The Book of Documents* is one of the Chinese classics.

are dispersed and made ready for reincorporation into a new development. The idea of this development is simple: the life cycle lives upon broken-down remnants of the dead and thus the constituent parts of the organism that endure pass over into new life.

Correlated with this is the prevailing Chinese idea that men are permeated by the soul of the land. These remnants of life, which go into the earth and come forth from it again, are also forces which influence the constitution of men. It is as if there were a reservoir of life, infusing the whole with a clearly defined atmosphere so strong that the dead, as long as they are not yet quite organically dissolved, exert a formative power, surpassing even that of race, as the European conceives of it. Obviously the inheritance from the parents is also taken into consideration in China. But this is always connected with the great heritage stored in the primeval ancestors who rest in the paternal soil. From here, too, comes the superstition which makes the Chinese wish always to be buried in his native land. He wishes to return again to the place where not only his bodily but also his psychic constitution has taken rise. Thus we see even those Chinese who have given up their Chinese nationality and taken service in foreign lands saving their last pennies, so that when they die their bodies may be returned to their ancient homeland. Hence, too, comes the often morbid homesickness of the Chinese when remote from the ancestral soil that contained and sustained him; also his ecstatic joy when he returns. Once I was with the poet, Hsü Chih-mo, when he returned to his homeland after a yearlong sojourn in Europe, and I shall never forget the words that burst from him: "This earth here, these rivers, these trees, they are my flesh and my blood, I come from them, I live on them, and now I am home again." Here it is evident how death, decay, and life constitute a cycle that is not just theoretically conceived, but directly sensed.

Yet beyond this vegetative soul, this corporeally living thing, still another soul exists which I have designated the animus. I do not say that it is higher, for that would be a comparative evaluation, but that it is intellectual, spiritual, or, to be still more clear, that it has the capacity for spirituality. For spirit, as such, is not a thing that man can produce from within himself, but something he must acquire during the course of life. And perhaps life exists simply in order to become spiritualized. For after death, according to the Confucian view, the animus still retains a kind of consciousness. It is not as if everything were over with the advent of death; rather, just as what is bodily does not immediately dissolve but keeps its form, so does the psychic, too. The two elements separate: the one remains with the corporeal and the other frees itself from it, yet remains somehow connected with it so that it retains a certain kind of perception. The dead, for example, still hear what is said in their presence—wherefore in China it is the custom to speak no evil in the death chamber but to say everything as if one were in the dead man's company, so that he will not be upset and will have time to complete his release from the corporeal.

In general a dynamic point of view is usual in China. The Chinese does not differentiate "substance" so much by measurement as we do, and what we call a substance is to him more likely a state of energy.

Thus, while spirit is not anything that exists substantially, it is also not something that does not exist, rather, it is a tendency toward consciousness. Therefore it has naturally a somewhat precarious existence—unless it has been so concentrated during life as to have built up, as it were, "a rarefied body," a body of thoughts and deeds, a body of a spiritual kind which can provide it with support, now when it must separate itself from the physical body which has been its helpmeet so far, but in which it can no longer find lodging. This psychic body is at first a very delicate thing; only by highest wisdom does it gain a support in itself beyond death.

Among ordinary people this must be taken care of by those who survive. Herein lies the significance of ancestor sacrifice. A sacrifice made for the ancestors means just this, that through pious thought the psychic essence of the dead person lives on in a state of animation. Every good thought sent to the one who has passed on gives him strength and saves him from flickering out into nothingness.[4] As a rule it is not supposed that this life, even though it does not end with death, is eternal; rather, a gradual dimming occurs, a second death. For the descendants think of their ancestors only so long as a living tradition about them exists among the survivors. Therefore in prominent families ancestor sacrifices are brought to more bygone generations than among ordinary people whose memories seldom reach back more than four or five generations. Here another idea may also come into play, namely, that after having lived in the beyond for some time the ancestors come back to the world. Indeed, in early times a succession of generations was supposed to occur in accordance with which those of one generation would sometimes be reincorporated in the generation after the next, the grandfather reappearing in the grandson, for example. Obviously we must not interpret this mechanically as meaning that the grandson is really the grandfather in person. It is better understood as a succession: something from the grandfather's generation lives on in the grandson, something of the grandfather's nature—not just a fortuitous resemblance but something of the grandfather's vital force—actually appears again in the grandson. So, after a certain time has passed, the ancestors return to the common spiritual reservoir, as it were, and from there, sooner or later, as stimulations and life energies, they once again become associated with the human bodies and corporeal souls that are coming into being.

This is approximately the Confucian idea. The only exception to it is that not all men are considered immortal in the same way.[5] The man who has harmonized his nature and brought his being to such a point of effectiveness that it gives forth power—we can call it natural magic power—which works in a creatively transforming way, such a man does not become a *Kuei*, a returner, but a *Shen*, that is, someone effective, a divinity. He becomes a hero and, as such, is bound up with

---

[4] A very similar thought is to be found in Fechner, who builds the whole of immortality on the idea that when the primary body decays an immortal body is built up by those who think about the dead person; thus, so to speak, a body of a higher order arises in which the dead person can live on.

[5] Incidentally, Goethe once expressed the same idea.

the whole culture; so long as it lasts he will last; he leads a
continuing life in the pantheon of that culture. Thus Confucius is still always thought of as presently existing, and not
only he but other great persons, too, as for example Yüeh
Fei, the true knight without fear or reproach. But these are
only the most highly developed people, those who have been
able to set into such continuous rotation the entelechy in-
vested in them that they remain creatively rooted in the context of the culture.

## The Taoist Interpretation

With Taoism we move a step further on. Taoism sees in
mankind nothing essentially different from the rest of life.
Man is just a separate species, a somewhat troublesome species perhaps, being endowed with the doubtful gift of consciousness and therefore capable of committing follies,
whereas other creatures live and die naturally by themselves.
For Taoism the problem is something else. It sees the rhythm
of life simply as a coming forth and a returning; coming forth
is being born, returning is death. But this rhythmic coming
forth and returning goes on continuously and so Lao-tzu says:

> See, all things however they flourish
> Return to the root from which they grew.[6]

This root, which is at the same time a seed, is the eternal
thing, it is life. And when they also say:

> The Valley Spirit[7] never dies.
> It is named the Mysterious Female.
> And the Doorway of the Mysterious Female
> Is the base from which Heaven and Earth sprang.
> It is there within us all the while;
> Draw upon it as you will, it never runs dry.[8]

what they mean is the waterfall of life, whose falling spray

[6] See Arthur Waley, *The Way and Its Power, A Study of the
Tao Te Ching and Its Place in Chinese Thought* (Boston & New
York: Houghton Mifflin Co., 1935), XVI, p. 162.
[7] *Ibid.*, p. 56. Called Valley Spirit because Tao, "like water,
'takes the low ground.'"
[8] *Ibid.*, p. 149.

maintains its form, not because the drops persist—since it is always made up of new drops—but because the conditions causing the drops to follow their path remain the same. And the souls of men are like this water that falls from heaven and ascends to heaven and is shaped by Tao. That is man's fate.

From this point of view, taking life and death too seriously really seems to be only a misunderstanding. So we find in reading Chuang-tzu that he looks forward to death with a light heart and that among other Taoists death is regarded simply as an easy parting.[9] For though consciousness, too, disappears in death, yet for them consciousness is not the highest thing; on the contrary, it is the festering wound from which men suffer throughout life. When consciousness comes to an end with death, it is as if a man tied by the foot were freed from his tether. A change in the feeling of selfhood is necessary for this, to be sure. So long as I identify myself with the transitory body, I will suffer from its transitoriness. For then I make the mistake of supposing that I shall pass away, whereas only the constituent parts that surround me will separate again. Thus for Lao-tzu, and for Taoism in general, the problem is for man to enlarge his feeling of self beyond the transitory into ever widening spheres, the spheres of the family, the nation, humanity, the world. For ultimately the existence of the man who can revolve with the sun and moon lasts as long as the sun and moon, and he who is beyond all becoming lives eternally. This is the same aspect that we found in Confucianism, only freed from human circumstances and carried over to the whole of nature.

## The Buddhist Interpretation

Buddhism goes a step beyond this, in that it identifies life with suffering. Here we will not go into Southern Buddhism

---

[9] *Chuang-tzu, Mystic, Moralist, and Social Reformer.* Translated from the Chinese by Herbert A. Giles (London: Bernard Quaritch, 1889). See the death of Chuang-tzu's wife and his colloquy with the skull.

—which has long been well known in Europe—but will describe only the rhythm of events as Northern Chinese Buddhism sees it. When a man is born he is not one substance but an aggregation of states involving material in motion. Something like a whirlwind that blows up dust. The eddy of dust seems to be an object existing in space, but in reality it is nothing, only a condition of atmospheric pressure which constantly gives rise to new eddies. And so long as new wind goes into eddies, new particles of dust will also be blown up and these whirls of dust will give the impression of lasting existence. Man is like this, so long as he lives. He is a whirling motion resulting from various causes of a physical and psychic nature; without being substantial, this still has lastingness, because one condition of motion necessarily brings on another: birth necessarily leads to development, man takes nourishment, he grows, he matures, he loves, then follows illness, then age, then death. But the cycle does not end there. As long as the causes of this cycle of motion are not exhausted, it will, whenever it comes into sight, repeat itself, like a whirlwind which becomes wholly invisible when it reaches a dustless place but raises up new dust when it re-enters a dusty area. We call this metempsychosis or the cycle of rebirth. But neither expression is entirely right. The prevailing idea in Tibet is that the soul passes successively through three different states after death. The strange look of transfiguration on all the death masks is due to this, at least on the masks of those who died quietly, without terror or shock. The peace which overspreads the faces of the dead comes from the fact that temporarily the world of appearance has vanished; and for a moment the nothingness beyond being and non-being has come to view. Now if the dead person can stay in this moment, he has reached nirvana. But this is rarely possible. Most persons sink down to another state, to where conscious images appear like dreams. At first the good ones appear, the divinities. These good divinities, as is clearly explained, do not exist in themselves but are only emanations of the person's own heart, which can now be seen as if outside. And after the good divinities—it is interesting to see how the psychic breakdown occurs—come the evil divinities.

But these also are not to be feared. They are the same powers as the good divinities, only seen from a different aspect. Like the former emanations of the heart, they are illusions. Both the good and the bad are produced from within the person himself and are therefore neither to be loved nor feared; actually they are no more than temptations that come up to lure him back into the world of appearances. Then follows the second stage, where the breakdown continues. The man turns away from the past. What happens now results from his actions in life: first, the results in the psychic realm, these are the heavens and hells. They are intermediate stages. (Eternal punishment in hell is known only to Christianity, which in this has betrayed its founder in the worst way.) But even these psychological effects of past lives gradually break down. Meanwhile the soul has become ever more dim and lost more and more of its consciousness. But obviously the eddy is still there, it is only for the time being no longer filled, it is a whirlwind without dust; and this arouses a feeling of misfortune in the soul. He who has not found the way to salvation now hungers and thirsts for existence. He has felt dissolution; everything corporeal about him has disintegrated; one layer after another has fallen from him and yet he has not lost the thirst for life. So he pursues existence again and once more approaches the real world. Wishful images come to him.

These hungry souls work their way to wherever a child is being engendered on earth and seek admission to new birth through the mother's body. For though the union of the masculine and feminine poles in the corporeal world is necessary, this by itself is still not enough to make a human being; at the moment of union one of these souls, who are always at hand thirsting for existence, must thrust its way into life again. This is also the reason why so many unwanted children are born. The children do not come from the parents' wish but from the wishes of these unfortunate souls who endeavor with deluded frenzy to force their way into existence —for delusion is, indeed, what drives them.

In Europe one often hears it said that the doctrine of reincarnation is especially reassuring because it gives the convic-

tion that man will return to the world again. That is a totally
unoriental thought. Reincarnation is the great burden under
which the oriental suffers. For it suggests to him not so much
life and the joy of living as death. As soon as a man re-
enters life, he faces death at the end. Thus he is reborn to
ever renewed death and to ever new forms of the horrible
and frightening which he must endure until finally released.
And this is where karma comes in: according to this idea
the soul eddy naturally seeks out the future body best suited
to its measure. The reincarnated man (who is thus not simply
a reconstitution of the past, being made up physically of entirely different forms and elements and retaining only the same
impulses as before) will seek out the physical capacities
through which he can best fulfill his central tendency. Thus
it happens that a man who has stolen jewels in this life will
be a jeweler in his future life, or, if he has been cruel, he
may become a lion. It is not true, as we are accustomed to
suppose, that this has anything to do with punishment. Karma,
in the final analysis, is not an ethical doctrine; it teaches
that every tendency, according to law, seeks to enhance itself and that this enhancement continues over and beyond
individual existence until it reaches the point where the great
reversal occurs. Only then is it dissolved and not until then
does the delusion cease. But where the delusion ends, there
is nirvana, the great peace. Nirvana is therefore not a purely
negative thing; it is simply a condition that is higher than the
condition of tension between opposites, a condition of oneness. Just for that reason, it is—for those who have their being
within the world of polar opposites—very difficult, if not impossible, to understand.

## The Role of Consciousness

The conception of life as a tendency to motion, interrupted
intermittently by death, is definitely a concept of highest interest scientifically. But this problem has another totally different aspect due to the special fact that we are not here concerned with a process which we observe only in plants and
animals, which takes place only in the external world, or even

only within the world of psychological experience; rather, life and the idea of death have special psychic connotations because it is I who am living, the ego that is conceiving of its own loss of life, its own death. And this ego-consciousness is what gives special tension to the problem. For it goes without saying that life, like any operating force, is so constituted that it cannot itself conceive any adequate reason for its own cessation. Hence the love of life, which inheres naturally in all that lives. The force that brings life to an end is abhorrent to life. For obviously life must, as it were, instinctively fear and be appalled at its own cessation, just because it is life. Moreover men are organized in such a way that consciousness (which is what we call occurrences in the cortex of the brain and perhaps in other regions of the body, too, when they are reflected on a different, incorporeal plane) is not only connected with the area of psychic phenomena which we call life, but also appears to us as *my* consciousness. That is, we are conscious of ourselves.

What is the ego? That is the great question. We may compare it to a point of light, which without extension in time yet moves forward in time. What it is cannot be explained but only experienced. We all know how the ego-experience differs from other experiences. And this ego is tied up with a complex of living events and identifies itself with them. I am my body, I am the sum or the harmony—however you want to put it—of the occurrences which enter my consciousness as living events in my body. The love of life is not just an anonymous force, but it is *my* love of *my* life, which throws a wholly new light on the problem, for then it is my fear and my resistance to the cessation of life that is seeking a solution.

Let us be as cool and severe about this as possible. It is not a matter of having great thoughts in the presence of death, suitably toned with strong feeling. These help very little to make the experience what it should be, for a strong feeling tone does not in the end necessarily agree with reality. We often have the strongest feelings with no connection to reality at all. Likewise, there are perhaps men who have died a wonderfully beautiful death, swept away from consciousness to the unconscious on wings of high feeling, as it were, who are yet far from having gained a victory. It just depends upon the questions: What about life? What about death? Is there a chance of our overcoming death? And if there is, what ways will actually lead us to it?

If we are to answer these questions, one thing is clear: we must subscribe completely to the modern attitude toward physical life. The medieval attitude which looked upon the earth as no more than a place of trial, and which yearned for deliverance from life, was a kind of self-betrayal. Naturally, it could be maintained only because it found support in the imaginary picture of a future heaven to which men hoped to be translated. But today we know that our capital in hand is our life in the body. We have no second, further life at our disposal. We know, too, that in all true religions this life in the body, this soul incarnate, uniformly plays a great part. This is not just a modern materialistic idea; in earliest Christendom the responsibility for man's fate after death was also laid upon the life in the body. Even in Buddhism—the whole aim of which is to release men from everything that life signifies because all living is suffering—the only weapon men have at their disposal with which to struggle is corporeal life itself. The conclusion to be drawn from this, even in the East, is that corporeal life must be valued, appreciated, and cared for. The senselessness of death (which has, indeed, no place in life) may quite likely have led in very early times—and perhaps not only then, but repeatedly—to men making attempts to find out whether death could not be done away with in general, or life simply continued *ad infinitum*. These attempts, although for the most part they cannot be refuted purely logically, hold little interest for us, because experience shows us that all those who have made them—from the earliest right up to the most modern times—always end by committing the *faux pas* of experiencing the "senselessness of death" in their own persons. Yet something attaches to these attempts which makes them seem, perhaps, not wholly meaningless. We have not, it is true, advanced far enough to be able to give a clear account of ourselves when confronted with the death of consciousness, or to boast that we already know about death— far enough to be able to die, as it were, not sloppily but appropriately. But since this is so, then I say, we must take care to obtain as much time as is needed to come to this stage during our life cycle. For, if we are snatched away prematurely, our death is not the right death, and it is naturally impossible that anything right should come of it.

So during the Sung dynasty we see efforts being made in different directions, in Buddhism, in Taoism, and even in Confucianism, to prolong life, and not just to seventy or eighty years, but for a much longer period. These methods made use of introspection to carefully observe the life processes as well as what furthers life and what hinders it. In this the life blood, the life in the blood, apparently played a great part. [They likened it to water.] And it was repeatedly said that water is essential for the soul and that, in order to prolong life, the fire of the spirit must penetrate into this water. "Water and fire complement each other" is an old magic saying in the *Book of Changes*[10] which contains the secret of life. And ultimately this idea is nothing other than the idea of baptism, which is on the one hand baptism with water and on the other hand baptism with the Holy Ghost and with fire. So we find, in the secret religious teachings of the Orient, a method for prolonging life by making the blood healthy, that is, by ridding it of its dross and overcoming the limitations and obstacles in its way, so that it can flow continuously and by this continuous flowing never fall behind the time. Because, as they think of it, blood is not just a mixture of chemical materials, but the soul is contained in it. Like Goethe, they say, "Blood is a very special fluid." When the blood is shed outwardly, it is accompanied by the soul, and even when no corporeal blood is shed, still the inward dissipation of this life fluid tends to disperse the soul and use up life. However, when this same blood, this entirely special fluid, fulfills its inner circulation without hindrance, then it constitutes the strength within strength and is for mankind the substratum of the soul, the substratum of corporeal life.

What then were the methods used to prolong life through

[10] *Shua Kua* in *The I Ching or Book of Changes*, Vol. 1, p. 292.

the purification, sanctification, and renewal of the blood? In China there are certain meditation practices which are of great interest when viewed in the light of recent research. In many ways the outer forms in which the instructions for them were given suggest alchemical formulas. Instructions are given for smelting the pearl of life, the gold pearl, the stone of wisdom, or whatever one chooses to call this elixir. Behind this Chinese alchemy (even though it occasionally prepared medical materials, which in so far as they worked are not to be scorned) we must not expect to find any scientific chemistry; this was rather a psychic technique. Indeed, it was a matter of activating certain psychic centers by concentrating attention on them, for these centers ordinarily sleep and precisely through their non-functioning bring about the cessation of life. But what does it mean to concentrate the attention?

Here we come to the secret of the whole practice. We know that attention is subject to our will. We have the power to direct our attention wherever we wish. But over and against this we know, too, that so endlessly much strength is needed for such an act of will that hardly more than a brief shift is possible. To fix our attention is beyond our power. That is, we may be able to force it, but then it will be unproductive attention and nothing will come of it. Some guidance independent of our own design is much better able to fix it. Yet so long as the attention is undirected, it is not a strength. Only directed and, as it were, collected, concentrated attention actually constitutes something creative in the life of the psyche, a power. And such attention must be directed toward the life centers, toward the system of activities that the blood keeps in motion, in such a way that they are awakened and set going, so that life flows again.

It is at this point that the magic power of imagery is brought into practice. Attention cannot be fixed voluntarily but it is possible to fix it by forming an image that evokes it. This image may be of different kinds: it may be either a representational summation, a visual image built up in the imagination —under some circumstances even a sound image—or else it may be a succession of words, not spoken aloud but visually conceived; there are various possibilities. But in any case this kind of attention-exciting image must exert an attraction. That is the magic of meditation, why meditation seeks to construct such images. Naturally the meditator himself must build up the images, for only so do they correspond to his nature and possess the power, drawn from within himself, to hold his attention. However, they have to be drawn up, so to speak, upon a certain ground plan, must tend in a certain direction, and many of these images are therefore so common that they can be used by almost all men, or at least by all men of the same cultural background. Through consciousness-attracting images like these, the attention is concentrated and the images become so established that they enter into connection with the life centers. Attention directed to these images even exerts an effect upon the bodily life as a result of which fluids are produced which circulate in the blood, and the blood, which may have been about to stagnate, is provided with new life energy; thus a new circulation of blood is brought about. This practice is combined with breathing exercises. These, however, are purely technical matters which do not concern us here. In any case, it is evident that what is involved is in principle the gradual, subtle perception, resulting from self-analysis, which meditates not upon itself but upon what may be forthcoming from the soul, from the blood. What follows is the building up of centers of strength of a psychic kind which are suited to work upon this psychic stuff and to effect an inner renewal of the blood through their suggestive power.

## Life-Renewing Forces in Nature

But besides this there is something else. Certain forces seem to exist in nature which are not always of the same strength throughout the course of the day and the year, but which seem to circle around the world from time to time like tidal waves. For example, the philosopher Meng-tzu said that such life-renewing forces are particularly strong in the time before daybreak and especially effective then if a person is in a deep and peaceful sleep. For, if his sleep is not deep, he is not detached enough to receive the cosmic forces. Such detachment can be achieved only through proper practice, but in so far as a man has it, he is enabled to receive the forces of cosmic life—to free himself, as it were, from the deposit of past days and go forth strengthened and refreshed to meet a new day of life. And this technique goes still a step further: if a man consciously gives himself over to the stream of time and does not remain on the bank reflecting on the past and future, permitting fear and hope to unsettle the soul, and if the soul concentrates its whole life in the present, in the here and now, allowing that which is passing to pass away and that which is coming to come, then the heart resembles a mirror, free of dust, in which things reflect themselves as they come and go, thus always calling forth the right reactions and not the false. This is, therefore, an endeavor not to suppress any psychic experience but to give everything that happens the opportunity of immediately eliciting the necessary reaction, so that the poisonous forces in the experiences may be eliminated.

Peace of soul, here operating as vital strength, is represented by Meng-tzu as possible in various ways. It depends upon the man himself. But although, according to this philosopher, such peace of soul is possible even upon low levels, all the different ways to it have one thing in common: a man must never tolerate the heaping up of disagreeable psychic stuff, but must always level it out with all possible speed. For unevened tensions constitute repressions and make inhibitions in the unconscious, which prevent the soul from taking free breaths of permanent renewal from the sources of strength in nature.

That is how the Chinese thought that life should be prolonged. In addition there were certain rules concerned with the training of the body which we might think of as being taken care of in our modern sports if an essentially different way of regarding the matter did not prevail in China. For bodily exercises such as these do not serve in China to establish athletic records. On the contrary, in China competitive physical exercise is considered a waste of life energy because it sets up an outer goal, not based upon the body but upon a vague popular idea; moreover it uses up a disproportionate amount of psychic strength. Yet, apart from this, physical exercise is cultivated in China; but always in such a way that the Why and not the material What is emphasized. It is harmony that counts most in this kind of exercise, not the greatness of the measure of the achievement. An arrow that hit the center was considered a good shot even if it did not pierce the leather surface of the target, for, as Confucius said, in shooting it is hitting the target that matters, not penetrating it. Physical exercise was, therefore, included in these efforts to prolong life, but only in the sense that it was conceived of as harmoniously training the body for its own inner purposes. Yet all that can be achieved in these ways is the avoidance of premature death, not dying before one's allotment of life strength runs out. For we all must die one way or another.

There is an idea among the Chinese that life has a natural boundary; the "heavenly years" are those permitted to a man when he does nothing to curtail his life. Life is also conceived as a given extension in time, with a beginning and an end. One cannot say that this is so because this life is predetermined. But the fullness, the duration, and also the rhythm of a life are laid down from the first moment on, just as the whole course of a curve may be reckoned from the first three points. Thus bodily life is also thought of as something thoroughly unified. Death does not come by chance, but every life has its limits set by nature, limits which correspond to the vitality and the rhythm of this particular life which enters only once into time as it does into space. This temporal limitation is neither good fortune nor bad; it is a fact, like the three dimensional extension of our spatial life, which is also simply accepted by us. Possibly some men are unhappy not to be taller; and others would like to be thinner; but these are inconveniences to which we resign ourselves without making them into problems. Similarly the duration of this physical life in time is no problem in itself if it is looked at rightly.

The point which turns into a problem here is that I want immortality. The body is mortal and does not experience its mortality as disagreeable; it just dies when the time comes. But the body has, so to speak, an inner aspect, it has consciousness, and consciousness imagines death before it happens. This is the idea of death with which men have been constantly preoccupied since the beginning of time, which has been, perhaps, one of the strongest forces in history. When we visualize all that has been produced by the idea of death, it is downright overwhelming. Not only whole religious systems, not only complete political organizations, not only—and this is strangest of all—wars and battles, wiping out millions of lives, have resulted from this idea, but when one considers the pyramids and other similar monuments that have resulted from this idea of death, this resistance to transitoriness, one sees its effects have gone so far that they reach almost into geological magnitudes.

What can be done about it? In Chinese there is a tradition, which by boldly taking the psyche apart sees what must be done. The philosophical belief of a man like Chuang-tzu was that he could, as it were, put himself to one side and observe the behavior of things with his "I" no longer confined to his body, but with a larger view.

This does not end the matter, though; if what we want is a sure position and not just to get the better of our feeling, then something additional is needed, namely, the detachment of the "I" from the body. This is the point on which all religions agree. The "I" wants life, but he who wishes to keep his life will lose it. This adherence of the "I" to life is, in a way, precisely what causes life to end, to be withdrawn from the "I." So the problem, as the Chinese see it, is to form a new body inside the earthly body. This is the problem of rebirth as it is also to be found in the esoteric tradition of Christianity in the first centuries, of which we no longer know anything today, at least in the Evangelical Church. Rebirth is not just a pious phrase and when Paul fought and struggled, not only to put off corruption, but also to put on incorruption, this was not an imaginary idea of some sort of new life in the flesh, which he would wrap about himself like a mantle; he had something entirely real in view. And so also among the Chinese we find the attempt to form a new body for the "I." But it is a very difficult thing and must be very carefully meditated throughout. This new body is not of gross material but, so to speak, a body composed of energy.

The attempt is to release these energies through exercises in meditation and concentration and to surround with them the seedlike entelechy which is latently present. Thus in the end it is no different from the formation of a grain of seed, but it is transferred from the physical plane. For what else is the seed but the entelechy of the tree, invisibly concentrated and yet not within the body, since the possibility of embodiment is always there. This concentration is a latent tension of forces, which, when the seed falls to the earth, will be stirred by the process of decomposition to a suitable new course of action. Thus it is a retrograde movement, which when it reaches utmost concentration makes release possible. The release occurs through the decomposition of the material surrounding the seed. The Chinese strove for something similar in the psychic realm, for the formation of a psychic seed. By surrounding this seed with bodily energies a concentration of latent strength is developed which now reaches a point where it is able to free itself from primary time, that is, from transitoriness.

Different images were used to express this in China. A holy man, sunk deep in meditation, may be depicted, for example, with a small child in his heart. This child will then be cared for and will finally rise on high through the orifice in the top of the skull. This is a reproduction in life of what will occur at death. The significance of this departure of the highest powers through the topmost orifice of the body is nothing other, when translated into modern language, than that we are here seeing things from a second order of time. For when, with the whole of life spread out before us, we consciously release ourselves from it, while still remaining bound up with material existence so far as energy is concerned, it means that we are able to reflect life, not in the usual sense, but in a pre-eminently strong and meditatively satisfying sense. And this may even increase by stages. For we do not actually live just in one time, but, as it were, in different shells of time—shells which resemble onion skins. For instance, I am conscious of seeing this chair. But now I can move my subject back one stratum and take this chair-observing subject as my object: look at myself as I observe the chair. Yes, and that goes on to eternity; how far the process can be carried is a matter of the individual's psychic force, of his ability to concentrate. Among the Chinese we find meditation practices which go a long way toward uniting the subject's potentialities for concentration with the making conscious of the meaningful dominants that exist in the ego monad. Such an occurrence was pictorially represented as if the supertemporal "I" released itself first from the meditating man, then sent forth five emanations, which, in turn, again each emitted five human reflections. Such a picture looks strange as a picture but it is meant to convey the serene fulfillment in time of a process liberating the "I" from the material body —which was all that existed at first.

Very serious and austere mental work is required for this. But not thought as we understand it in the West as a purely intellectual exercise. Among us, thinking and being are spoken of as irreconcilable opposites. But this Chinese thinking is conceived of as active, as thought so concentrated that an effect is produced through it in the world of being. In Chinese the sign for "to think" is a square field with a heart (that is, consciousness) under it, thus, an area in which consciousness participates. Thoughts are conceived as sounds arising in consciousness. They are, so to speak, sound images issuing from the consciously worked-over field. These, of course, are concepts and ideas of which we can discover the meaning only with difficulty. Yet our own philosophical concepts are also only very figurative and inexact. But what concerns us here is the real work of achieving independence from this life while still alive. Moreover, this independence is not purely theoretical but practical; it contains within itself, just as the grain of seed does, something which we can (following Goethe) call an entelechy, a force with an entirely definite rhythm, a completely definite direction, and all that accompanies that. An entelechy in this sense is like a small self-enclosed world system. And the concept exists throughout Chinese thought—in Confucianism as well as in Taoism, or Buddhism—that now, during the course of his lifetime a man makes whatever psychic and corporeal dispositions he has been endowed with into a harmonious whole, unifying it and giving it form from the center outward.

Naturally this means the formation of an immensely strong force if it succeeds. But the question is, will it succeed? The possibility exists that a man may not be able to hold together the psychic entities united in him; occasionally one or another of these beings may escape and take a trip in the dream world on its own. This kind of happening, which may bring men into touch with departed spirits or the spirits of non-human creatures, actually does not give the Chinese objects for serious belief so much as it gives them material for a multiplicity of entertaining fairy tales.

## The Formation of the Higher State

But such things happen only rarely, and the goal is a unification of the psyche through consistent exercise. The presupposition is that this entelechy contains within itself a higher state, capable of viewing not only the past but also the future, and therefore that it has a kind of intuition superior to intellect as such. This higher state, however, is still, as it were, underdeveloped at our present stage of life. It is an extraordinary thought that what is highest, most intuitive, should have to be educated and shaped by a consciousness which, by comparison, is in itself a much lower thing; thus the divine—if we can use that expression here—is something in man that requires the achievement of humanity before it can develop. What is highest must to begin with be shaped and informed through the achievement of consciousness. This was taken very seriously among the Chinese. Expressions which spring and bubble forth involuntarily from the unconscious, which in Europe are often—or sometimes, anyway—considered particularly inspired, are not especially valued in China. Rather, they are considered wasted powers, undeveloped opportunities for the birth of eternal life which, just because they have not yet concentrated themselves, finally scatter again.

Thus a man must make some acquaintance with the after-death condition during his lifetime, and we have the opportunity for this in sleep, for then the soul dwells in the liver. By this the Chinese means, not in the brain, not in consciousness, but in the vegetative part of man. And deep sleep, the complete absence of consciousness, is a condition very closely related to the after-death condition. This is the time when it is valuable for a man to educate his dreams; through educating dreams a man educates himself for life after death. For the wise man no longer dreams; he is no longer subject to these images taking form chaotically in visual or aural phantasies. Rather, he is so in harmony with happenings in the world that in sleep, or deep sleep, these last timid vestiges of consciousness fall away from him completely. Then like clear water in which no images appear at all, but which can be seen through to the bottom, his sleep too is entirely clear and clean.

So we come here to the third "I," the spiritual "I," which is higher than the physical and psychical. That the psychical "I" can develop so far as it does is possible only through this third "I" which, in contradistinction to the individual "I," is completely universal. This "I" is bound neither to the body nor to the psyche; it is the great "I" of humanity, the world "I." To the degree that one's own psychic entelechy vibrates in the rhythm of this "I," and the "I"-experience is transposed into it—not only momentarily but for deep periods of strengthening rest—one succeeds in experiencing the after-death condition in a way which no longer excites fear.

The task of life is therefore to prepare for death, not in the sense of doing a given number of good deeds according to the book, in order to get into heaven later, but in such a way as to engender in oneself a condition which, freed from the finite, represents the infinite—in such a way as to center the "I" in this infinite, eternal condition. This is a withdrawal from the world, so to speak. Naturally there is a point where the psychical "I" has to release itself; that is, there comes a death. And this is the death that is bound up with the becoming of something new, the death that now guards against a further death. This point is similar to that of birth. For birth is indeed a great revolution, heaven and earth reverse themselves for men then, they change places. The new birth is a kind of spiritual recentering wherein heaven and earth again change places; what was formerly over becomes under and what was under becomes over, thus making possible a new form of existence which is eternal. A man who has reached this point will not fear death any more; he will consider it like sleep, as a physiological occurrence which befalls all men in common and which can be the more easily borne the less importance one gives to it as a process. And now in life, too, because he is as it were one reborn, he has an essentially different attitude. He acquires a gravity in regard to eternal things, and he takes the passing of temporal things lightly; it no longer engages him very deeply. For the Taoist this enjoins an ironical and humorous bearing, a smiling at all earthly goings on. But for the Confucian it means sublimity as is shown in the fact that the reborn man comes down from the highest heights to the place where he is and fulfills the duties associated with this place in a practicable way, not from special virtue or from the necessity of so acquiring merit, but simply because this is the manner of participating in life that befits him now. He no longer needs to go to the beyond, for in the here he is already in the beyond. This beyond is not separated from the here by either time or space; it is the Tao, it is the meaning, which penetrates alike all being and becoming; it is the gravity which sanctifies; it is this that no longer allows death to seem a fearful thing, that makes life into eternity.

*Translated from the German by Jane A. Pratt*

# THE RESURRECTION
# OF THE BODY

## NORMAN O. BROWN

The path of sublimation, which mankind has religiously followed at least since the foundation of the first cities, is no way out of the human neurosis, but, on the contrary, leads to its aggravation. Psychoanalytical theory and the bitter facts of contemporary history suggest that mankind is reaching the end of this road. Psychoanalytical theory declares that the end of the road is the dominion of death-in-life. History has brought mankind to that pinnacle on which the total obliteration of mankind is at last a practical possibility. At this moment of history the friends of the life instinct must warn that the victory of death is by no means impossible; the malignant death instinct can unleash those hydrogen bombs. For if we discard our fond illusion that the human race has a privileged or providential status in the life of the universe, it seems plain that the malignant death instinct is a built-in guarantee that the human experiment, if it fails to attain its possible perfection, will cancel itself out, as the dinosaur experiment canceled itself out. But jeremiads are useless unless we can point to a better way. Therefore the question confronting mankind is the abolition of repression—in traditional Christian language, the resurrection of the body.

We have already done what we could to extract from psychoanalytical theory a model of what the resurrected body would be like. The life instinct, or sexual instinct, demands activity of a kind that, in contrast to our current mode of activity, can only be called play. The life instinct also demands a union with others and with the world around us based not on anxiety and aggression but on narcissism and erotic exuberance.

But the death instinct also demands satisfaction; as Hegel says in the *Phenomenology*, "The life and knowledge of God may doubtless be described as love playing with itself; but this idea sinks into triviality, if the seriousness, the pain, the patience and the labor of the Negative are omitted."[1] The death instinct is reconciled with the life instinct only in a life which is not repressed, which leaves no "unlived lines" in the human body, the death instinct then being affirmed in a body which is willing to die. And, because the body is satisfied, the death instinct no longer drives it to change itself and make history, and therefore, as Christian theology divined, its activity is in eternity.

At the same time—and here again Christian theology and psychoanalysis agree—the resurrected body is the transfigured body. The abolition of repression would abolish the unnatural concentrations of libido in certain particular bodily organs—concentrations engineered by the negativity of the morbid death instinct, and constituting the bodily base of the neurotic character disorders in the human ego. In the words of Thoreau: "We need pray for no higher heaven than the pure senses can furnish, a purely sensuous life. Our present senses are but rudiments of what they are destined to become."[2] The human body would become polymorphously perverse, delighting in that full life of all the body which it now fears. The consciousness strong enough to endure full life would be no longer Apollonian but Dionysian—con-

[1] Hegel, G. W. F., *Phenomenology of Mind*, tr. J. B. Baillie, 2nd ed. (London: G. Allen & Unwin, 1931), p. 81.

[2] Thoreau, *A Week on the Concord and Merrimack Rivers;* cf. Read, H., *Icon and Idea* (Cambridge: Harvard University Press, 1948), p. 139.

sciousness which does not observe the limit, but overflows; consciousness which *does not negate any more*.

If the question facing mankind is the abolition of repression, psychoanalysis is not the only point of view from which the question can and should be raised. We have already indicated that the question is intrinsic to Christian theology. The time has come to ask Christian theologians, especially the neoorthodox, what they mean by the resurrection of the body and by eternal life. Is this a promise of immortality after death? In other words, is the psychological premise of Christianity the impossibility of reconciling life and death either in "this" world or the "next," so that flight from death—with all its morbid consequences—is our eternal fate in "this world" and in "the next?" For we have seen that the perfect body, promised by Christian theology, enjoying that perfect felicity promised by Christian theology, is a body reconciled with death.

In the last analysis Christian theology must either accept death as part of life or abandon the body. For two thousand years Christianity has kept alive the mystical hope of an ultimate victory of Life over Death, during a phase of human history when Life was at war with Death and hope could only be mystical. But if we are approaching the last days, Christian theology might ask itself whether it is only the religion of fallen humanity, or whether it might be asleep when the bridegroom comes. Certain it is that if Christianity wishes to help mankind toward that erasure of the traces of original sin which Baudelaire said was the true definition of progress,[3] there are priceless insights in its tradition—insights which have to be transformed into a system of practical therapy, something like psychoanalysis, before they are useful or even meaningful.

The specialty of Christian eschatology lies precisely in its rejection of the Platonic hostility to the human body and to "matter," its refusal to identify the Platonic path of sublimation with ultimate salvation, and its affirmation that eternal

[3] Baudelaire, *Mon coeur mis à nu.* Cf. Marcuse, H., *Eros and Civilization* (Boston: Beacon Press, 1955), p. 153.

life can only be life in a body. Christian asceticism can carry punishment of the fallen body to heights inconceivable to Plato; but Christian hope is for the redemption of that fallen body. Hence the affirmation of Tertullian: *Resurget igitur caro, et quidem omnis, et quidem ipsa, et quidem integra*—The body will rise again, all of the body, the identical body, the entire body.[4] The medieval Catholic synthesis between Christianity and Greek philosophy, with its notion of an immortal soul, compromised and confused the issue; only Protestantism carries the full burden of the peculiar Christian faith. Luther's break with the doctrine of sublimation (good works) is decisive; but the theologian of the resurrected body is the cobbler of Görlitz, Jacob Boehme. When Tillich and Barth finally get round to the substance of things hoped for, their eschatology, they will have to reckon with Boehme. Meanwhile, as neoorthodox theology plunges deeper into the nature of sin and death, Boehme's *theologia ex idea vitae deducta* is neglected except by the lonely mystic and revolutionary Berdyaev.[5]

Whatever the Christian churches do with him, Boehme's position in the Western tradition of mystic hope of better things is central and assured. Backward he is linked, through Paracelsus and alchemy, to the tradition of Christian gnosticism and Jewish cabalism; forward he is linked, through his influence on the romantics Blake, Novalis, and Hegel, with Freud. We have argued that psychoanalysis has not psychoanalyzed itself until it places itself inside the history of Western thought —inside the general neurosis of mankind. So seen, psychoanalysis is the heir to a mystical tradition which it must affirm.

Mysticism, in the mind of the general public, is identified with that flight from the material world and from life . . . which, from the psychoanalytical point of view, may be termed Apollonian or sublimation mysticism. But there is in the Western tradition another kind of mysticism, which can

[4] Tertullian, *De Carnis Resurrectione*, p. 63. Cf. Mead, G. R. S., *The Doctrine of the Subtle Body in Western Tradition* (London: J. M. Watkins, 1919), p. 111.

[5] Berdyaev, N., *The Destiny of Man*, 3rd ed. (London: G. Bles, 1948), p. 64.

be called Dionysian or body mysticism, which stays with life, which is the body, and seeks to transform and perfect it. Western body mysticism—a tradition which urgently needs reexamination—contains three main strands: the Christian (Pauline) notion of the "spiritual" body, the Jewish (cabalistic) notion of Adam's perfect body before the Fall, and the alchemical notion of the subtle body.[6] All of these strands unite in Boehme, and even a little knowledge of the real Boehme . . . makes it plain that Boehme and Freud have too much in common to be able to dispense with each other.

Boehme, like Freud, understands death not as a mere nothing but as a positive force either in dialectical conflict with life (in fallen man), or dialectically unified with life (in God's perfection). Thus, says Benz, "Our life remains a struggle between life and death, and as long as this conflict lasts, anxiety lasts also."[7] In Boehme's concept of life, the concept of play, or love-play, is as central as it is in Freud's; and his concept of the spiritual or paradisical body of Adam before the Fall recognizes the potent demand in our unconscious both for an androgynous mode of being and for a narcissistic mode of self-expression, as well as the corruption in our current use of the oral, anal, and genital functions. It is true that Boehme does not yet accept the brutal death of the individual physical body, and therefore makes his paradisical body ambiguously immaterial, without oral, anal, and genital organs; and yet he clings obstinately to the body and to bodily pleasure, and therefore says that Adam was "magically" able to eat and enjoy the "essence" of things, and "magically" able to reproduce and to have sexual pleasure in the act of reproduction. Boehme is caught in these dilemmas because of his insight into the corruption of the human body, his insight that all life is life in the body, and, on the other hand, his inability to

---

[6] Mead, *The Doctrine of the Subtle Body in Western Tradition;* Scholem, *Major Trends in Jewish Mysticism;* Gray, *Goethe the Alchemist.* Cf. Savage, "Jung, Alchemy and Self," in *Explorations: Studies in Culture and Communication, No. 2* (Toronto: University of Toronto Press, 1954), pp. 14–37.

[7] Benz, E., *Der vollkommene Mensch nach Jacob Boehme* (Stuttgart: W. Kohlhammer, 1937), p. 138.

accept a body which dies. No Protestant theologian has gone further; or rather, later Protestantism has preferred to repress the problem and to repress Boehme.

Oriental mysticism also, to judge from Needham's survey of Taoism or Eliade's study of Yoga,[8] has reached the same point. Needham (quoting Maspéro) is right in stressing that the Taoist quest for a more perfect body transcends the Platonic dualism of soul and matter. But Needham's enthusiasm for Taoism as a human and organismic response to life in the world must be qualified by recognizing that the Taoist perfect body is immortal: Taoism does not accept death as part of life. . . .

Modern poetry, like psychoanalysis and Protestant theology, faces the problem of the resurrection of the body. Art and poetry have always been altering our ways of sensing and feeling—that is to say, altering the human body. And Whitehead rightly discerns as the essence of the "Romantic Reaction" a revulsion against abstraction (in psychoanalytical terms, sublimation) in favor of the concrete sensual organism, the human body.[9] "Energy is the only life, and is from the Body. . . . Energy is Eternal Delight," says Blake. . . .

The "magical" body which the poet seeks is the "subtle" or "spiritual" or "translucent" body of occidental mysticism, and the "diamond" body of oriental mysticism, and, in psychoanalysis, the polymorphously perverse body of childhood. Thus, for example, psychoanalysis declares the fundamentally bisexual character of human nature; Boehme insists on the androgynous character of human perfection; Taoist mysticism invokes feminine passivity to counteract masculine aggressivity; and Rilke's poetic quest is a quest for a hermaphroditic body. There is an urgent need for elucidation of the interrelations between these disparate modes of articu-

[8] Needham, J., *Science and Civilization in China*, Vol. II (Cambridge: Cambridge University Press, 1956), pp. 139–54. Needham seems to underestimate Occidental body mysticism; cf. *op. cit.*, p. 464, the only reference to Boehme. See also Watts, "Asian Psychology and Modern Psychiatry," *American Journal of Psychoanalysis*, XIII (1953), pp. 25–30.

[9] Whitehead, A. N., *Science and the Modern World* (Cambridge: Cambridge University Press, 1927), pp. 93–118.

lating the desires of the unconscious. Jung is aware of these interrelations, and orthodox psychoanalysts have not been aware of them. But no elucidation results from incorporation of the data into the Jungian system, not so much because of the intellectual disorder in the system, but rather because of the fundamental orientation of Jung, which is flight from the problem of the body, flight from the concept of repression, and a return to the path of sublimation. Freudianism must face the issue, and Freud himself said: "Certain practices of the mystics may succeed in upsetting the normal relations between the different regions of the mind, so that, for example, the perceptual system becomes able to grasp relations in the deeper layers of the ego and in the id which would otherwise be inaccessible to it."

The resurrection of the body is a social project facing mankind as a whole, and it will become a practical political problem when the statesmen of the world are called upon to deliver happiness instead of power, when political economy becomes a science of use-values instead of exchange-values—a science of enjoyment instead of a science of accumulation. In the face of this tremendous human problem, contemporary social theory, both capitalist and socialist, has nothing to say. Contemporary social theory (again we must honor Veblen as an exception) has been completely taken in by the inhuman abstractions of the path of sublimation, and has no contact with concrete human beings, with their concrete bodies, their concrete though repressed desires, and their concrete neuroses.

To find social theorists who are thinking about the real problem of our age, we have to go back to the Marx of 1844, or even to the philosophers influencing Marx in 1844, Fourier and Feuerbach. From Fourier's psychological analysis of the antithesis of work and pleasure Marx obtained the concept of play, and used it, in a halfhearted way to be sure, in some of his early utopian speculations. From Feuerbach Marx learned the necessity of moving from Hegelian abstractions to the concrete senses and the concrete human body. Marx' "philosophic-economic manuscripts" of 1844 contain remarkable formulations calling for the resurrection of human nature, the appropriation of the human body, the transformation of the human senses, and the realization of a state of self-enjoyment. Thus, for example, "Man appropriates himself as an all-sided being in an all-sided way, hence as total man. [This appropriation lies in] every one of his human relationships to the world—seeing, hearing, smell, taste, feeling, thought, perception, experience, wishing, activity, loving, in short, all organs of his individuality."[10] The human physical senses must be emancipated from the sense of possession, and then the humanity of the senses and the human enjoyment of the senses will be achieved for the first time. Here is the point of contact between Marx and Freud: I do not see how the profundities and obscurities of the "philosophic-economic manuscripts" can be elucidated except with the aid of psychoanalysis.

Psychoanalysis, mysticism, poetry, the philosophy of organism, Feuerbach, and Marx—this is a miscellaneous assemblage; but, as Heraclitus said, the unseen harmony is stronger than the seen. Common to all of them is a mode of consciousness that can be called—although the term causes fresh difficulties —the dialectical imagination. By "dialectical" I mean an activity of consciousness struggling to circumvent the limitations imposed by the formal-logical law of contradiction. Marxism, of course, has no monopoly of "dialectics." Needham has shown the dialectical character of Whitehead's philosophy, and he constantly draws attention to dialectical patterns in mystical thought.[11] The goal of Indian body mysticism, according to Eliade, is the "conjunction of contrarieties" (*coincidentia oppositorum*). Scholem, in his survey of Jewish mysticism, says, "Mysticism, intent on formulating the paradoxes of religious experience, uses the instrument of dialectics to express its meaning. The Kabbalists are by no

---

[10] Marx, K. and Engels, F., *Kleine ökonomische Schriften* (Berlin: Dietz, 1955), p. 131; cf. pp. 127–37.

[11] Needham, "A Biologist's View of Whitehead's Philosophy," in Schilpp (ed.), *The Philosophy of Alfred North Whitehead*, pp. 241–72; Needham, *Science and Civilization in China*, II, 75–77, 291, 454, 467.

means the only witnesses to this affinity between mystical and dialectical thinking."[12]

As for poetry, are not those basic poetic devices emphasized by recent criticism—paradox, ambiguity, irony, tension —devices whereby the poetic imagination subverts the "reasonableness" of language, the chains it imposes? And from the psychoanalytical point of view, if we, with Trilling, accept the substantial identity between poetic logic (with its symbolism, condensation of meaning, and displacement of accent) and dream logic, then the connection between poetry and dialectics, as defined, is more substantially grounded. Dreams are certainly an activity of the mind struggling to circumvent the formal-logical law of contradiction.[13]

Psychoanalytical thinking has a double relation to the dialectical imagination. It is, on the one hand (actually or potentially), a mode of dialectical consciousness; on the other hand, it contains, or ought to contain, a theory about the nature of the dialectical imagination. I say "actually or potentially" because psychoanalysis, either as a body of doctrine or an experience of the analysand, is no total revelation of the unconscious repressed. The struggle of consciousness to circumvent the limitations of formal logic, of language, and of "common sense" is under conditions of general repression never ending . . . "Dialectical" are those psychoanalysts who continue this struggle; for the rest, psychoanalytical terminology can be a prison house of Byzantine scholasticism in which "word-consciousness" is substituting for consciousness of the unconscious. . . .

And even if we take Freud as the model of psychoanalytical consciousness, we have argued that at such crucial points as the relation between the two instincts and the relation between humanity and animality, Freud is trapped because he is not sufficiently "dialectical." Nevertheless, the basic struc-

[12] Eliade, M., *Le Yoga* (Paris: Payot, 1954), pp. 110, 258, 269; Scholem, G. G., *Major Trends in Jewish Mysticism* (New York: Schocken Books, 1941), p. 218.
[13] Cf. the role of paradox in philosophy: Wisdom, J. O., *Philosophy and Psycho-Analysis* (Oxford: B. Blackwell, 1953), pp. 169–81, 248–82.

ture of Freud's thought is committed to dialectics, because it is committed to the vision of mental life as basically an arena of conflict; and his finest insights (for example, that when the patient denies something, he affirms it) are incurably "dialectical." Hence the attempt to make psychoanalysis out to be "scientific" (in the positivist sense) is not only vain but destructive.[14] Empirical verification, the positivist test of science, can apply only to that which is fully in consciousness; but psychoanalysis is a mode of contacting the unconscious under conditions of general repression, when the unconscious remains in some sense repressed. To put the matter another way, the "poetry" in Freud's thought cannot be purged away, or rather such an expurgation is exactly what is accomplished in "scientific" textbooks of psychology; but Freud's writings remain unexpurgatable. The same "poetical" imagination marks the work of Róheim and Ferenczi as superior, and explains why they are neglected by "scientific" anthropologists and psychoanalysts. The whole nature of the "dialectical" or "poetical" imagination is another problem urgently needing examination; and there is a particular need for psychoanalysis, as part of the psychoanalysis of psychoanalysis, to become conscious of the dialectical, poetical, mystical stream that runs in its blood.

The key to the nature of dialectical thinking may lie in psychoanalysis, more specifically in Freud's psychoanalysis of negation. There is first the theorem that "there is nothing in the id which can be compared to negation," and that the law of contradiction does not hold in the id. Similarly, the dream does not seem to recognize the word "no." Instead of the law of contradiction we find a unity of opposites: "Dreams show a special tendency to reduce two opposites to a unity"; "Any thing in a dream may mean its opposite." We must therefore entertain the hypothesis that there is an important connection between being "dialectical" and dreaming, just as

[14] For the positivist approach to psychoanalysis, see Kris, "The Nature of Psychoanalytical Propositions and Their Validation," pp. 239–59; Frenkel-Brunswik, "Psychoanalysis and the Unity of Science," pp. 273–347; Pumpian-Mindlin (ed.), *Psychoanalysis and Science* (Stanford: Stanford University Press, 1952).

there is between dreaming and poetry or mysticism. Furthermore, in his essay "The Antithetical Sense of Primal Words" Freud compares the linguistic phenomenon of a hidden (in the etymological root) identity between words with antithetical meanings; he reveals the significant fact that it was the linguistic phenomenon that gave him the clue to the dream phenomenon, and not vice versa. It is plain that both psychoanalysis and the study of language (philosophical and philological) need a marriage or at least a meeting.

And, on the other hand, Freud's essay "On Negation" may throw light on the nature of the "dialectical" dissatisfaction with formal logic. Negation is the primal act of repression; but it at the same time liberates the mind to think about the repressed under the general condition that it is denied and thus remains essentially repressed. With Spinoza's formula *omnis determinatio est negatio* in mind, examine the following formulations of Freud: "A negative judgment is the intellectual substitute for repression; the 'No' in which it is expressed is the hall-mark of repression. . . . By the help of the symbol of negation, the thinking process frees itself from the limitations of repression and enriches itself with the subject-matter without which it could not work efficiently." But: "Negation only assists in undoing one of the consequences of repression—the fact that the subject-matter of the image in question is unable to enter consciousness. The result is a kind of intellectual acceptance of what is repressed, though in all essentials the repression persists."

We may therefore entertain the hypothesis that formal logic and the law of contradiction are the rules whereby the mind submits to operate under general conditions of repression. As with the concept of time, Kant's categories of rationality would then turn out to be the categories of repression. And conversely, "dialectical" would be the struggle of the mind to circumvent repression and make the unconscious conscious. But by the same token, it would be the struggle of the mind to overcome the split and conflict within itself. It could then be identified with that "synthesizing" tendency in the ego of which Freud spoke, and with that attempt to cure, inside the neurosis itself, on which Freud came finally to place his hope for therapy. As an attempt to unify and to cure, the "dialectical" consciousness would be a manifestation of Eros. And, as consciousness trying to throw off the fetters of negation, the "dialectical" consciousness would be a step toward that Dionysian ego which does not negate any more.

What the great world needs, of course, is a little more Eros and less strife; but the intellectual world needs it just as much. A little more Eros would make conscious the unconscious harmony between "dialectical" dreamers of all kinds—psychoanalysts, political idealists, mystics, poets, philosophers—and abate the sterile and ignorant polemics. Since the ignorance seems to be mostly a matter of self-ignorance, a little more psychoanalytical consciousness on all sides (including the psychoanalysts) might help—a little more self-knowledge, humility, humanity, and Eros. We may therefore conclude with the concluding words of Freud's *Civilization and Its Discontents:*

> Men have brought their powers of subduing the forces of nature to such a pitch that by using them they could now very easily exterminate one another to the last man. They know this—hence arises a great part of their current unrest, their dejection, their mood of apprehension. And now it may be expected that the other of the two "heavenly forces," eternal Eros, will put forth his strength so as to maintain himself alongside of his equally immortal adversary.

And perhaps our children will live to live a full life, and so see what Freud could not see—in the old adversary, a friend.

# THE MYSTIC UNION:
# A SUGGESTED BIOLOGICAL
# INTERPRETATION

## ALEXANDER MAVEN

The mystic union has been variously interpreted by those who have experienced it. By most religious mystics it has been thought of as being a spiritual union with God or the Divine, thus partaking of the supernatural, while by most non-religious or pantheistic mystics it has been thought of as such a union with the universe and within the realm of the natural.

In addition to these differences in interpretation, there are differences in description of the experience. Several recent writers (Happold, 1963, pp. 44–45; Laski, 1962, pp. 449–50; Schoeps, 1966, p. 157; Winski, 1965, pp. 76–77) on mysticism have called attention to the fact that most mystics in relating their experience of the mystic union have described it as occurring in either one or the other or both of two contrasting ways. I suggest that both interpretations may be mistaken but that all three of the descriptions may be in part correct.

In support of this suggestion I point to the, perhaps, more significant fact that each of those ways of describing the experience is analogous to a description of the union of sperm and ovum. In that biological union the sperm penetrates or is absorbed by the ovum and dissolves; its protoplasm merges and its chromosomes pair off with the like parts of the ovum. The result is that the ovum is transformed from a gamete into a zygote and the sperm ceases to exist as a separate entity but continues to exist as an integral part of the zygote.

Bearing that description in mind, let us now consider how mystics have described the mystic union. Some mystics, mostly Western ones, have said that the Divine spirit enters the soul and uniting with it transforms and immortalizes it. Others, including most Eastern mystics, have said that the soul or self enters the Divine "like a drop of rain falling in the ocean" and therein dissolves and merges with the Divine, thus losing its separate identity and becoming one with the Divine. Still others, few in number, have said that in the mystic union the soul both is entered by and enters the Divine. An example of the last type of description was given by St. Thomas Aquinas (Underhill, 1915, p. 141), who wrote "Here the soul in a wonderful and unspeakable manner both seizes and is seized upon, devours and is herself devoured, embraces and is violently embraced; and by the knot of love she unites herself with God, and is with Him as the Alone with the Alone."

The analogies between these several descriptions of the mystic union and the foregoing description of the union of sperm and ovum are obvious and so close as to suggest the possibility that the experience of the mystic union in its various forms may be a "playback" of a record of the mystic's biological conception as it might have been experienced, respectively, by the ovum, by the sperm, and by both together. (Evidence of the existence of memory in unicellular organisms is reported by Halstead and Rucker, 1968.)

Besides suggesting how all three of the descriptions given by mystics could be true in spite of the fact that the first two seem to be contraries and the third seems to be paradoxical, this suggested interpretation of the experience of mystic union offers possible explanations of three characteristics of the experience attested to by most, if not all mystics: its immediacy, its ineffability, and its immortalizing effect.

Mystics are almost unanimous in saying that the experience

is more immediate than any ordinary experience, so immediate that its reality cannot be doubted. Some even have said the reality disclosed by mystical experience is the only reality, all else being illusion. Their awareness of the experience has been said to be beyond sensing, perceiving, conceptualizing, reasoning, or understanding and unlike anything remembered or imagined. It is, the mystics say, pure intuition, pure consciousness. All this seems tantamount to saying that the awareness is beyond the functioning of a nervous system and a brain. And that, I submit, would be true of any awareness of a unicellular organism such as a gamete or a zygote. If such an organism can consciously or unconsciously experience anything, it must be by some means other and more basic than a nervous system or brain, whether or not it is something physical—some form of extrasensory perception perhaps.

> All that is implied by the words "mind" and "mentality" is unthinkable without there being a tangible structure with which to associate it. The brain clearly specializes in mind; but it is not proven that the brain has a monopoly of it. No one would quarrel with so bald a statement now, but it has not always been so. There is, of course, nothing tangible about the mind: it is a function, not an entity, and for this reason the word "mentality" is often preferred (Roddam, 1966, p. 120).

And if, as we must assume, the unicellular organism is capable of recording its experiences somehow so that they can be "played back," it may well be that the record would be duplicated in every cell of the multicellular organism that develops from the zygote. That duplication might account for the felt immediacy of a "playback" which has led some mystics to say that they felt the experience "in the very marrow of their bones."

Mystics are also nearly unanimous in saying the experience of mystic union is ineffable. But paradoxically they seem to be able to say a lot about it. Some writers on mysticism attempt to explain this paradox by saying that the experience is ineffable while it is happening but can be talked about when it is remembered. But that does not explain why it is ineffable while it is being experienced. I suggest the reason may be simply that if the mystical experience is a "playback" of the experience of the mystic's biological conception it is experienced as being ineffable because the original experience of conception, having occurred prior to the mystic's learning a language, had no verbal component. The "playback" in the mystical experience therefore also lacks a verbal component and is so experienced. But the "playback" can be described when it is later remembered.

The feeling of immortalization that characterizes the mystic union may also be explainable in terms of the union of sperm and ovum. In the situation in which conception occurs, failure of a gamete to unite with an opposite other means death. But the zygote which results from union is at least potentially immortal in the sense that the spark of life it represents might be passed on to subsequent generations indefinitely.

A fourth characteristic of the mystic union as reported by many is that it is accompanied by extremely pleasurable feelings: usually ecstasy and bliss.

Remembering that for most non-mystics probably the nearest approach to such feelings they ever experience occurs during sexual intercourse, I suggest that the sexual union of sperm and ovum may also be accompanied by those feelings. In view of the general precariousness of life it seems reasonable to suppose that, to insure its survival, obedience to the demands of instinct would be reinforced by being self-rewarding, particularly in such an important instance as biological conception is for forms of life that reproduce sexually.

The instinct in this case would be that of the gamete for union with an opposite other. This suggests that the memory of the experience of union might be an inherited memory as well as a memory of the individual's own conception. If there is any inherited memory, it would seem highly probable that the event of conception would be included in such memory, having been repeated in every generation of mankind and its pre-human ancestors, presumably, over a period of hundreds of millions of years.

This instinct of the gamete for union might also account for the longing for unity referred to in the following passage (Schoeps, 1966):

> If we examine the essential content common to all the developed religions we know, we might perhaps cautiously suggest that everywhere we find the striving for a lost unity. Religion always proceeds from an existential dichotomy between man and the world, between man and God or the gods. Man longs for unity, longs to overcome the dichotomy; wholeness rather than division seems to him necessary for living. But—and this is the crucial element—he can never achieve in reality the unity he seeks. Thus the essence of religion may be seen as springing from contradiction, at the focus and source of which stands the dichotomy of life itself.

If the longed-for unity can never be achieved, the longing either is meaningless or has been misinterpreted. But if the longing is interpreted as the instinctive urge of the gamete for union, it becomes meaningful since unity is achieved in every event of biological conception.

This interpretation is intended to apply only to the experience of the mystic union. It leaves unexplained the many other mystic experiences that have been reported.

One such other experience frequently reported by mystics is that of interior light:

> All at once without warning of any kind, I found myself wrapped in a flame-colored cloud. For an instant I thought of fire, an immense conflagration somewhere close by in that great city; the next I knew that the fire was within myself. Directly afterward there came upon me a sense of exultation, of immense joyousness accompanied or immediately followed by intellectual illumination impossible to describe. Among other things, I did not merely come to believe, but I saw that the universe is not composed of dead matter, but is, on the contrary, a living Presence; I became conscious in myself of eternal life. It was not a conviction that I would have eternal life, but a consciousness that I possessed eternal life then; I saw that all men are immortal; that the cosmic order is such that without any peradventure all things

work together for the good of each and all; that the foundation principle of the world, of all the worlds, is what we call love, and that the happiness of each and all is in the long run absolutely certain . . . (James, 1902, quoting R. M. Bucke)

This passage contains reference to enough of the characteristics of the experience of the mystic union to suggest that the experience it records might have the same source and be explainable in the same way as the mystic union experience. Beyond the knowledge that ". . . all living things are electrical. All living cells are essentially batteries" (Komarek, 1966), I have not been able to learn whether there is any verifiable reason for thinking that the union of sperm and ovum might, at least sometimes, give rise to, or be accompanied by, the experience of light. But I would not be surprised if someone, perhaps some biochemist or biophysicist, were to find such a reason if he should turn his attention to doing so.

Speculative as it is and based on the unproved assumption, suggested by analogies, that human gametes are capable of experiencing the event of union and of recording that experience so that it can be "played back," this analysis may not seem convincing, especially to those who prefer to regard the mystic union as supernatural. This suggested biological interpretation is naturalistic. Perhaps future investigation can provide scientific evidence for proof or disproof of this speculative hypothesis.

#### REFERENCES

JAMES, W. *Varieties of Religious Experiences* (New York: Random House, 1902), p. 390.

HALSTEAD, W. C. & RUCKER, W. M. Memory, a molecular maze, *Psychology Today*, 1968, 2, 1, 40.

HAPPOLD, F. C. *Mysticism* (Baltimore: Penguin Books, 1963).

KOMAREK, SR. E. V. Cited by J. Lear in *Saturday Review of Literature*, June 4, 1966, p. 57.

LASKI, M. *Ecstacy* (Bloomington, Ind.: Indiana University Press, 1962).

RODDAM, J. *The Changing Mind* (Boston: Little, Brown & Co., 1966).

SCHOEPS, H. *The Religions of Mankind* (Garden City, N.Y.: Doubleday & Co., 1966).

UNDERHILL, E. *Practical Mysticism* (New York: E. P. Dutton & Co., 1915).

WINSKI, N. *Mysticism for the Millions* (Los Angeles: Sherbourne Press, 1965).

# THIS IS IT

## ALAN W. WATTS

The most impressive fact in man's spiritual, intellectual, and poetic experience has always been, for me, the universal prevalence of those astonishing moments of insight which Richard Bucke called "cosmic consciousness." There is no really satisfactory name for this type of experience. To call it mystical is to confuse it with visions of another world, or of gods and angels. To call it spiritual or metaphysical is to suggest that it is not also extremely concrete and physical, while the term "cosmic consciousness" itself has the unpoetic flavor of occultist jargon. But from all historical times and cultures we have reports of this same unmistakable sensation emerging, as a rule, quite suddenly and unexpectedly and from no clearly understood cause.

To the individual thus enlightened it appears as a vivid and overwhelming certainty that the universe, precisely as it is at this moment, as a whole and in every one of its parts, is so completely *right* as to need no explanation or justification beyond what it simply is. Existence not only ceases to be a problem; the mind is so wonder-struck at the self-evident and self-sufficient fitness of things as they are, including what would ordinarily be thought the very worst, that it cannot find any word strong enough to express the perfection and beauty of the experience. Its clarity sometimes gives the sensation that the world has become transparent or luminous, and its simplicity the sensation that it is pervaded and ordered by a supreme intelligence. At the same time it is usual for the individual to feel that the whole world has become his own body, and that whatever he is has not only become, but always has been, what everything else is. It is not that he loses his identity to the point of feeling that he actually looks out through all other eyes, becoming literally omniscient, but rather that his individual consciousness and existence is a point of view temporarily adopted by something immeasurably greater than himself.

The central core of the experience seems to be the conviction, or insight, that the immediate *now*, whatever its nature, is the goal and fulfillment of all living. Surrounding and flowing from this insight is an emotional ecstasy, a sense of intense relief, freedom, and lightness, and often of almost unbearable love for the world, which is, however, secondary. Often, the pleasure of the experience is confused with the experience and the insight lost in the ecstasy, so that in trying to retain the secondary effects of the experience the individual misses its point—that the immediate *now* is complete even when it is not ecstatic. For ecstasy is a necessarily impermanent contrast in the constant fluctuation of our feelings. But insight, when clear enough, persists; having once understood a particular skill, the facility tends to remain.

The terms in which a man interprets this experience are naturally drawn from the religious and philosophical ideas of his culture, and their differences often conceal its basic identity. As water seeks the course of least resistance, so the emotions clothe themselves in the symbols that lie most readily to hand, and the association is so swift and automatic that the symbol may appear to be the very heart of the experience. Clarity—the disappearance of problems—suggests light, and in moments of such acute clarity there may be the physical sensation of light penetrating everything. To a theist this will naturally seem to be a glimpse of the presence of God, as in the celebrated testimony of Pascal:

The year of grace 1654,
Monday the 23rd of November, St. Clement's day. . . .

From about half past ten in the evening
until about half past twelve, midnight,
    FIRE
God of Abraham. God of Isaac. God of Jacob
    not of the philosophers and the wise.
Certainty, joy, certainty, feeling, joy, peace.

Or in a case quoted by William James:

> The very heavens seemed to open and pour down rays
> of light and glory. Not for a moment only, but all day
> and night, floods of light and glory seemed to pour
> through my soul, and oh, how I was changed, and every-
> thing became new. My horses and hogs and everybody
> seemed changed.

But clarity may also suggest transparency, or the sense that
the world confronting us is no longer an obstacle and the
body no longer a burden, and to a Buddhist this will just as
naturally call to mind the doctrine of reality as the ungraspable, indefinable Void (*sunyata*).

> I came back into the hall and was about to go to my seat
> when the whole outlook changed. A broad expanse
> opened, and the ground appeared as if all caved in. . . .
> As I looked around and up and down, the whole uni-
> verse with its multitudinous sense-objects now appeared
> quite different; what was loathsome before, together with
> ignorance and passions, was now seen to be nothing else
> but the outflow of my own inmost nature which in itself
> remained bright, true, and transparent.[1]

As one and the same pain may be described either as a hot
pang or as a cold sting, so the descriptions of this experience
may take forms that seem to be completely opposed. One person may say that he has found the answer to the whole mystery of life, but somehow cannot put it into words. Another
will say that there never was a mystery and thus no answer to
it, for what the experience made clear to him was the irrelevance and artificiality of all our questions. One declares
himself convinced that there is no death, his true self being
as eternal as the universe. Another states that death has simply

[1] Yüan-chou (*d.* 1287), quoted by Suzuki, *Essays in Zen Buddhism*, Vol. 2, p. 92.

ceased to matter, because the present moment is so complete that it requires no future. One feels himself taken up and united with a life infinitely other than his own. But as the beating of the heart may be regarded as something that *happens* to you or something that you *do,* depending on the point of view, so another will feel that he has experienced, not a transcendent God, but his own inmost nature. One will get the sense that his ego or self has expanded to become the entire universe, whereas another will feel that he has lost himself altogether and that what he called his ego was never anything but an abstraction. One will describe himself as infinitely enriched, while another will speak of being brought to such absolute poverty that he owns not even his mind and body, and has not a care in the world.

Rarely is the experience described without metaphors that might be misleading if taken literally. But in reading Bernard Berenson's *Sketch for a Self-Portrait* I came across a passage which is one of the simplest and "cleanest" accounts of it I have ever seen.

> It was a morning in early summer. A silver haze shimmered and trembled over the lime trees. The air was laden with their fragrance. The temperature was like a caress. I remember—I need not recall—that I climbed up a tree stump and felt suddenly immersed in Itness. I did not call it by that name. I had no need for words. It and I were one.[2]

Just "It"—as when we use the word to denote the superlative, or the exact point, or intense reality, or what we were always looking for. Not the neuter sense of the mere object, but something still more alive and far wider than the personal, and for which we use this simplest of words because we have no word for it.

It is especially difficult to find the right means of expression for the experience in the cultural context of Christianity. For while this enlightenment comes just as much to Christians as to anyone else, the Christian mystic has always been in danger of conflict with the defenders of orthodoxy. Christian

[2] Bernard Berenson, *Sketch for a Self-Portrait* (New York: Pantheon Books, 1949), p. 18.

dogmatics insist firmly upon the radical difference between God and his created universe, as between God and the human soul. They insist upon God's eternal opposition to and abhorrence of evil and sin, and, since these are very present realities, upon the effective salvation of the world only at the end of time. Even then, hell will remain forever as the state of permanent imprisonment and torment for the forces of evil. Nevertheless, the doctrine of omnipotence—that nothing, not even sin, can happen without the permission of God's will—makes it possible even in this difficult framework for the Christian mystic to express the unspeakable doctrine that "sin is behovable, but all shall be well, and all shall be well, and all manner of thing shall be well."[3]

The Christian sense of the reality of evil and of time and history as the process of overcoming evil remains with us so strongly even in the post-Christian intellectual climate of today that we have difficulty in accepting the "cosmic consciousness" as more than an inspiring hallucination. Admissible it may be as the vision of some "far-off divine event" in the future, but with our progressive view of the world it seems impossible to accept it as a vision of the way things *are*. Even in the description which Bucke gives of his own experience there is a significant use of the future tense:

> All at once, without warning of any kind, I found myself wrapped in a flame-colored cloud. For an instant I thought of fire, an immense conflagration somewhere close by in that great city; the next, I knew that the fire was within myself. Directly afterward there came upon me a sense of exultation, of immense joyousness accompanied or immediately followed by an intellectual illumination impossible to describe. Among other things, I did not merely come to believe, but I saw that the universe is not composed of dead matter, but is, on the contrary, a living Presence; I became conscious in myself of eternal life. It was not a conviction that I would have

[3] Dame Julian of Norwich (c. 1342–1414), *Revelations of Divine Love*, xxvii. Ed. Grace Warrack. London, 1949. "Behovable" has the sense of "playing a necessary part." Compare the celebrated passage in the Roman liturgy of Holy Saturday, "O truly necessary sin of Adam, which the death of Christ has blotted out! O happy fault, that merited such and so great a redeemer!"

eternal life, but a consciousness that I possessed eternal life then; I saw that all men are immortal; that the cosmic order is such that without any peradventure all things work together for the good of each and all; that the foundation principle of the world, of all the worlds, is what we call love, and that the happiness of each and all is *in the long run* absolutely certain. The vision lasted a few seconds and was gone; but the memory of it and the sense of the reality of what it taught has remained during the quarter of a century which has since elapsed.[4]

Nevertheless, the "consciousness that I possessed eternal life *then*" corresponds to the Buddhist realization that "all things are in Nirvana from the very beginning," and that the enlightenment or awakening is not the creation of a new state of affairs but the recognition of what always is.

Such experiences imply, then, that our normal perception and valuation of the world is a subjective but collective nightmare. They suggest that our ordinary sense of practical reality—of the world as seen on Monday morning—is a construct of socialized conditioning and repression, a system of selective inattention whereby we are taught to screen out aspects and relations within nature which do not accord with the rules of the game of civilized life. Yet the vision almost invariably includes the realization that this very restriction of consciousness is also part of the eternal fitness of things. In the words of the Zen master Gensha:

> If you understand, things are such as they are;
> If you do not understand, things are such as they are—

this "such as they are" being the utterly unproblematic and self-sufficient character of this eternal now in which, as Chuang-tzu said,

> A duck's legs, though short, cannot be lengthened without discomfort to the duck; a crane's legs, though long, cannot be shortened without discomfort to the crane.

For in some way the vision seems to come about through accepting the rightness of the fact that one does not have it,

---

[4] Quoted from a privately printed account of the experience by William James, *Varieties of Religious Experience* (London, 1929), p. 399. Italics mine.

through being willing to be as imperfect as one is—perfectly imperfect.

Now it is easy to see how this way of seeing things might be acceptable in cultures without the sense of hope and history, how, indeed, it might be the only basis for a philosophy that would make life tolerable. Indeed, it is very probable that the "historical dynamism" of the Christian West is a rather recent theological discovery, for we can no longer sing, without qualms of the social conscience, the *laissez-faire* hymn which says:

> *The rich man in his castle, the poor man at his gate,*
> *He made them high or lowly, and ordered their estate—*

and then go on to exclaim:

> *All things bright and beautiful, all creatures great and small,*
> *All things wise and wonderful, the Lord God made them all!*

But, even though it may be exploited for this purpose, the experience itself is in no sense a philosophy designed to justify or to desensitize oneself to the inequalities of life. Like falling in love, it has a minimal connection with any particular cultural background or economic position. It descends upon the rich and the poor, the moral and the immoral, the happy and the miserable without distinction. It carries with it the overwhelming conviction that the world is in every respect a miracle of glory, and though this might logically exclude the necessity to share the vision with others and awaken them from their nightmare the usual reaction is a sense, not of duty, but of sheer delight in communicating the experience by word or deed.

From this new perspective the crimes and follies of man's ordinary nightmare life seem neither evil nor stupid but simply pitiable. One has the extraordinarily odd sensation of seeing people in their mean or malicious pursuits looking, at the same time, like gods—as if they were supremely happy without knowing it. As Kirillov puts it in Dostoyevsky's *The Possessed,*

> "Man is unhappy because he doesn't know he's happy. It's only that. That's all, that's all! If anyone finds out

he'll become happy at once, that minute. . . . It's all good. I discovered it all of a sudden."

"And if anyone dies of hunger," [asks Stavrogin], "and if anyone insults and outrages the little girl, is that good?"

"Yes! And if anyone blows his brains out for the baby, that's good too. And if anyone doesn't, that's good too. It's all good, all. It's good for all those who know that it's all good. If they knew that it was good for them, it would be good for them, but as long as they don't know it's good for them, it will be bad for them. That's the whole idea, the whole of it! . . . They're bad because they don't know they're good. When they find out, they won't outrage a little girl. They'll find out that they're good and they'll all become good, every one of them."[5]

Ordinarily one might feel that there is a shocking contrast between the marvellous structure of the human organism and its brain, on the one hand, and the uses to which most people put it, on the other. Yet there could perhaps be a point of view from which the natural wonder of the organism simply outshines the degrading performances of its superficial consciousness. In a somewhat similar way this strange opening of vision does not permit attention to remain focussed narrowly upon the details of evil; they become subordinate to the all-pervading intelligence and beauty of the total design.

Such insight has not the slightest connection with "shallow optimism" nor with grasping the meaning of the universe in terms of some neat philosophical simplification. Beside it, *all* philosophical opinions and disputations sound like somewhat sophisticated versions of children yelling back and forth— " 'Tis!" " 'Tisn't!" " 'Tis!" " 'Tisn't!"—until (if only the philosophers would do likewise) they catch the nonsense of it and roll over backwards with hoots of laughter. Furthermore, so far from being the smug rationalization of a Mr. Pangloss, the experience has a tendency to arise in situations of total extremity or despair, when the individual finds himself without any alternative but to surrender himself entirely.

[5] Dostoyevsky, *The Possessed,* pp. 240–41. Trans. Constance Garnett (Modern Library, New York, 1936).

Something of this kind came to me in a dream when I was about eight years old. I was sick at the time and almost delirious with fever, and in the dream I found myself attached face-downward and spread-eagled to an immense ball of steel which was spinning about the earth. I knew in this dream with complete certainty that I was doomed to be spun in this sickening and terrifying whirl forever and ever, and the conviction was so intense that there was nothing for it but to give up—for this was hell itself and nothing lay before me but a literal everlastingness of pain. But in the moment when I surrendered, the ball seemed to strike against a mountain and disintegrate, and the next thing I knew was that I was sitting on a stretch of warm sand with nothing left of the ball except crumpled fragments of sheet metal scattered around me. This was not, of course, the experience of "cosmic consciousness," but simply of the fact that release in extremity lies through and not away from the problem.

That other experience came much later, twice with intensity, and other times with what might be called more of a glow than a brilliant flash. Shortly after I had first begun to study Indian and Chinese philosophy, I was sitting one night by the fire, trying to make out what was the right attitude of mind for meditation as it is practiced in Hindu and Buddhist disciplines. It seemed to me that several attitudes were possible, but as they appeared mutually exclusive and contradictory I was trying to fit them into one—all to no purpose. Finally, in sheer disgust, I decided to reject them all and to have no special attitude of mind whatsoever. In the force of throwing them away it seemed that I threw myself away as well, for quite suddenly the weight of my own body disappeared. I felt that I owned nothing, not even a self, and that nothing owned me. The whole world became as transparent and unobstructed as my own mind; the "problem of life" simply ceased to exist, and for about eighteen hours I and everything around me felt like the wind blowing leaves across a field on an autumn day.

The second time, a few years later, came after a period when I had been attempting to practice what Buddhists call "recollection" (smriti) or constant awareness of the immediate present, as distinct from the usual distracted rambling of reminiscence and anticipation. But, in discussing it one evening, someone said to me, "But why *try* to live in the present? Surely we are always completely *in* the present even when we're thinking about the past or the future?" This, actually quite obvious, remark again brought on the sudden sensation of having no weight. At the same time, the present seemed to become a kind of moving stillness, an eternal stream from which neither I nor anything could deviate. I saw that everything, just as it is now, is IT—is the whole point of there being life and a universe. I saw that when the *Upanishads* said, "That art thou!" or "All this world is Brahman," they meant just exactly what they said. Each thing, each event, each experience in its inescapable nowness and in all its own particular individuality was precisely what it should be, and so much so that it acquired a divine authority and originality. It struck me with the fullest clarity that none of this depended on my seeing it to be so; that was the way things were, whether I understood it or not, and if I did not understand, that was IT too. Furthermore, I felt that I now understood what Christianity might mean by the love of God —namely, that despite the commonsensical imperfection of things, they were nonetheless loved by God just as they are, and that this loving of them was at the same time the godding of them. This time the vivid sensation of lightness and clarity lasted a full week.

These experiences, reinforced by others that have followed, have been the enlivening force of all my work in writing and in philosophy since that time, though I have come to realize that how I *feel,* whether the actual sensation of freedom and clarity is present or not, is not the point— for, again, to feel heavy or restricted is also IT. But with this point of departure a philosopher is faced with a strange problem of communication, especially to the degree that his philosophy seems to have some affinity with religion. People appear to be under the fixed impression that one speaks or writes of these things in order to improve them or do them some good, assuming, too, that the speaker has himself been improved and is able to speak with authority. In other words, the philosopher is forced into the role of preacher, and is in turn expected to practice what he preaches. Thereupon the truth of what he says is tested by his character and his morals—whether he shows anxiety or not, whether he depends upon "material crutches" such as wine or tobacco, whether he has stomach ulcers or likes money, whether he loses his temper, or gets depressed, or falls in love when he shouldn't, or sometimes looks a bit tired and frayed at the edges. All these criteria might be valid if the philosopher were preaching freedom from being human, or if he were trying to make himself and others radically better.

In the span of one lifetime it is, of course, possible for almost every human being to improve himself—within limits set by energy, time, temperament, and the level from which he begins. Obviously, then, there is a proper place for preachers and other technical advisers in the disciplines of human betterment. But the limits within which such improvements may be made are small in comparison with the vast aspects of our nature and our circumstances which remain the same, and which will be very difficult to improve even were it desirable to do so. I am saying, therefore, that while there is a place for bettering oneself and others, solving problems and coping with situations is by no means the only or even the chief business of life. Nor is it the principal work of philosophy.

Human purposes are pursued within an immense circling universe which does not seem to me to have purpose, in our sense, at all. Nature is much more playful than purposeful, and the probability that it has no special goals for the future need not strike one as a defect. On the contrary, the processes of nature as we see them both in the surrounding world and in the involuntary aspects of our own organisms are much more like art than like business, politics, or religion. They are especially like the arts of music and dancing, which unfold themselves without aiming at future destinations. No one imagines that a symphony is supposed to improve in quality as it goes along, or that the whole object of playing it is to reach the finale. The point of music is discovered in every moment of playing and listening to it. It is the same, I feel, with the greater part of our lives, and if we are unduly absorbed in improving them we may forget altogether to live them. The musician whose chief concern is to make every performance better than the last may so fail to participate and delight in his own music that he will impress his audience only with the anxious rigor of his technique.

Thus it is by no means the main work of a philosopher to be classed with the moralists and reformers. There is such a thing as philosophy, the love of wisdom, in the spirit of the artist. Such philosophy will not preach or advocate practices leading to improvement. As I understand it, the work of the philosopher as artist is to reveal and celebrate the eternal and purposeless background of human life. Out of simple exuberance or wonder he wants to tell others of the point of view from which the world is unimaginably good as it is, with people just as they are. No matter how difficult it may be to express this point of view without sounding smug or appearing to be a wishful dreamer, some hint of it may be suggested if the philosopher has had the good fortune to have experienced it himself.

This may sound like a purpose, like a desire to improve, to those who insist upon seeing all human activity in terms of goal-seeking. The trouble is that our Western common sense is firmly Aristotelian, and we therefore believe that the will never acts except for some good or pleasure. But upon analysis this turns out to say no more than that we do what we do, for if we *always* do what pleases us—even in committing suicide—there is no means of showing what pleases us apart from what we do. In using such logic I am only throwing a stone back to the glass house from which it came, for I am well aware that expressions of mystical experience will not stand the test of logic. But, unlike the Aristotelian, the mystic does not claim to be logical. His sphere of experience is the unspeakable. Yet this need mean no more than that it is the sphere of physical nature, of all that is not simply conceptions, numbers, or words.

If the experience of "cosmic consciousness" is unspeakable, it is true that in trying to utter it in words one is not "saying" anything in the sense of conveying information or

making a proposition. The speech expressing such an experience is more like an exclamation. Or better, it is the speech
of poetry rather than logic, though not poetry in the impoverished sense of the logical positivist, the sense of decorative
and beautiful nonsense. For there is a kind of speech that
may be able to convey something without actually being able
to say it. Korzybski ran into this difficulty in trying to express
the apparently simple point that things are not what we *say*
they are, that, for example, the word "water" is not itself
drinkable. He formulated it in his "law of nonidentity," that
"whatever you say a thing *is,* it *isn't.*" But from this it will
follow that it isn't a thing either, for if I say that a thing is a
thing, it isn't. What, then, are we talking about? He was trying to show that we are talking about the unspeakable world
of the physical universe, the world that is other than words.
Words represent it, but if we want to *know* it directly we
must do so by immediate sensory contact. What we call
things, facts, or events are after all no more than convenient
units of perception, recognizable pegs for names, selected
from the infinite multitude of lines and surfaces, colors and
textures, spaces and densities which surround us. There is
no more a fixed and final way of dividing these variations
into things than of grouping the stars in constellations.

From this example, however, it is certainly clear that we
can point out the unspeakable world, and even convey the
idea of its existence, without being able to say exactly *what*
it is. We do not know what it is. We know only that it is. To be
able to say what it is we must be able to classify it, but obviously the "all" in which the whole multiplicity of things is
delineated cannot be classified.

The sphere of "cosmic consciousness" is, I believe, the
same as the unspeakable world of Korzybski and the seman-
ticists. It is nothing "spiritual" in the usual sense of abstract
or ideational. It is concretely physical, yet for this very reason
ineffable (or unspeakable) and indefinable. "Cosmic" consciousness is a release from self-consciousness, that is to say
from the fixed belief and feeling that one's organism is an
absolute and separate thing, as distinct from a convenient
unit of perception. For if it becomes clear that our use of the

lines and surfaces of nature to divide the world into units is
only a matter of convenience, then all that I have called myself is actually inseparable from everything. This is exactly
what one experiences in these extraordinary moments. It is
not that the outlines and shapes which we *call* things and use
to delineate things disappear into some sort of luminous void.
It simply becomes obvious that though they may be used as
divisions they do not really divide. However much I may be
impressed by the difference between a star and the dark space
around it, I must not forget that I can see the two only in
relation to each other, and that this relation is inseparable.

The most astonishing feature of this experience is, however, the conviction that this entire unspeakable world is
"right," so right that our normal anxieties become ludicrous,
that if only men could see it they would go wild with joy,

> *And the king be cutting capers,*
> *And the priest be picking flowers.*

Quite apart from the difficulty of relating this sensation to
the problem of evil and pain, there is the question of the
very meaning of the assertion "All shall be well, and all shall
be well, and all manner of thing shall be well." I can say
only that the meaning of the assertion is the experience itself. Outside that state of consciousness it has no meaning, so
much so that it would be difficult even to believe in it as a
revelation without the actual experience. For the experience
makes it perfectly clear that the whole universe is through
and through the playing of love in every shade of the word's
use, from animal lust to divine charity. Somehow this includes even the holocaust of the biological world, where
every creature lives by feeding on others. Our usual picture
of this world is reversed so that every victim is seen as offer-
ing itself in sacrifice.

If we are to ask whether this vision is true, we may first answer that there are no such things as truths by themselves: a
truth is always in relation to a point of view. Fire is hot in
relation to skin. The structure of the world appears as it
does in relation to our organs of sense and our brains. Therefore certain alterations in the human organism may turn it

into the sort of percipient for which the world *is* as it is seen in this vision. But, in the same way, other alterations will give us the truth of the world as it appears to the schizophrenic, or to the mind in black depression.

There is, however, a possible argument for the superior truth of the "cosmic" experience. Its basis is simply that no energy system can be completely self-controlling without ceasing to move. Control is restraint upon movement, and because complete control would be complete restraint, control must always be subordinate to motion if there is to be motion at all. In human terms, total restraint of movement is the equivalent of total doubt, of refusal to trust one's senses or feelings in any respect, and perhaps its embodiment is the extreme catatonic who refuses every motion or communication. On the other hand, movement and the release of restraint are the equivalent of faith, of committing oneself to the uncontrolled and unknown. In an extreme form this would mean the abandonment of oneself to utter caprice, and at first sight a life of such indiscriminate faith might seem to correspond to a vision of the world in which "everything is right." Yet this point of view would exclude all control as wrong, and thus there would be no place in it for the rightness of restraint. An essential part of the "cosmic" experience is, however, that the normal restriction of consciousness to the ego-feeling is also right, but only and always because it is subordinate to absence of restriction, to movement and faith.

The point is simply that, if there is to be any life and movement at all, the attitude of faith must be basic—the final and fundamental attitude—and the attitude of doubt secondary and subordinate. This is another way of saying that toward the vast and all-encompassing background of human life, with which the philosopher as artist is concerned, there must be total affirmation and acceptance. Otherwise there is no basis at all for caution and control with respect to details in the foreground. But it is all too easy to become so absorbed in these details that all sense of proportion is lost, and for man to make himself mad by trying to bring everything under his control. We become insane, unsound, and without foundation when we lose consciousness of and faith in the uncontrolled and ungraspable background world which is ultimately what we ourselves are. And there is a very slight distinction, if any, between complete, conscious faith and love.

# From THE MAGUS

## JOHN FOWLES

Then there was no clearly situated and environmented self; there was the star, not closer but with something of the isolation a telescope gives; not one of a pattern of stars, but itself, floating in the blue-black breath of space, in a kind of void. I remember very clearly this sense, this completely new strange perceiving of the star as a ball of white light both breeding and needing the void around it; of, in retrospect, a related sense that I was exactly the same, suspended in a dark void. I was watching the star and the star was watching me. We were poised, exactly equal weights, if one can think of awareness as a weight, held level in a balance. This seemed to endure and endure, I don't know how long, two entities equally suspended in a void, equally opposite, devoid of any meaning or feeling. There was no sensation of beauty, of morality, of divinity, of physical geometry; simply the sensation of the situation. As an animal might feel.

Then a rise of tension. I was expecting something. The waiting was a waiting for. I did not know if it would be audible or visible, which sense. But it was trying to come, and I was trying to discover its coming. There seemed to be no more star. Perhaps he had made me close my eyes. The void was all. I remember two words, Conchis must have spoken them: glisten, and listen. There was the glistening, listening void; darkness and expectation. Then there came a wind on my face, a perfectly physical sensation. I tried to face it, it was fresh and warm, but I suddenly realized, with an excited shock, not at anything but the physical strangeness of it, that it was blowing on me from all directions at the same time. I raised my hand, I could feel it. The dark wind, like draft from thousands of invisible fans, blowing in on me. And again this seemed to last for a long time.

At some point it began imperceptibly to change. The wind became light. I don't think there was any visual awareness of this, it was simply that I knew the wind had become light (perhaps Conchis had told me the wind was light) and this light was intensely pleasing, a kind of mental sunbathing after a long dark winter, an exquisitely agreeable sensation both of being aware of light and attracting it. Of having power to attract and power to receive this light.

From this stage I moved to one where it dawned on me that this was something intensely true and revealing; this being something that drew all this light upon it. I mean it seemed to reveal something deeply significant about being; I was aware of existing, and this being aware of existing became more significant than the light, just as the light had become more significant than the wind. I began to get a sense of progress, that I was transforming, as a fountain in a wind is transformed in shape; an eddy in the water. The wind and the light became mere secondaries, roads to the present state, this state without dimensions or sensations; awareness of pure being. Or perhaps that is a solipsism; it was simply a pure awareness.

That lasted; and then changed, like the other states. This state was being imposed on me from outside, I knew this, I knew that although it did not flow in on me like the wind and the light, it nevertheless flowed, though flowed was not the word. There was no word, it arrived, descended, penetrated from outside. It was not an immanent state, it was a conferred state, a presented state. I was a recipient. But once again there came this strange surprise that the emitters stood all around me. I was not receiving from any one direction, but from all directions. Though once again, direction is too physical a word. I was having feelings that no language based on concrete physical objects, on actual feeling, can describe. I think I was aware of the metaphoricality of what I felt. I knew words were like chains, they held me back; and like walls with holes in them. Reality kept rushing through; and yet I could not get out to fully exist in it. This is interpreting what I struggled to remember feeling; the act of description taints the description.

I had the sense that this was the fundamental reality and that reality had a universal mouth to tell me so; no sense of divinity, of communion, of the brotherhood of man, of anything I had expected before I became suggestible. No pantheism, no humanism. But something much wider, cooler and more abstruse. That reality was endless interaction. No good, no evil; no beauty, no ugliness. No sympathy, no antipathy. But simply interaction. The endless solitude of the one, its total enislement from all else, seemed the same thing as the total interrelationship of the all. All opposites seemed one, because each was indispensable to each. The indifference and the indispensability of all seemed one. I suddenly knew, but in a new hitherto unexperienced sense of knowing, that all else exists.

Knowing, willing, being wise, being good, education, information, classification, knowledge of all kinds, sensibility, sexuality, these things seemed superficial. I had no desire to state or define or analyze this interaction, I simply wished to constitute it—not even "wished to"—I constituted it. I was volitionless. There was no meaning. Only being.

But the fountain changed, the eddy whirled. It seemed at first to be a kind of reversion to the stage of the dark wind breathing in on me from every side, except that there was no wind, the wind had been only a metaphor, and now it was millions, trillions of such consciousnesses of being, countless nuclei of hope suspended in a vast solution of hazard, a pouring out not of photons, but nöons, consciousness-of-being particles. An enormous and vertiginous sense of the innumerability of the universe; an innumerability in which transience and unchangingness seemed integral, essential and uncontradictory. I felt like a germ that had landed, like the first penicillin microbe, not only in a culture where it was totally at home, totally nourished; but in a situation in which it was infinitely significant. A condition of acute physical and intellectual pleasure, a floating suspension, a being perfectly adjusted and *related;* a quintessential arrival. An intercognition.

At the same time a parabola, a fall, an ejaculation; but the transience, the passage, had become an integral part of the knowledge of the experience. The becoming and the being were one.

# POSTSCRIPT:
# PSYCHICAL RESEARCH IN RELATION TO HIGHER STATES OF CONSCIOUSNESS

## W. G. ROLL

Psychical research does not exist in a vacuum. Like any other organized human activity, it is a response to individual and social needs. Knowledge of these needs may prepare us for the years ahead. As a point of departure for the next decade, Marshall Berman, New York University, has this to say: "For a great many Americans, particularly young Americans, the 1960s were a time in which two of the deepest streams of consciousness—self-consciousness and social consciousness—converged. The radical vision and energy of the sixties aimed at a fusion of ideas and experiences which the fifties had found either unrelated or incompatible: political freedom and personal ecstasy, activism and mysticism, voter registration drives and mind-expanding drugs, sit-ins and love-ins."[1] The effort at this fusion caused people to "look harder and deeper at once into themselves and into the institutions and environment they lived in. They sought both to expand the self and open it up, and to create a society in which the self could survive." Many experienced a conflict with existing society because it compels us "to play roles and fulfill functions that cut us off from our deepest feelings and needs: it alienates us from ourselves."

From "Psychical Research in the Seventies," by W. G. Roll, *Psychic*, March–April, 1971. Reprinted by permission.
[1] The New York *Times Book Review*, February 22, 1970, p. 1.

If this view is correct, how can the conflict be resolved? How can a fusion be achieved between the needs for "activism and mysticism" or for "political freedom and personal ecstasy?" And in what sense can the self be expanded and opened up? The answers to these questions hinge on the nature of the human self. The behavioral sciences identify the self with the body, and its needs with organic needs only modified by the environment. We regard ourselves as a species which emerged victorious in the fight for survival, and we see the fight continuing among ourselves, if not for physical survival, then for individual ascendancy. Our educational, professional and commercial institutions all reinforce personal achievement in competitive situations. Recreational activities often follow the same theme, whether at the Miss America stage, the Rose Bowl or whatever arena we attend. Although there are times when cooperative relationships override individual concerns, the mold is essentially the same since the group we belong to is usually set against another group. The context may be anything from the battlefield to the church which excludes members of other races.

If this picture of human beings as separate egos is accurate, there cannot be any actual expansion of the self. The search for ways to "open up" the self and satisfy its need for "activism," "mysticism," etc., are then to be explored in terms of ego functions—such as adolescent rebelliousness, perhaps with artistic and pathological overtones—which present-day psychological and sociological techniques may be able to accommodate. But if the self in some real sense encompasses its social and physical environment, science and technology cannot be expected to respond to its needs until they recognize the possibility of an extrasomatic self. The question is whether it can be shown that the human self extends beyond the borders of its organism.

## Psi Field and Field Consciousness

Psi phenomena such as extrasensory perception and psychokinesis indicate that people are connected with each other and with their physical environment in ways additional to those familiar to science. It has been suggested that psi fields exist around people and objects which are similar to (perhaps identical with) known fields and which interact with these to produce psi phenomena. The possibility that psi phenomena can be explained within the framework of modern physics has aroused lively interest among parapsychologists and physicists and promises to spur new research developments in the 1970s.

The idea that a person's ESP abilities can be understood in terms of fields surrounding his body does not necessarily imply an extrasomatic self. The interaction between a person's psi field and a closed pack of ESP cards on a desk in front of him by itself is no more evidence of an expanded self than the interactions of electromagnetic fields which enable him to see the desk. If an idea, emotion or object is to be accepted as part of a person's self, it must somehow be incorporated into his self-consciousness, into the experience he has of his "I." Similarly, the contents of the unconscious are likely to be regarded as part of the self to the extent that they can be brought into awareness.

If the psi field and the other fields making up our environment are experienced as part of the self, we may define such an experience as one of "field consciousness." Experiences of field consciousness (FC) have been reported near the moment of death, during psychedelic drug trips, as a result of meditation and in other altered states of consciousness.

A. Govinda, an exponent of Tibetan Buddhism says that in states of absorption, human consciousness "is not bound to one direction (of time), like the body and its senses."[2] Also, "while in meditation space seems to expand . . . in the higher stages of absorption the experience of the infinity of space immediately leads to the experience of the infinity of consciousness. After the elimination of all thing- and form-ideas or representations, space is the direct and intuitive object of consciousness."[3]

[2] "Time and Space and the Problem of Free Will," *Main Currents,* March–April 1970, Vol. 26, No. 4, pp. 112–15, p. 113.
[3] "The Conception of Space in Ancient Buddhist Art and Thought," *Main Currents,* January–February 1970, Vol. 26, No. 3, pp. 76–81, p. 78.

By themselves experiences of this kind do not prove that field consciousness occurs though they may be highly convincing to the person who has them and more "real" than the world of ordinary sense perception.

There are two approaches to the problem of whether FC experiences represent an expansion of the self into the environment in fact or only in fancy. We can examine psi occurrences and determine whether they are associated with FC experiences, and we can examine FC experiences and explore for psi phenomena that might be related to them. The former approach would include studies of persons with marked psychical abilities, such as mediums and sensitives, to determine whether the use of these abilities coincides with experiences of field consciousness. The latter approach would take as its starting point the FC experiences, say of yogis and Zen teachers, to determine whether these experiences result in increased psi capacities.

When a sensitive "reads" a target person, he often identifies with that person, sometimes to the point of losing sight of the borders between the two personalities. The FC experience, as a rule, is not consciously sought by the sensitive but seems to result from the use of his psychical abilities. Usually the experience is restricted to the person or situation the medium is responding to at the moment. Occasionally its scope is wider. The British medium "Mrs. Willett" once said at the end of a mediumistic session, "It's so heavenly to be out of myself—when I'm everything, you know, and everything else is me."[4]

Mrs. Eileen J. Garrett (*Theta* 22 and 25)* said that when she practiced her mediumship, "I have an inner feeling of participating, in a very unified way, with what I observe—by which I mean that I have no sense of I and any other, but a close association with, an immersion in, the phenomena. The 'phenomena' are therefore not phenomenal while they are in process; it is only after the event that the conscious mind,

---

[4] Gerald William, Earl of Balfour: "A Study of the Psychological Aspects of Mrs. Willett's Mediumship, and of the Statements of the Communicators Concerning Process," *Proc.* S.P.R., Vol. 43 (1935), p. 218.

* See Appendix.

seeking to understand the experience in its own analytical way, divides up the unity which, after all, is the nature of the supersensory event."[5]

In the same way that FC experiences may arise as by-products of ESP, persons whose main goal is the achievement of the FC state often report the development of psychic powers as side effects. W. Y. Evans-Wentz says that in Tibet telepathy is regarded as "a quite ordinary outcome of a disciple's *yogic* training."[6] Swami Akhilananda makes a similar statement.[7] Govinda refers to FC moments of "full awareness and 'wakedness'" as experiences of "clairvoyant states."[8] But many yogis and others who teach the attainment of such experiences warn that ESP incidents should not be regarded as a substitute for this. The value of ESP is a function of the extent to which it serves the attainment of the FC state.

There is good reason then for taking seriously the view that there may be a close relation between psi phenomena and FC experiences. ESP incidents during FC experiences indicate that the latter may not be occult illusions but represent actual expansion of the self into the objective world of space and time: ESP and other psi phenomena may provide the empirical validation of self-expansion. Conversely, if the FC experience encompasses the psi field, this is likely to give a richer meaning to psychical research. Indeed, if ESP is involved in the FC experience, then it is likely that this experience can be better understood and perhaps achieved more easily through a fuller understanding of ESP.

[5] E. J. Garrett, *Awareness* (New York: Creative Age Press, Inc., 1943), p. 113.

[6] *The Tibetan Book of the Great Liberation,* Oxford University Press, 1968, p. 253.

[7] *Hindu Psychology,* Routledge & Kegan Paul, 1948, p. 149.

[8] "Time and Space and the Problem of Free Will," *Main Currents,* March–April 1970, Vol. 26, No. 4, pp. 112–15, p. 114.

## Mind in Matter

A medium being tested at the P.R.F.* is handed a concealed object belonging to a target person. Holding this, the medium proceeds to describe events in the life of that person. This type of ESP, known as object association (or "psychometry"), has long been familiar to researchers. Sir Oliver Lodge said that "it appears as if we left traces of ourselves, not only on our bodies, but on many other things with which we have been . . . associated, and that these traces can thereafter be detected by a sufficiently sensitive person."[9] From a parapsychological point of view, there may be no sharp border between self and environment, between mind and matter.

The idea that mind and matter are not separate entities is now also expressed by biologists and physicists. For instance, A. A. Cochran suggests that what we regard as the inanimate physical world may possess life and mind properties in a rudimentary form. He goes a step further and specifies where in the physical world mind properties may be found. "Man is both matter and mind, while atoms and the fundamental particles of matter are both particles and waves. If one suspected that a rudimentary degree of life were possessed by all matter, he would naturally suspect that the dual aspects of man are a direct result of the dual aspects of the matter from which he is made, and that the mind of man and the wave properties of an electron are two extremes of the same thing: the mind properties of matter."[10] He pursues this idea by exploring the wave properties of the elements which constitute living organisms. It appears that carbon, hydrogen, nitrogen and oxygen which make up about 99 per cent of the atoms in protein have relatively high wave predominance compared to other chemical elements. (By this it is meant

* See Appendix.

[9] "Report on Some Trance Communications Received Chiefly Through Mrs. Piper," *Proc.* S.P.R., Vol. 23, 1909, 127–85.

[10] A. A. Cochran, "Mind, Matter, and Quanta," *Main Currents*, Vol. 22, March–April 1966, No. 4, pp. 79–88.

that only few of the atoms absorb or emit energy at any given time, with the result that their total energy is stable.) Cochran suggests that this may explain how living and conscious organisms can result from aggregations of such elements.

If the physical surroundings of the organism can be said to possess mind properties, it may become easier to explain how consciousness can expand into the environment. This in turn suggests that findings about the physical world may also explain characteristics of the mental world and vice versa. For instance, the psychological laws of association may have a close parallel in object association where physical objects that have been contiguous apparently remain connected, the strength of the associations depending on the "laws" of recency, frequency, etc.—this explaining why a sensitive is more likely to respond by ESP to events associated with the psychometric objects that are recent or recurrent. The concept of (psi) fields surrounding physical objects is an example of a physical concept being used increasingly often in psychical research. If people as well as apparently inanimate physical objects and places are the center of psi fields, this may throw light, among other things, on the supposed ability of persons who have achieved the FC experience to evoke this in others and on the effects which places or objects ("relics") connected with such persons are said to possess. With present-day concepts and research procedures it becomes possible to extract such claims from myth and folklore and examine them in the light of science.

## Consciousness Control

Psychical researchers and others interested in exploring FC experiences were greatly encouraged in the 1960s by the discovery that these seem to be associated with certain brain wave patterns. Joseph Kamiya at the Langley Porter Neuropsychiatric Institute in San Francisco found that yogis and Zen teachers showed a greater amount of brain waves in the alpha frequency during FC experiences than persons who had no such experiences. He then attempted to train ordinary subjects to produce alpha by connecting a buzzer to his electro-encephalograph (EEG) which sounded whenever the alpha wave was dominant. Kamiya found that many people could learn to prolong the alpha periods by listening to the buzzer and that they reported FC experiences during these times.[11] This "bio-feedback" work, which has spread to studies of other brain waves and autonomic functions such as heart rate and breathing, accelerated greatly when it was found that increased conscious control over them may bring psychological and medical benefits.

Parapsychologists were quick to respond to the possibility that these measurements were related to a person's psi abilities. Their interest centered on the alpha brain wave since this seemed to be associated with mental states generally held conducive to ESP receptivity, whether these consisted in mild states of relaxed awareness or intensive FC experiences. Several recent parapsychological studies have suggested a relationship between ESP and alpha waves.

In the 1970s this research can be expected to embrace other methods for achieving the FC state, including traditional yogic and Zen practices, either in isolation or combined with psychophysiological techniques. Since the environment may play a role in FC experiences, there will probably be work with controlled surroundings, including manipulation of climatic conditions, light and sound. The personality of the FC trainee is also likely to be a factor. Research for the best method to achieve the FC state is likely therefore to take account of his psychological characteristics.

## Science, the Self and Survival

The relation between the human self and the physical world was examined by Lawrence LeShan in the second William McDougall Lecture on Psychical Research at Duke Univer-

---

[11] J. Kamiya, "Operant control of the EEG alpha rhythm and some of its reported effects on consciousness," in C. T. Tart (ed.) *Altered States of Consciousness* (New York: Wiley, 1969), pp. 507–18.

sity, "Human Survival of Biological Death."[12] LeShan found that the descriptions of the universe by modern physicists were strikingly similar to the accounts by so-called mystics. A group of physicists to whom LeShan showed a collection of about sixty quotations from the two groups were unable to tell them apart. An example from the collection illustrates LeShan's point: ". . . the reason why our sentient, percipient, and thinking ego, is met nowhere in our world picture can easily be indicated in seven words: because it is ITSELF that world picture. It is identical with the whole and therefore cannot be contained in it as part of it." The quotation is from the German physicist, Erwin Schrödinger.[13]

This approach brings the survival question into new perspective. In the space-time continuum of field theory a physical entity is considered part of a larger pattern and not primarily a discrete object. From a field theoretical point of view the human self is not contained within the life span of its body. All objects and events exist always in the total field which constitutes the universe. This was not true in the Newtonian universe. In the older picture of the world, which is close to the common-sense view, ordinary macroscopic objects were separate entities with finite careers.

Field theory, LeShan says, implies survival of the self of bodily death as clearly as Newtonian physics implies its termination. But LeShan is quick to recognize that this is of little interest if survival does not involve continuation of consciousness. The question then hinges on the relation between the conscious self and the physical space-time continuum. As an answer, LeShan points to the similarity between the description of the universe by modern physicists and FC experiences as reported from many cultures and periods. Usually as a result of lengthy training designed to still discursive thinking while simultaneously retaining consciousness, the self is experienced as limitless and identical with the universe. The

[12] The title was the same used for an article in *Main Currents*, Vol. 26, No. 2, November–December 1969, pp. 35–45.

[13] R. Fischer (ed.), *Interdisciplinary Perspectives on Time* (New York: New York Academy of Science, 1967), p. 16.

common sense notion of the self as restricted to and dependent on the body is seen as an illusion.

In the past, psychical researchers have usually thought of survival as a continuation of the ego in a nonphysical world. Studies of the survival of a person's memories and personality traits, as manifested through a medium or in a reincarnation subject, are part of this approach. In the years ahead, research into survival is likely to expand and at the same time find a firmer basis in physical science. If survival occurs, this may be within the fabric of the physical universe and survival may range from the continuation of the consciousness of ordinary life to field consciousness where the self merges into the universal continuum. With this increase of possibilities, the research approach is also likely to widen. Procedures that may establish continuation of a self identifiable in terms of memories and personality traits, may not detect the continuation of a self which has merged with the universal field system. For the person who has reached the FC state, survival after death may entail the *loss* of memories and personality traits rather than their continuation. We should therefore predict failure in communicating with deceased persons who have reached this state. Here, the best time to explore survival would be before death, during FC experiences. Out-of-the-body experiences when consciousness also extends beyond the living body are promising topics, too, for the survival researcher.

If it should be found that field consciousness transcends space-time barriers, including the moment of death, survival after death could in effect be reached before. Achieving the state of consciousness which survives death would become a this-world undertaking and not only something for the future when death is near: attainment of the FC experience would be training for death. And death itself, far from being the dreaded termination of consciousness, would become the opportunity for its permanent expansion—uninterrupted by the demands of brain and body.

## Complementarity

If science and personal experience were to verify the self-environment union, this would not entail a denial of the experience of separations, of the awareness of "I" as distinct from "you." It would, however, bring us back to the question posed by Berman—whether the two "streams of consciousness" can be integrated.

J. Robert Oppenheimer uses a concept from modern physics to deal with the two aspects of human nature: "These two ways of thinking, the way of time and history and the way of eternity and timelessness, are both parts of man's efforts to comprehend the world in which he lives. Neither is comprehended in the other nor reducible to it. They are, as we have learned to say in physics, complementary views, each supplementing the other, neither telling the whole story."[14]

The point about complementarity is that two things cannot be true or valid at the same time. Thus a subatomic entity acts under certain conditions as a wave and under other conditions as a particle, but never as a wave and particle at the same time. In the words of Werner Heisenberg, "These different pictures are . . . correct if one uses them in the right place, but they contradict each other, and therefore one designates them as complementary to each other."[15] Similarly, a person may be able to gain the FC experience and also live and conduct himself as an individual among others.

Meister Eckhart, a medieval German priest said: "The soul has something within it, a spark of supersensual knowledge that is never quenched. But there is also another knowledge in our souls, which is directed toward outward objects; namely, knowledge of the senses and the understanding: this hides that other knowledge from us. The intuitive, higher

[14] J. R. Oppenheimer, *Science and the Common Understanding* (New York: Simon and Schuster, 1966), p. 69.
[15] *Main Currents*, Vol. 26, Number 3, January–February 1970, p. 70.

knowledge is timeless and spaceless, without any here and now."[16]

This duality does not entail a split existence, but a more coherent one. The periods of field consciousness may provide an integrative basis for everyday living, leading to a more fulfilling and more responsible existence in relation to one's social and physical environment. Such an existence, in turn, is likely to result in more frequent and richer FC experiences.

The impact of the complementary approach will be particularly significant for science. Scientific observation involves a subject-object dichotomy—though one may be aware on theoretical or experiential grounds of a basic unity. Field consciousness may direct science toward exploring the basic man-world unity, and science in turn may help to understand and activate field awareness.

## Religion as Applied Science

"Christian faith proceeds . . . on the assumption that extrasensory communication regularly takes place between God and man. . . . The Christian who is unwilling to affirm the occurrence of telepathy must give up praying or be called a fool!"[17] This opinion by Howard Wilkinson, Chaplain of Duke University Chapel, is representative of views held by an increasing number of religious leaders, as shown by their involvement in such groups as the Churches Fellowship for Psychical Study in Great Britain and Spiritual Frontiers Fellowship in the U.S.A. (at Evanston, Illinois).

But many clergymen, wanting to avoid conflicts with accepted scientific beliefs, have ignored ESP and PK occurrences—the "miracles" of an earlier day, when they were seen as signs of godliness. Also ignored are the FC experiences of the founders and saints of the great religions, the visionary or

[16] R. Otto, *Mysticism East and West,* translated by B. L. Bracey and R. C. Payne (New York: The Macmillan Co., 1932), p. 35.
[17] H. C. Wilkinson, "Parapsychology and Religion," *Parapsychology Today* (edited by J. B. Rhine and Robert Brier), 1968, pp. 223–28.

mystical experiences which told them that man is part of a divine or universal relationship.

During the 1960s many clergymen saw the church's main role as consisting in social action. This sidestepped the issue of religious belief at the same time as it supported a religiously toned life of sacrifice and aid to others. It did not satisfy the need for an opening or expansion of the self, felt particularly strongly among the young who had experienced (or simulated) the FC state during drug experiences, at rock festivals, etc.

Our social institutions and action programs failed in other ways. Edward B. Fiske, writing in The New York *Times* says: "The war in Vietnam, the failure of the civil rights movement and other recent events have led young persons to a serious questioning of the authority of science, reason and technology—the very values with which religion had attempted to reach an accommodation.

"Their reaction has led, among other things, to a new interest in Eastern religion, astrology, witchcraft, drugs, spiritualism and other phenomena that were presumably incompatible with modern scientific knowledge. The result is that society is undergoing a profound mystical and religious revival that is taking place almost entirely outside the religious institutions that presumably should be the first to recognize its significance."[18] Fiske sees the commune movement as a "modern expression of most of the ideals of classical monasticism" and the drug culture as "at least partly a search for new modes of reality . . . that has obvious links with traditional Christian mysticism." In the same vein, he points to the "liturgical nature" of rock music.

Many churchmen urge the institutions with which they are associated to respond to this religious revival. But their traditional approaches and dogmas have often proved irrelevant. The choice is not indiscriminately to resurrect the past or substitute current fads. Science and technology should not be blindly rejected but, on the contrary, should be focussed on

[18] "Religion in the Age of Aquarius," December 25, 1969.

the issue at stake: the nature and reach of the human self and consciousness.

In recapturing its role, religion in the 1970s can be expected increasingly to rely on empirical observation and testing. For instance, if prayer involves a telepathic relationship, studies that increase our understanding of telepathy should also help to increase the efficiency of prayer. This is true whether we think of prayer as communication between man and God as distinct entities or as parts of the same continuum.

In this approach, traditional as well as new rituals and dogmas become hypotheses to be verified or falsified. By isolating the real from myth and superstition, psychical research will be an important anti-pollutant. Tests of the claims connected with witchcraft, spiritualism, drugs and astrology have begun and will continue in the effort to sift the genuine from the spurious.

As medicine and engineering rest on physiology and physics, religion is likely to depend increasingly on psychical research and on other branches of science and technology which focus on the human self.

One of the most important by-products of our technological society may be leisure time. In the past sustained inward explorations were mainly for the affluent or for those who chose the life of the monastery. Now many persons have more free time than they can spend meaningfully. If safe methods can be developed to enable the ordinary person to have some degree of the FC experience within a reasonably short time, an increasing number of persons are likely to seek it. Our churches, temples and religious retreats could then regain their function as places for actual, experiential communion between man and a universal or divine principle.

If religions were to open their doors and dogmas in this way, we would see an ecumenical movement embracing not only different religions but science and technology as well. By guiding technology to the service of the relationship between man and the larger pattern of which he may be part, religion could become one of the most vital of the applied sciences.

## Conclusion

On one of the last days of the old decade, on December 30, 1969, the Parapsychological Association, the international professional society for psychical researchers, was accepted as an affiliated organization by the American Association for the Advancement of Science. This can be expected to bring increasingly closer relations between parapsychology and the established sciences.

Psychical research long ago adopted the scientific method. But until recently it seemed that the explanation of psi phenomena would be divorced from the world picture of the physical sciences. As ESP emerges into clearer focus, however, it no longer seems a response to a nonphysical world but on the contrary a response to the physical world in all its extension. And the experiences of yogis and others, often thought to contradict the world picture of science, now appear to support it. Conversely, the space time continuum of modern physics, generally held to be a mathematical abstraction, can apparently be verified by direct experience.

In our projection into the 1970s, psychical research takes in a wider scope of human nature and experience than it previously did. If the environment is encompassed within the human "psyche," it is inevitable that its systematic study also will expand. Historically, psychical research included studies of altered states of consciousness. (Some of the pioneering work in hypnosis was done in the late nineteenth century at the London Society for Psychical Research.) Indeed the FC experience figures prominently in the classic of the field, F. W. H. Myers' *Human Personality and Its Survival of Bodily Death*.[19] The scope of "parapsychology" was more restricted, since the work tended to isolate ESP and PK from the psychophysical matrix of which they seem part. Where these phenomena earlier appeared to be manifestations of hidden eddies in some realm of existence outside direct experience, as in a "collective unconscious," they seem now to

[19] New York: Longmans, Green and Co., 1904.

belong in a universe that is an integral part of the human self and can be directly experienced.

In the years ahead, explorations of the self will be integrative and therefore interdisciplinary. They will bring together physicists, psychical researchers, psychophysiologists, religious leaders and workers from other professions. Indeed the work could not succeed without a dedicated interdisciplinary approach.

If the borders between self and environment can be made to disappear, this is likely to have profound effects on man's attitude to his environment, both social and physical. If the self is experienced as actually embracing other people, self-consciousness becomes social consciousness. Race and generation gaps and the other divisions which keep people apart and in angry confrontations cannot then be easily sustained. So also with the physical environment: pollution and other acts defacing nature will be more difficult to commit if they are seen, literally, as acts of self-destruction.

If the indications I have outlined about the human self are in the right direction, if "inner" and outer space are basically synonymous, its exploration will be more exciting and meaningful to man than any other he could undertake.

*"We shall not cease from exploration . . ."*
T. S. Eliot, FOUR QUARTETS


# SUGGESTIONS FOR FURTHER EXPLORATION


## BOOKS

In addition to reading the books from which the preceding selections have been taken, the following titles are recommended. Their "classification" is simply a matter of convenience and should not be understood in a strict sense.

LITERARY CRITICISM

*The Way Down and Out,* John Senior, Cornell University Press, 1959

*The Heresy of Self Love,* Paul Zweig, Basic Books, 1968

LITERATURE

*Childhood's End,* Arthur Clarke, Ballentine Books, 1953

*Franny and Zooey,* J. D. Salinger, Little, Brown, 1961

*Island,* Aldous Huxley, Bantam Books, 1963

*Lilith,* J. R. Salamanca, Bantam Books, 1961

*Stranger in a Strange Land,* Robert A. Heinlein, Avon Books, 1961

METALINGUISTICS

*Language in Thought and Action,* S. I. Hayakawa, Harcourt, Brace & World, 1949

*Language, Thought, and Reality,* Benjamin Lee Whorf, MIT Press, 1956

*Tomorrow and Tomorrow and Tomorrow,* Aldous Huxley, Signet, 1964

MYSTICISM

*Awakening to the Good,* Claire Myers Owens, Christopher Publishing House, 1958

*Mysticism,* Evelyn Underhill, Dutton, 1961

*Mysticism and Philosophy,* W. D. Stace, Lippincott, 1960

*Mysticism: Christian and Buddhist,* D. T. Suzuki, Harper, 1957

*Mysticism East and West,* Rudolf Otto, Macmillan, 1970

*Mystics and Zen Masters,* Thomas Merton, Farrar, Straus & Giroux, 1967

*The Western Mystical Tradition,* Thomas Katsaros and Nathaniel Kaplan, College and University Press, 1969

PARAPSYCHOLOGY AND OCCULTISM

*A Search for the Truth,* Ruth Montgomery, Bantam Books, 1968

*Astrology: The Space Age Science,* Joseph Goodavage, Signet, 1967

*Edgar Cayce—the Sleeping Prophet,* Jess Stern, Doubleday, 1967

*Psychic Discoveries Behind the Iron Curtain,* Sheila Ostander and Lynn Schroeder, Prentice-Hall, 1970

*The Challenge of Psychical Research,* Gardner Murphy, Harper & Row, 1961

*The Morning of the Magicians,* Louis Pauwels and Jacques Bergier, Stein & Day, 1964

*The Reach of the Mind,* J. B. Rhine, Apollo, 1947

*The Seth Material,* Jane Roberts, Prentice-Hall, 1970

PHILOSOPHY

*The Phenomenon of Man,* Teilhard de Chardin, Harper, 1961

*Thus Spake Zarathustra,* Friedrich Nietzsche, Modern Library, 1954

PSYCHEDELICA

*High Priest,* Timothy Leary, New American Library, 1968

*LSD: The Consciousness Expanding Drug,* David Solomon, Putnam, 1964

*Psychedelics,* Bernard Aaronson and Humphrey Osmond, Anchor, 1970

*The Doors of Perception/Heaven and Hell,* Aldous Huxley, Harper Colophon 1963

*The Politics of Ecstasy,* Timothy Leary, Putnam, 1968

*Varieties of Psychedelic Experience,* Jean Houston and Robert E. L. Masters, Holt, Rinehart and Winston, 1966

PSYCHOLOGY

*Basic Writings of C. G. Jung,* ed. V. S. de Laszlo, Modern Library, 1959

*Love's Body,* Norman O. Brown, Random House, 1966

*The Science of Being and the Art of Living,* Maharishi Mahesh Yogi, Allied, 1963

*Toward a Psychology of Being,* Abraham Maslow, Van Nostrand, 1968

*Turning on,* Rasa Gustaitis, Signet, 1969

*Varieties of Self-Realization,* Claire Myers Owens (in press)

PSYCHOPHYSIOLOGY

*Altered States of Consciousness,* Charles T. Tart, John Wiley, 1969

*Biological Basis of Religion and Genius,* Gopi Krishna, N.C. Publishing Co., 1971

*Brain and Consciousness,* Hartwig Kuhlenbeck, S. Karger, 1957

*By the Late John Brockman,* John Brockman, Macmillan, 1969

*Ecstasy,* Marghanita Laski, Indiana University Press, 1962

*The Ghost in the Machine,* Arthur Koestler, Macmillan, 1968

*Preconscious Foundations of Human Experience,* ed. William E. Galt, Basic Books, 1964

RELIGION

*Autobiography of a Yogi,* Paramhansa Yogananda, Philosophic Library, 1946

*I and Thou,* Martin Buber, Scribner, 1958

*Knowledge of Higher Worlds and Its Attainment,* Rudolf Steiner, Anthroposophic Press, 1936

*The Courage to Be,* Paul Tillich, Yale University Press, 1956

*The Two Hands of God,* Alan W. Watts, Braziller, 1963

*Varieties of Religious Experience,* William James, University Books, 1936

*Vedanta and the Western World,* ed. Christopher Isherwood, Harper, 1951

SOCIOLOGY

*A Serious Call to an American (R)Evolution,* Jerome Ellison, Berkeley Medallion, 1971

*Eros and Civilization,* Herbert Marcuse, Vintage, 1962

*Ideology and Utopia,* Karl Mannheim, Harcourt, Brace and World, 1936

*One Dimensional Man,* Herbert Marcuse, Beacon, 1964

*The Greening of America,* Charles Reich, Random, 1970

UTOPIANISM

*American Dreams,* Vernon L. Parrington, Jr., Brown University, 1947

*Anarchism,* George Woodcock, Penguin, 1963

*Heavens Below,* W. H. G. Armytage, University of Toronto Press, 1961

*The Story of Utopias,* Lewis L. Mumford, Boni and Liveright, 1922

*Utopians and Utopian Thought,* ed. Frank E. Manuel, Houghton Mifflin, 1966

# PERIODICALS

*Fate*
500 Hyacinth Place
Highland Park
Chicago, Illinois 60035

*International Journal of Parapsychology* and *Parapsychology Review*
Parapsychology Foundation, Inc.
29 West 57th Street
New York, New York 10019

*Journal for the Scientific Study of Religion*
The Society for the Scientific Study of Religion
3812 Walnut Street
Philadelphia, Pennsylvania 19104

*Journal for the Study of Consciousness*
844 San Ysidro Lane
Santa Barbara, California 93103

*Journal of the American Society for Psychical Research*
5 West 73rd Street
New York, New York 10023

*Journal of Humanistic Psychology*
Box 11173 Station A
Palo Alto, California 94306

*Journal of Parapsychology*
Box 6847 College Station
Durham, North Carolina 27708

*Journal of Thanatology*
The Foundation for Thanatology
630 West 168th Street
New York, New York 10032

*Journal of Transpersonal Psychology*
P.O. Box 4437
Stanford, California 94305

*Main Currents in Modern Thought*
Center for Integrative Education
12 Church Street
New Rochelle, New York 10805

*Psychedelic Review*
4034 20th Street
San Francisco, California 94114

*Psychophysiology*
Society for Psychophysiological Research
951 East Lafayette Street
Detroit, Michigan 48207

*R. M. Bucke Newsletter*
R. M. Bucke Memorial Society
1266 Pine Avenue West
Montreal, Canada

*Spring*
Spring Publications
Suite 306
130 East 39th Street
New York, New York
A journal of archetypal psychology and Jungian thought.


# ORGANIZATIONS

ANALYTICAL PSYCHOLOGY CLUB OF NEW YORK, INC.
130 East 39th Street
New York, New York 10016
Promotes the work—called analytical psychology—of Carl Jung and publishes *Spring* magazine.

AMERICAN SOCIETY FOR PSYCHICAL RESEARCH
5 West 73rd Street
New York, New York 10023
Publishes *Journal of the American Society for Psychical Research*.

ASSOCIATION FOR HUMANISTIC PSYCHOLOGY
416 Hoffman Street
San Francisco, California 94114
Provides an excellent listing of Growth Centers around the country.

ASSOCIATION FOR RESEARCH AND ENLIGHTENMENT
Atlantic Avenue and 67th Street
Virginia Beach, Virginia 23451
(Mr. Hugh Lynn Cayce, Director)
ARE was founded to preserve and continue the work of Edgar Cayce.

BACKSTER RESEARCH FOUNDATION, INC.
165 West 46th Street
New York, New York
(Mr. Cleve Backster, Director)
Cleve Backster has rediscovered (through polygraph studies) the ancient Indian claim of primary perception in plants.

BIOFEEDBACK SOCIETY INFORMATION EXCHANGE
Department of Experiential Physiology
Veterans Administration Hospital
Sepulveda, California 91343
(Dr. Barbara Brown, Co-ordinator)

CENTER FOR INTEGRATIVE EDUCATION
12 Church Street
New Rochelle, New York 10805
The Center publishes *Main Currents in Modern Thought*.

ESALEN INSTITUTE
Box 31389
San Francisco, California 94131
(Mr. Michael Murphy, President)
The Esalen Catalogue is an education in itself.

FOUNDATION FOR MIND RESEARCH, INC.
315 East 86th Street
New York, New York 10028
(Dr. Jean Houston Masters, Director)
The Foundation's main concern is non-drug inducement of psychedelic/transcendent experiences.

FOUNDATION FOR RESEARCH ON THE NATURE OF MAN
402 Buchanan Boulevard
Durham, North Carolina
(Dr. J. B. Rhine, Director)
The emphasis is on parapsychology.

FOUNDATION FOR THE STUDY OF CONSCIOUSNESS
1812 Delancy Place
Philadelphia, Pennsylvania 19103
(Mr. Arthur Young, President)
Publishes *Journal for the Study of Consciousness*.

KUNDALINI RESEARCH FOUNDATION
10 East 39th Street
New York, New York 10016
Promotes the work of Gopi Krishna to synthesize science and religion.

LIFWYNN FOUNDATION
52 South Morningside Drive
Westport, Connecticut 06880
Established by Trigant Burrow to provide the social setting for group-analysis investigations and basic problems of consciousness.

PARAPSYCHOLOGY FOUNDATION, INC.
29 West 57th Street
New York, New York 10019
Publishes *International Journal of Parapsychology*.

PSYCHICAL RESEARCH FOUNDATION
Duke Station
Durham, North Carolina 27706
(W. G. Roll, Project Director)
Publishes *Theta*, a journal concerned with the possibility of life after death.

PSYCHOSYNTHESIS RESEARCH FOUNDATION
Room 1902
40 East 49th Street
New York, New York 10017

Promotes the psychotherapy system—called psychosynthesis—of Dr. Robert Assagioli of Italy.

R. M. BUCKE MEMORIAL SOCIETY
1266 Pine Avenue West
Montreal, Canada
(Dr. Raymond Prince, President)

Concerned with comparative study of mystical states.

SELF-REALIZATION FELLOWSHIP
Center Department
3880 San Rafael Avenue
Los Angeles, California 90065
(The Rev. Mother Daya Mata, President)

Founded by Paramhansa Yogananda "to teach the individual man the way to personal contact with God."

THE SOCIETY FOR COMPARATIVE PHILOSOPHY, INC.
S.S. Vallejo
Box 857
Sausalito, California 94965
(Dr. Alan W. Watts, President)

SPIRITUAL FRONTIERS FELLOWSHIP
800 Custer Avenue—Suite No. 1
Evanston, Illinois 60202

Encourages the churches to explore mystical, psychical and paranormal experience.

STUDENTS INTERNATIONAL MEDITATION SOCIETY
1015 Gayley Avenue
Los Angeles, California 90024
(Mr. Jerry Jarvis, Director)
also
27 Concord Avenue
Cambridge, Massachusetts 02138

Promotes the teaching—called Transcendental Meditation—of Maharishi Mahesh Yogi.

SUFISM REORIENTED
1290 Sutter Street
San Francisco, California

Promotes the teaching of Meher Baba.

THEOSOPHICAL SOCIETY IN AMERICA
P.O. Box 270
Wheaton, Illinois 60187

A world-wide organization to promote spirituality and brotherhood in man.

WESTERN BEHAVIORAL SCIENCES INSTITUTE
1150 Silverado
La Jolla, California 92037

Provides an excellent listing of Growth Centers around the country, as well as an annotated Film List.

## GROWTH CENTERS

Growth centers (of which Esalen Institute is the prototype) are springing up rapidly. For the address of those in your locality, see "Association for Humanistic Psychology" and "Western Behavioral Sciences Institute" under ORGANIZATIONS.

## TAPES, RECORDS AND FILMS

Write for the catalogs.

ASSOCIATION FOR RESEARCH AND ENLIGHTENMENT
Atlantic Avenue and 67th Street
Virginia Beach, Virginia 23451

BUCKS COUNTY SEMINAR HOUSE, INC.
Erwinna, Pennsylvania 18920

ESALEN INSTITUTE
Box 31389
San Francisco, California 94131

NOUMEDIA CO.
P.O. Box 750
Port Chester, New York 10573

PORTOLA INSTITUTE, INC.
1115 Merrill Street
Menlo Park, California 94025

WESTERN BEHAVIORAL SCIENCES INSTITUTE
1150 Silverado
La Jolla, California 92037

## USEFUL GUIDES

1. "The Psychology and Physiology of Meditation and Related Phenomena," Beverly Timmons and Joe Kamiya, *Journal of Transpersonal Psychology,* Vol. 2/No. 1, Spring 1970.

An excellent bibliography of books and articles which seem to indicate a convergence of science and religion.

2. "Whole Consciousness Catalog," January 1970 Supplement to *Whole Earth Catalog,* Baba Ram Dass.

Ram Dass is the former Dr. Richard Alpert of the Psychology Department at Harvard University. He and his colleague, Dr. Timothy Leary, were expelled from the university for their experiments with

LSD. Subsequently Alpert gave up drugs in favor of yoga. The Supplement is available for $1 from:

> Portola Institute, Inc.
> 1115 Merrill Street
> Menlo Park, California 94025

3. *Toward a Catalog of: Ways People Grow*, Vol. 1

A paperback book (Ballentine) by Severin Peterson that indicates the enormous diversity and richness with which people grow. It gives a clear, accurate introduction to forty-one ways of growth, which include spiritual disciplines, psychotherapies and other approaches that do not fit a simple category. Also included is a directory of ways people grow that classifies and annotates several hundred persons, processes, places and publications.

4. "Eupsychian Network II," *Mother Earth News*, Henry Winthrop, No. 7, January 1971.

A list (based on the one first compiled by Abraham Maslow) of movements, organizations, books, periodicals, etc., that "tend to foster communal and spiritual values that enable men to realize their fullest potential . . ."

# ABOUT THE AUTHORS

U. A. ASRANI is assistant professor of physics, emeritus, at Benares Hindu University, India.

ERIKA BOURGUIGNON is professor of anthropology at Ohio State University. From 1963–68 she was director of a project titled Cross-Cultural Studies of Dissociational States under the auspices of the National Institute of Mental Health.

NORMAN O. BROWN is professor of classics at Cowell College, University of California, Santa Cruz. His radical reinterpretation of Freud, *Life Against Death,* became an underground best seller and emerged as one of the most-discussed books of its time. *Love's Body* is a continuation of that voyage begun in *Life Against Death.*

RICHARD MAURICE BUCKE (1837–1902) was a Canadian doctor and psychologist. His spontaneous experience of cosmic consciousness at age thirty-five led to a life concerned with understanding the nature of the illumination-event. Dr. Bucke was the author of *Cosmic Consciousness.*

ROBERT S. DE ROPP is a biochemist who has done research on cancer, mental illness and the biochemistry of the brain. His books include *Drugs and the Mind* and *Science and Salvation.*

ROLAND FISCHER is a biologist of the Fleeting Moment. He holds the position of research professor of experimental psychiatry and psychopharmacology in the Department of Psychiatry, Ohio State University. He has authored some 180 research papers, book chapters and monographs on biology and behavior in general, and experiential pharmacology in particular.

JOHN FOWLES is a well-known British novelist, author of *The Collector* and *The French Lieutenant's Woman.*

ANAGARIKA GOVINDA was born in Germany in 1898. His interest in Buddhism led him to India, where he became a member of the Tibetan Buddhist Order. He now lives in the foothills of the Himalayan Mountains with his wife.

JEAN HOUSTON and ROBERT E. L. MASTERS are the authors of *The Varieties of Psychedelic Experience* and *Psychedelic Art,* and are directors of The Foundation for Mind Research in New York City. Prof. Houston also teaches in the philosophy department of Marymount College at Tarrytown, New York.

ALDOUS HUXLEY (1894–1963) was one of the major thinkers and mind-explorers of this century. It was Huxley's competition with Sir Humphrey Osmond to find a neutral term for consciousness-expanding substances that led to the invention (by Osmond in 1957) of the word "psychedelic." In that respect and many others, Huxley is a father of the consciousness (r)evolution now underway. His major books include *Doors of Perception* and *Brave New World*.

G. RAY JORDAN is chairman of the Department of Religious Studies at San Diego State College. From 1946–47 he conducted special research in religion and psychology of religion under Gerald Heard. Since then he has carried on special research in Zen under various Buddhist monks and teachers, while continuing a career in teaching.

DEMETRI P. KANELLAKOS is a senior research engineer at the Radio Physics Laboratory of Stanford Research Institute, Menlo Park, California, and a practitioner of transcendental meditation. He has lectured on the psychobiology of TM, and since March 1970 has been promoting scientific studies on the effects of TM on the individual at Stanford Research Institute and elsewhere.

DURAND KIEFER is a retired naval officer. In 1959, with no previous religious or psychological training, he embarked on a private empirical investigation of supra-rational consciousness. He now travels widely in study of higher states of consciousness.

STANLEY KRIPPNER is a director of the Dream Laboratory at Maimonides Medical Center in Brooklyn, New York. He is also senior research associate for the department of psychiatry there. He is the author of more than one hundred articles and research papers, some of which have appeared in *LSD in Action, Psychedelics: Their Uses and Implications,* and *Psychedelic Art*.

R. D. LAING is a British psychoanalyst and psychiatrist whose work has dealt with schizophrenia, different kinds of families and psychedelic drugs. He is now chairman of the Philadelphia Association Limited in London, an organization concerned with implementing his theories in society. His books include *The Divided Self* and, most recently, *Knots*.

ABRAHAM MASLOW (1908–70) was one of the prime movers in the emergence of modern psychology, helping to establish the humanistic "third force" in psychology in the mid-1950s. In the late 1960s, he and others brought forward a "fourth force" in the study of man, transpersonal psychology.

EDWARD W. MAUPIN has a Ph.D. in psychology. A past director of the resident program at Esalen Institute, he has focussed increasingly on the psychology of the body as a means for organizing higher states of consciousness. He now practices the Rolf method of Structural Integration and pursues a natural life on a farm in British Columbia.

ALEXANDER MAVEN is a retired federal civil service employee of tht Army Audit Agency. He currently lives in St. Petersburg, Florida.

P. D. OUSPENSKY (1878–1947) was a Russian mathematician and philosopher. He met G. I. Gurdjieff in 1915. Soon afterward he published *Tertium Organum,* and thereafter he devoted himself to the study of developing greater consciousness in man. His last work is *The Psychology of Man's Possible Evolution.*

CLAIRE MYERS OWENS is the author of *Awakening to the Good,* an account of her spontaneous mystical experience, and *Discovery of the Self.* Her latest work, *Varieties of Self-Realization,* examines the higher and highest states of consciousness as exhibited in famous people throughout history.

WALTER N. PAHNKE (1930–71) was active in research with psychedelic drugs. He was the Director of Clinical Sciences Research at the Maryland State Psychiatric Research Center in Baltimore, Maryland.

RAYMOND PRINCE is assistant professor of psychiatry at McGill University. He was one of the organizers and is presently president of the R. M. Bucke Memorial Society, which is concerned with the comparative study of mystical states.

W. G. ROLL is project director of the Psychical Research Foundation in Durham, North Carolina, which engages in research on the question of survival of personality after death. He is also editor of *Theta,* a quarterly bulletin devoted to the work of the Foundation. In 1964 he was president of the Parapsychological Association, which he helped found in 1957 and for which he edited the *Journal of Parapsychology.*

CHARLES SAVAGE, M.D., is associate director of the Maryland State Psychiatric Research Center in Baltimore. He also holds the position of assistant professor of psychiatry at Johns Hopkins University. Dr. Savage has published about thirty papers dealing with psychopharmacology, psychoanalysis and cross-cultural studies.

CHARLES T. TART is associate professor of psychology at University of California, Davis. The editor of *Altered States of Consciousness,* his research currently involves psychic and paranormal experiences. In preparation are books on out-of-the-body experiences and the varieties of human consciousness.

ARTHUR WALEY (1889–1966) was a British writer and sinologist who translated many Chinese and Japanese literary works. *Three Ways of Thought in Ancient China* is his best-known book.

KENNETH WAPNICK practices clinical psychology at Harlem Valley State Hospital in Wingdale, New York, where he is assistant chief psychologist. His current professional interests include therapeutic investigations of schizophrenic families and their children.

ALAN WATTS helped introduce Zen to the Western world. He is the author of many books on religion and philosophy, including *Psychotherapy East and West* and *The Book*.

ROGER W. WESCOTT is chairman of the anthropology department at Drew Unversity in Madison, New Jersey. A prolific writer, he has authored a dozen books and more than one hundred articles, reviews and commentaries. In addition, he writes and translates poetry.

KENNETH WALKER (1883–1966) was a British surgeon, author of many medical and philosophical works, and a disciple of G. I. Gurdjieff. He wrote about his reactions to the Russian mystic in *Venture with Ideas*. His last works were *The Unconscious Mind, The Conscious Mind* and *The Making of Man*.

JOHN WHITE, editor of this book, is a writer and college teacher. He lives in Cheshire, Connecticut.

RICHARD WILHELM (1873–1930) was a German professor and theologian whose major concern was sinology. He spent many years in China as a missionary.

# ANCHOR BOOKS

## PSYCHOLOGY

# ANCHOR BOOKS

## PHILOSOPHY

12Ab

PHILOSOPHY *(cont'd)*

# ANCHOR BOOKS

## RELIGION

15Ab

15Bb

## RELIGION (*cont'd*)

15Cb